Eldercare, Distributive Justice, and the Welfare State

SUNY Series in the Political Economy of Health Care

Eldercare, Distributive Justice, and the Welfare State

Retrenchment or Expansion

Edited by
Derek G. Gill and Stanley R. Ingman

State University of New York Press

Published by
State University of New York Press, Albany

For information, address State University of New York Press,
State University Plaza, Albany, N.Y. 12246

Production by M. R. Mulholland
Marketing by Bernadette LaManna

Library of Congress Cataloging-in-Publication Data

Eldercare, distributive justice, and the welfare state : retrenchment
  or expansion / [edited by] Derek G. Gill and Stanley R. Ingman.
    p.   cm. — (SUNY series in the political economy of health
  care)
    Includes bibliographical references and index.
    ISBN 0-7914-1765-4 (alk. paper). — ISBN 0-7914-1766-2 (pbk. :
  alk. paper)
    1. Aged —Care—Cross-cultural studies.   2. Aged—Care—Government
  policy—Cross-cultural studies.   3. Aged—Services for—Government
  policy—Cross-cultural studies.   I. Gill, Derek.   II. Ingman,
  Stanley R.   III. Series.
  HV1451.E44   1994
  362.6'3—dc20   93-18518
                                                                  CIP

10 9 8 7 6 5 4 3 2 1

Contents

Foreword

This Gill and Ingman volume provides a variety of readers with material which has been sadly lacking in the literatures of sociology, economics, social welfare, health policy and gerontology. Each of these disciplines will read this book from different perspectives, with different agendas, and for different purposes; however, each of them will find much that is new, or focused in new ways.

The editors asked the authors to place elder care in each of their countries within the broader characteristics of the welfare state and to address collectivism versus individualism and distributive justice. With this focus, the authors have provided the reader with a cross-national comparative collection of essays, on various national eldercare models.

Further, the editors' Introduction and Epilogue have created a cohesive whole from these divergent contributions. This accomplishment is even more noteworthy given the inclusion of many countries with which the majority of readers will be less familiar. For example how often does one have the opportunity to read about eldercare in Iceland or even Switzerland, or given the welfare state focus to read about Italy and Japan in the same volume with Sweden, France, Germany, Canada and the U.S. and to read analyses of systems in Poland and the former USSR? As the editors themselves state: "The societies chosen, therefore, provide an opportunity to explore the influence of individualism vs. collectivism, equity, uniformity, public accountability, distributive justice, residual vs institutionalized forms of the welfare state in a number of different social systems each with their own socio-historical precedents upon which welfare mechanisms were built."

This book is an important contribution to the current state of knowledge; but, it will probably be even more important ten to fifteen years from now as scholars, policy makers, researchers and academics search for material to assist in explaining how these societies have arrived at their, then, positions. The timing of this volume captures most of the chosen countries at what is likely to be viewed as a watershed period relative to the welfare state from that future vantage point.

With the exception of France and Italy, each of the other countries have seen dramatic political events since 1989 which would appear to have long term effects on eldercare and the welfare state in the countries. These authors have captured Sweden at the beginning of fiscal reform which claims to see U.S. "tax reform" as far-sighted despite its potentially negative effect on Sweden, the most fully developed example of the institutionalized welfare state. Germany is developing a new state as a result of reunification which must attempt to balance the capitalistic individualism of the old West Germany with the collective socialism of the previous East Germany. Poland is emerging from its initial rush to capitalism following independence from the former USSR and is beginning to reconsider its more socialistic premises. Iceland's rapid shift toward an institutionalized welfare state based on its historic collectivism and the capital generation by its strategic position during the "Cold War," threatens to be slowed as its geography becomes less important to the post-Cold War "West." Switzerland's rudimentary welfare state may be either further constrained or stimulated by the likely economic impact of the EEC on its mechanism to stabilize employment, namely the influx and exodus of guest workers as currently determined by the Swiss. The states of the former USSR are in the most dramatic state of flux, but are also the most difficult to analyze because of the extreme needs for simultaneous capital accumulation for survival and the history of collective activities within the sphere of their former socialistic welfare states. Japan has very rapidly moved from familial eldercare, to free medical care in 1973, to co-payment and other constraints, to the institutionalized welfare state by 1982, to most recently fully articulated plans for tremendous expansion to their eldercare programs by 1996. Canada has been experiencing both economic and constitutional crises both of which also threaten its health and eldercare programs despite their deep roots in the Canadian psyche. Finally as noted by the editors, U.S. elections seem to hold little promise, regardless of party, for either institutionalizing the welfare state or expanding or even coordinating eldercare. Certainly, a national health care policy, which would increase coverage and decrease the incidence of personal bankruptcies, seems especially unlikely given the strength of the health insurance industry as it continues to lobby against even the existent modicum of public health care insurance.

This book will surely stand the test of time given the significance of each of the events noted above to the history of the world. I wish there were some way that these essays could benefit the developing nations, but faced with the traumas of starvation, resource depletion and corruption, both internal and external, it seems unlikely. However, perhaps there are some lessons to be learned about how not to industrialize, modernize and marginalize which may be or become instructive. In any case Gill and Ingman are to be commended for their selection of countries, their framing of the question, their insightful epilogue and their sense of history.

Betty Havens
Manitoba Health
Winnipeg, Manitoba

Preface

When this volume appears in print more detailed information may be available about President Clinton's plan for changes in the American Health Care System. In this work the authors from eleven different countires have described the medical and social services which provide care for the elderly within the broader context of each country's welfare state system. All authors touch upon the broader aspects of medical and social care provisions, including the major policy issues of distributive justice, access, equity, uniformity and public accountability. These issues are also discussed in both the introduction and epilogue. Hopefully, this discourse and the detailed comparative examination of the eleven countries' systems of social and medical care will provide guidelines with which a continuing assessment and debate of the Clinton proposals can be conducted. As will be clear from many of the chapters covering countries such as West Germany, the former Soviet Union, Sweden, Italy, France and of course the United States; what has been called the crisis of the welfare state its very raison d'être, is being questioned. Yet the provisions for the elderly are deemed inadequate in many societies, and the continued increase in the proportion of elders among the population are exhausting existing services, just as the need for additional support of the frail elderly becomes more apparent. Hence, the second part of the title of this volume; Retrenchment or Expansion. If adequate service provision for the elderly is to be made available to this and future generations of older people, it is difficult to see how this might be accomplished without continuing expansion and development of the welfare state.

The editors wish to acknowledge their enormous debts to mentors, friends, and colleagues. Tim Diamond, Jon Hendricks, Georgia Walker and Ilsa Lottes reviewed the Introduction and Epilogue suggesting improvements and elaboration of the arguments, and we gratefully acknowledge their input. Isidor Wallimann and Martin Jaeckel played important supportive roles to facilitate the completion of this volume. From the outset the ideas and ultimate framework was enthusiastically supported by the then editor of the series, Ray Elling. The editors wish to acknowledge their deep thanks for the support, advice and encouragement provided by this distinguished scholar throughout the development of this book.

Véronique Ingman has played a unique editorial role in this and in other volumes we have jointly produced over the last ten years. In this volume, Véronique and Martha Hipskind were meticulous in their editorial role as individual chapters arrived. Véronique, with her special linguistic skills and general scholarship, assisted the editors in integrating context and content into the volume. Xiao Mei Pei devoted many hours to the detailed compilation and ordering of materials. Our secretarial staff at the Texas Institute for Research and Education on Aging at the University of North Texas and the Texas College of Osteopathic Medicine, Elizabeth Tucker and Kay Branum, and Mary Pat Armstrong and Sue Hahn of the Department of Sociology and Anthropology at the University of Maryland Baltimore County were persistent and patient in deciphering the untidy manuscripts that sometimes appeared. We would like to thank our mentors, colleagues and friends, too numerous to mention, which included the faculties of the Medical Research Council at the University of Aberdeen 1966-74, the Section of Behavioral Sciences and the Department of Sociology at the University of Missouri-Columbia 1974-90, the Department of Sociology and Anthropology at the University of Maryland Baltimore County since 1986, and the University of North Texas/Texas College of Osteopathic Medicine from 1990. Nevertheless, our mentors must be singled out for special note, for Derek Gill, Raymond Illesley and Gordon Horobin, the Medical Research Council, Medical Sociology Research Unit, Aberdeen, and for Stan Ingman, Ray Elling, Burkhardt Holzner, Ian Lawson and Carroll Estes.

Derek Gill
Stan Ingman

Introduction

In the concluding chapter of her book entitled *Aging in Early Industrial Society: Work, Family and Social Policy in Nineteenth Century England* Quadagno (1982) states...."The general trend in research on older people has been to study them in isolation, independent of the economy, the polity and the general structure of society. A central theme in the literature has been adjustment to old age or changing social roles in later life, the expectation being that adjustment should vary according to residence, gender, race, or some other exogenous factor". In her analysis of the changing status of the elderly and changes in their economic, familial and employment circumstances during the agricultural and industrial revolutions, the need to integrate and interpret changes in the broader infrastructure of the social system was clearly demonstrated if understanding of the changing condition of the elderly was to be generated.

The essays, commissioned for this volume, are an attempt to describe and understand the situation of the elderly today taking into account three major political, economic, and social variations of service provision which can be observed in a number of different national settings. In all developed and most developing societies the welfare state exists or is being introduced but the extent of welfare provision varies substantially. Elderly care varies accordingly, with some countries—Sweden, Denmark and Holland—providing high levels of income support, medical care, sheltered housing in a variety of forms and social services designed to prevent social isolation and the maintenance of community involvement, while others such as the U.S., the former USSR and Poland provide limited social support, income and services. The variation in services and support for the elderly in different countries reflects, at least in part, the extent of development of the welfare state in different national settings. This variation in the degree of development of the welfare state is in turn affected by the political, economic and social values which predominate in different societies. Different degrees of commitment to the principles of collectivism versus individualism for the resolution of social problems differ between—say—the USA and Sweden.

The contributors to this volume were asked to examine the provision for care of the elderly in their respective countries in the light of the broader characteristics of the welfare state of which services to the elderly were a part. Contributors were asked to address the issues of collectivism versus individualism and distributive justice. Apart from these suggestions, each contributor was free to examine the current state and/or development of elderly care in the way which best explicated the current circumstances and levels of service provision in his/her country. Such 'loose' instructions were expected to and did provide a variety of issues and emphases in describing and analyzing the provision for the elderly in each country.

In the introduction the editors choose to develop a framework of concepts and perspectives which would establish links between elderly care, distributive justice and the welfare state to demonstrate the interaction effects between 'the economy, the polity and the general structure of society' and the condition of the elderly. Then follows the accounts of each contributor's analysis of the provision and extent of services for the elderly in each selected country. Finally in an epilogue we will try to show how and in what ways the concepts developed in the introduction—equity, uniformity, public accountability, individualism, collectivism, institutional or residual welfare state orientation, 'high' or 'low' wage economies—apply to and help to explain the variation in provisions for the care of the elderly in each of the societies represented.

The Welfare State and Distributive Justice: Concepts and Perspectives

Most societies operate some form of a welfare state to protect citizens against expected or unexpected interruptions of social existence such as old age or illness. For the elderly a range of services and provisions are necessary if the complex mix of social, economic and medical problems often associated with old age are to be ameliorated or prevented. A single volume cannot hope to explore all aspects of the welfare state which impinge upon the condition of the elderly. For example, we devote almost no attention to the nature, characteristics and exchange relationships between family units at different stages of the life cycle. Our major focus is therefore restricted to the supports and services which societies provide, qua society, which serve to illustrate varying degrees of commitment to systemic measures designed to meet the needs of the elderly in different countries.

The extent of support for the elderly tends to be related to the overall development of the welfare state. Welfare state development may also be linked to the degree to which collectivist as opposed to individualistic value systems predominate in a given social system. The consequences of this broad distinction are best illustrated by applying these categories to the provision of medical care. While the needs of the elderly are many and varied and medical and social care must often be provided in an integrated and coordinated manner if needs are to be met, the elderly—because of reductions in earning power—often cannot afford medical services without outside assistance. The distinction between collectivist and individualist oriented societies is particularly useful in examining the allocation of scarce resources and the ways in which national health policies are or were formulated to provide care for the elderly.

A social system which operates with an individualistic orientation may be defined as one which emphasizes the duties and responsibilities of individuals to provide for their medical care; a social system which operates with a collectivist orientation is one which emphasizes the duties and responsibilities of the society at-large to provide medical care for all. Embedded in this distinction is the notion that persons who failed to provide for their medical care are the victims of unfortunate natural events or are, simply, failures. Conversely, those who are able to make adequate provision for their own medical care are successful in the normal economic exchanges of the market place. In a collectivist orientation the financing of medical care is decommodified. Services are made available at zero cost at point of delivery so that those unable or least able to bear the costs of medical care and associated social services necessary for the maintenance of a social existence are not barred from access. The dichotomy between individualist and collectivist orientations is never complete. Most societies use a mix of both orientations in the delivery of medical care services. In Britain a small private sector, providing medical care for those wealthy enough to afford private insurance premiums persists and, in the public sector prescription charges, a regressive tax, clearly antithetical to a collectivist orientation, were introduced to dissuade both patients and primary care practitioners from overutilizing drug therapies for the treatment of minor illness episodes.

In the USA the care of the elderly is largely financed by federal and state governments although co-payments and deductibles are so significant that elderly Americans now pay more out-of-pocket expenses for medical care than they did in 1964, before Medicare was introduced, and that controlling for cost in real terms. But the fiscal situation is made more complex by the confusing mix of public and private funding for other sectors of the medical care industry. Tax rebates to large employers cost more to the country annually than the whole funding of Medicaid, the scheme which provides coverage for the medically indigent. Both Medicare and Medicaid use regulations and policies whose purpose is to drive down hospital and physician costs in the provision of care to the elderly and the medically indigent. Additional financial confusion arises from the fact that somewhere between 30 and 37 million Americans have no medical care insurance and a further 15 million or so (some estimates go as high as 50 million) are deemed to have inadequate insurance coverage. Hospitals, particularly those in the public sector, must absorb the costs of treating the uninsured when they are hospitalized. The need to cover the cost of treatment of uninsured patients is threatening the very existence of American public hospitals as a recent study from the National Association of Public Hospitals (1991) demonstrates most clearly. The problems of the public hospitals are exacerbated even further, since for many Americans without medical insurance the emergency rooms of public hospitals represent their only source of medical care.

A further factor adding to the increasing cost of medical care in the United States is related to profit. In both the hospital sector and the third party payer market a significant proportion of insurance coverage and medical services are offered on a private-for-profit basis. Costs for medical care are driven upwards by the need to generate and maintain healthy profits for the investors who provide the financing for private-for-profit health insurance companies and proprietary hospitals. Profits and other unnecessary administrative overhead (Woolhandler and Himmelstein, 1991; U.S. G.A.O., 1991), stemming from the large number of third party payers competing in the insurance market, are increasingly recognized as economic factors which in part explain the thirteen percent of the GNP absorbed by medical care in the United States—more than any other country in the western world—while leaving significant segments of the American population without access to medical care.

Of major import and clear relevance to the present project is the extent to which commodification of medical care is a significant component of a country's medical care system and the degree of medical dominance which impinges on both policy issues and the day-to-day administration, management and provision of medical care. There seems to be a clear link between commodification and medical dominance. A fee-for-service payment mechanism for the reimbursement of professional services is a central feature of the commodification of medical care and also seems to enhance the degree of medical dominance within a given medical care system. Nursing homes, for example, might more appropriately be named nursing hospitals since, as Diamond (1986) has so clearly demonstrated, institutionalized care of the elderly is dominated by a medical model of treatment and procedures, rather than by concepts which would enable nursing hospitals to be real homes. A fee-for-service system treats medicine as a commodity like any other in market exchange. Providers charge what the market will bear and consumers are expected to choose between alternative service providers in accordance with the usual principles of economic exchange, quality, cost and effectiveness. It is now, however, generally recognized that the consumer, i.e. the patient in medical care exchanges has little ability to exercise real choices (Gill and Horobin, 1972; Waitzkin and Stoeckle, 1976; Gill, 1978). Physicians control an esoteric body of knowledge inaccessible to the patient which determines both input and outcomes. Physicians decide not only what is wrong with the patient but what treatment modalities are appropriate to ameliorate or cure the disease condition. Under these circumstances, particularly in a system based on a fee-for-service financing mechanism the costs of the input/outcome equation are determined by only one party to the relationship, the physician.

At the interface between medical and social systems of care medical decisions often determine the extent to which non-medical services may be provided to meet the complex mix of social and medical care necessary to alleviate the problem to be addressed. This is particularly important in geriatric care since declining biological and bodily functions can in part be compensated by the provision of social services whose purpose is to support elderly persons in their current environments through procedures which compensate for declining bio/social abilities. Services for the elderly, therefore, are likely to be affected by the degree of commodification within a medical care system and the element of medical dominance which controls the circumstances in which services are provided. What is to be done?

Decommodification of medical care services would be a first and essential step. This would not, however, deal with the problem of medical dominance in the total array of service provision for the elderly which involves a complex mix of medical and social services if the needs of the elderly are to be adequately dealt with. What follows is a brief outline of a different form of distributive justice which, it is suggested, more adequately and fairly spreads the cost of elderly care and creates the opportunity to generate adequate service provision.

Two principles, uniformity and equity and one process, the direct public accountability of the medical profession through the body politic to the population it serves, would lead to the decommodification of medical care and reduce the element of medical dominance. Uniformity implies the provision of uniform quality of medical services in all geographic locations. Although the USA, for example, possesses a highly favorable physician/population ratio of approximately 400:1 (a higher number of physicians per unit of population than most other Western societies), residents of inner city ghettos and sparsely populated districts often are unable to gain access to medical care, while the suburbs are often over-supplied with physician services. Even what many authorities regard as a current and growing over-supply of physicians in the U.S. has not assured the migration of physicians to all under-served areas.

The second principle, that of equity, requires that medical services should be provided in such a way that no one is barred from access to them. Funding of such a medical care delivery system is probably best dealt with through direct taxation, perhaps with a component of co-payment or deductibles for those in the top quartile of incomes. The U.S. system of taxation is just about the most regressive in the Western world. Indirect taxation is an important component of both State and Federal government and, of course, is a serious burden for the least well-off. Direct taxation is only mildly progressive and the loopholes are so large that wealthy people may pay little in income tax if they employ competent tax consultants. (Some wealthy people, frequently in the public eye, may not take advantage of all the loopholes so that they may present a favorable public image.) Social Security, a significant charge on low wage occupations, is only mildly progressive.

The third component in the decommodification of medical care would entail the public ownership of hospitals, nursing homes, the medical supply and drug industries and the primary care sector. Physicians would be placed on salary, like most other health care workers; a mechanism which has much potential for reducing medical care costs, as the HMO experiment has shown.

But above all, public ownership of the medical care industry would generate a degree of public accountability in medicine. The body politic would control and be responsible for the allocation of resources to the medical care sector. If nothing else such a procedure could prevent the expensive and unnecessary duplication of medical technologies where, presently, hospitals compete with one another for physician services by offering doctors the full array of high technology procedures to ensure adequate staffing. The city of Denver, for example, has 12 hospitals, 11 of which operate CAT scanners. Current logic forces the question: What is wrong with the 12th hospital? Current data do not enable one to state precisely how many CAT scanners are needed in Denver, but 11 are certainly well above the medical need of the catchment area. Similar arguments apply to the duplication of cardio-vascular surgical units, transplant facilities, intensive care units, with the additional problem that underutilization may also jeopardize clinical outcomes (Enthoven and Kronick, 1991).[1] How irrational it is to attempt to influence distributive decisions through the crude and impersonal process of the market place which takes no account of the medical care needs of the population to be served. Far better to introduce a system where planners, administrators, providers and representatives of the population to be served, exercise their collective wisdom and judgment to determine the allocation and distribution of medical and social services. Morally, the generation of profits from the fear, pain and suffering of people's illnesses and diseases is an obscenity. It is only through adoption of the principles briefly outlined above that the obscenity of private-for-profit medical care can be eradicated.

Any serious attempt to decommodify medical care in the current political climate in the U.S. is unlikely. While interest groups as diverse as organized labor, CEOs of large corporations and representatives of the elderly favor the introduction of a universal form of medical insurance other forces in U.S. society—the health insurance industry, some physicians, pharmaceutical and medical manufacturing companies, the owners of private-for-profit hospitals and nursing homes (where 70-75% of providers are for-profit entities)—prefer the status quo but with an expansion of public sector funding to enable the less-well-off to purchase medical insurance. Opinion polls suggest that many Americans are dissatisfied with the present medical care system and are willing to support the introduction of reforms aimed at providing a national health insurance program even if it involves higher taxes. Nevertheless the combination of political forces and other pressure groups to form an effective coalition to enforce health insurance reform is yet to be achieved and is unlikely to emerge in the foreseeable future.

This reluctance to address the problems of the provision of medical care in the U.S. seems to be part of a more general lack of commitment to intervene publicly in other areas where the welfare structure is wanting. Public schools are under-financed precisely in those geographic areas where the deprived and the underprivileged are concentrated and where additional resources are needed to combat a wide combination of social insults, unemployment, under-employment, inadequate housing, etc., etc. Western capitalism's most obvious failure is its response or rather lack of response to the dips and swings of the trade cycle. The West seems to have little response to the breakdown of Eastern European economies other than to tacitly accept a massive growth in unemployment in those countries. Domestically Western societies seem equally incapable of eliminating unemployment but provide varying degrees of financial support to the unemployed and some make available re-training schemes for workers made redundant. Moreover, it is only in countries with a highly developed welfare state that unemployment pay and retraining schemes indemnify workers against a sharp reduction in standards of living.

Variations in unemployment insurance illustrate very well the differences in financial support for the unemployed in European welfare states.

Only Belgium pays unemployment benefits permanently but the rate declines with time unemployed. Only Holland, Ireland and Britain provide unlimited income support once unemployment is exhausted by supplementary social security payments, but at very low levels. In the U.S. jobless benefits are unstandardized and vary widely from state to state. Benefits only last for 26 weeks and recently only 42% of Americans out of work were getting benefits compared with 75% in the mid-1970s recession. Tighter eligibility requirements and difficulty in extending benefits beyond the 26-week period in all but a few states account for this reduction of almost a half (*Sun*, June 4, 1991:5). While all developed societies incorporate some degree of welfare provision into their socio-economic structure, the dichotomy between countries with a

TABLE 1

Unemployment Insurance for a Single Person Aged Less than 50 Years

	Maximum duration (months)	% of gross wages Rate (%)	Ceiling on insurable wages (as 1988)**
Belgium	unlimited	60-40+	0.8
Germany	22*	63++	1.7
France	19*	75-57'	5.0
Holland	36*	70	1.8
Italy	6	15"	0.7
Denmark	30*	90	0.8
Ireland	15	85'	1.2
Britain	12	flat	-
Spain	24	80-60+	0.9
Portugal	6*	65	2.6
Greece	8*	65	0.7
Sweden	14	80#	1.1

*Depending on employment record
**as proportion of average OECD production worker's earnings
+ rate declines with time unemployed
++ rate of net wages
' rate is declining function of wage
" 66% in case of redundancy
flat rate payments fixed at 80% of average wage in industry.

Reprinted in The Economist, May 11th, 1991:57 Source: OECD

highly developed welfare state in contrast to those where welfare provision is at a low level is clearly useful to the task we are undertaking. Adequate geriatric care which attempts to meet the social, economic and medical needs of the elderly will be most likely in countries with a well-developed welfare state in which the principles of distributive justice in terms of equity, uniformity and public accountability, influence or control the way in which services to the elderly are delivered.

This distinction between 'high' and 'low' levels of the welfare state is formalized in an article discussing relationships between equality, social solidarity and the Welfare State by Weale (1990). Weale distinguishes between 'high' and 'low' welfare state provision under the terms, respectively, the *institutional* and the *residual* form of the welfare state, in the following ways:

The paradigm of the institutional welfare state is the form of provision that we find in Sweden. High levels of public provision and low levels of private provision are typical in the fields of health care and education. In the field of income maintenance, the emphasis is upon earnings-related benefits built upon a substructure of flat-rate benefits paid from general taxation and not related to occupational provision. The market remains the basic device by which goods and services are allocated and investment decisions made, but it is complemented by an extensive series of policies for countering unemployment, raising the skill levels of the workforce and negotiating "solidaristic" wage bargains that narrow differentials. The paradigm of the residual welfare state remains the United States, with the exception of education provision and some aspects of the social security system. But in the United States there is little public provision for those otherwise able to pay for themselves. There are no family benefits, there is no compulsory health insurance coverage, and the earnings-related social security system still leaves considerable incentives for better-paid workers to take out private coverage.

Further, institutional welfare states tend to share certain characteristics in common:

The Scandinavian and the Continental welfare states share a range of features: access to universal benefits is high and to means-tested benefits is low; the share of "minimum income" benefits in total benefits is low; and the proportion of the Gross Domestic Product devoted to social policy is high. There are differences, of course. The Scandinavian welfare state devotes a higher proportion of its resources to full employment benefits and is more skewed toward meeting current need than matching past contributions, and there are significant differences in management and control. However, both forms seem to contrast with the Anglo-American form of residualism in which access to universal benefits is low and access to means-tested benefits high, and in which the share of "minimum income" benefit in total benefits is high (475-6).

In the case of the elderly the frailties of illness and old age, with the exception of those who die in early old age, are the almost inevitable consequences of the aging process. In the chapters which follow readers can judge for themselves the extent to which each society approaches the institutional or residual forms of welfare state provision.

While the distinction between institutional and residual forms of the welfare state provides a further conceptual tool for comparative analysis, we must also be aware of the large societal and economic circumstances which distinguish countries and that generate very different economic bases upon which welfare systems are erected. Until recently the major differences in terms of macro-economic organization were to be found between the 'state capitalism' of the former USSR and its Eastern European satellites and the 'mixed' economies of Western Europe and North America.[2] Today 'state capitalism' in the former Iron Curtain countries is rapidly being dismantled, although it remains to be seen how the populations of for example former Eastern Germany, Poland and even the USSR will react to the introduction of market forces which will steeply increase the costs of food, housing, education and other basic amenities which formerly were controlled to provide a low but essentially guaranteed standard of living. Presumably the forms of welfare provision associated with 'state capitalism' will also disappear. In most cases this may not be a severe loss since medical and social services were often under-funded compared with western countries operating an institutionalized form of the welfare state. In the case of occupational safety and health services, but not anti-pollution programs, formerly East Germany had the most intensive and effective set of provisions in Europe with the single exception of Sweden (Elling, 1986). As unification proceeds it will be interesting to see if the East German example prevails and the well-developed system of OSH provision is adopted throughout all of Germany.

Indeed, the future stability of the former Communist countries is further threatened by the geopolitics consequent upon the annexation of former independent territories (Latvia, Lithuania and Estonia) and the imposition of a 'Soviet' identity upon a landmass containing enormous ethnic and cultural variations which constituted the Union of Soviet Socialist Republics. Will the collectivist ideology, however imperfectly embedded in the 'state capitalism' of Russia and its former satellites, be entirely swept aside or will welfare states re-emerge in the previous territories of Eastern Europe as they begin to re-build and re-arrange their socio-economic structures to accommodate to the new circumstances following the breakdown of Communism? Who knows? Who would be silly enough to attempt predictions upon what will happen in Eastern Europe?

Are the sources of this dilemma to be found only in the distortions of 'state capitalism' in Eastern European societies? Are such circumstances also to be found in Western and North American societies where equally threatening disjunctions to the social order exist and which must be addressed if these societies are to continue to prosper? At this juncture another dichotomy, that between 'high' and 'low' wage economies, may be relevant to the second theme represented in the title of this work—retrenchment or expansion of the welfare state. Westerners object to the lack of political freedom and expression in Communist countries as do the inhabitants of the USSR, Poland, Hungary, Bulgaria and so on. The inhabitants of these countries similarly object to the limited supply of consumer goods and the low standard of living in Communist regimes. Lack of consumer goods in Eastern Europe is, at least in part, a consequence of the 'low' wage economies of these countries. Under 'state capitalism' 'low' wages represent a form of forced saving which finances state expenditures on large armed forces, support for Communism world-wide and high investments in 'prestige' projects such as space exploration. These forced savings clearly divert current and capital resources from consumer industries. Ultimately guns and satellites are no substitute for butter and better housing and the populations so deprived seek redress through social, economic and political change.

In Western Europe and North America 'low' wage economies most certainly exist while others could be described as 'high' wage economies. In the 'low' wage economies, segments of the population are relatively or absolutely deprived. Moreover, while 'low' and 'high' wages may not be characteristic of all economic segments or classes in a given society the presence and persistence of a 'low' wage segment will have serious implications for social and welfare provision. If the 'low' wage sector also persists throughout the life-cycle then all seven ages of man will remain relatively deprived.[3] Poverty in old age is most often the consequence of low pay and/or interrupted employment throughout the adolescent and adulthood work experience as well as earlier childhood deprivation.

Barry (1990:524-5) has described the characteristics and consequences of 'high' and 'low' wage economics in the following terms:

> Some countries (e.g., Sweden and West Germany) have a high minimum wage...and then seek to give the work force sufficient training to make its members profitably employable at that wage. In such a set-up, nobody in full-time employment will have an unacceptably low income, provided that there is an adequate scheme of child benefit. For then full-time pay will be enough for everyone to live on.

> This approach has much to commend it. To insist that every full-time job should pay a "living wage" makes eminently good sense economically as a way of forcing firms to make efficient use of labor. It is also, I believe, morally obnoxious that people in full-time employment should require their pay to be supplemented to bring it up to a level that is regarded in their society as constituting a decent amount to live on. By the same token, it is also, I suggest, morally obnoxious that firms that pay low wages should in effect be publicly subsidized.

Nevertheless, some countries, such as Britain and the United States, have gone down the low-wage path. Thus, in the past ten years in Britain, the minimum wage legislation covering traditionally low-wage areas (e.g., catering) has been abolished, and the new jobs that have been created have been in precisely such low-wage service occupations, while the jobs that have been lost have tended to be semi-skilled ones with adequate rates of pay. Faced with an economy in which a substantial proportion of jobs fails to pay enough to live on, a government that accepts an obligation to avoid stark poverty (and wishes to ensure that being employed compares favorably with being unemployed) has only two choices. One is the Poor Law approach of making up household income where it falls short of the official poverty level, and this is that approach that has been followed in Britain and (less systematically through the food stamp program) in the United States.

The relationship between poverty and low pay in the United States is well-documented by a recent study by the Food Research Action Center (1991) of a survey of poor people conducted in 1989 when the Federal Government defined a family as poor if its total income was $9,885 or less for a family of three and $12,675 or less for a family of four. The study found that almost 12 million children (18 or under) or one in five lived in poor families. In almost two-thirds of these the 'family' (including single parent families) included at least one worker. Nevertheless, two in five poor children live in families in which the father is present.

To put the reality of low pay into clearer perspective consider the following: a single parent family headed by a female (almost 90% of single parent families are headed by a woman) with two children, one school-age, one pre-school. (Currently minimum wage is $4.25 per hour—$3.75 per hour in 1989). Assume a minimum wage job for eight hours per day, five days per week, 50 weeks per year.

Income	*Poverty Line: Family of Three*
$8,500	$9,885

This income, $1,385 below the poverty line, it is suggested is simply insufficient to cover rent of a two-bedroom apartment, travel expenses to work, baby-sitting for the pre-school child and to provide a minimally acceptable standard of living. Savings for holidays and retirement would be out of the question. If this family is to avoid stark poverty, then government assistance is essential and in the U.S. programs such as Aid to Families with Dependent Children and the Special Supplemental Food Program for Women, Infants and Children and the Food Stamp Program are in effect devices to subsidize inadequate wages, unemployment pay or social security benefits. All these programs require elaborate staffing by administrators and case workers yet the CCHIP revealed 37% of those eligible for food stamps were not receiving them, and, of those eligible for WIC, 55% were not receiving WIC benefits. Not only are these programs inefficient, they also must be serviced by batteries of administrators and case workers who apply strict tests of eligibility before these forms of relief are available to poor people.

As Woolhandler and Himmelstein (1991:1253–1256) have demonstrated, the administrative structure of the American health care system is increasingly inefficient as compared with Canada's national health program and even more dramatically expensive when compared with the administrative costs of the British National Health Service. "In 1987 health care administration cost between $96.8 billion and $120.4 billion in the United States, amounting to 19.3 to 24.1 percent of total spending on health care or $400 to $497 per capita. In Canada, between 8.4 and 11.1 percent of health care spending ($117 to $156 per capita) was devoted to administration." Many factors are involved, additional costs generated by the production of profit in the private-for-profit health insurance sector, the fragmented and complex payment structure, competition among insurers, and the obverse of economies of scale consequent upon the duplication of administrative costs through the multiplicity of third-party payers. Even more bizarre is the increase in costs associated with attempts to improve the efficiency with which medical care services are provided: "The United States spent 37% more in real dollars in health administration in 1987 than in 1983. The recent quest for efficiency has apparently amplified inefficiency. Cost-containment programs predicated on stringent scrutiny of the clinical encounter have required an army of bureaucrats to eliminate modest amounts of unnecessary care. Each piece of medical terrain is meticulously inspected except that between the inspectors' feet."

No study which examines the administrative overhead in the U.S. social system compared with the 'costs' for the delivery of social services to the poor, the elderly, the disabled and other disadvantaged groups has been completed with anything like the credibility, universal estimates and sophistication of Woolhandler and Himmelstein's study of the medical care system. Logico-deductive reasoning would, however, suggest that many of the factors generating waste and inefficiency in the medical care system are likely to be duplicated in the social care system. We have already noted that 70-75% of nursing homes in the U.S. are operated on a private-for-profit basis. The costs of long-term institutional care are therefore higher than would be the case if such services were provided on a non-profit basis. Waste consequent upon administrative inefficiency and unnecessary duplication of service agencies may also apply to the social service sector. In 1987, the list of social service agencies operating in Boone County in Missouri included 180 different organizations providing services and counseling to the area's inhabitants. The total catchment area covered a population of 100,000, an average of roughly one agency for every 550 inhabitants. Many of these agencies had full time administrative and clerical staff while others used largely volunteer staff. The mix of public, quasi-public and volunteer effort in the social service arena may well represent an extremely high administrative cost per unit of expenditure on clients and services to clients. Certainly many charities including the United Way have been criticized for the high proportion of administrative and other costs deducted from each dollar before donations are passed on to private, quasi-public or public agencies involved in the amelioration or assistance of the deprived and the under-privileged. Attempts, therefore, to compensate individuals and families in the 'low' wage sector through social services seem to mirror the inefficiencies of medical care provision including Medicare and Medicaid, the latter whose purpose is to protect the vulnerable in the medical care system.

The circumstances of people in the 'low' wage sector is made even more deplorable by the absence of affordable housing. Rental units for low-income families are a scarce resource in the U.S. compared with other Western societies. In Britain, notwithstanding the sale of council housing to sitting tenants, the stock of low-rental public housing can represent 20-30% of the total housing stock. In some Scottish cities, e.g. Aberdeen, almost 50% of families are housed in rental properties owned by the local authority in which the rents are affordable to low-wage earners. A recent report by the Center on Budget and Policy Priorities entitled "A Place to Call Home: The Crisis in Housing for the Poor—Baltimore, Maryland," (one of a series of similar studies in 10 other cities, including Birmingham, Detroit, Milwaukee, San Francisco and Buffalo) found that 1) four out of five poor households (those earning less than $10,000) in the Baltimore area pay more than 30% of their income for housing—the maximum considered affordable under federal standards. 2) 60% of poor white households and 54% of poor black households spend at least half their income on housing, and 3) many households with incomes of $10,000-$30,000 spend 30% or more on housing, while only 1% of those with incomes higher than $60,000 pay that much. A spokesperson for the Baltimore Housing Authority stated that the number of subsidized housing units has remained the same over the last decade and that the number of households on the waiting list is 30,000 with many remaining on the waiting lists for up to 10 years before they get subsidized housing. (Barancik and Sheft, 1991)

A significant number of low-cost housing units in towns and cities can contribute to the maintenance of an independent existence for elderly persons. Some units can be converted or specially designed to provide accommodations for the frail elderly who would otherwise require long-term institutional care. Such units can be grouped around day-care centers, dining rooms and staff made available to provide intermittent or continuing domestic services, social and medical care services.

The Reagan era, characterized by an enormous increase in defense spending, turned America from a creditor to the largest debtor nation in the Western world and managed to attack and reduce welfare expenditures, particularly entitlement programs. Federal support for education, never a large component of central government expenditure in the USA compared with other Western countries, was reduced and more costs shifted to the states. But of all public allocations for the common good, expenditures on public housing were reduced the most drastically. Disbursement of the sum available to support the development of subsidized housing was fraught with corruption and inappropriate use of HUD funds throughout much of the eighties further reducing the money available to build low-income housing. Retrenchment of the Welfare State was indeed a priority of the Reagan administration.

Some might object to discussion of issues such as low wages, administrative inefficiencies throughout the medical and social service care sector, inadequate public housing and the relationship between low pay and poverty in a set of readings designed to examine the plight of the elderly and the services available to them in a number of different countries. The point is, however, that resources are finite. Even Sweden, which competes with Holland for the title of the most advanced welfare state in the Western world, is beginning a process of retrenchment of its social services, although the planners argue that a reduction in standards will not be noticeable since current provisions are already most generous.

Even the brief comments presented here on the U.S. welfare system demonstrate the degree of underdevelopment of its medical and social care systems and the cut-backs of the Reagan administration (and the apparent continuation of such policies under President Bush) have made the situation even more desperate. More, rather than less, allocation of the GNP to the welfare sector is essential if the 'tail' of poverty, of real as well as relative deprivation, is to be reduced in American society. In this context it should be clear that services and support for the elderly must be viewed, not in isolation, but in relation to the total organization of welfare services and support to all under-privileged groups in American society. It is, therefore, not sufficient to study the care of the elderly in isolation. The extent to which retrenchment or development of the welfare state characterizes service provision in different countries is important to our understanding of the ways in which geriatric care is provided now and the circumstances under which it will be supported in the foreseeable future.

In a similar vein it is also important to note the dominant aspects of economic activity which operate in the various nation-states under review. A detailed analysis of the economic system in each country to be discussed and compared would be an impossible undertaking in a single collection of readings. Nevertheless, following Offe (1984) some broad categories under which labor power is organized and rewarded may be useful, particularly in identifying those aspects of economic activity which distinguish between 'high' and 'low' wage economies. The social labor power of industrial societies tends to be distributed between different sections and rewarded differently in the various segments of economic activity.

Offe (1984) identifies four such sectors, the monopoly, competitive, and state sectors and a final somewhat differently constituted sector of residual labor power. The *monopoly sector* is characterized by a high degree of organization of the capital and labor market. Price competition is relatively minimal. Labor costs are a small proportion of total costs but wages are high since the unions are strong and labor costs can be passed on through price increases. But even here, international competitive forces are beginning to impact, mostly through international wage competition as well as varying rates of fringe benefits charged against, for example, the automobile industry in different national settings.[4] Nevertheless in internal markets (i.e. not including imports or where imports are limited by quotas) increased costs can be passed on through price increases consequent upon the monopolistic or oligopolistic supply situation. In the *competitive sector* price competition is greater but still limited since many of the goods and services are produced and sold to the monopoly sector which can again influence prices. Trade unions tend to be less well-organized, cover fewer members of the work force and have less bargaining power both economically and within the larger trade union movement. "The competitive sector is dependent upon the monopoly sector...because the room for maneuver of small and medium-sized businesses is determined both qualitatively and quantitatively by the degree to which they are able to function as suppliers and distributors for the large corporations for whose patronage they can only compete" (Offe, 1984:37).

Apart from the absence or near absence of price competition the *state sector* has characteristics of both the monopoly and competitive sectors. In state bureaucracies and institutions civil servants or salaried employees are remunerated through sovereign political organization principles rather than those of exchange. Salaries are paid through government receipts, but to some extent the state must take account of wages and salaries in the private sector since it must compete with the private economy for labor power. Trade unions exist but their power to operate in constraint of trade is often severely reduced or even eliminated. Nevertheless, while wage bargaining may not be conducted in accordance with the normal principles of conflict between employers and employees characteristic of the private sector, the notion of a fair wage has often influenced payments to certain categories of state workers to compensate for their loss of ability to strike. Postal workers, for example, in the United States, not only benefit from security of employment but also receive better wages than other occupational categories whose work can be described at best as semi-skilled.

In the *residual labor power sector* market mediated relationships are either eliminated or of limited and indirect influence. Work performed in this sector is virtually decommodified. The payments received by categories such as old-age pensioners, the unemployed, the disabled, college students, and drafted servicemen are transfer payments which are determined directly by political and administrative decisions rather than by economic forces. Employment in the armed forces may be indirectly affected by the broader state of the economy. During periods of depression employment in the army may be very attractive compared with no employment at all, but the amount of remuneration is still a political and administrative decision. The work of full-time housewives as feminist theorists have so ably demonstrated, is outside the forces of the marketplace.

While these distinctions in terms of the four sectors are useful they are not distinct categories. There is considerable overlap in at least three sectors, the competitive, the state sector and the residual labor power sector. In the state sector state industries and services may be in competition albeit limited, with the competitive sector. The Federal Postal System must compete with UPS and Federal Express, for example. Nevertheless the degree of competition is lessened by the need of the state sector to maintain the service component in its operation. The Federal Postal System is unable to control costs by eliminating distributions to areas either nationally or internationally "uncompetitive." The Postal Service must deliver to all of Alaska as well as to addressees in remote areas all over the globe. Federal Express can and does limit its operations to areas which are easily serviced. Many small businesses in the competitive sector and some oligopolies in the monopoly sector are dependent upon government contracts for some or even all of their profits. A good example is the so-called defense industry where all profits may be derived from tax revenues or the sale of weapons and weapons systems to overseas customers.

But it is in the residual labor power sector that Offe's analysis (1984) seems the least effective. It is probable that many service industries would be unable to operate without the labor of old age pensioners, high school and college students and housewives. Part-time work in the last two decades is an important contributor to service industries as varied as real estate, fast food restaurants, super markets and large numbers of organizations which service the needs of the underclass in both urban and rural settings.

In the service industries an independent existence based on even full time work may be impossible. Even for a single person a gross salary of $12,000 per annum (after taxes and other stoppages and an allowance for minimal expenses) could hardly be called a living wage and the preservation of an independent existence and lifestyle is likely impossible. In the residual labor power sector it is not surprising that we find a concentration of members of the work force in categories such as old age pensioners, high school and college students and housewives.

This introduction to the readings which follow has attempted to identify major concepts which will guide the reader through an evaluation of each country's system of care for its older citizens. The concepts outlined above may or may not be applicable to a particular society, but we suggest that the basic concerns associated with distributive justice and the extent of the welfare state and therefore service provision, are issues that are implicit or explicit in the organization of elderly care. Moreover, these issues are in turn associated with the nature of each society's social and economic infrastructure, the way in which rewards are distributed and the emphasis upon individualistic or collectivist solutions to the problems to be addressed in complex modern industrial or industrializing social systems. In an epilogue we will try to show how and in what ways each of the concepts developed here—equity, uniformity, public accountability, individualism, collectivism, institutional or residual welfare state orientation, 'high' or 'low' wage economics—apply to and help explain the variation in provisions for the care of the elderly in each of the societies represented.

Selection of Countries

Starting in the late seventies and continuing throughout the eighties a number of countries, notably the United States and Britain, began to reduce their commitments to the welfare state. In both countries reduction in the extent of welfare provision was accompanied by attacks on trades unionism possibly associated with the declining fortunes of liberal, socialist and social democratic political forces. The degree to which political conservatism increased its power base was of course not uniform and the shift to the right was muted if the welfare state was well established in the major sectors of social, medical and economic activity.

Countries were selected to illustrate the differing degrees of contemporary welfare state provision and its consequences for care of the elderly *and* to illustrate the different socio-historical circumstances under which the welfare state had developed in a variety of national settings. A focus upon European and North American nations seemed appropriate to compare and contrast the fairly extensive differences in welfare provision between societies at relatively similar levels of socio-economic development and loose but important socio-historical ties across the Atlantic. Sweden and the USA represent, if not polar opposites, nations in which the degree of welfare state development may be contrasted in terms of extensive against limited welfare provisions. France, Western Germany, Italy and Switzerland represent different points on the continuum between the advanced and limited welfare state systems of Sweden and USA. Canada, particularly in the medical care sector, leans more toward the European as opposed to the USA end of the continuum, yet its major trading partner is the United States and many Canadian industries are dependent upon American investments. In light of the above, comparisons between the various European communities, between them and the North American societies and between Canada and the USA may be particularly fruitful for exploring the relationships between the extent of welfare provision, distributive justice and care of the elderly in countries with fairly similar democratic institutions and economic systems.

The former USSR and Poland represent societies which, until recently, differed markedly from European and North American nations in their political, social and economic institutions and underlying ideologies. The USSR and Poland, although purporting to provide governments representing the interests of the working class were in fact organized as state capitalist societies. In such circumstances government determines the ways in which the surplus product is distributed. To what degree will state capitalist governments be prepared to direct scarce resources to the welfare state and elderly care?

At first sight it might appear strange to include Iceland and Japan when contrasting the development of the welfare state, care of the elderly and the ways in which issues of distributive justice are dealt with in different national settings. In the case of Iceland the rationale stems from the amazing rapidity with which a complex welfare state apparatus, particularly with respect to the elderly, was developed between 1890 and the present day which also encompassed a socio-historical transition from virtually a feudal to a modern economy over the same period. All the Scandinavian countries have well developed welfare state systems and Iceland's historic ties to the Nordic countries may have provided examples of what could be accomplished if a commitment to protect the deprived and underprivileged is accorded high priority. Nevertheless, the Icelandic experience must be nearly unique and for this reason is of interest.

In a similar way Japan is also an example of a society subject to very rapid change over a limited period—say the last 100 years. After establishing an Empire over virtually all of the Far East and the Central Pacific followed by defeat in World War II, in the 1980s Japan was one of the leading economic powers of the late twentieth century. This rapid rate of change was associated with—for a limited period—the emergence and powerful impact of a left wing movement which encouraged the development of a welfare state apparatus. Subsequently, the working class movement lost power but the initial welfare state structure remained, albeit at a less effective and less interventionist level.

The societies chosen, therefore, provide an opportunity to explore the influence of individualism vs. collectivism, equity, uniformity, public accountability, distributive justice, residual vs. institutionalized forms of the welfare state in a number of different social systems each with their own socio-historical precedents upon which welfare mechanisms were built. It is to be hoped that these comparative perspectives will help to clarify the relationships between elderly care, the welfare state and distributive justice and to indicate the extent to which further expansion, steady state, or retrenchment of welfare systems must prevail if the needs of the elderly are to be adequately met.

Notes

1. Enthoven and Kronic (1991:2533-5) state... "We have a proliferation of costly specialized services that are underutilized... in 1986, more than one third of the hospitals in California doing open-heart surgery performed fewer than 150 operations, the minimum annual volume recommended by the American College of Surgeons (Los Angeles Times, December 27, 1988) and such differences in utilization are accomplished by wide differences in charges... "For example, in L.A. in 1986 one hospital performed 44 coronary artery bypass grafts with an 11.4% death rate and median charges of $59,000, while another hospital performed 770 coronary artery bypass grafts with a 38% death rate and median charges of $16,000 (*Los Angeles Times*, July 24, 1988:3).

2. The notion of "state capitalism" is a more accurate description of the economics of Russia and its former Eastern European satellites than the descriptor communist. Communism implies a form of government structure in which authority is nested in the hands of organized working class groups. In the previous Iron Curtain countries a political apparatus representative of little more than its own membership constructed an elaborate state bureaucracy which controlled production, the allocation of scarce resources as well as day-to-day aspects of social, political and economic life of its populations. Throughout such societies the distribution of economic surplus was controlled, not through the mechanisms of the market place, but by decisions made by

and handed down throughout the state bureaucratic structure—a form of "state capitalism" rather than a form of distribution in which distributive justice issues were related to the broad needs of the total collectivity.

   3. William Shakespeare. As You Like It. Act II scene VII

"Jacques" All the world's a stage,
And all the men and women merely players,
They have their exits and their entrances,
And one man in his time plays many parts,
His acts being seven ages. At first the infant,
Mewling and puking in the nurse's arms.
Then, the whining schoolboy with his satchel
And shinning morning face, creeping like snail
Unwilling to school. And then the lover,
Sighing like furnace, with a woeful ballad
Made to his mistress' eyebrow. Then, a soldier,
Full of strange oaths, and bearded like the pard,
Jealous in honour, sudden, and quick in quarrel,
Seeking the bubble reputation
Even in the canon's mouth. And then in justice,
In fair round belly, with good capon lin'd,
With eyes severe, and beard of formal cut,
Full of wise saws, and modern instances,
And so he plays his part. The sixth age shifts
Into the lean and slipper'd pantaloon,
With spectacles on nose, and pouch on side,
His youthful hose well sav'd, a world too wide
For his shrunk shank, and his big manly voice,
Turning again toward childish treble, pipes
And whistles in his sound. Last scene of all,
That ends this strange eventful history,
Is second childishness and mere oblivion,
Sans teeth, sans eyes, sans taste, sans everything.

   4. Today the power of the unions in the U.S. is limited. Less than 20% of the labor force is unionized and their bargaining power is limited by "a quirk in federal labor law under which employers cannot fire a worker who strikes legally but can give the striker's job and paycheck to a permanent replacement (*Sun*, July 18, 1991)." In the last 10 years a number of large U.S. companies have used this tactic for breaking legal strikes—Hormel, TWA, Continental, Eastern Airlines, Phelps Dodge, International Paper and Greyhound. President Reagan was able to dismember PATCO through this legal facility which abrogates the right of working people to withhold their labor. Most other industrialized countries outlaw this practice.

   On July 17, 1991 the House passed a bill which would ban the permanent replacement of workers striking over economic issues. Predictably the proposed bill will face much stiffer opposition in the Senate where conservative forces, whether Democrat or Republican, predominate. Equally predictable, Bush has vowed to veto such legislation should it reach his desk.

In the absence of a political party that represents the interests of the working class in national politics, the only protection that U.S. workers can hope for is trades unionism. Without the ability to withhold their labor the working class is powerless to bargain effectively against the interests of capital to reduce labor cost in the pursuit of profit maximization. Clearly exploitation of the working class in the U.S. is more extreme than the situation in most other Western societies—with the possible exception of South Africa.

References

Barancik, S. and M. Sheft (1991) A Place To Call Home: The Crisis in Housing for the Poor, Baltimore, Maryland. Center on Budget and Policy Priorities, Washington, DC:p. 92.

Barry, B. (1990) The welfare state versus the relief of poverty. Ethics:100,: 503-529.

Community Childhood Hunger Identification Project: A Survey of Childhood Hunger in the United States (1991). Food Research and Action Center, Washington, D.C. Executive Summary.

Diamond, T. (1986) Social policy and everyday life in nursing homes: a critical ethnography. In Ingman, S. R., and Gill, D.G. Geriatric Care and Distributive Justice: Cross-National Perspectives. *Soc. Sci. & Med.*, 23, No. 12. Special Issue 1267-1278.

Elling, R. H. (1986) *The Struggle for Workers' Health: A Study of Six Industrialized Countries.* Baywood, New York: pp. 498. see especially Chapter 9, East Germany and German History, 229-282.

Enthoven, A. C., and R. Kronick, (1991) Universal health insurance through incentive reforms. *J.A.M.A.*, 265, No 19:2532-2536.

Gill, D. G. (1978) Limitations upon choice and constraints over decision-making in doctor-patient exchanges. In: *The Doctor-Patient Relationship in the Changing Health Scene.* Ed. E. B. Gallagher. DHEW Pub. No. (NIH) 78-183:141-156.

Gill, D. G. and G. W. Horobin (1972). Doctors, patients and the state: Relationship and decision-making. *Soc. Rev.* 20:4:505-520 (new series).

National Association of Public Hospitals (1991). *America's Safety Net Hospitals: The Foundation of Our Nation's Health System.* Gage, L. S., V. B. Weslowski, D. P. Andrulis, E. Hunt, and A. B. Camper, Washington, D.C.:pp. 127.

Offe, C. (1984). *Contradictions of the Welfare State*, Ed. J. Keane. MIT Press. Mass.:pp. 310.

Quadagno, J. (1982) *Aging in Early Industrial Society: Work, Family and Social Policy in Nineteenth Century England,* Academic Press, New York, pp. 210.

Sun, (Baltimore) June 4, 1991:5

Sun, (Baltimore) July 18, 1991:11A

United States General Accounting Office (1991). *Canadian Health Insurance: Lessons for the United States.* G.A.O./H.R.D.-91-90. Washington, D.C.:pp. 85.

Waitzkin, H., and J. D. Stoeckle (1976) Information on the micro politics of health care: Summary of an ongoing research project. *Soc. Sci & Med.* 6:263-276.

Weale, A. (1990) Equality, social solidarity, and the welfare state. *Ethics:100*:473-488.

Woolhandler, S., and D. V. Himmelstein (1991). The deteriorating administrative efficiacy of the U.S. health care system. *New England Journal of Medicine, 324*:1253-8.

1

Sweden: Ideals and Realities of Old Age Care in the Welfare State

Gerdt Sundström and Mats Thorslund

Introduction

In Sweden, nearly all old age care is publicly provided, under public control, and guided by legislation. The "official" aims for the care of the elderly are to assure the elderly of a secure financial situation, good housing, and service and care according to needs (Thorslund, 1989). The public help which the individual receives shall contain an element of choice and options for the recipient and shall maintain high standards.

An explicit principle of equity further implies that the service and care provided by public agencies shall be influenced only by "needs." All the elderly should have equal access to these welfare goods regardless of where they live, regardless of purchasing power, or other factors.

The disparity between public statements at the national level and down-to-earth reality is often great (and not only with regard to the situation of the aged population). The intent of this article is therefore twofold: to describe the organization of Swedish old age care and its principles, and to convey an idea of the limits of equity, the relative lack of uniformity and problems of public accountability that prevail "inside" the national "average" in a modern welfare state.

The Authorities Responsible

Overall responsibility for the various elements of the care of the elderly rests with the state. Government and Parliament legislate and formulate guidelines for how the elderly shall be cared for and who shall bear responsibility for the various services.

Sweden's municipalities (284 in all) are responsible for the social services, and the county councils (23) for health care and medical services. The boards of both these bodies are locally elected, and they enjoy an internationally unique degree of autonomy (though the other Nordic countries are comparable). They levy taxes and spend money at their own discretion. Most services are provided locally, and it is hard for the national government to monitor these authorities. To be sure, there is national legislation as to what shall be provided and how, but this legislation is only a framework, and elusively vague for those who seek concrete guidance.

In the area of old age care, mainly two pieces of legislation apply, both of a recent date. Thus, in 1982 the new Social Services Act (Social-tjänstlagen) came into effect. This framework legislation emphasizes the right of the individual to receive public sector service and help at all stages of his life. Everyone who needs help to support himself in his day-to-day existence has the right to claim assistance if his "needs cannot be met in any other way" (a stipulation of the Social Services Act that may be interpreted differently).

In 1983 a new Health and Medical Services Act (Hälso-och sjuk-vardslagen) came into effect. According to this Act, health care and medical services aim to maintain a good standard of health among the entire population and to provide care of equal terms for all. Responsibility for the running and shaping of health and medical care rests mainly with the 23 county councils and the three metropolitan municipalities of Malmö, Gotland and Göteborg.

From these laws themselves and the extensive work that preceded, especially the first law, one can extract a number of general aims for the care of the elderly, mentioned initially (finances, housing and service-care).

Both laws stress that help shall be given in settings as "normalized" as possible. This means that old people should be helped to remain at home for as long as possible, and in principle no one can be forced to move to an institution due to extensive needs for personal care. Most municipalities have one or more cases where they have to provide around-the-clock home making services.

The autonomy of local administrations and direct elections of local politicians in conjunction with the "loftiness" of the legislation related to social services, health care, and medical care allows the municipalities and the county councils very great freedom to plan and organize their own services in Sweden.

The autonomy of these two levels of local government also means that services for and the care of the elderly have, to a certain extent, come to be organized differently in various parts of the country. Thus, the number of institutional beds in relation to the size of the local population and the scope of home making services and home nursing care, for example, can vary considerably. There are great variations between urban and rural areas, to the disadvantage of the former.

On the other hand, the general principles of the Swedish welfare state regarding the care of the elderly are the same nationwide: namely that care of and services for the elderly are primary public sector responsibilities, and that care shall be given by trained and qualified staff.

The outcome in practice of the general principles of democratic provision of help and support in combination with declarations of respect of individual choice and needs can be studied in a number of areas. We will not cover economic provision, even if there is notable inequity in the pension system. We select the areas of housing, in-the-home care and institutional care of different varieties for our analysis.

Pensions and Allowances

The Swedish system of national pensions and housing allowances is designed to give elderly people financial security. The national pensions scheme covers a basic pension (folkpension), payable to everyone regardless of previous working income, and a supplementary pension (ATP) based on income from gainful employment. A special partial pension makes it possible for employees and self-employed persons aged 60-64 to combine part-time work with a pension.

Usual retirement age is 65 in Sweden. However, one can start to draw the old-age pension from one's 60th birthday or postpone receipt until one reaches 70. The amount received is lower if payments are begun early and higher if they are delayed.

Swedish citizens residing in Sweden are entitled to the full basic pension, as are, on certain conditions, Swedish citizens domiciled abroad and foreign nationals in Sweden. To be eligible for the ATP pension, both Swedes and foreign citizens must have had an income higher than the base rate for a least three years. The size of this pension is calculated on the basis of average pensionable income during a person's 15 best-paid years.

A recipient of the basic pension may be entitled to a municipal housing allowance. This is a means-tested benefit and the rules for eligibility are determined by the municipality. In 1988, 31% of old-age pensioners received this type of benefit.

The housing allowance is only one of a wide range of main and supplementary benefits which can be combined with the basic and ATP pensions (for full range see diagram overleaf). Pension amounts are set by the government each year and are calculated according to a base amount which is related to the consumer price index. In approximate terms, the combined basic and ATP pension for a person with an average industrial worker's salary will equal just over 70% of his earlier net income.

Yet, within this general picture there are noticeable variations. Especially among the oldest and among women, quite a few are at or just above the minimum provision of the general basic pension (folkpension). This would be due to their not having been in paid employment or a few might also have been self-employed persons who earlier chose to "contract out" (particularly farmers). Even among those who retire right now, a fifth of the women are in this precarious situation. Men are usually found in the more advantageous pension categories, but also within these, women receive lower amounts (thanks to the generally higher incomes of men, that produce higher supplementary pensions).

In practice, virtually all the elderly are above the poverty line. No one needs welfare assistance, and very few among the aged complain about economic problems in various surveys. It remains, though, that for some of the elderly, poverty is not very far away. It would still be correct to say that the welfare state has abolished one of the classic poverty traps: old age is no longer synonymous with misery for many aged persons.

Housing

The main concept steering the care of the elderly in Sweden today is that the elderly shall be enabled to continue living in their own homes as long as possible. The fact that the proportion of elderly people in institutions has fallen is a result of this political ideology prevailing in Sweden and many other countries. According to this ideology it is felt that both human and financial benefits can be reaped by reducing institutional residence in favor of helping the elderly to remain living at home.

Most elderly people in Sweden (92%) live in ordinary homes and around half are owner-occupiers. The general standard of housing is high, with most elderly people living in modern, warm homes with well-equipped kitchens, hot and cold running water, and an indoor toilet. Nevertheless, the policy that as many as possible shall remain living at home creates a demand for ordinary dwellings to be adapted and for sufficient care and help in the home when the elderly person can no longer manage on his own. Municipalities therefore carry out home adaptations in order to minimize such difficulties as stairs and thresholds. The costs of these amenities are heavily subsidized or free.

According to the terms of the Social Services Act other forms of housing shall be available to those who can no longer live at home.

Sheltered Accommodations

In 1988 some 41,000 people lived in sheltered accommodations (servicehus) owned and managed by the municipality. Such accommodations take the form of apartments in buildings containing 20-100 housing units, most of which were built during the 1970s and 1980s. The availability of sheltered accommodation, allocation policies, and thus the age and fitness range of the tenants, vary from municipality to municipality. In a fifth of the municipalities there is no accommodation of this kind. The tenants are for the most part pensioners who have ordinary rent contracts with the municipality. The apartments consist of 1-3 rooms plus kitchen and bathroom. Subsidized municipal home-making services are available to residents (after means-testing) in the same way as they are available to those living in ordinary homes. Usually, there is a restaurant in the building, as well as activity rooms, chiropody services, etc. The number of apartments in service homes increased by some 3,000 in 1988.

Old-Age Homes

In 1988 there were some 900 municipal old-age homes with around 44,000 places for elderly people unable to cope at home even with the aid of the home making and nursing services. Many old-age homes are old, with the majority dating from before 1965. In line with the policy that as many old people as possible shall remain living in their own homes, the construction of old-age homes started to decline during the 1970s and almost completely ceased during the following decade. In 1988 the number of places decreased by some 2,000.

Most residents of old-age homes live in small single rooms (approximately 10-15 m^2) with their own toilets. Residents may bring their own furniture with them. Meals are served communally at set times. Various types of facilities and activities are available. Care is provided around-the-clock by regular staff. The monthly fees charged by old-age homes are income-related.

Group Dwellings

During recent years, group dwellings have become an alternative to institutions for persons with great need of care and supervision. There are group dwellings for persons with physical handicaps, psychological problems and many other conditions. Most common, however, are group dwellings for persons with senile dementia. "Group dwellings" usually means a small housing collective for 6-8 persons, in which each resident has his own room, shares communal areas, and has access to service and care provided by resident staff around-the-clock.

In 1988 there were around 1,000 persons living in group dwellings. Previously in Sweden there was no suitable form of housing or care for persons with senile dementia. Experiences of group dwellings have been favorable hitherto and all municipalities and county councils are currently planning an expansion of group dwelling capacity during the coming years.

Home Making Services

The municipalities are responsible for the home making services ("home help") which supply help with shopping, cleaning, cooking, laundry, personal hygiene and nursing (the first four items constitute 80% of the time budget of these services), to those elderly persons living in their own homes who cannot cope on their own. The fees charged for these services vary

FIGURE 1

Number of Persons Receiving Homemaking Services 1964-1988

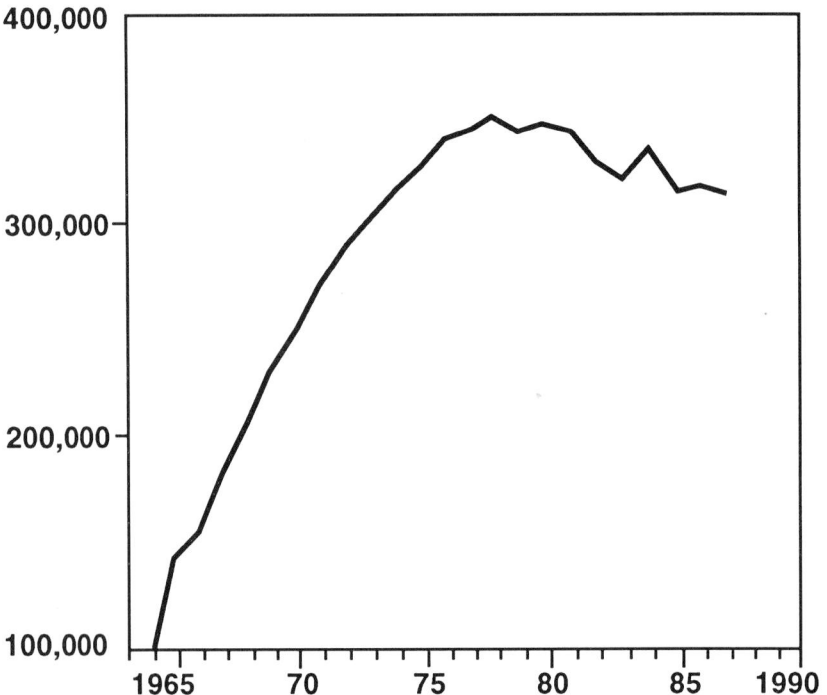

Source: Thorslund, 1990

FIGURE 2

Number of Hours of Help Given in the Public Homemaking
Services to Elderly and Handicapped

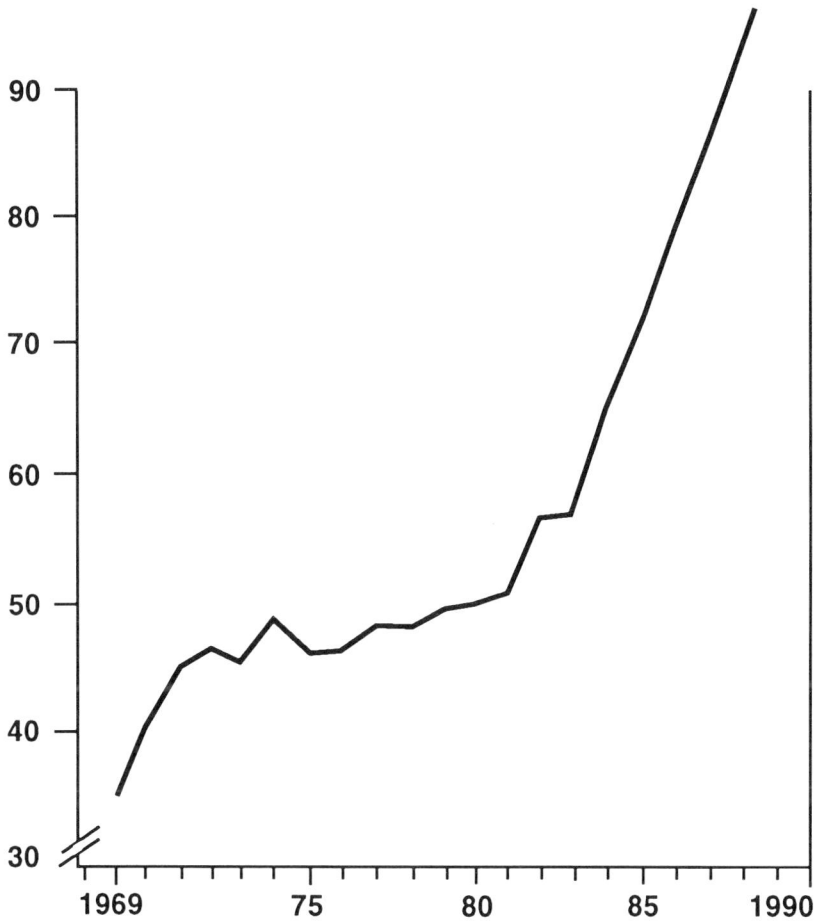

Source: Thorslund, 1990

between municipalities and according to the number of hours of help needed
and the income of the recipient. Help is also available during the evening, at
night, and on weekends. Most municipalities today, for example, provide
night patrols which include both nursing and "home help" staff.

Since the mid-1960s the number of handicapped and elderly people who receive home making services has more than trebled. The numbers of people receiving help increased particularly during the late 1960s and the 1970s, only to decrease somewhat during the 1980s. It is pensioners under the age of 80 and persons under 65 who now receive less help. In 1988 nearly one fifth of Sweden's old-age pensioners (65+) received some form of home making services.

Although the number of recipients of home making services has dropped over the last decade, the total number of hours of home help given to the elderly and handicapped has risen greatly, and the 35 million hours of home making services given in 1969 has grown to over 93 million in 1988. Recipients receive on average a greater number of hours than previously, with fewer people receiving just one or two hours per week. This is a result of decisions taken in an attempt to trim back and rationalize services, to concentrate resources on certain groups of the population—here, the very oldest in the population.

Other forms of service and care are often given in combination with "home help." Most municipalities offer chiropody, hair care, food services (meals-on-wheels), help with bathing, snow-clearing, and day care units for elderly persons with senile dementia or other impairments.

All Swedish municipalities run a transportation service for those elderly and handicapped people who are unable to use ordinary public transportation. Eligibility for this service is established after a needs test, but coverage and charges vary from one municipality to another.

Home Nursing

A growing proportion of the total resources of the medical services in Sweden is being consumed by the elderly. Home nursing, the county council service which provides community-based nursing as an alternative to institution-based care, has been expanded during the 1970s and 1980s. In 1987 there were over 5,000 district nurses (calculated as number of full-time posts) in the country, representing a three-fold increase since the mid-1970s. The number of assistant nurses and district physicians has also increased significantly in recent years.

Most elderly people living at home see the district nurse or doctor at a clinic or office. Home visits to those who have difficulty in getting to their local clinic are paid mainly by district nurses and assistant nurses. The former divide their time between clinic-based care and home visits while the latter spend most of their time out on home calls.

A government inquiry has recommended that around half of all district nurses and all assistant nurses who treat elderly patients at home should be

FIGURE 3

Number of General Practitioners and Visiting Nurses
(As Working Years) 1974-1988

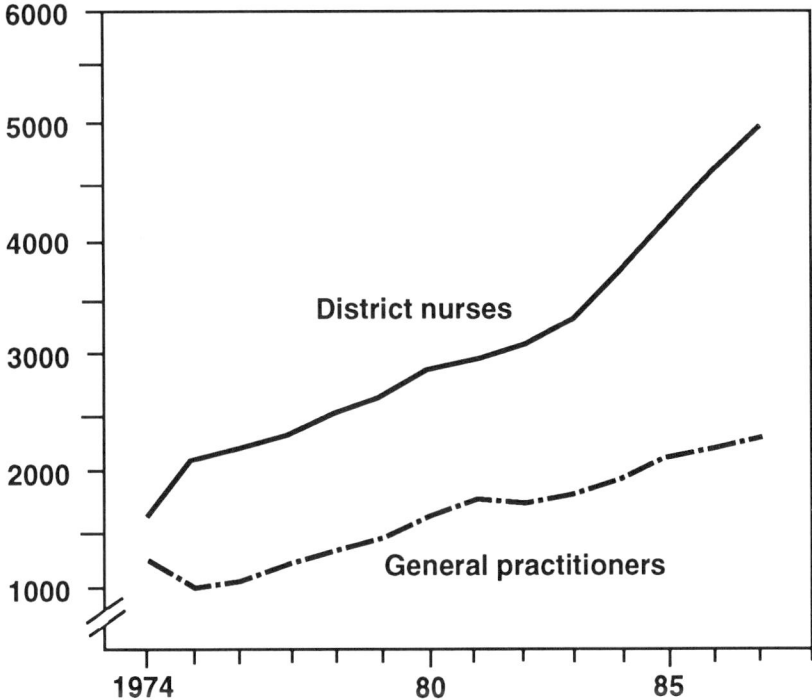

Source: Thorslund, 1990

transferred from the county councils, who presently run health services, to the municipalities, who run the "home help" services. If this reform is carried out, the municipalities will be responsible for both services. The present system, under which the "home help" and home nursing services are run by different authorities, had demonstrated many problems, such as difficulties in cooperation, lack of continuity in visits to the elderly, and gaps in the information on individuals passed from the staff of one service to that of the other.

Long-Term Care

Many elderly patients need care and rehabilitation that is difficult to give at home. In 1988 there were 49,000 beds for somatic long-term care (geriatric wards and nursing homes). Geriatric wards are often linked to general hospitals. Here the aim is to rehabilitate and send the elderly patient home as soon as possible. Such wards also offer the opportunity for so-called relief care, whereby the patient is admitted for a certain time to allow the family taking care of the patient at home to have some relief and rest, and respite care, when patients spend certain regular periods in the wards according to a fixed schedule.

"Nursing homes" provide care for longer periods under more home-like conditions. In Sweden, three general types of nursing homes have developed. "Central" nursing homes are usually attached to a geriatric department and function essentially as an annex. These seem to be diminishing in importance. "Local" nursing homes are usually independent of hospitals and come under the organizational auspices of the primary care system, with the district physician usually having referral authority. At present the number of beds in such local nursing homes is being increased. Finally, 4% of all beds in long-term care are private nursing homes.

During the 1980s both the total number of beds and the number of days of somatic short-term care have decreased, the number of beds being around 36,000 in 1988. On the other hand, the proportion of days of care consumed by the elderly has risen continuously during the 1980s. In 1985, 54.6% of all days of care within the somatic short-term care sector were accounted for by persons in the 75+ age group (6.3% of the total population). There are many developments behind this trend. One is the rise in the number of the elderly. Another is the fact that geriatric medicine has become more highly developed. It is, furthermore, often difficult to discharge elderly patients whose medical treatment has been completed if they cannot be cared for at home and if there is a shortage of beds in long-term institutions to which they should otherwise be transferred for more appropriate care. Such elderly patients consequently remain in ordinary somatic short-term wards.

Variations in the Provision of Old Age Care

The foreigner who comes to Sweden often cherishes the notion that "at least" the welfare state has managed to provide equally well for all segments of the population and that there is an even "spread" of welfare arrangements, locally, regionally, and nationally.

These assumptions need to be scrutinized, upheld as they are by Swedes as well. Until recently, there were no comprehensive data collected on the services mentioned, and no one had an overview of the availability of home making services, institutions and sheltered housing. When data were collected and systematized it therefore was a surprise to find that variability is large indeed. Probing the issue at the municipality level we first noted that

FIGURE 4

"Home Help" to the Aged 65+ and 80+, Swedish Municipalities 1985. Percentages.

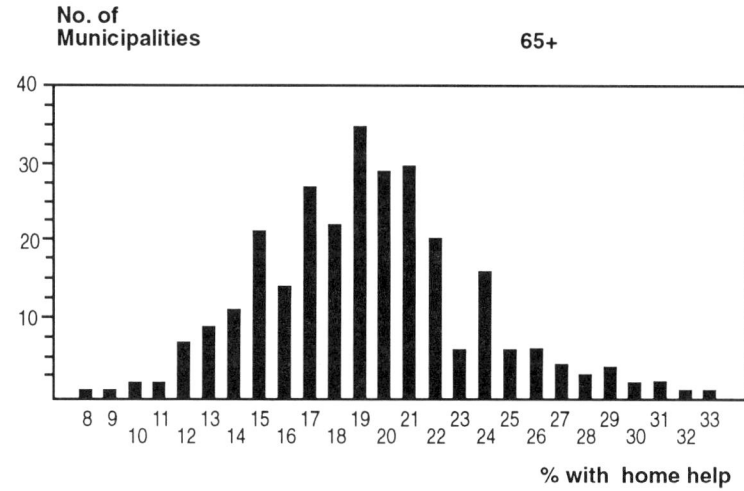

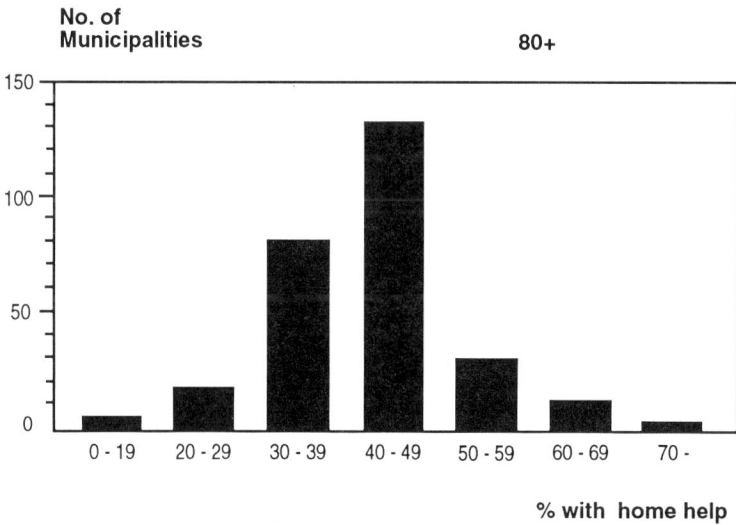

Source: Berg and Sundström, 1989

home making services differ considerably. This is shown in Figure 4 for all the aged and the very old (80+).

On average, 19% received home making services in 1985, but there were municipalities that provided only 8% of their aged with the service, while others provided more than 30% with the same service. More was provided to the oldest (80+): 43% benefitted from the service, but also for them variation was large. One municipality provided as many as 80% of the 80+ group with these services and one as little as 17%.

We already mentioned that the average input of "home help" hours per client is being raised. It must be remembered that the average is very unequally distributed: in many municipalities a tenth of the clients use about half of all hours that are provided. Nevertheless, the tendency is to put highest priority on the frailest and neediest among the elderly. Furthermore averages vary greatly between the municipalities. In some, the clients may get less that 150 hours/year, in others more than 400 hours/year!

One must also assess the differential needs structure. Home making services are used primarily by those who live alone. The proportion of the non-institutionalized elderly that lives alone has increased considerably in the post-war years, and is now probably higher in Sweden than in any other country (except Denmark, with a slightly higher rate), with 34% of the 65+ and 44% of the 80+ group living wholly on their own. It is more common in urban areas and more among women (for example, 7 out of 10 women 80+ in Stockholm live alone) but generally it varies much between municipalities for reasons that are not well understood. It is therefore not possible to evaluate home making services (Figure 4) at "face value." Analyses indicate that also when these facts are taken into consideration, variation in provision continues to be large.

The provision of institutional care has declined drastically over the last 20 years, taken at the national average and relative to the number of needy elderly (Sundström, 1987; Thorslund, 1988).

In Sweden, institutions for the elderly encompass both old-age homes and long-term care (above). As can be seen in Figure 5, the municipalities perform very differently in this area as well. Especially noteworthy are the variations for the old-old as nearly all residents in these institutions are 80 years old or more. Increasingly, they suffer not only from somatic impairments but also from mental confusion.

In this context it can be mentioned that the same variations or even greater ones apply for sheltered accommodations. Conceivably, one kind of care (institutional) might substitute for another (in-the-home care) to "even out" local variations. Yet, when this possibility is put to test it proves that variations are just as large when it comes to "total" old age care. This is shown in Figure 6. This construct is the simple sum of coverage rates for

FIGURE 5

Institutional Coverage for Persons 65+ *and* 80+,
Swedish Municipalities 1985. Percentages.

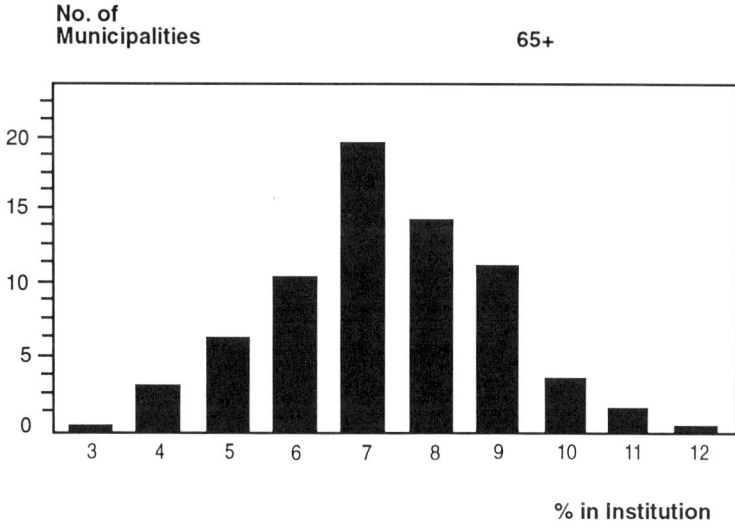

**No. of
Municipalities**

65+

% in Institution

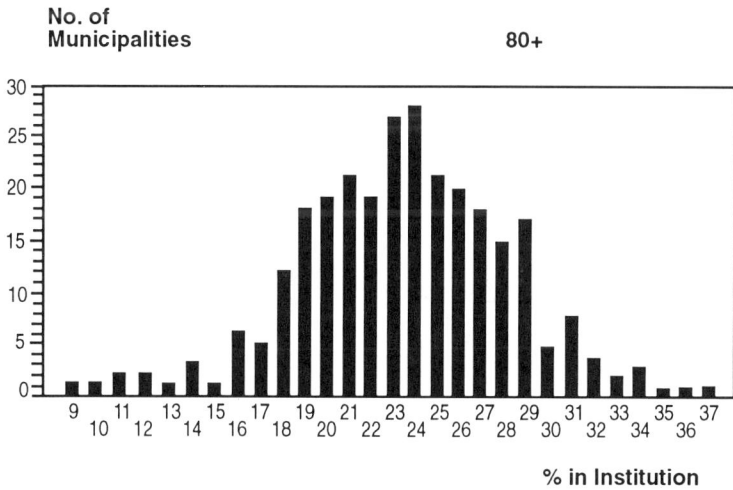

**No. of
Municipalities**

80+

% in Institution

Source: Berg and Sundström, 1989

FIGURE 6

Total Old Age Care (Institutional and "Home Help" Coverage)
for Persons 65+ and 80+. Swedish Municipalities 1985. Percentages.

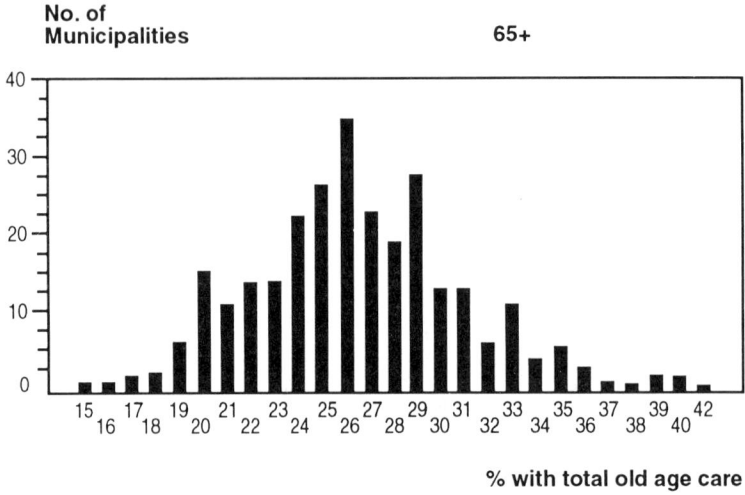

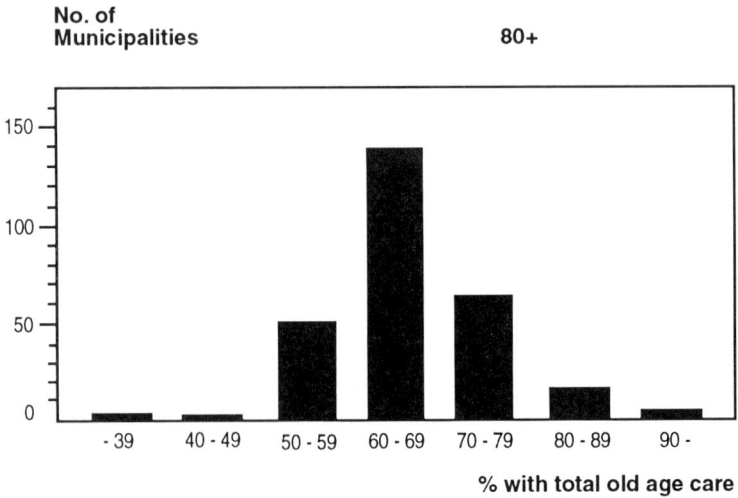

Source: Berg and Sundström, 1989

home making services and institutional care as the individual old person can benefit from only one of them at any time. The national variation is from less that 30% of the old-old in one municipality to 100%.

It is harder to explain than describe these patterns. The proportion of the elderly that live alone is a good predictor of coverage of home help services just as the proportion of old people, at large, predicts the total amount of old age care. (Living alone does not explain total costs of old age care as costs of home making services make up just a minor item in the total budget.) Regional and economic factors explain part of the variations as well. Contrary to what one may expect, the rural and poor municipalities provide better coverage. This is made possible thanks to the tax redistribution system operating between municipalities in Sweden. Thus, political composition of the municipalities explains very little about service coverage. The tax redistribution policy demonstrates the level of national political consensus about old age care in this country (Berg and Sundström, 1989).

However, it is difficult to come up with a "rational" explanation of these variations. To some degree, municipalities may long since have established norms for what is "reasonable" provision, which creates a historical continuity. There is a stability in the patterns of provision for the epoch 1965-1985. But even if historical explanations may once have had a rationale in "reality," that rationale is often no longer true decades later.

Data from one municipality indicate that there are great variations inside it as well: Looking at the oldest old (85+) it has been observed that in one year the proportions who received home making services varied between 36% and 71% in the local parishes. Much the same held for the chance to get a home visit by the visiting nurse, even if these two to a degree offset each other (Thorslund, 1990b).

Still, from all these variations it does not follow that elderly persons live in neglect and misery in some areas. A number of local and national studies all bear witness to the fact that very few of the aged have unsatisfied needs for help and support. To some degree this may be explained by mechanisms of adaptation, but probably more by the family that in the welfare state is still the most important provider of care and therefore is likely to act as a "buffer" (Sundström, 1987; Hokenstad and Johansson, 1990).

All the above evidence is at the aggregate level, but there are also individual data for assessments of issues of equity. To grasp this we may look at factors that determine use of home making services and those that influence moves to institutional care. A few studies shed light on this.

From data on home making services it becomes clear that disability (IADL) and living alone are the two most important factors to explain who is a user. Disability weighs somewhat more for women, living alone more for men (Sundström, 1984; Thorslund, 1990a). This is consistent with the kind of evidence we already have suggested. The individual data also permit us to assess the impact of social class: Is this a service for the poor and for the working class rather than for the affluent?

The evidence is that social class does not seem to influence the provision and/or use of the home making services in Sweden. To be sure, old workers use the service more often and get more hours per recipient but this is due to their greater frailty (they also die earlier). When comparing elderly of the same health status these differences vanish.

It should be kept in mind that these services are a citizen's right, but only for those who need it. Interviews with the administrators of the service also disclose that they are often unaware of the social class of the users. Nor do administrators have an extensive knowledge of the social network that usually exists around their clients. There are no indications that clients with access to an offspring nearby get less or no help, in contrast with the British situation (Sundström, 1986). Thus, there are no evident signs of "discrimination" so far on either social or family grounds.

Turning to those who move to institutional care a very different picture emerges, and one with which observers in other countries are also familiar. In institutions there is a surplus of women, of persons who lack family support (i.e. the never-married, the childless, and those on the lower rungs of the social ladder (Samuelsson and Sundström, 1987)). In other words, these are persons who in many respects are underprivileged. One might even interpret the tendency to shift emphasis from institutional care to care in the "community" as a shrinkage in choice for the marginal groups where there still was a "choice" (though a difficult one for some of them) to move to an institution.

The strength of these predictive factors are illustrated by local data from Dalby: for persons at the age of 40 (in 1942-1943) one could predict who would 30-40 years later move to an institution. To make a reasonable guess one needs to know gender, marital status and social class—but nothing about health. Non-married working class women had a chance (risk) of 3 in 10 to move before the age of 80, married men (at 40)—regardless of class—a near zero-risk (Samuelsson and Sundström, 1986).

Summary and Conclusions

Sweden has, to summarize, in international comparison still a very comprehensive system of old age care, with extensive coverage. Even the cut-backs described above cannot change this basic fact. Furthermore, there is legislation to back up demands on these services and to provide equally well to everyone according to needs and on equal terms.

Yet, in reality there are differences. Mainly these are "geographic" rather than of a social or class nature. The large variations—and hence inequalities—are hard to explain rationally and therefore may be in a sense more palatable than if they were products of class injustice. At the same time there are great local variations even inside administrative units. Taken together, this suggests that welfare bureaucracies have less than perfect control over the services they provide. In a situation where needs grow drastically and funds are restricted, this becomes politically unacceptable and appears to be a sign of inefficient use of the resources.

The new social legislation in 1982 also gave users of social services the legal right to appeal to higher administrative courts if they were dissatisfied with decisions on, for example, home making services or institutional care in their municipality. This is the only formalized way to demand "public accounts" in the sphere of old age care. Yet, few elderly use this appeal privilege and, most likely, many more who could choose not to appeal. At the same time, most users of the home making services express their satisfaction. (Sundström and Cronholm, 1988).

Other differences in the provision of services and care have also been mentioned. Especially social and medical services cater for those weak in social resources and in particular those who live alone. Only with those who move to institutions are there indications that social class influences use, though it might be misleading to see this as segregation. Parts of the population may—as surveys indicate—rather view institutional care as a welfare item (though, or course, one prefers not to have to use it).

For a number of years, social and medical resources have been placed under an ever stricter mandate to care for the neediest. Everything indicates that these tendencies are reinforced and can be expected to continue in this way. One development that is already underway—a remarkable achievement by Swedish standards—is the spread of cooperative or even fully private (for profit and non-profit) service-homes for the aged. These are marketed as alternatives to and in clear reaction to the dominant public enterprises in this area. There are also private entrepreneurs that set up firms to provide home making services. In addition, there are groups of the elderly who demand the funds to administer their own home making services now.

Taken together, all these developments appear to lead the Swedish welfare state into a more "traditional" and mainstream kind of benign state. In the future, the publicly organized and financed system of care will tend to focus primarily on those weak in social and economic resources, and who cannot care for themselves.

References

Berg, S. and Sundström, G. (1989). Kommunal och regional variation inom äldreomsorgen, Rapport 70, Instituet för gerontologi, Jönköping.

Hokenstad, M.C. and Johansson L. (1990). Caregiving for the elderly in Sweden: Program challenges and policy initiatives. In *Aging and caregiving: Theory, research and policy,* (Eds. Bigel D. and Blum A.). Sage, San Francisco. In press.

Samuelsson G. and Sundström G. (1986). Att flytta till institution i slutet av livet. *Socialmedicinsk tidskrift,* vol. 63(5-6): 257-263.

Sundström G. (1988). Ending one's life in an Institution. A note on Swedish Findings. *International Journal of Aging and Human Development,* vol. 27 (2):81-88.

Sundström G. (1984). De Gamla, Deras anhöriga och hemtjänsten. Rapport i socialt arbete 22. School of Social Work, University of Stockholm.

Sundström G. (1987). Old Age Care in Sweden: Yesterday, Today, Tomorrow? Swedish Institute, Stockholm.

Sundström G. and Cronholm I. (1988). Hemtjänsten. De äldsta vårdtagarna och omsorgsapparaten. Rapport 68, Institutet för gerontologi, Jönköping.

Thorslund M. (1990a). The increasing number of very old people will change the Swedish model of the welfare state. Submitted.

Thorslund M. (1988). The de-institutionalization of care of the elderly: some notes about implementation and outcome of a Swedish case study. *Health Policy,* 10:41-56.

Thorslund M., Norström T. and Wernberg K. (1990). The utilization of home help: A multivariate analysis. Submitted.

Thorslund M. (1989). Care of the elderly in Sweden. Fact sheet. *Svenska Institutet.* In press.

Thorslund M. (1990b). Om uppsökande verksamhet för äldre. Submitted.

2

Long-Term Care for the Aged in Germany (FRG): Structure and Prospects

Martin Jaeckel

Introduction

The current situation and the prospects for long-term care (LTC) services for the elderly in Germany are determined by several components, some of which are similar to the situation in the United States, while other components differ. The components that are basically similar are two: the pressure of demographic developments, in particular the rapid increase of the proportion of the old-old in the population; and the location of LTC services in the existing financing structure, somewhere between the provisions for general health insurance and those for social assistance/welfare. The resulting pressures and ambiguities constitute the common elements in the situation, the generic problem which LTC planning and policy seek to address. The differences in the situation, on the other hand, consist of certain cultural and institutional patterns which characterize each society's approach to dealing with social welfare matters. These structural differences tend to extend into the resulting solutions, i.e. the nature and design of the LTC system to come.

In both Germany and the United States, public discussion of the topic is beginning to focus on the financing aspects, in particular the prospects for some form of public financing of LTC. In both countries, the existing financing mechanisms are grossly inadequate, when compared with the burgeoning need. As the proportion of the elderly and especially the old-old increases, so do the numbers and proportions of the chronically ill and the functionally impaired. With these continuing increases, the unmet need for long-term care begins to approach the dimensions of a societal disaster.[1] At the level of the individual, the costs of nursing home care (of anything longer than three months) constitute a financial catastrophe.[2] There is increased risk that, sometime during one's remaining lifetime, there will be the need for LTC in some form.[3] Furthermore, the risk is widespread, and is not restricted to any specific group or social class. This kind of situation—the widespread risk of the occurrence of a catastrophic event—is the classic situation for the development of some form of risk-pooling, i.e. population-based LTC insurance, as the best way to share the burden between those directly affected and those not.

Both countries, Germany and the United States, are currently witnessing the initial development of a limited market for commercial LTC insurance, as well as the introduction of legislative proposals for more inclusive public financing for LTC. The discussion of the particular form that LTC insurance should take is central to the future development of LTC services in both countries. In the case of Germany, the issue is likely to be shaped by several kinds of conditions:

1. the historically evolved general approach to social welfare issues;
2. the fragmented institutional structure of the voluntary sector within which most LTC services are delivered; and
3. the current configuration of organized constituencies and interest groups, together with the information and arguments which they are able to marshall on the issue.

Financing questions are not the be-all and end-all of long-term care, but they are the current focus of public discussion in both countries. Decisions which are pending on this dimension are certain to shape the structure, the availability and the quality of LTC services for some time to come. We shall, therefore, make the financing and insurance issue the general focus of our review of the current situation with respect to LTC in Germany, and of our assessment of the most likely direction of development.

Historical Background

As a political force, the aged in Germany are not a powerfully organized constituency; they are the recipients of social policy, rather than its source. Although their numbers and voting power are increasing, the social policies which affect their welfare are mainly developed by others, mostly from within the infrastructure of service agencies operating on their behalf,—not as the result of grassroots social movements and related political activity.[4] Furthermore, public discussion and development of the LTC topic in Germany has to be seen in the context of the existing cultural and institutional traditions for dealing with social welfare issues. Among the industrial nations of the world, Germany (as is well known) was one of the early leaders in developing public policies to provide major forms of social protection for its population; in particular, a system of income security in old age, and statutory health insurance (Rimlinger,1971). Characteristically, however, these policies were introduced by central administrations at least as concerned with protecting the viability of a German nation state (the war-making powers of the state, the status and security of the civil service, the stability of the family, the social position of various occupational groups) and with counter acting the growing influence of worker/ socialist parties, as with the welfare and life conditions of the individual members of the population at large (Deppe,1989). Generically speaking, the German approach to welfare issues has followed what has been designated the "conservative" or "corporatist" model of a social welfare regime (Esping-Andersen, 1990).

At present, public coverage for the major types of risk is almost universal; it extends to more than ninety percent of the population. And there are some egalitarian trends as well (Bonner Almanach, 1989). But historically, public policies for the social protection of member citizens have tended to promote the preservation of the existing status differentials in the social and political order (Baier,1977). The allocation of benefits has paralleled the social and economic organization of the major constituent groups. There are separate public pension plans and administrations for blue collar and for white collar workers, for civil servants, and for members of special occupational groups (miners, railroad workers, farmers and farm workers, sailors and fishermen). And there is an even greater proliferation of health insurance schemes and carriers, ranging from community-wide insurance organizations to sickness funds denominated by industry and occupational type.

Within the German corporatist model of social welfare, individuals' participation in the workforce constitutes the primary basis for their claims to the main kinds of statutory entitlements (unemployment, sickness and disability, social security, and workmen's/accident insurance). By and large, this is of course true in other industrial societies as well. But there is a difference in emphasis. In Germany, non-participants in the workforce can establish their claims to public/statutory support only in a derivative sense—as former or future participants, as dependents of participants, or as members whose support from other intermediate institutions (the family; the church; local communities; and the voluntary sector) does not suffice. The latter type of assistance is called social assistance ("Sozialhilfe"); and its character as a back-up system is enunciated in what is called the "substitution principle" ("Subsidiarität"), i.e. the precedence of local and individual sources of assistance, before broader public funds come into play. Since the 1960s, statutory social assistance has been expanded and broadened to include several different kinds of support: general income supplements; supplements to cope with various life exigencies; as well as assistance in the form of personal services in kind, and defined by the needs of the situation, and not by categorical restrictions (Flamm, 1980).

The Institutional Context

Traditionally, much of the delivery of LTC services (for aged and non-aged alike) has been organized as a form of local community assistance, in part provided by various groups in the voluntary sector. The emphasis has been on ambulatory care, and on services which combine household assistance with personal and with basic nursing care. Much of the work was of low intensity; it combined volunteer, low-paid and part-time efforts into outreach networks; and it was conducted as a form of community service. A good part of the funding, however, came from the same source which also covers the costs of institutional care (for the needy)—the "special life situations" category of social assistance mentioned above ("Hilfe in besonderen Lebenslagen").[5] For the more serious cases of physical and mental debilitation, LTC is also being provided in separate wards in general hospitals and in certain hospitals specializing in psychiatric care (Dieck, 1989). And in the past, these services have been carried, at least in part, as marginal burdens within the regular health insurance system.

In an attempt to cope with the increasing demographic and epidemiological pressures, certain expansions and improvements in LTC benefits were introduced into regular health insurance in recent years. Beginning in January of 1991, those in need of skilled care are eligible for up to 25 home-care visits a month (for DM 750,- altogether), up to a cost of DM 9000,-a year. And conversely, those chronically disabled who organize their own helpers can draw up to DM 400,- a month for the purpose. To protect caregivers and next-of-kin, statutory health insurance also provides for up to four weeks of respite care a year (either at home or in a LTC facility), at a cost of up to DM 1800. Caregivers/next-of-kin are also eligible for certain tax benefits and for enhancements in the provisions for their own social security pensions (in their old age).

The problem is that these and other improvements only cover part of the existing and constantly expanding need. At best, these entitlements cover only a fraction of the expenses generated by year-round long-term care. Based on the experience with the recent benefit upgrades, health planners are becoming increasingly aware of the magnitude of the LTC problem, and are beginning to see the limits in the conventional system of financing care. Since acute care and hospital costs are increasing rapidly as well, resistance is building up among the carriers (the statutory health insurance bodies) to further expansion of service benefits to the elderly—especially in view of the fact that regular health insurance for retirees/pensioners is already being subsidized (to the extent of the former employer contribution) by the other participants in the system. The feeling is growing that some form of general across-the-board solution, rather than continued piecemeal improvements, is required for the financing of LTC.

Current Proposals for the Financing of Long-Term Care

Public discussion of the issue of LTC insurance has waxed and waned periodically since it was first initiated in a position paper by the society for worker welfare (Arbeiterwohlfahrt) in 1976. Since 1984, several proposals have been launched on how to organize the financing for LTC.[6] The current legislative proposals are basically two. Culturally speaking they revolve around the question of who is deemed responsible for supplying the required protection against anticipated LTC costs in later life. One proposal, submitted by the state of Baden-Württemberg and supported by the insurance industry, is centered on the idea that individuals should provide for themselves, i.e. that they should buy LTC insurance with contributions taken from their (earned) income, and that they should build up drawing rights which can be utilized in old age. The current version of the proposal suggests that the purchase of minimum coverage (benefits in the amount of DM 1500,- per month) be required for all Germans who are 45 or older (Bundesrat, 1990a). The benefits would take the form of indemnity payments, which the recipient could use for institutional or for ambulatory (home based) care. Although enrollment would be compulsory, the policies would be bought individually and from insurance companies in the private sector. Many users would of course purchase more than the minimum coverage, since nursing home care actually costs about twice as much (currently about DM 2900,-monthly for basic care).

Since passage of this legislation would create a huge new volume of guaranteed business for the health and life insurance companies in the private sector, it is strongly supported by the insurance industry. Seen in the context of the dominant corporatist tradition in Germany, however, the proposal represents somewhat of an innovation. By and large, Germans are used to institutionalist solutions on such matters. To support their case, and to try to sway those used to other models for protection against general risks, the proponents argue that the alternative modes of financing LTC, namely reliance on federal taxes, or on the existing structure for social insurance (i.e. payroll deductions), would overload either or both of these systems. The social insurance approach, it is further argued, suffers from an inherent weakness, namely that what is called the "contract between the generations" ("Umlageverfahren"), i.e. the promise that future workers will pay for the entitlements accumulated by future retirees, will be increasingly difficult to fulfill. Basically, the backers of this proposal are using arguments about current fiscal pressures to draw support from within the health insurance system, and from the federal social security bureaucracy, both of which are anxious to avoid expanding the scope of the burdens they impose on taxpayers and on the payroll tax system.

To deal with the problem of those who do not have sufficient discretionary income to pay for the envisioned premiums (currently estimated at about DM 50,- a month), the proposal includes provisions for subsidies from the usual public sources of social assistance. To which the critics reply, that this will create a two-class system of payers (i.e. those who have only minimum coverage, partly paid for by public sources, vs. those who have better coverage, paid for privately); that it will perpetuate the tendencies toward a two-class system of treatment and care; and that it does not take care of the bulk of the actual burdens, i.e. the large number of cases who are currently forced into the spend-down and pauperization process.

The alternative proposal, put forth by the state of Rheinland-Pfalz in 1986 and again in the summer of 1990, starts at the other end (Bundesrat, 1990b). It is predicated on the responsibility of society as a whole to protect its weaker members. But in this view, it is not society in general, as represented by the central government, but rather society as a composite of traditional forms of solidarity and assistance (the existing forms of voluntary and informal help at the community level, and local, state and federal forms of cost-sharing and support), which is taken to be the carrier of a wholistic approach to protection against need. The proposed law is very explicit about the various kinds of need for LTC and of ways to supply the needed care. It sets several substantive priorities: strengthening of the informal support network ("neighborhood help"); provision for the economic protection of caregivers (including contributions toward their pensions); and the prevention of the spend-down and pauperization process for the institutionally housed (mainly by setting the income subsidies at a high enough level).

It is the orientation to the total situation of those who need LTC which underlies the second bill's formulations, combined with the utilization of the several forms of social assistance and care that are already in place. The bill envisions financial transfers from all the segments of the existing system of social security, and the maintenance and expansion of the existing (largely voluntary sector-based) network for the delivery of needed LTC services.

Culturally, the Rheinland-Pfalz proposal represents the continuation and extension of the corporatist model of providing for social welfare needs. It is fairly explicit on the need to guarantee a whole range of substantive LTC services, and to accommodate the client's preferences in the selection of the actual forms of assistance. Finally, although it is not overly explicit on the sources of the required financing, the proposal does indicate that the burden should be carried by a combination of federal and local/state sources (i.e., general taxation at various levels).

Implementation Issues: Barriers and Difficulties

A key issue which the two alternative proposals raise is where the envisioned financing mechanism is to fit into the existing institutional structure. Much depends on how the requisite funds are to be raised, pooled, allocated and distributed.

The market-based (compulsory) individual insurance model contained in the Baden-Württemberg proposal, for example, would normally be administered within the private sector (i.e., by life and health insurance companies). But there is resistance among government planners to supporting legislation that would directly expand the private-sector bureaucracies and their control over the formation and use of large new amounts of capital (the pooled reserves which would accumulate from designated contributions). The proponents of this solution are hence modifying their plan, and are seeking to locate the further development of the envisioned legislation in the federal Ministry of Labor and Social Affairs, which is the traditional location for the coordination and supervision of general (and compulsory) health insurance. Logically, LTC insurance could be introduced as another part of general health insurance, or as a separate but parallel form of compulsory insurance also based on payroll deductions. Apart from the thorny question of whether employers are currently willing to take on the additional burden of contributing to such a scheme, however, there are historical and cultural barriers which would have to be overcome before such an innovation could be implemented.

The problem is that health insurance has traditionally been oriented to helping to overcome "sickness" (in German, it is called "Krankenversicherung", "sickness insurance"). Culturally and legally, "sickness" is defined as a condition which impairs the capacity to function at work, and which can be treated and cured (Flamm, 1980; and Frankfurter Rundschau, 1991a). Both of these components (the prospects of recovery and of returning to the labor force) must be given for statutory health insurance to apply. Long-term care, on the other hand, is currently not defined as linked to rehabilitation of either kind. The goals of the requisite social assistance are defined to be "integration" into the community and custodial and remedial care (basically palliative measures), rather than "treatment" in the technical sense. Thus, as current practices stand, a joining of general health and of LTC insurance would either restrict the latter to mainly medical (or medically certified) conditions, or force a cultural redefinition and expansion of what health and related welfare insurance are about. But for now, such a general redefinition is not very likely. Even the labor unions, which traditionally tend to favor the expansion of social welfare measures, are not taking a very strong stand on the issue (Baecker, 1990). For now it seems they prefer a solution based on general taxes, rather than further increases in payroll deductions.

Conversely, the prospects for the implementation of the generalized social assistance model (i.e. national insurance based on need) suffer from the lack of organization and integration in the existing social-organizational base. As noted earlier, the existing institutional infrastructure for the delivery of LTC services is severely underdeveloped. It is divided into community organizations and the voluntary sector on one side, and specialized sub-units of the healthcare system on the other. The voluntary sector itself is fragmented: it consists of a whole set of distinct service agencies, each with historically entrenched ties to certain social and religious groups, and not overly inclined to cooperate with each other. These agencies are: the Workers' Welfare League ("Arbeiterwohlfahrt"); the Catholic, the Protestant, and the Jewish service associations ("Karitas"; "Diakonisches Werk" and "Jüdischer Wohlfahrtsverband", respectively); the German Red Cross; and the (non-aligned) German General Mutual Aid Society ("Deutscher Paritätischer Wohlfahrts-Verband").

Most German states and larger communities do have some type of institution which serves as the logistical base for the delivery of a range of ambulatory community-based services. These are typically called community or social service stations ("Gemeindedienst," "Sozialstation"). But the staffing of these services is very inadequate, both in terms of scope as compared with the need (especially among the elderly), and in terms of the background and training of the staff. Sample calculations have shown that the average amount of time a social service worker has available to devote to the hypothetical "average" older person in the territory is one minute a day (ibid.). And a recent survey which the national association of public and private social service agencies conducted of its member organizations and service centers showed considerable variations in the conditions under which the work was being done, and severe deficits in the staff's preparation (BMfJFFG, vol 195, 1987). Many are volunteer or part-time workers and very poorly paid. And the majority have practically no professional training for the kind of service in which they are engaged (ambulatory work with the elderly). Although there are variations in the level of training provided in the various states, the degree of professionalization in the field of LTC for the elderly is very uneven, and in the beginning stages overall.[7]

To attempt to superimpose a system of "national" LTC insurance (which would be unified at least in terms of the standards of "need" and of eligibility) on this variegated infrastructure would be a difficult undertaking, especially since the actual sources of funding would have to be several (according to the Rheinland-Pfalz proposal: the states and communities, as well as the general federal budget and several national social welfare institutions). For now, none of the corresponding levels of the political structure has given indications of anything approaching the political will required to implement this scheme.[8]

The general conclusion toward which this review of the situation seems to lead is that what Germany is facing, with respect to the development of LTC financing and services, is basically a problem of cultural lag. The general electorate's awareness of, and mobilization on the issue is barely incipient. It is mainly social policy planners and the higher-level staff of the service infrastructure who are debating the issue, and they are hampered in their efforts by the dominant corporatist tradition.

The corporatist (conservative institutionalist) tradition, it seems, asserts itself at both ends of the spectrum. On the one hand, the attempt to assimilate and add LTC insurance to the existing system of health insurance runs up against the employment-related nature of such insurance. Historically and culturally, German health insurance was designed to restore one's capability to work. It is carried by contributions made by employers and the employed, both of whom resist additional financial burdens for the sake of a category ("the aged"), which for now they view as not involved in the production process (especially manufacturing) and, therefore, as separate from themselves.

Conversely the attempt to generalize the social assistance model and to create a kind of national LTC insurance based on need runs up against the limitations inherent in the traditional multi-level infrastructure for providing and funding such services. The implementation of outright universal LTC insurance (i.e. direct provision/guarantees of such services to individuals by the federal government) would require the adoption of corresponding collectivist assumptions and political beliefs. As long as both the delivery of LTC services and a major part of the requisite funding are controlled by the intermediate political and voluntary sector institutions traditionally considered as appropriate for dealing with "need," such an innovation is not very likely. Although some feminist groups and social scientists who are engaged in research on poverty do propagate the universalist national insurance solution, the resonance among the general public and among the major political constituencies (the political parties, employer organizations and labor unions, insurance companies, and state and federal bureaucracies) has been weak (Frankfurter Rundschau, 1991a).

In point of fact, recently the proponents of the compulsory social insurance model have succeeded in locating the federal-level planning for LTC financing with the Ministry of Labor and Social Affairs.[9] Given the prior declarations on the issue by the incumbent minister, Norbert Bluem, this preliminary political decision does tend to focus the public discussion of LTC insurance on payroll deductions as the financing vehicle. But at the same time, the topic is being segregated from planning for the health insurance sector in general, which is being transferred to the new Ministry for Health (Frankfurter Rundschau, 1991b).

Outlook and Prospects

The immediate prospects for the passage of legislation to establish generic public LTC insurance in Germany are not good. New proposals keep surfacing, recently (in October of 1990) in particular a renewed call by Norbert Bluem, the CDU minister for Labor and Social Affairs, to locate LTC insurance within the existing institutional structure for dealing with health-related expenditures (the multifarious sickness funds mentioned earlier). Employers, however, and their representation in the political parties (i.e. the CDU and especially the FDP) tend to resist these additional expenditures, as do the sickness funds themselves and the related federal agencies. In my estimation, the LTC financing issue will continue to percolate and be filtered through various federal agencies and reports, probably until the next federal election (in 1994). By that time it will presumably have reached sufficient crisis proportions, and will have to be settled between the communities and states, who are the main current carriers, and the federal government and allied social insurance institutions.

In the meantime, further public discussion and development of the issue is hampered by three general conditions, each of which tends to create its own delays.

1. The first of these is the lack of reliable baseline information on the overall dimensions of the problem, such as estimates of the scope of the the various kinds of need, and of the types of services available and required. The relative absence of general information of this kind is somewhat surprising in a highly-developed industrial economy such as Germany, with a fairly strong tradition of centralized public planning in other service sectors. It is accounted for in part by the corporatist segmentation of the LTC service sector noted earlier,—especially the fragmentation of the voluntary sector between several traditional agencies, each with separate clienteles. By and large, these organizations treat information on the scope and organization of their services as part of their control and jurisdiction, and make it nearly impossible for the federal government to collect general statistics on the topic. The deficit in representative information on LTC is probably also due to a general tendency, in private and in public sector bureaucracies, to concentrate on information which bears on what is viewed as central to the German economy, namely the production process (especially the manufacturing sector). The latter is seen as the driving force in the German economy's successful and export-led development since World War II. Issues such as the social welfare of the elderly pale when compared with questions pertaining to the training and technical proficiency of the (manufacturing) labor force, its composition and productivity, and the appropriate compensation and fringe benefits required to keep it at peak performance. Social welfare and insurance problems of the

elderly are viewed as derivative issues, along with those of other social dependents, and are hence treated as such.

In any event, the federal government's strategy for dealing with the situation is two-pronged. On the one hand, it has in recent years commissioned a variety of demonstration projects which highlight model efforts in the realm of social policies for the aged. This includes studies of adult day care centers; caregiver/LTC client relationships; the retirement transition/ social network planning for older women; and in particular, demonstration projects to develop estimates of what the current costs of institutional over and against home-based long term care actually come to be. And on the other hand, it has commissioned a baseline representative study to determine the scope of the need for LTC (levels and definitions of impairment; extent of the institutional as well as the home-based LTC populations; linkages to physical and medical health problems; and the like). However, since this national study has only just gotten underway, the results will not be available for several years to come. Furthermore, the discussion and development of the design for this study have become embroiled in another controversy, namely the question of whether federal-level emphasis (and funds) should be placed on enabling the elderly to develop their own "competence" to engage in self-help; or alternatively, on fostering and supporting the traditional forms of caregiving and service for those whose capability for independently managing their households and their personal care has already deteriorated. To some extent, the ideological debate and concerns over this issue have already overlaid the original question, which was to establish the scope of the existing need.[10]

2. A second general constraint on public discussion of the LTC financing issue devolves from the assessment (among experts) of the demographic developments to come. Both West and East Germany have birth rates among the lowest in the world. Current projections of the size and composition of the German population a generation or two from now are sobering in two respects. The total population is expected to decrease (ultimately by about twenty percent before stabilizing); and the proportion of the elderly in the population (those 60 years old and above) is expected to rise, to about 37% of the population by the year 2030 (Wingen, 1988). This in turn implies a severe worsening of the aged dependency ratio, i.e. the number of pensioners to be carried by the members of the, by then, strongly decreasing labor force. Given historical examples of pay-as-you-go developments occurring in other social security systems, notably in the U.S., both experts and several interested publics are decrying the folly of engaging in new kinds of entitlements, the ultimate extent of which cannot (at present) even be accurately assessed.

There are of course theoretical solutions to this general problem, such as raising the nominal age for retirement (Schmaehl, 1988). But these kinds of questions, as well as the estimated effects of possible future migration within the Common Market, are not at issue. The main point is that the indicated fears about the fiscal soundness of the German social security system reinforce the currently dominant conservative fiscal approach, i.e. the resistance to and postponement of the introduction of new entitlements (for the elderly) of any kind.

3. A last major factor in the situation is the economic and social impact of German Re-Unification. This recent series of events has added a fairly large number of relatively impoverished retirees to the German social security, and health and social welfare systems. For East German retirees, the main problem is that their public pension incomes tend to remain relatively stable (and at a low level), whereas the prices for essential goods (such as housing, basic food such as bread, and also health care, much of which used to be subsidized by the state, or even provided free of charge) are beginning to approximate the higher levels charged in the West (Schwitzer,1990). Analogous gaps and deficiencies obtain in the (institutional) long-term care sector. Although in principle retirees in the former DDR were guaranteed direct entitlements to LTC services by the state, the actual rendering of such care occurred at a much reduced level of outlays and of services (when compared with the FRG). Thus on both counts, income as well as LTC protection in old age, the first order of business, from the reconstituted federal government's point of view, is to introduce the subsidies and federal supplements which are needed to raise East German seniors' life conditions to a politically more tolerable level. Only then will there be time and political leeway to consider more general reforms.

The rapid economic collapse of the East German regime in the summer and fall of 1990 has also tended to discredit the collectivist social policies and ideals which that government had fostered. The collectivist notion that the central government as the agent of society should directly and universally be responsible for the acute and the long-term health care needs of the individual citizen is not likely to survive the blend of the two systems. Nor will, to any great extent, another achievement of "collectivist" social policy: public compensation for child care for working mothers.

Conclusion

Overall, the implementation of public (or compulsory) LTC insurance and the related expansion and modernization of the LTC delivery system will probably require several more years of review and debate. The federal government's immediate fiscal plans for social policies are dominated by the expenditures which are currently being incurred in raising social welfare payments for East German recipients to somewhere near West German levels. In point of fact, both public and private-sector budgets are being extended altogether by the investments and subsidies needed to rationalize and rebuild the economic infrastructure of East Germany (in agriculture and mining, and the manufacturing, energy and chemical industries). The considerable expansion of public as well as private sector expenditures required for these investments and for measures to ameliorate and deal with the resulting unemployment can be expected to shape the federal government's overall fiscal priorities for several years to come. Once these fiscal deficits are reduced, the question of publicly guaranteed LTC entitlements, and related issues in the distribution of service delivery and financing burdens, will come to focus in clearer form.

On balance, I would expect the payroll-based social insurance approach to, in time, become the accepted major vehicle for the financing of long-term care. This expectation is based on the historical experience with the introduction of social insurance for protection against the other major risks of industrial life—sickness and disability, accident/workmen's compensation, unemployment insurance and income protection in old age. It is quite possible that this reform will only come in incremental stages—viz. the measures included in the German health (insurance) reform of 1989 and the (already legislated) social security reform of 1992. But it is clear that the variety of LTC insurance proposals currently being launched by various political constituencies will keep public attention focused on the issue. With time, the realization should grow among the general electorate that the older population's rights to protection against the major risks are based on their previous participation in the process that creates industrial society's wealth in the first place, and in the process of rearing the human beings whose efforts are maintaining the society altogether.

The current delay in the implementation of an overall LTC financing system does mean that the volume of underlying unmet needs among the elderly will continue to grow. This delay allows some time for the development of a negotiated consensus among the organized constituencies involved, concerning generalized entitlements for this increasingly visible public need. Overall, the German cultural model of a negotiated public order for meeting publicly identified needs will most likely continue to assert itself. The general situation is complicated by the fact that, to some extent, the general health care and the long-term care markets are both controlled by the same provider organizations and political jurisdictions (Dieck,1989). Given the cost containment and consolidation pressures currently operating in these markets, part of the indicated reforms and transformations will probably be negotiated within and between these controlling organizations, as well as with the public at large.

Notes

1. Depending on the definitions and estimation procedures used, the estimates for the total number of elderly in need of some form of LTC (in the FRG) range from about 1,850,000 (Social-data-study, BMfFFG vol. 80) to about 2,100,000 persons (overview article, Frankfurter Rundschau, 1991a).

2 The average monthly cost of basic nursing home care in Germany is currently estimated to be about DM 2900,-.

3. For the U.S., estimates range from a probability of .35 to one of .45. For details, see the Pepper Commission Report (USGPO), issued in September of 1990.

4. For another assessment, see Tews, 1989.

5. This latter type of assistance also covers other kinds of situations, such as childbirth and maternity, training and relocation, and even medical bills in general.

6. For a listing of these proposals, see the overview article by the Frankfurter "Arbeitsgruppe Armut und Unterversorgung", Frankfurter Rundschau, 1991a.

7. Historically speaking, Germans appear to have relied on a historical surplus of unattached untrained women for many of these services. See Rueckert, 1987.

8. The state with the best-developed LTC infrastructure, Baden-Württemberg, itself favors the mixed private-sector/ compulsory social insurance model.

9. In the weeks following the federal German elections of December 1990, the victorious CDU/FDP coalition decided to break up the former Ministry for Youth, Family, Women and Health, which had been responsible for most federal social policies, and to create separate ministries focused on Youth and Women, on Families and the Aged, and on Health.

10. See the RFP announced for the study by the BMfFFG in January of 1990.

References

Baecker, G. 1990. *Soziale Absicherung bei Pflegebedürftigkeit.* WSI des DGB, Summer 1990.

Baier, H. 1977. Herrschaft im Sozialstaat: Auf der Suche nach einem soziologischen Paradigma der Sozialpolitik, KZfSS vol. 19, Supplement, 128–142.

Bonner Almanach 1989. Bonn 1989/90.

BMfJFFG 1987. Bundesministerium für Jugend, Familie, Frau und Gesundheit. *Bestandsaufnahme der ambulanten sozial- pflegerischen Dienste (Kranken- und Altenpflege, Haus- und Familienpflege) im Bundesgebiet.* Schriftenreihe des BMfJFFG Band 192 (Kohlhammer).

Bundesrat 1990a. Long-Term Care Insurance Bill introduced May 28, 1990. (Drucksache 367/90), Bonn.

Bundesrat 1990b. Long-Term Care Insurance Bill introduced June 6, 1990. (Drucksache 425/90), Bonn.

Deppe, H.-U. 1989. "The State and Health" *Social Science and Medicine*, vol. 28, no. 11, 1159–1164.

Dieck, M. 1989. Long-Term Care for the Elderly in Germany. *Caring for an Aging World: International Models for Long-Term Care, Financing and Delivery* (ed. T. Schwab), 96-161. New York (McGraw-Hill)

Esping-Andersen, G. 1990. *The Three Worlds of Welfare Capitalism*. Princeton (Princeton University Press).

Flamm, F. 1980. *Sozialwesen und Soziale Arbeit in der Bundesrepublik Deutschland.* 3rd ed.n, Frankfurt/M. Landesregierung Baden-Württemberg 1988. Bericht der Kommission Altern als Chance und Herausforderung, Stuttgart.

Frankfurter Rundschau 1991a. Overview article on Long-term Care. January 5, 1991, p. 8.

Frankfurter Rundschau 1991b. January 25, p. 10.

Rimlinger, G. 1971. *Welfare Policy and Industrialization in Europe, America and Russia.* New York (Wiley).

Rückert, W. 1987. *Die demographische Herausforderung an die Altenhilfe.* Kuratorium Deutsche Altershilfe, Köln.

Schmaehl, W. 1988. Erwerbsleben, Ausscheiden aus dem Erwerbsleben und Leben im "Ruhestand" - Veränderungen und Aufgaben aus oekonomischer Sicht. Landesregierung Baden-Württemberg 1988, 77-98.

Schwitzer, K.- P. 1990. Altenreport '90: Zur sozialen Lage von Altersrentnerrinnen und Altersrentnern in der DDR. Blätter der Wohlfahrtspflege (Deutsche Zeitschrift für Sozialarbeit), vol 137, Oktober/November.

Tews, H.- G. 1989. *Die Ergraute Gesellschaft* (2nd ed.n), 144–188. Deutsches Zentrum für Altersfragen, Berlin.

Wingen, M. 1988. Altern heute und morgen—demographische Entwicklungen. Landesregierung Baden-Württemberg 1988, 23–34.

3

Coping with Unemployment and Poverty While Increasing Capital Accumulation: Social Policy in France during the 1980s

Isidor Wallimann

Introduction

During the eighties, most industrialized nations were confronted with a "new" set of social and economic problems. For the most part, these problems were intimately linked to developments in the labor market: unemployment reached its highest levels since World War II and, for many, salaries no longer covered subsistence needs adequately. Astonishingly high numbers of long-term unemployed joined the ranks of the ever-rising numbers of the working poor and the homeless, both individuals and families.

Amidst persistent reports of record profits and an unexpectedly long upswing in the business cycle, the number of homeless and working poor continued to grow, or stabilize at best, while the unemployed increasingly turned into an abandoned mass of people no longer useful for the extraction of surplus value. Instead, needy but inexpensive, vigorous and more youthful immigrant populations often supplied the labor force needed to fill the inadequate number of jobs 'reopened' or newly created during the latter part of the eighties. Profits, in turn, skyrocketed; so did speculative and economically unproductive transactions in ever more world-wide stock markets, leveraged and other buyouts and real estate activity increased. While profits became abundantly available for productive economic activity—although insufficiently used for this purpose—the political climate turned increasingly oppressive. For example, the state cut welfare state provisions and tended to 'criminalize' or 'hospitalize' the homeless. In addition, by 'criminalizing' petty theft and other illegal but victimless forms of deviance such as the petty sale of drugs the state also increased oppression.

The developments, briefly sketched above, are not particular to the United States, but exist in countries such as the United Kingdom, Germany, Switzerland, The Netherlands and France. Unfortunately, relatively little is known outside France of French social policy in general, and of the ways by which France has dealt with the issues discussed above.

The first part of this chapter outlines the characteristics of the French social insurance system and some of the tendencies for changing this system. The second part focuses more on the general organization of social services and programs designed to improve the long-term unemployment problem, particularly the national guaranteed minimum income program for social integration.

The French Social Insurance System

Although France, like other industrializing countries, was engaged in combatting disease and illness on a national level during the 19th century, its social security system (in a larger sense) was created somewhat later than that of other countries. While Bismarck's Germany, threatened by the advent of socialism, instituted health insurance and pension schemes during the 1880s, similar developments in France did not begin until 1930. The adoption of health insurance was facilitated by a law (passed in 1901) which allowed for the free formation of associations and non-profit organizations. During this period, numerous private organizations emerged offering various forms of insurance to specific groups on a non-profit basis.

On April 30, 1930 the legal foundation was laid for a large-scale insurance scheme covering such events as illness, maternity, disability, old age and death. Just as with Bismarck's social legislation, low income workers in industry and commerce were the prime beneficiaries of this national insurance program, and payments into the system were shared equally between employer and employee, amounting to 4% of the wage or salary for each. In addition to the national insurance program, a national family assistance program was established by law in 1932. Such programs existed before. However, they were not universal and were dependent on the benevolence of employers who, acting in response to trends in Catholic social policy, supplemented the income of those with family obligations. By the beginning of World War II in 1939, the family assistance program was extended to cover not only the families of wage and salary earners but all families. After World War II (in 1945) with pressure from the left, France reorganized and expanded the national insurance program resulting in what today is known as the *régime général* which includes the vast majority of the population, namely all the wage and salary earners in commerce and industry. The remaining population, i.e., specific occupational groups or classes, is covered by special insurance organizations which are not part of the *régime général*. The *régime général*, then, is a first attempt at providing large-scale and homogeneous insurance coverage to the largest possible number of individuals. In the past, it has gained in importance, since the percentage of wage and salary earners has been increasing steadily (Dupeyroux, 1988), and it also has been expanded. In addition to social insurance coverage and the family assistance program of 1945, injuries incurred at work began to be covered in the *régime général* as early as 1946, and coverage was extended to everyone in the *régime général* for retirement (in 1948) and in 1966 for health insurance. Contrary to the previous national insurance system, the present one does not allow individuals to choose freely the insurance organization through which they wish to be insured. A wage or salary earner in industry or commerce, for example, cannot be insured through the farmers' insurance organization, and vice versa. He must obtain coverage through the *régime général*.

Today, the social insurance system has three basic pillars according to which risks are being categorized. They are old age, illness and family. While the first pillar provides for such things as retirement benefits (even for mothers who had never engaged in wage labor but who had been in charge of caring for five children below 16 for at least nine years) and insures against the cost incurred by death; sickness or illness insurance covers such things as illness, invalidity and accidents at work. Under the family pillar, assistance (in various instances including maternity) is provided to families as well as to orphans and single parents.

Although the total insurance system rests on the three pillars mentioned, it is neither the case that there is only one single insurance organization nationwide nor that all individuals are members of the same organization. For each pillar, special insurance organizations or funds exist within each pillar (see Table 1).

As can be seen, the French insurance system subdivides people according to occupational groups (or, depending on the perspective and definitions, social classes). This segmentation is greatly facilitated by the private nature of these organizations. Based on the law of 1901, the various insurance organizations are non-profit associations which, although supervised by government, are accountable to their insured members. In addition, the insurance organizations of the different occupational groups consist for the most part of a conglomerate of 'local' organizations coordinated for purposes of national policy. Since 1967, each pillar also has its national organizations to further facilitate the national integration. In turn, the various national organizations (of the *régime général*) are themselves integrated into a union of national organizations within the social security system. Since the collection of insurance premiums for all three pillars is (for the *régime général*) the duty of special 'local' organ-

TABLE 1

The Pillars of the French Social Insurance System and Its Groups

Approx. No. of Members	Member Categories	Old Age	Illness	Family
13 million	Wage and salary earners in commerce and industry (régime général)	Own organization (CNAV) (régime général)	Own Organization (CNAM)	Shared organization (CNAF)
1.6 million	Businessmen, craftsmen, professionals (self-employed)	Several organizations of their own depending on group (CANCAVA) (ORGANIC)	Own organization (CNAM)	Shared organization (CNAF)
2.4 million	Farmers and agricultural workers	Own organization (MSA)	Own organization (MSA)	Own organization (MSA)
4.2 million	Public sector employees functionaries, various occupations	Several organizations of their own most of which have a special status (régimes spéciaux)	Several organizations of their own all of which have a special status (régimes spéciaux)	Shared organization (CNAF)

Sources: Dupeyroux (1988:158), Ray and Dupuis (1988:270), Ministère (1979)

izations—payment of benefits and collection of premiums being separated for all—the *régime général's* national 'collection' organization is also a member of this union (Besnard, 1982).

Aside from the fact that other countries usually do not organizationally separate the collection of premiums from the remittal of payments, the social insurance system is more uniformly organized for the entire population. Thus, Germany, Switzerland, the USA (and, as a rule, all or most modern welfare states) tend towards having one insurance system covering all citizens irrespective of their class or occupation. This is also true for health insurance where states such as Sweden, Great Britain, Germany, albeit not the USA or Switzerland, tend to provide coverage against illness for the entire population. It must be concluded, therefore, that the French welfare state is very unique in that it covers the entire population for old age and illness by means of an insurance system which is not only more "decentralized" but also organized more around the occupation or social class of individuals.

How, then, it may be asked, can national uniformity in covering the entire population be achieved? The answer is that, unlike other countries with a more centralized and unified insurance system, coverage is not entirely uniform. To the extent that uniformity is present, this has been achieved mainly through two strategies. First, each and every member of society must contribute, albeit to different insurance organizations. Secondly, all insurance organizations are controlled by the various ministries. Thus, the Ministry of Agriculture, for instance, controls and supervises the farmers' and agricultural workers' insurance organizations, while the wage and salary earners' insurance organization (*régime général*) is under the control of the Department of Social Affairs and Employment (Ministère 1982a; 1982b). Some national uniformity and coordination of the social insurance system is, therefore, made possible through legislation, negotiation and policy formulation at top levels of the government, involving the participation of several ministries. Yet, except for some minimum standards to which all insurance organizations must conform, many differences and inequalities in the provision of benefits and payments of contributions between the various occupational groups or classes persist.

From what has been outlined above, it can be concluded that the French welfare state is also unique in the following way. Although it has managed to extend and guarantee coverage against all major risks to the entire population— which is, for instance not true for the USA and Switzerland (Sommer, 1978)— it has done so by maintaining unequal treatment of the population covered. In its unequal treatment, it further tends to distinguish itself from other welfare states by treating equally the population along various occupational or class lines.

While this system tends to provide individuals with the necessary financial resources in times of need[1]—being certainly one of the most elaborate social insurance systems in the world—it, nonetheless, remains insufficient for some. Those insufficiently covered by the system for one reason or another, must resort to other sources of income, particularly welfare. Six categories of welfare can be distinguished: medical aid, support for the elderly, support for the handicapped, aid to children, aid to homes for various groups and measures against poverty (Dupeyroux, 1988).[2]

In addition to the insurance system in which membership is mandatory, it is possible to become a voluntary member of other organizations for supplemental coverage.[3] These insurance organizations, although non-profit in character, are less constrained by government and insure mostly (but not always) against illness (Dupeyroux, 1980: 88-89; Ancelin, 1976).

Strains in the Social Insurance System

Although it is mandatory for every active individual in the work force to be insured through the appropriate organization, contributions as well as benefits (except for the legally specified minimum) still differ from one occupational group or class to another. Thus, not all individuals are treated equally within the insurance system, and this 'discrimination' directly reflects the individuals' employment or class status, i.e. the privileges and particularities associated with their economic positions. Historic in origin, these privileges and particularities have, thus, also come to be 'preserved' within the national insurance system. Longstanding government efforts and a tendency towards unification (harmonization) do exist but the goal of a unified system in terms of premiums and benefits has not been reached. Thus, the self-employed or those working in agriculture pay different contributions and receive different benefits as, for example, the wage and salary earners organized in the *régime général*. The same holds true for the members of the special associations (*régimes spéciaux*) that cover groups such as government employees, railroad personnel, miners, and merchant mariners. Although everyone is obliged to contribute somewhere, there is a ceiling beyond which a smaller percentage (or none at all) of one's wage or salary is deducted or contributed by the employer to the insurance fund (Ministère, 1979; Dupeyroux, 1980: 88-89).

This inequality tends to violate the principle of solidarity on a national level, a notion which has also been of importance in France's welfare state history and politics. As such, it explicitly rejects the idea that social security rests on a social contract whereby benefits relate directly to payments made into the system. This policy does favor distributive justice (Schorr, 1965: 2). However, there are some policies that undercut justice. In contemporary France, the more affluent (such as the self-employed) maintain some of their privileges in the social insurance system by virtue of the fact that they are permitted to form and shape quite autonomously their own insurance organization and its operation. Similarly, the relative disadvantages resulting from the agricultural workers and farmers' economic status is reflected in the benefits they receive and the premiums they can afford to pay within their social insurance organization.

Consequently, in France probably more so than in other countries, the differential treatment of various groups within the social insurance system has often led to political contention. Particularly in times of economic crisis, when contributions decrease and needs increase, questions about the 'fairness' of the present insurance system arise. Should the entire wage, salary or income not be subject to the same deductions and employer contributions? As is the case with the income tax system, should the contribution rate not be progressive instead of regressive? Should those who as a result of their occupation or class are privileged, and who belong to insurance organizations providing them with better coverage, not be compelled to pass on some of their privileges to the more disadvantaged groups? These are some of the questions raised in debates addressing the unequal treatment of the various groups involved in the national insurance system. However, there is presently no evidence that the national insurance system's basic structure will be modified, nor that the Mitterrand government could politically abolish the remaining vestiges of privilege inherent in France's national insurance system (Catrice-Lorey, 1983).

Aside from questions relating to the ability to pay and the extent to which the principle of solidarity is being realized, changes in the economy's occupational structure (and the associated demographic changes) further introduce strains into the social insurance system. Some of these changes have been significant enough as to endanger the very viability of various insurance organizations. Thus, their viability has been threatened by the generally shrinking base of contributors in some groups, while there has not been a corresponding decrease in these groups' pool of beneficiaries. Conversely, related to the shrinking base of contributors, the age of beneficiaries in some insurance organizations is considerably higher. Thus, in addition to the shrinking base of contributors, these organizations tend to be faced with above-average costs (Dupeyroux, 1988: 191).

Since some groups' insurance organization is being financially threatened by demographic changes, a compensating mechanism has been developed (based on legislation passed in 1974) to compensate various insurance companies for their demographic losses. Of course, such compensations do not occur in a political vacuum and can become issues of conflict and debate. Involved in the demographic compensation mechanism are various insurance organizations as well as the national government (in part through its national solidarity fund). Of the amount passing from various 'donor' insurance organizations to 'recipient' organizations, the largest share comes from wage and salary earners in commerce and industry and is absorbed, e.g, by the farmers' and agricultural workers' insurance organizations or other major recipient groups such as ORGANIC, CANAVAC, and the Miners (Dupeyroux, 1988: 291; Ministère, 1979: 64).

Due to the growth in long-term unemployment and low-wage employment, the insurance system's revenues declined. This was coupled with the sectorial economic and demographic shifts described above. With this situation, new attempts to 'reform' the system have been made. Reforms were primarily aimed at reducing cost by curtailing privileges, while making the system more uniform. Thus, some groups organized within the *régimes spéciaux* have been induced, usually not without some administrative coercive power, to negotiate a merger with the *régime général*. Usually, such reorganization implied that a relatively privileged position within the *régimes spéciaux* is sooner or later lost for a less privileged position in the *régime général*. The tendency to privatize certain industries has the same effect. Since employees of private enterprises are organized in the *régime général*, the privatization of state enterprises also implies a loss of insurance privileges derived from employment in the public sector. Whatever the tactics chosen, the tendency to unify the system is motivated by the possibility to cut the cost of social benefits, i.e., to reduce the general wage level by reducing indirect wages.

The above described tendency towards a more unified system particularly affects the pillar concerned with old age. In the illness pillar a significant degree of uniformity has already been achieved, primarily through voluntary, mutual agreement. Thus, many functionaries are now in their own association (CNAM) and many independent health insurance organizations have established significant financial relations with these associations. Therefore, the degree of uniformity is much greater in the illness and family pillar than in the old age pillar.

While a greater uniformity and a more equal treatment—albeit by lowering the general wage level—has been one of the Mitterrand government's objectives, significant irregularities and a lack of social solidarity continue to exist in collecting social insurance premiums. First, there is the reluctance—well-known in the history of social policy—among self-employed businessmen to pay social insurance premiums. Second, among self-employed professionals, there is a significant interest in underreporting income. As a result, insurance premiums also fall short of what they would be with correctly reported income. Presently, the instruments available to the government are insufficient to enforce an adequate collection of premiums. Collecting social insurance premiums from self-employed professionals is made even more arduous by the fact that it is not linked to the collection of income taxes.

Economic Crisis

Unemployment, one of the foremost indicators of economic crisis, has risen considerably in the 1980s. Comparatively speaking, France experienced a relatively low level of unemployment during the 1970s, when approximately 2-3% were recorded for the first half and 4-6% for the second half of the decade. With the recession of 1981/83, and the additional structural changes introduced in such areas as coal, steel and automobile production, the official unemployment rate jumped to about 10% in 1985 (Dupeyroux, 1988:295). From March 1984 to March 1989, the registered number of unemployed rose from approximately 2.47m to 2.51m after having peaked at approximately 2.68m in March 1987. However, the number of registered new jobs only grew from about thirty thousand (March 1985) to fifty thousand (March 1989), while the number of newly listed unemployed rose from about 308,000 to 360,000 during the same period of time. In addition, from March 1985-89, temporary employment workers grew in number from approximately 220,000-480,000 (SES 1989a: 16). Against this history of sustained high-level unemployment, long-term unemployment also has risen. According to Dupeyroux (1989: 1019), the unemployed have, on average, registered 333 days in 1987 and 346 days in 1988. In 1987, 811,352 (827,530 in 1988) were registered for more than one year, while 336,103 (355,523 in 1988) were even registered for more than two years. Consequently, Dupeyroux concluded that long-term unemployment is directly associated with increasing levels of marginalization and homelessness.

Much of France's unemployment has statistically been relabeled as 'early retirement,' which grew significantly with unemployment. According to Gaullier (1988: 40), 42.6% of those employed in the private sector are in early retirement. Their age ranges between 55 and 65. The number of early retirees had risen from about 100,000 in 1975 to some 800,000 in 1983, when the private sector employed some 12m individuals. The ratio of unemployed/early retirees had narrowed from about 11.2 (in 1975) to 2.3 (in 1983) (CERC, 1985: 225). Guillemard (1986: 272) reports that the number of early retirees remained at 807,777 in 1984 and declined thereafter to 463,300 in 1989 (Dupeyroux, 1988: 1033). Despite the very high level of early retirement and persistent high levels of unemployment during the eighties, the number of work permits (of various kinds) granted to foreigners also remained relatively high. The number granted fell from 300,100 in 1982 to 233,883 in 1983 and to 203,555 in 1987. In 1988, however, it had again risen to 340,732 (SES 1989a: 13, 1984: 16). To some extent, then, older segments of the labor force were replaced by a younger immigrant labor force. As such, this tendency to suppress the general wage level, and to increase productivity by employing—despite economic crises—even more desperate segments of the world population is documented for capitalist economies (see also Wallimann, 1988; 1984). France, even under Mitterrand, is here no exception.

Using 1980 as the point of departure (index = 100), the net national product gained about 21% by the end of 1988. Corporate profits (after depreciation), however, grew by 160% in real terms, while all salaries and wages increased only about 12%. Also, income to households only grew some 16%, while the profit (after depreciation) of small businesses (individual owners) improved about 7%. In sum, what occurred was a redistribution of the nation's income in favor of big capital, and at the expense of small entrepreneurs and employees (CERC, 1989).

In France, the minimum wage (SMIC) was introduced in 1969. It is supposed to be adjusted to the cost of living (CPI) as well as to the general economic development and growth (in real terms). Only in rare exceptions (e.g., for individuals between the ages of 16 and 18) may wages fall below the SMIC level. In this case, the SMIC is 10-20% lower than the regular allocation of F5,074.24/month (July 1989). Taking 1980 as the base year (index=100) again, the SMIC index was at 174.7 in 1989 (March), while the CPI index stood then at 175.4 (SES 1989a: 26). Clearly, the minimum wage does not adequately reflect the growth in productivity, and barely keeps up with the rising cost of living. Additionally, the rise in the 'real' cost of living for minimum wage recipients is higher than indicated by the index, since they are likely to spend a greater share of their income on food, shelter, clothing, transportation than the 'average consumer' reflected in the CPI. Minimum wage recipients therefore are bound to be considerably more vulnerable to stark increases in the price of housing, food and clothing, thus making them more prone to poverty and homelessness (working poor, homeless families).

The percentage of the population subject to the minimum wage rose after 1982. In firms employing more than 10 individuals, 6.2% received minimum wage in 1982, 9.7% in 1985 and 7.0% in 1988. Nationwide—all firms included—11.1% of all employees received minimum wage in 1987 and 9.7% in 1988. In general, the following additional facts must be noted:

- firms of over 500 employees had only 1.5% of employees on minimum wage in 1988
- 40% of minimum wage recipients are less than 26 years old
- women and workers receive minimum wage twice as often as men or other employees
- while men receive a minimum wage primarily at the beginning of their careers, women often do so for a prolonged period of their careers (SES 1989a; 1989b; 1988)

In sum, the persistently high level of unemployment, (especially long-term unemployment), the number of early retirees, the needy and primarily young (imported) immigrants, the altered distribution of national income, and the increasing number of individuals on minimum wage, all combine to threaten the existence of a growing portion of France's population. Ever larger numbers are joining the ranks of the poor and the homeless.

Coping with Crisis: Financial Aspects

As a result of the economic and social problems experienced during the 1980s, the total amount of money allocated to social protection has increased. This sum reached 25.9% of the Gross Domestic Product(GDP) in 1981, 28.2% in 1985 and 27.7% in 1988. During these years, however, the share financed by premiums and specific taxes (on income, profits, cars, alcohol, pharmaceutical advertisements and tobacco) increased, while that of general government funds decreased (Commission, 1989b: 29,37,39,69; SESI 1989; 1987). Although this has not changed the level of disposable income in the economy as a whole, it most certainly has negatively affected the disposable income of lower level income groups, particularly those whose earnings are relatively close to the subsistence level. This is the case for two reasons: first, because of the social insurance system's income ceilings—above which, to the extent that they still exist, no premiums must be paid—and, second, the regressive nature of the taxes involved.

While premiums have increased, (e.g. for the old age insurance) and ceilings lifted to increase revenues (e.g. for the health and family insurance), reductions in benefits were also introduced, affecting the health sector, the unemployed and the aged whose pension, for instance, has been indexed to the CPI (Dupeyroux, 1988: 303-4, 446).

Finally, it must be reiterated (see also Wallimann, 1986) that the social insurance system in France, to an uncommonly high degree, is financed through premiums of which employers pay an unusually high share. In general, the role of income taxation for the entire area of social protection must be termed minimal (Dupeyroux, 1988: 91-5, 216). Furthermore, total insurance premiums and income taxes withheld from employees together result in a 'tax rate' (for singles only) which is only slightly progressive (Dupeyroux, 1988: 232). Thus, total withholdings will amount to 44.28% for a yearly income of F100,000 and only 57.8% for an income of F1,500,000.

Coping with Crisis: Ideas and Programs

The source of the crisis can be located in economic and labor market developments. With millions of individuals unemployed and threatened in their existence, various coping mechanisms were developed. One such mechanism was to lower the retirement age in 1982 (March) in an attempt to lower official unemployment statistics. Other programs were designed to facilitate early retirement for those between 55-60 years of age. Early retirement often was negotiated through contracts involving parties such as industry, the unions, the social insurance system and various ministries of the state. Thus, the already low labor participation rate for the 55-64 year olds in France, dropped from 69.9% in 1979 to 50.1% in 1985 (Guillemard, 1989). However, the pensions for the increasing overall number of retirees were also financed in part by funds outside the old age insurance system, such as the national employment fund, the national solidarity fund and the special old age allocation fund (SESI, 1988a).

The cost of unemployment, including the cost to promote employment, increased already with the recession in the 1970s. From 1973-1980, an average yearly increase of 19.1% was recorded. This growth continued at a rate of about 9-10% from 1980-1985. Aside from the increased cost of financing early retirees and the much larger number of unemployed, significant sums were spent on job related training (Dupeyroux, 1988: 967-8). Numerous programs were developed and expanded for this purpose in and outside industry, just as firms have received various financial incentives to retain individuals and to create jobs in specific areas of skill and production. Furthermore, employment programs designed for certain age groups were created and expanded. For instance, the public work and non-profit organization oriented program (TUC) was conceived for youths between the ages of 16 and 21. Since its inception in 1984, the TUC has benefited more than one million youths while the age limit has been raised to 25. Of the participants, 87% were unemployed when they entered the program. Participation may last for up to one year and is intended to integrate individuals into the labor market. However, 47% still were unemployed upon termination of the program (Schmidt, 1988), a fact that points to the severity of long-term unemployment.

The precariousness of the labor market has also led to new concerns, problem solving inquiries and strategies. Poverty, "new" and "old," increasingly became an issue, as did the search for ways to protect the long-term unemployed from becoming impoverished and excluded from social participation (Adair, 1988; Kergoat, 1988; Rabanes, 1988). While "only" 16.3% of those looking for work were long-term unemployed in 1975, this percentage had risen to 47.8% in 1986. Reflecting the increased level of early retirement, long-term unemployment increased for all age groups except those over fifty. However, while it had affected women more in 1973, by 1986 proportions had approximately been reversed such that "only" 46.5% of all women looking for work were long-term unemployed (Sibille and Rayssac, 1989). The latter development, not unknown to social policy and labor market analysts in other countries, reflects the shift in sectorial employment towards increased low wage and service related occupations.

Given the changes on the labor market and the corresponding challenges to French social policy, developments and coping mechanisms in France were increasingly compared to those in other countries. In particular, the need was felt to introduce reforms that would officially and effectively guarantee a minimum existence for all those who, for one reason or another, did not (or no longer did) qualify for social insurance benefits or who were in danger of being totally excluded from productive activity and marginalized by society. Coping mechanisms in countries such as the Netherlands, the Federal Republic of Germany, and even the negative income tax experiments in the U.S. became of interest (Milano, 1988; Ray and Dupuis, 1988).

In France, experience in combining the minimum income with social integration was gained through a mulitplicity of projects—many of them on the local level—during the years prior to 1989. The public interest employment project (TUC) has already been discussed. Additionally, the following may be mentioned, although the list must remain incomplete:

* programs for the local integration of women
* programs for local, social integration
* programs designed to provide participants with a specific skill or work-related practicum (Sibille and Rayssac, 1989)
* programs for supplemental local resources, of which the projects in the city of Besançon and the Belfort region, for instance, are well-known (Belorgey, 1988; Mariller and Janvier, 1988; Mouranche, 1988).

Based on such experience, and as a result of increasing and persisting pressures, numerous social policy analysts began to suggest that a national guaranteed minimum income be implemented. In December 1988, the guaranteed minimum income law for social integration (the RMI) was passed by the French legislature with a large multi-partisan majority (Ministère, 1989).

The RMI program is administered on a local level in conjunction with funds transferred from the national level. Before addressing the RMI program in more detail, the regional and local administration of social services will briefly be discussed.

The Regional and Local Organization of the French Welfare State

It is characteristic of today's welfare states that aside from the financial arrangements of the social insurance system, a large number of social services have been created, some of which primarily administer the benefits to which individuals are entitled under the national insurance system. Other social services, however, are of a different nature. Thus, the various insurance organizations are by law entitled to spend a certain percentage of their funds on providing the population with social services unconnected to the administration of benefits. Aside from these services, and those provided by various non-profit organizations and enterprises, the most significant supplier of social services is the government. A large number of social workers therefore are employed by the government. Through its regional and 'departmental' prefect the central government extends its powers to the regions and the 'departments' (France's roughly 100 geographic and administrative subdivisions). Thus, on the regional level, and under the authority of a regional prefect, there exists the Regional Administration for Health and Social Affairs (DDASS). The Ministry of Solidarity, Health and Social Protection is supervising, coordinating and/or delivering social and medical services through both the DRASS and DDASS. The regional agency (DRASS), however, has no administrative control over the various DDASS agencies in the region. Rather, DRASS is responsible for both the supervision of some of the social insurance organizations falling under its regional jurisdiction, and the planning of new facilities and services. It also oversees the proper implementation and application of social policy legislation and supervises the training of social service professionals such as social workers, educators, and activities directors. The DDASS, on the other hand, establishes, coordinates and supervises social services. Services range from prevention against illness, disease and drug addiction to aid to children, the aged and the handicapped. It is also here where hospitals, retirement homes, and clinics for the mentally ill are supervised with regard to their management. It is not possible to explain in great detail here the range and type of services provided; it must simply be said that the social services offered vary widely and are closely coordinated. What must be mentioned, however, is that unlike the social insurance system, general government taxes are used to finance these services. The central government directly foots part of the bill while financing almost all of the balance of services indirectly through local jurisdictions. Therefore, DDASS is accountable not only to the Ministry of Solidarity, Health and Social Protection but also to the General Council of the 'department.' The General Council, a body without legislative power, takes care of administrative 'everyday business' in the department.

When it came to power in 1981, the Mitterrand government pursued a policy of national solidarity and decentralization. Decentralization, a political novelty on the French political scene since the law of March 1982, was to bring the country a step further toward base participation and democratization. Social services and the ways to administer them were increasingly to be determined by all parties involved: clients, social workers, unions, government, etc. In other words, together with decentralization, a process altering the ways in which social services are delivered was to be implemented. Thereby real or important needs of people were to be both met and met more effectively. Together with the redistribution of tasks, i.e., those that remain with the central government and those that should become the responsibility of the 'departments', the large majority of the social services now delivered fell under local, i.e., departmental control (Wallimann, 1986).

The Guaranteed Minimum Income for Social Integration (RMI)

At the departmental level the RMI is administered by the family insurance pillar's local branch (CAF). At the national level, the CAF branches are merged in the national organization of the family insurance pillar known as the CNAF which obtains the RMI funds directly from the central government. However, while the guaranteed minimum income portion is directly financed through the central government, programs to socially integrate RMI recipients must be financed locally, such as through the DDASS, municipalities, public non-profit organizations, and charity. Thus, the national RMI program is directly linked to decentralization and strongly incorporates the idea of a 'social contract.' Supervised by the prefect, central government RMI funds must be matched by local level social services, a process in which the DDASS plays an important role in the deliverly, initiation, coordination and supervision. Accordingly, each RMI recipient negotiates and signs an individually tailored contract in which the kind of activity designed to enhance social integration is specified. A department may have several committees for local integration engaged in approving RMI contracts, and in monitoring them after the prefect's signature has been obtained. All such committees, however, are coordinated on the level of the department by the departmental committee for integration and are staffed by representatives of the state, such as the DDASS, local government and various public and social service related organizations. The central government (through the prefect) and the DDASS can intervene and use their sanctioning power if contracts are violated.

The RMI program attempts to reach all those who do not (or no longer do) qualify for benefits within the traditional social insurance and social services system and who have an insufficient income. To obtain the RMI is a right, albeit with obligations. At the time the RMI was implemented, it was estimated that France had some 420,000 long-term unemployed, many of whom did not receive unemployment benefits. Some 500,000 households had an income below the RMI level. And while some 400,000 individuals were totally without any social insurance, about 200,000 did not have a stable residence (Ministère, 1988a).

Administratively, it is assumed that individuals in need will take the initiative in filing an RMI application. However, numerous private and governmental social services may 'motivate' and 'aid' individuals in filing and in determining an activity designed to enhance social integration (CLI, 1989). In order to ascertain that the applicant does not qualify for benefits outside RMI (which might be more generous), the local CAF (i.e., local organization of the family insurance fund), who also transfers the cash benefits to RMI recipients, screens the application. The social services facilitate social integration by providing both case-specific polyvalent services and an integration-enhancing activity for the RMI recipient. The latter can consist of gainful employment, training, field practicum (usually in non-profit enterprises) and/or some educational effort to enhance coping skills and literacy. Integration enhancing activities are subject to negotiation, since the individual's background, needs, interests, skills and abilities are to be taken into account (Lejeune, 1988; Ministère, 1988a). The resulting written contract is subsequently approved by the prefect and supervised by the local committee for integration. The social integration part of the RMI, therefore, is not to be equated with the familiar 'workfare' or 'public works' programs. Rather, it must be viewed as a society-wide 'experiment' in social pedagogy while guaranteeing subsistence. Furthermore, the RMI regulations do not include a fixed hourly 'effort' or 'work' for the cash amount received. Initially, a RMI contract is valid for three months, to be renewed for 3-12 months by the prefect. Thereafter, approval is given on a 3-12 months basis by the prefect upon recommendation of the local committee for integration.

The RMI program is to be evaluated nationwide within the first three years. The collection of data has begun on the local level. Although this is inconclusive, the following patterns evolved (Mairie de Paris, 1988; DDASS, 1989; DRASS 1989a; 1989b):

- the majority of RMI recipients are single.
- the majority of RMI recipients are men (single parents, mostly women, primarily obtain aid under the social insurance's family pillar).
- about 25% are less than 30 years old, a majority of them being women. About 20% are more than 50, and about 5-10% over 60. This indicates that many young individuals have not been reached by other programs to combat unemployment. Equally, these figures show that old age insurance and early retirement schemes have not been able to reach all to guarantee them minimum subsistence.
- only about 35% of all RMI recipients received support from the CAF previously.
- some 75% are French nationals.

- some 75% are victims of long-term unemployment, of which some 50% received no unemployment benefits.
- some 8% lived in collective housing, some 43% lived with families or friends and some 40% were renting, while 4% owned residential property.

The number of RMI applications strongly varies with the level of regional unemployment. In both the Rhône-Alpes region and the 'department' of Paris they constitute about 0.5% of the population (DRASS, 1989; Mairie de Paris, 1989). In the vast majority of cases, applicants have a strong desire to find permanent employment. From May through August, a total of 1,492 RMI contracts were drawn up in the 'department' of Paris but only 690 of them were signed. In the department of the Rhône (Lyons and surroundings), a similar picture emerges. From January through August 1989, the committees for social integration examined only 1,398 (22%) of the 6,302 cases who qualified for RMI payments, and only 484 cases were signed as RMI contracts in the same period, pointing to significant delays at various administrative levels.

The RMI minimum income is set at F2,000/month (July 1, 1989). Depending on other resources and income, a single individual typically received a transfer of about F1,600-1,700 (DRASS, 1989a; Mairie de Paris, 1989). The RMI minimum income compares with other benefits as follows (Liaisons sociales, 1989):

- F5,074/month = minimum wage (SMIC) (20% less for youths from 16-17 years of age; 10% less for youths 17-18 years of age)
- F2,832/month = minimum pension
- F2,105/month = benefits for long-term unemployed (AFD) below 55 years of age (for a limited period)
- F2,918/month = benefits for long-term unemployed (AFD) above 55 years of age (for a limited period)
- F2,712/month = benefits for pregnant women without children
- F3,616/month = benefits for single parent with one child

As can be seen from this comparison, there is a very strong built-in pressure to have an economic and social status other than that of an RMI recipient. In general, it must be said that the French social insurance system strongly "punishes" individuals for not taking part in the labor market and, therefore, blames individuals indirectly for being in their situation (even if their circumstances are structurally caused) (see also Ray and Dupuis, 1988). Thus, RMI recipients, in practice are making less than half the minimum wage. However, they are not expected to engage in a social integration activity full time. At prevailing exchange rates, the RMI minimum of F2,000 amounts to about US $330-370/month in cash transfers.

In accordance with the pressure to rapidly become a regular member of the work force, during the first 6 months of his/her status an RMI recipient may retain part of any additional income earned. For example, for the first F500 in additional income, the RMI recipient would have no deductions in his cash transfers. F500 are deducted with an additional income of F1500, while F900 are deducted if the additional income reaches F2000/month. Thus, the RMI recipient is materially rewarded and motivated to find quickly some form of gainful employment high enough to leave the RMI program. Implicit in this mechanism is the assumption that there is no significant structural unemployment.

Bottlenecks and Problems with the RMI

It is not possible here to give a detailed discussion of all difficulties associated with the RMI program. The following, then, is a list of difficulties present and to which attention must be paid in any future evaluations of the program:

- At F2,000/month, the RMI minimum income is set far too low, particularly since RMI recipients, being of an advanced age, can no longer draw on family resources as easily as is the case with youths. Therefore, there is a considerable incentive to engage in the 'black' labor market or in 'illegal' activities to make a living, with the consequences that the secondary social problems and costs that incur to society also increase.
- According to information from a local committee on poverty in Lyons, many eligible families and individuals do not apply for the RMI or have not yet been reached by social service agencies to submit applications. Thus, the CAF estimates that about 24% of eligible families knowingly refrained from applying. This in turn suggests again that many RMI eligibles could be engaged in work outside the "normal" boundaries of the economy and the social insurance system.
- That many have refrained from applying may also be associated with the great effort involved for the low level of benefits to be expected and the high level of public scrutiny and control over one's personal life to be accepted. Indeed, the RMI's institutional mechanisms resemble the pedagogically minded, inquisitive community based welfare boards of earlier times, and are quite removed from the 'spirit' embodied in mechanisms such as the negative income tax.
- Accordingly, the application consists of filling out a huge questionnaire and of documenting authorities in various ways. Aside from the demeaning 'beggar role' and the disclosure of privacy involved, this may practically be an insurmountable task for many, particularly if they are illiterate or

'disorganized'. It is no surprise, then, that many refrain from applying or that their application fails to pass the various hurdles (Commission, 1989a: 95).

• However, even if applications do successfully pass the bureaucratic hurdles, the local committees for social integration have not been able to swiftly process them. In part, this is an initial problem of 'getting started.' However, the problem primarily lies in the bureaucratized way of doing social work which has been characteristic for France (Wallimann, 1986). Social services are insufficiently prepared to work for the open milieu and to engage in community type of social work. The RMI program calls for a kind of social work and services delivery tradition which in many ways must first be established and sufficiently expanded. The need to establish and to drastically expand the horizontally connected social services in the community has become paramount (Moreau, 1988).

• Because social services have been unable to generate enough social integration type projects capable of accommodating the various RMI recipients, relatively few RMI contracts have been signed considering the large number of eligible applicants still to be accommodated. While it is possible that RMI recipients obtain cash transfers for three months without engaging in a social integration activity for three months, it is unlikely that the RMI program will be able to meaningfully enroll but a small percentage of eligible applicants in a social integration type activity. Of course, this bottleneck may be overcome should the labor market sufficiently improve in the future. (For additional social integration projects see Lejeune, 1988).

Conclusions

Recently, *The New York Times* ran an article which characterizes developments in France during the 1980s quite accurately: "Rather than tending to their home market, they (the state controlled French companies, I.W.) are aggressively buying abroad, both in Europe and the United States. Some, like Renault, are positioning themselves for the economic union of Europe in 1992; others, like Rhône-Poulenc, are pursuing the grander goal of a top-ranking in their industry, world wide." (*The New York Times*; July 22, 1990)

As was shown before, the 1980s saw a redistribution of income in favor of capital, at the expense of wage and salary earners as well as small entrepreneurs and recipients of social insurance benefits. Significant pressure was applied to lower the general wage level, both in its direct (real wages) and indirect components (social insurance benefits, social services). Instead of making productive use of the increased volume of capital accumulated, capital has been increasingly exported and used for various speculative ventures as well as unproductive mergers. Despite record profits and stock market indexes, the eighties have also shown 'record' unemployment and poverty levels.

By not including sufficient levels of productive and infrastructural investments, and by dividing up very unequally the amount of work available, France has chosen one of the most costly, and dissatisfying, ways of dealing with economic change and labor market transformation. Unemployment is the most costly way to redistribute work, if both the primary cost of unemployment benefits and the secondary costs (personal and public) such as medical care, social services, the criminal justice system, and psychological and physical well-being are considered.

Rather than aggressively pursuing a policy to increase and distribute employment, France has aggressively pursued a policy of disfranchising large segments of the working population. This is evident in the levels of unemployment (short and long-term) and early retirement. As a consequence, and in addition to the general losses incurred to employees by redistributing income in favor of capital, select but large segments of the working population were additionally compelled to absorb the huge material and immaterial cost of unemployment and early retirement.

The *secondary* strategies adopted by France to cope with the *secondary* cost of unemployment to society, programs such as TUC, CLR, RMI and an elaborate set of social services for the poor and the homeless—tend to be both very costly and oppressive. Oppressive both because of the bureaucratic means-testing approach usually involved, and the pedagogic, inquisitive and patronizing attitudes institutionalized in programs such as the RMI.

During the 1980s, then, France has pursued a social policy that weakened the social and economic position of employees in general, and disfranchised a large segment of the population. In doing so, although capitalist societies usually praise themselves for being highly efficient, France adhered to a policy pattern which tends to be both inefficient and ineffective. To be sure, this is not an unusual social policy pattern for capitalist countries, France included. Why is it that France, and other capitalist countries, usually prefer the more ineffective, inefficient and costly—but more oppressive—social policy approaches to approaches that are obvioulsy less costly, more efficient, more effective and less oppressive? Social policy research has only insufficiently dealt with this question.

Notes

This research was made possible by a grant from the European Council. For their support, I am obliged to the DRASS and the DDASS in Lyon, to several ministries in Paris and to the Department of Sociology at Syracuse University. Specifically, I'd like to thank H. Orbach, A. Delarue, J.-M. Reynaut, I. Besnard, J.L. Besnard, D. Herholtz and M. Coad.

1. Unemployment insurance is organized outside this system.

2. Welfare (aide sociale) is not financed out of the insurance system but by the central and local government, whereby central government payments favor poor over rich areas. Despite decentralization, the *aide sociale* provided by the department (*département*) remained about four times the volume of that provided by the central government. From 1979-1985, the total volume of welfare (*aide sociale*) funds spent almost doubled. (SESI 1988b; Ministère 1979: 65).

3. The mandatory supplemental retirement insurance is excluded here since the distinctions between it and the national insurance systems are becoming increasingly blurred.

References

Adair, Philippe (1988). "Pauvreté, nouvelle pauvreté: L'analyse de l'aide sociale à Amiens," *Revue française des affaires sociales* 42 (Nr. 4, Oct.-Dec.): 9–36.

Ancelin, J. ed. (1976). *Cross-national Studies of Social Service Systems: French Reports,* Vols 1 and 2. New York: Columbia University School of Social Work.

Belorgey, Jean-Michel (1988). *La gauche et les pauvres*, Paris: Syros.

Besnard, J.L. (1982). *Panorama de la décentralisation.* Paris: Association Professionnelle des Directeurs Régionaux et Départementaux des Affaires Sanitaires et Sociales.

Catrice-Lorey, A. (1983). "Social Security and the State in France: What Management Autonomy Should the Institution Enjoy? *International Social Security Review* 2: 191–206.

Centre d'étude des revenus et des coûts (CERC) (1989). *Constat de l'évolution récente des revenus en France (1985-1988)*, Nr. 93 (2nd trimester). Paris: CERC.

_____. (1985). *Les revenus des Français: La croissance et la crise (1960-1983).* Quatrième rapport de synthèse. Paris: CERC.

Commission des comptes de la sécurité sociale (1989a July). *Les comptes de la sécurité sociale.* Paris: Commission des comptes de la sécurité sociale.

_____. (1989b January). *Les comptes de la sécurité sociale* (January). Paris: Commission des comptes de la sécurité sociale.

Commissions locales d'insertion (CLI) du Rhône (1989). "Instructeurs des demandes de revenu minimum d'insertion (RMI)" (brochure available at DDASS, Lyon).

Direction des affaires sanitaires et sociales (DDASS, Lyon) (1989). "Note sur la situation de l'application sur le revenu minimum d'insertion dans le Rhône au 31 Août 1989," paper dated Sept. 8.

Direction régionale des affaires sanitaires et sociales (DRASS, Lyon) (1989a). "Les bénéficiaires du revenu minimum d'insertion en région Rhône-Alpes," statistic dated July 19.

_____. (1989b). "Profils des bénéficiaires du R.M.I. (informations recueillies entre mars et juillet 1989)", statistics.

Dupeyroux, Jean-Jacques (1988). *Droit de la sécurité sociale.* Paris: Dalloz.

_____. (1980). *Droit de la sécurité sociale.* Paris: Dalloz.

Gaullier, Xavier (1988). *La deuxième carrière: Âges, emplois, retraities.* Paris: Seuil.

_____. (1986). "Âge et emploi: Les salariés âgés et la fin de carrière," *Revue française des affaires sociales* 40 (Nr. 1; Jan-March): 69–76.

Guillemard, Anne-Marie (1989). "The Trend Towards Early Labour Force Withdrawal and the Reorganization of the Life Course: A Cross-national Analysis," in Johnson, Paul et al. (eds). *Workers Versus Pensioners: Intergenerational Justice in an Aging World*, pp. 164–180. Manchester: Manchester University Press.

_____. (1986). *Le déclin du social.* Paris: Presses Universitaires de France.

Kergoat, Michelle (1988). "Le complément d'insertion sociale et professionelle," *Revue française des affaires sociales* 42 (Nr. 4, Oct.-Dec.): 37–57.

Lejeune, Rémi (1988). *Revenu minimum: Réussir l'insertion.* Paris: Syros.

Liaisons sociales (1989). *Barème social périodique* (July 31). Paris: Liaisons sociales.

Mairie de Paris (1988). "Les expériences étrangères de revenu minimum," *Mardis Chaligny,* December.

Mariller, Noëlle and Janvier, Guy (1988). "Les programmes gouvernementaux de lutte contre la pauvreté et la précarité," *Revue française des affaires sociales* 42 (Nr. 2, April-June): 23–33.

Milano, Serge (1988). *La pauvreté absolue.* Paris: Hachette.

Ministère des affaires sociales et de la solidarité nationale (1982a). *Le budget de la sécurité sociale: maladie famille-vieillesse en 1983.* Paris: Ministère des affaires sociales et de la solidarité nationale.

_____. (1982b). *Orientations principales sur le travail social.* Paris: Ministère de la solidarité nationale.

Ministère de la santé et de la sécurité sociale (1979). *Le ministère de la santé et de la sécurité sociale.* Paris: Ministère de la santé et de la sécurité sociale.

Ministère de la solidarité, de la santé et de la protection sociale (1989). *Revenu minimum d'insertion: Loi no.88-1088 du 1ᵉʳ décembre 1988 et textes d'application* (édition mars 1989, bulletin officiel no.89.6): Paris: Ministère de la solidarité, de la santé et de la protection sociale.

_____. (1988a). *Le revenu minimum d'insertion: guide d'information des organismes instructeurs.* Paris: Ministère de la solidarité, de la santé et de la protection sociale.

_____. (1988b). *Contrat d'insertion* (document). Paris: Ministère de la solidarité, de la santé et de la protection sociale.

Moreau, Roland (1988). "Réussir le revenu minimum," *Revue française des affaires sociales* 42 (Nr. 3, July-Sept.): 73–81.

Mouranche, Sylvie (1988). "Le revenu minimum garanti: Quelques études françaises récentes," *Revue française des affaires sociales* 42 (Nr. 2, April-June): 55–61.

Rabanes, Philippe (1988). "Formation et traitement social du chômage: La politique française et les objectifs communautaires," *Revue française des affaires sociales* 42 (Nr. 4, Oct.-Dec.): 59–94.

Ray, Jean-Claude and Dupuis, Jean-Marc (1988). *Analyze économique des politiques sociales.* Paris: Presses Universitaires de France.

Schmidt, Nicolas (1988). "Les travaux d'utilité collective: Évaluations et évolutions," *Revue française des affaires sociales* 42 (Nr. 3, June-Sept.): 49–62.

Schorr, A.L. (1965). *Social Security and Social Services in France.* U.S. Department of Health, Education, and Welfare (Social Security Administration, Division of Research and Statistics, Research Report No.7), Washington, 1965: p. 2.

Service des études et de la statistique (SES) (1989a). *Statistique du travail,* bulletin mensuel (July). Paris: Ministère du travail, de l'emploi et de la formation professionnelle.

_____. (1989b). *Premières informations,* Nr. 128 (June). Paris: Ministère du travail, de l'emploi et de la formation professionnelle.

_____. (1988). *Premières informations,* Nr. 86 (June). Paris: Ministère du travail de l'emploi et de la formation professionnelle.

_____. (1984). *Statistique du travail,* bulletin mensuel (December). Paris: Ministère du travail, de l'emploi et de la formation professionnelle.

Service des statistiques, des études et des systèmes d'information (SESI) (1989). *Le compte de la protection sociale de 1981 à 1988,* Nr. 141 (June). Paris: Ministère de la solidarité, de la santé et de la protection sociale.

_____. (1988a). *Les nouveaux bénéficiaires du minimum vieillesse en 1986*, Nr. 131 (Nov). Paris: Ministère de la solidarité, de la santé et de la protection sociale.

_____. (1988b). *Dépenses d'aide sociale: Évolution 1979-1985*, Nr. 116 (April). Paris: Ministère des affaires sociales et de l'emploi.

_____. (1987). *La protection sociale de 1959 à 1985,* Nr. 85 (Feb.). Paris: Ministère des affaires sociales et de l'emploi.

Sibille, Hugues and Rayssac, Gilles-Laurent (1989). "Le chômage de longue durée," in Sibille Hugues (ed.) *Les politiques d'emploi à l'épreuve du chômage de longue durée.* Paris: Syros.

Sommer, Jürg (1978). *Das Ringen um soziale Sicherheit in der Schweiz.* Ruegger: Diessenhofen.

Wallimann, Isidor (1988). "Evaluating the Swiss Welfare State: A Review Essay," *Journal of Sociology and Social Welfare* 15 (2): 143–154.

_____. (1986). "Social Insurance and the Delivery of Social Services in France: Organization, Class Structure and Problems of the French Welfare State," *Social Science & Medicine* 23 (12): 1305–1317.

_____. (1984). "The Import of Foreign Workers in Switzerland: Labor-Power Reproduction Costs, Ethnic Antagonism and the Integration of Foreign Workers in to Swiss Society." Pp. 153–175 in Louis Kriesberg (ed.), *Research in Social Movements, Conflict and Change*, Vol. 7. Greenwich, CT: JAI Press.

4

The Development of Geriatric Services for Elderly Icelanders: Pursuing Equity and Uniformity

G. Darryl Wieland

Introduction

The Republic of Iceland is an island nation in the North Atlantic close to the Arctic Circle. With a tiny population of one-quarter million, Iceland has often been overlooked due to its small size and isolation. While its newfound global strategic importance and the recent political summit have brought it some media notice, modern Icelandic society has received comparatively little international academic attention either alone or in comparative research. This is all the more remarkable in that Iceland's social development has occurred so quickly and recently compared to other Western nations.

Icelanders living today have witnessed major shifts from subsistence to full industrialization, famine and poverty to health and prosperity, and political dependency to full independence. The social changes these shifts have wrought have occurred within the context of a common culture, language and religion, a long and distinct historical and literary tradition, and a fairly discrete population stock. The social diversification and stratification attendant with industrialization have been registered, but the centripetal elements of social organization and dominant political ideology have lent support to development of the welfare state. Thus, class differences in access to the benefits of society (e.g., income and services) are not as marked as in larger, more heterogeneous industrial states. In particular, government -initiated, cooperative, and voluntary efforts to secure an equitable distri- bution of adequate and accountable health and social services to all

Icelanders have achieved considerable implementation and a broad base of commitment. Perhaps in this regard, Iceland is the paradigmatic Nordic welfare society.

We have previously outlined the historical position of the elderly and the development of geriatric services in Iceland (Wieland and Pálsdóttir, 1986). In the present chapter, the current and planned geriatric service system in Iceland is described in conjunction with projected need and demand. The aging of the Icelanders is challenging policy-makers, service professionals, volunteers, and familial caregivers to modify this system. The services system is being modified within the context of changing social and cultural values. These values emphasize disparate themes of individualism (personal responsibility, autonomy, and independence) and collective rights and obligations. The political and ideological underpinnings of the geriatric service system will be explored. In particular, I address the question of the future relationship between public and private, and formal and informal support of elderly Icelanders, because—given a society of such structure and scale—the extension of formal geriatric services will largely be adapted to the capabilities and preferences of dependent elders and their families.

Social Transitions and the Elderly Population

Epidemic, famine and natural disaster have reigned so prominently throughout much of Iceland's history that many periods are named and primarily remembered for them. In particular, Iceland's long decline between the 13th to the late 18th centuries was marked by increasing isolation from the rest of Europe, a worsening climate, frequent periods of plague and illness, famine linked to volcanic eruptions, and finally emigration (Jónsson, 1944; Bjarnar, 1965). During that time the population dropped from as many as 100,000 at the close of the island's commonwealth period (874-1264 AD) to less than 40,000 in the middle-late 1800s (Tomasson, 1977).

Fundamental socioeconomic changes began rapidly in Iceland with its gradual acquisition of political and economic rights, and the emergence of an export industry built upon fishing. These developments began in earnest only in the later 19th century, and resulted in the elimination of the plagues and famines of past years, a substantially improved living standard, and a quickly expanding population. What is remarkable about the demographic and epidemiologic transition in Iceland is the recency and relative speed of these fundamental structural changes. The turn-of-the-century fisheries, though labor intensive, required seasonal labor, and much of the population was of a landless *cottar* class unassured of continuous gainful employment. As one government report (dated 1901) put it:

The lifestyles here are the same year after year, except that increasing numbers come from the hinterlands to the coastal villages each year. But as the population grows, there is less work for each person. For this reason there is great poverty and much distress particularly if the fishing goes badly (Icelandic Public Health Reports 1901-1904: 26; quoted in Magnússon, 1989: 143).

Although native historians have marked the beginnings of industrialization in Iceland at the turn of the century with the arrival of large engine-driven fishing crafts (Thorleifsson, 1973), the elimination of widespread poverty really did not occur until World War II. The war brought full independence from Denmark, occupation by the British and Americans, and abundant, well-paid work at the behest of the occupying forces. During these years many of the landless *cottars* became sedentary middle-class wage earners.

The improvement in the standard of living is represented by changes in housing during this time. More than half of all dwellings in 1900 were simple turf-houses. By 1930, turf-covered huts still accounted for a quarter of domestic dwelling structures in Iceland. The war and post-war periods saw the virtual elimination of this traditional structure, and the housing of the population in high-quality, convenience-filled flats and single family homes, most owner-occupied (Kristinsson, 1975).

The recency of these changes has meant that Iceland has carried many characteristics of a peasant society well into the present century. Several of these characteristics are of relevance in connection with this chapter, and will be expanded upon below: a) the completion of the demographic transition has only recently occurred, signalled by its fertility rate, which (although now dropping) was and is among the highest of developed societies [this presages a large elderly "boom" in the early through mid-2000s]; b) the traditionally high social valuation of labor for its own sake in the elderly cohort (as well as the need for most able-bodied elderly to supplement their fixed incomes in a generally inflationary economy) contributes to a relatively high labor force participation of elderly Icelanders today; and c) the ideology of social equality, which has been strongly shaped by the material and social deprivations of the first part of the century and earlier (as well as culturally more fundamental presuppositions) has continued to serve as the basis of broadly supported social programs such as those deployed for elderly Icelanders.

Completion of the Demographic Transition

With the recession of epidemic illnesses and famine early in the present century (see Wieland and Pálsdóttir, 1986), life expectancy in Iceland improved dramatically, largely attributable to the great reduction in infant mor-

FIGURE 1

Life Expectancy 1860-1984

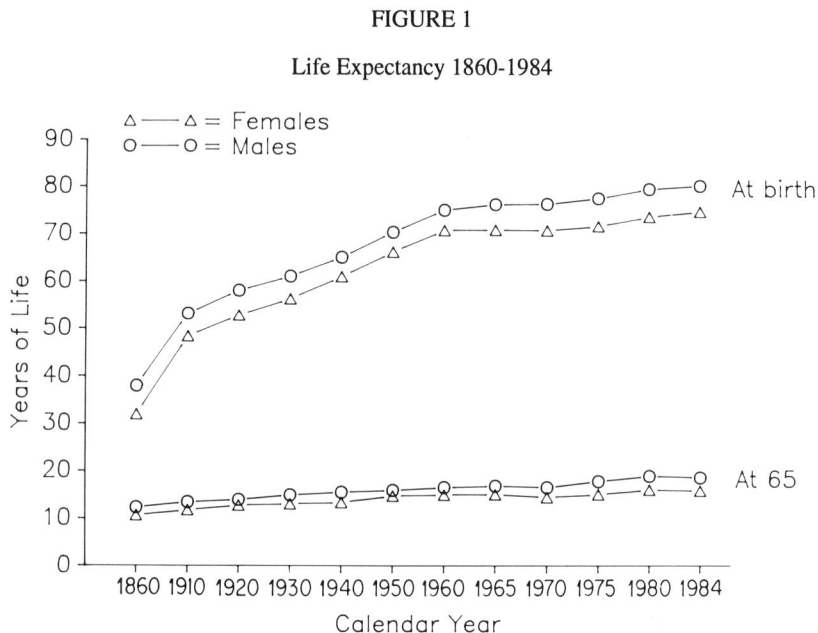

tality (Figure 1). Natural increase has accounted for steady population growth (37% from 1960 to 1985)—a period during which the population in the other Nordic countries has grown more slowly (about 12%). The final stage in the demographic transition (Davies, 1985) has only lately occurred in Iceland, with the decline in fertility[1], slowing population growth, and increase in the crude death rate due to population aging. In 1960, Icelandic women on the average bore over four live infants each, compared to the contemporaneous rate in Western Europe (Ireland excepted), which ran about 2.5 to 2.7 live births. As can be seen in Figure 2, fertility in Iceland (dropping to 1.9 in 1985) is closing on but still above that of the other Nordic countries (Planning Committee, 1987). The obvious implications for the age structure of the population from 1960 to 2025 are manifest in Figure 3 (Planning Committee, 1987). By 1980, Iceland was the "youngest" of the Nordic countries, with only 10% of its people aged 65 or older, compared to Finland (12.1%), Denmark (14.5%), Norway (14.9%), and Sweden (16.4%). Correspondingly, the crude death rate in Iceland (661.4 deaths per 100,000 in 1984) is somewhat lower than that of Finland (986.2), Denmark (1,141.6), Norway (1,068.6), and Sweden (1,125.8).[2] As fertility converges with the experience of the other Nordic countries, so will the crude death rate, population growth, and age structure of Iceland.

FIGURE 2

Fertility in the Nordic Countries, 1960-84

● Denmark   ○ Finland   ■ Iceland   □ Norway   △ Sweden

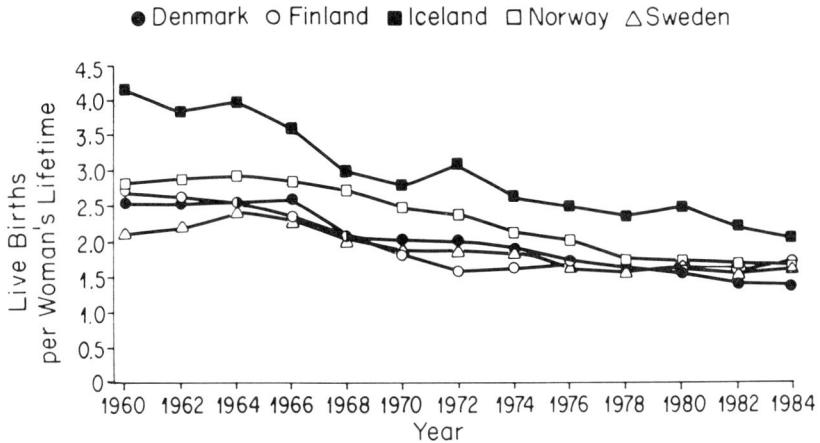

Workforce Participation and the Moral Value of Labor

One of the hallmarks of modern Icelandic society has been the nearly full employment of its workforce. Unemployment is considered a social problem of the highest order, and, because of fear of political consequences, few post-war governments have dared let the rate rise much above one percent, preferring to risk unstable prices and foreign indebtedness. The relationship between unemployment and wage levels (the so-called Phillips curve) has been difficult to detect in Iceland since the beginning of the Depression. The period from 1928 to 1940 saw little change in wages, but considerable unemployment, while since 1940, unemployment has been very low, but wages have changed greatly (Eggertsson, 1975). During the last ten years, unemployment in Iceland (0.3 to 1.3%) was well below that of the other Nordic countries (Nordic Council of Ministers, 1987). As Icelanders will point out, their pattern of labor is also unique, with an unusually large proportion of workers having second or third jobs, seasonal employment, and frequent overtime workdays (Planning Committee, 1987, p. 80).

While most Icelanders today see economic necessity as controlling the intensity with which they pursue their work, it is also true that work for Icelanders carries a positive moral valuation whose roots lie in the experience of the first half of the century. The industrialization of the fisheries in Iceland was roughly concurrent with the country's economic emancipation (Thorleifsson, 1973). Briefly put, while some Icelanders began to profit from

G. *Darryl Wieland*

FIGURE 3

Population by Age Groups, 1960-2020

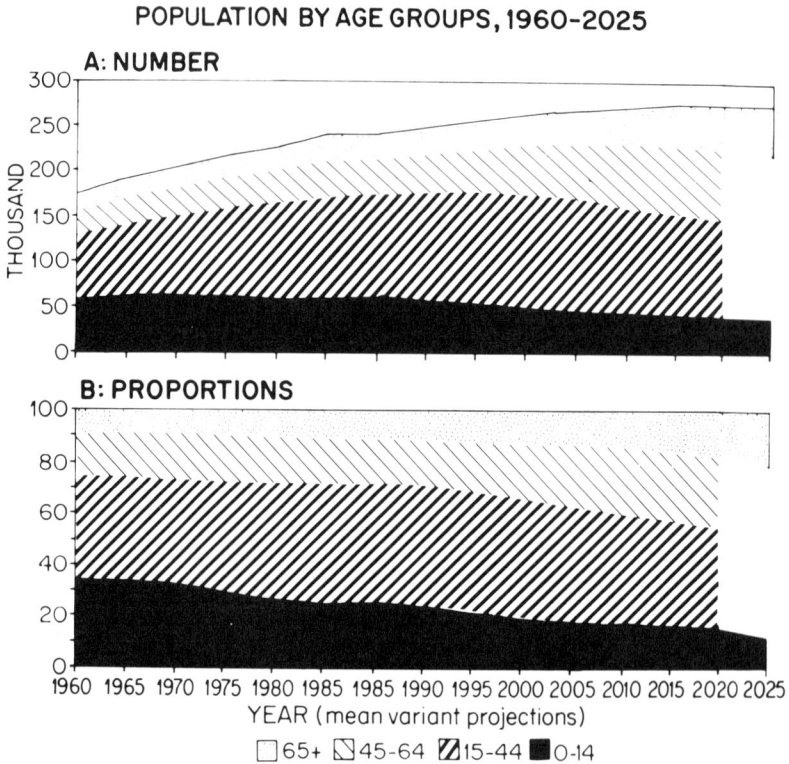

POPULATION BY AGE GROUPS, 1960-2025

the export and import trade in which they were gradually beginning to share, up to the early-middle 1940s, many were not included in the nascent cash economy, and subsisted mostly under barter principles. (The poor standard of living of this class is attested above.) They pursued the seasonal and occasional labor consistent with the mode of production of sundry harvests. As Magnússon (1989) puts it:

> Almost all trading and most kinds of work involving most Icelanders of the *cottar* class was based on the principles of credit (not cash) economy…For them money was something that circulated above their heads and could not be connected either with work or with work capacity…They lived in a world where their place in the hierarchy of

social structure often seemed given in advance and where saving…just did not make sense.

Magnússon asserts that the weak economic position of the *cottar* class meant that most could see no point whatsoever in mixing the meaning of work with the accumulation of capital. Rather, their notion of "respectable" work rested on traditional ideas of subsistence, personal independence and obligation, provision to dependents, and self-respect. Productive labor was that which produced consumable goods. Labor had to be carried through to survive, and proper respect for labor was necessary for survival with dignity.

Because the economic transition to a cash economy and to general prosperity has been so recent, these attitudes toward work are still strong. They are held by many elderly Icelanders who have witnessed these changes, and, while transformed, notions of the moral and social virtues of labor are promulgated throughout the society. Nevertheless, variations of these ideas and attitudes go to the heart of the distinctions between the ideologies of the middle and working classes, and—to some extent—between older and younger cohorts.

While these distinctions obviously arose with industrialization and political and economic emancipation, they received a further, important boost during the war. What many Icelanders found lacking in the "respectability" of work for the British and Americans during the war was the lack of connection between the quality and product of the "work" performed, and the wages paid. The individual qualities of inventiveness, endurance, and productivity were needed to influence uncertain outcomes of traditional subsistence. Yet the new work (*bretavinna*) was based on high regular wages and comparatively obscure standards of productivity which seemed to undermine these traditional values (i.e., the principles of a cash economy were finally replacing the indigenous barter-subsistence economy). Substantial cash income could now be earned via "work" having at best an uncertain moral valuation, by "workers" with or without high social esteem. Older Icelanders will often speak of their work histories in such moral terms, and disconnect the "value" of their toil from money:

> This is in a few words the story of my working life. On that matter I want to say this: I always got great pleasure out of work, and in the toil of everyday life I've got many good friends and companions—not one single enemy. But work never made me wealthy; I was always poor (from an interview with a worker born circa 1885, in Daníelsson 1959, p. 67, quoted in Magnússon, 1989: 152).

Given Iceland's recent socioeconomic transformation and associated values, it should not be surprising that elderly Icelanders today maintain a relatively high rate of workforce participation, even given a well-developed retirement pension and social security system. In 1980, over 70% of Icelanders aged 65 to 69 were fully or partly employed, while over 40% of those 70 to 74 and 15% older than 75 retained jobs (Ministry of Health and Social Security, 1982). At the same time in Europe and North America, only about 20 to 22% of males and 6 to 8% of females over 65 were "economically active" (World Health Organization, 1984). This noted, it must be pointed out that in Iceland, as elsewhere, the real earning power of elderly remaining in the workforce declines steadily from the sixth decade, suggesting both that the better-off among the aged leave the workforce and that the remainder work because they must (the latter observation increasingly attested to by Icelanders).

Political Action and the Ideology of Social Equality

The independence movement in Iceland was the primary focus of political action throughout the coincident industrialization at the turn of the century. Impetus was given to party differentiation both by the patent social and economic inequalities brought about in industrialization, and by the Great Depression, which had quite traumatic social and political effects (Blöndal, 1973). The differentiation of political parties began in earnest in the first twenty years of independence (from 1918). Notable in these developments was the growth of parties to the left of the nascent urban middle-class, whose Independence Party has ever since represented the center-right boundary of Icelandic party politics. An agrarian-progressive party emerged early and is still active, and socialist and communist parties developed with the support of intellectuals and workers. The direction and terms of political discourse were abruptly transformed by the allied occupation beginning in 1940, which—as described above—almost eliminated unemployment, and infused money into the economy, considerably raising the standard of living among the workers.

With modernization, the society is becoming stratified in a manner similar to other Western developed countries, yet from the beginning of the century to the present, many Icelanders display what has been called a "lack of consciousness" of inequality, or otherwise maintain that class differences are "not important" in Iceland (Broddason and Webb, 1975). In fact, the ideology of equality in Iceland probably crystallized, like the ideology of work, with the indigenous social inequalities introduced with independence and industrialization (see Magnússon, 1986). Accelerated development resulted in substantial mobility, as recruitment to new, well-paid, or high prestige occupations has drawn heavily on children from non-elite occupational groups.[3] Thus, Icelanders have often misidentified equality of opportunity with the absence of social stratification. But the ideology of social equality has been an important base of social and political action in Iceland.

Others have observed how the inwardness of insular, pioneer societies such as Iceland's fosters a pervasive and self-conscious sociocultural conservatism in the face of what is perceived as exogenic change (Lipset, 1963; Tomasson, 1980). In Iceland, this worldview motivates such typically Icelandic preoccupations as the conservation and defense of the language (which remains remarkably similar to Old Icelandic), "levelling" when class distinctions are perceived between social groups or categories, and to attribute perceived inequalities of particular people to primarily individual and/or family characteristics.[4] With regard to social action directed toward or affecting elderly Icelanders en masse, older Icelanders have benefitted from the apperception of growing inequality through the modernization period. The quick development of new occupational and high-income niches led not only to high mobility among the young, but held in train an intergenerational stratification with respect to older workers who were correspondingly less socially mobile. This age stratification was exacerbated by the Depression, and became the object of remedial social legislation, including workers' compensation, sickness and unemployment insurance, and old-age and retirement packages (see Wieland and Pálsdóttir, 1986; Hansen, 1975). It is important to note that these early comprehensive programs were installed from 1903 through 1936, well before the modern period of prosperity, and that they were put in place with a broad spectrum of social and political support—with even the Independence (center-right) Party playing a decisive role.

Current Health and Social Status of Elderly Icelanders

The standard of living enjoyed by elderly Icelanders mirrors that of the general population, and is related to the ongoing workforce participation and income supplementation of the aged, and the health and functional status of the group. To a considerable extent, elderly Icelanders have shared in the economic prosperity which first was realized during the 1940s, and has been precariously maintained ever since. In addition to their high rate of work-force participation, their economic security is in great part due to the various public and cooperative pension and income supplementation programs put in place largely prior to the boom years of the war (see below, and Wieland and Pálsdóttir, 1986). Among other factors discussed above, the visibility of older Icelanders in the workforce has at least partially prevented the formation of pervasive negative attitudes toward elderly Icelanders as a "dependent" class—a putative characteristic of modernization in other societies. Generational conflict over jobs is a moot issue, both because work is plentiful and because the work pursued by the oldest in the workforce tends not be the most highly paid and desired. Nevertheless, elderly Icelanders have paid a price for the full-employment policies adopted by the government since the war. Price instability throughout this period has made it very difficult for most Icelanders to accumulate substantial savings aside from home equity, and a large proportion retire with no income other than the basic social security pension. Other pension plans and supplements also yield fixed incomes. While pensions (like wages) have been subject to cost-of-living adjustments, economic security has been a public concern, and issues of collective bargaining with government for cost-of-living increases rank high in political discourse.

For the population as a whole, the balance between the traditional indicators of health and the expenditure of resources would appear very favorable. As seen in Figure 4, the ratio of per capita health expenditures to per capita productivity is representative of the average for 23 developed nations, with both expenditures and productivity slightly higher than average. (While Iceland expends over 10% of its national product on health services, it should be noted that it makes almost no outlays to military forces, raising the proportion of public expenditures on health, education and welfare to about 60%.) Among these developed countries, Iceland ranks high in physician availability (ahead of the U.S., Sweden, France, and West Germany), and highest in minimizing infant mortality (6 per 1,000 births) and increasing life expectancy (at 77 for both sexes, a tie with Japan). With particular respect to life expectancy at 65 (a measure more reflective of the standard of health and health care of the older population), Iceland in the 1980s is a leader of the developed nations with a male rate of over 15 years and a rate for female exceeding 19 years (Organization for Economic Cooperation and Development, 1987). A European study of intra-national inequalities in health status and access rated the Icelandic health system as the most equitable of the developed countries studied (Research Working Group, 1982).

Disease specific registers and health organization statistics indicate a disease burden in the general and elderly populations not unlike Iceland's Scandinavian neighbors. [5] This is indicated by the great shift of mortality to the oldest groups. While in 1900, approximately 21% (males) and 30% (females) of deaths in Iceland occurred among those aged 65 and over, by 1980 deaths of elderly men and women constituted 64.5 and 76.5% of the total (Hagstofa Islands, 1985). The 1984 pattern of causes of death demonstrates the new importance of chronic diseases, i.e., heart disease (33.7% of deaths), cancer (24.6%), respiratory diseases (11.7%), and stroke (8.2%). These four causes of death account for approximately three-quarters of all deaths in each of the Nordic countries (Nordic Council of Ministers, 1987).

What is left in gauging the current health and functional status of elderly Icelanders is an indirect interpretation of demographic, geographic, and services utilization statistics. Figure 4 helps account for Icelanders by re-

FIGURE 4

Population Groups (Total, > 65, and > 80) by Region, 1984

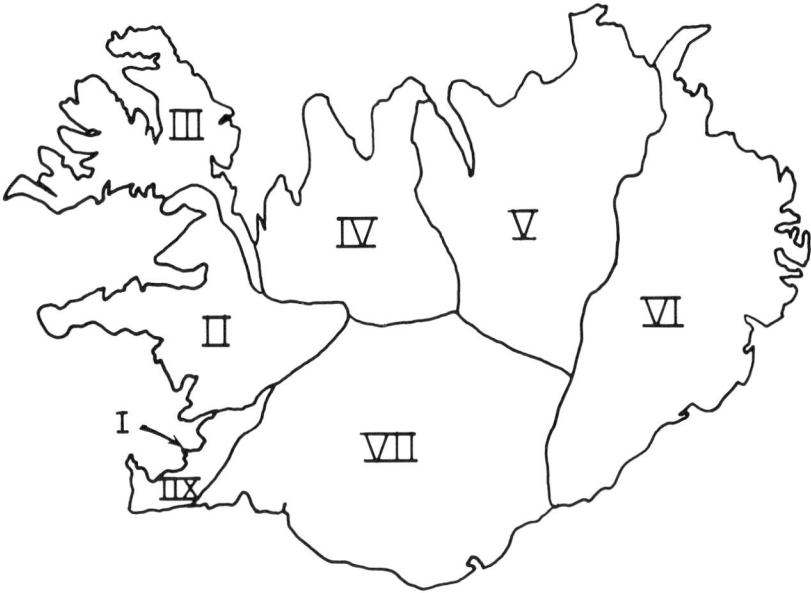

Region (see map)	Number (%) of total population in region		Number (%) of total > 65 population in region		Number (%) of total > 80 population in region		Number of institutional* beds (% of total) in region		Ratio of beds to population > 80
I. Greater Reykjavík	88,500	(36.9)	11,445	(47.0)	2,682	(45.6)	1500.5	(38.8)	1:1.8
II. West	14,974	(6.2)	1,398	(5.7)	381	(6.5)	271	(7.0)	1:1.4
III. Westfjords	10,418	(4.3	936	(3.8)	277	(4.7)	147	(3.8)	1:1.9
IV. Northwest	10,769	(4.5)	1,220	(5.0)	341	(5.8)	195	(5.1)	1:1.7
V. Northeast	25,982	(10.8)	2,737	(11.2)	714	(12.1)	466	(12.1)	1:1.5
VI. Eastfjords	13,095	(5.5)	1,235	(5.1)	306	(5.2)	187.5	(4.9)	1:1.6
VII. South	20,140	(8.4)	1,949	(8.0)	463	(7.9)	539	(14.0)	1:0.9
IIX. Reykjanes	56,202	(23.4)	3,460	(14.2)	724	(12.3)	555	(14.4)	1:1.3

* Beds in sheltered and service flats, old age homes, and skilled care

Source: (Hagtidindi 1/1985)

gion and age group. As can be seen, the distribution of the > 65 population varies somewhat from that of the total. Specifically, elderly Icelanders are over-represented in the major urban area of Reykjavík (close to half live there), and, to a lesser extent, in the Northeast (which contains the second largest urban and service center, Akureyri).

FIGURE 5

Total *Per Capita* Health Expenditures vs. *Per Capita* Production
in 23 Developed Countries (1982 U.S. Dollars)

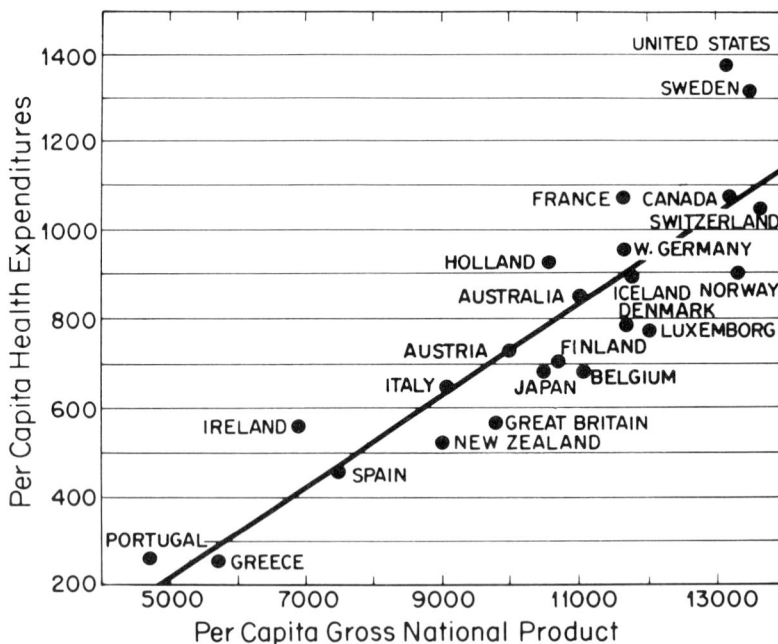

Factors accounting for this distribution were considered at some length in our earlier paper (Wieland and Pálsdóttir, 1986), although the causes and patterns of internal migration of the various age groups are not fully understood. The historically greater level of health and social services availability in the urban area may well account for a concentration of many frail elders in Reykjavík (Planning Committee, 1987, p. 121; Jónsson and Halldorsson, 1981; Johnsen, 1979). At the same time, many others with a variety of service needs remain in rural areas and coastal towns and villages. The above mentioned occupational and class mobility among the young has led to their relocation for education and work to the urban area and to the circuminsular coastal towns which are the mainstay of the fisheries. Together with the increasing workforce involvement of women outside the household and related changes in domestic group structure (see below), this mobility in the traditional natural or informal support network of elderly has increased the service needs of the aged Icelanders around the country. Recognition of these trends has led to the most recent initiatives directed toward elderly people in coastal settlements and rural areas (see below).

Existing and Planned Geriatric Services

The Pension and Social Security System

Iceland's pension, social security, and health insurance and services systems have previously been described in some detail (Wieland and Pálsdóttir, 1986). The Icelandic economy has a large central government sector accounting for approximately a third of the national income, and health and welfare programs represent about 40% of all public expenditures. The social security system, which is financed chiefly from general revenues, consists of basic social security insurance of residents of Iceland, and of supplementary pension funds which have come into creation over the years via special legislation and collective bargaining. Basic social security insurance consists of three parts: categorical pensions (e.g., old-age, disability, children's and widows' pensions, motherhood benefits), workers' compensation, and national health insurance.

National Health Insurance

National health insurance itself covers all residents of Iceland (including aliens, the retired, the never-employed and the unemployed), and is financed and administered on two levels. First, local municipalities and rural districts each maintain for residents a local health insurance fund, which is largely underwritten by the state Social Security Institute. Local funds pay for hospitalization (up to 12 months per 2-year period) and general medical care prescribed by physicians. Local funds cover ambulatory care and prescribed medications minus small co-payments and deductibles. For elderly Icelanders, those receiving only basic old-age pensions receive half the cost of most dental work; those that meet income tests for pension supplementation receive 75% coverage, and institutionalized elderly receive full dental coverage. Transportation in Iceland is still difficult and expensive, and its inadequacies affect most isolated persons who may require emergency access to health and other services. In response, the local funds cover necessary travel costs for both patients and health care providers (Ministry of Health and Social Security, 1982).

The second level of national health coverage is administered directly by the Social Security Institute, and financed entirely by general revenues. This supplemental health insurance extends full coverage to hospital stays in excess of those covered by the local funds. Further, it fully covers the long-term care of the mentally ill, developmentally disabled, and chronically ill. This supplemental coverage provides for almost all of the formal institutional and community-based long-term care delivered to elderly Icelanders.

The Health and Social Services System

Iceland is divided into eight health regions (Figure 4), each headed by a health area physician. These areas are subdivided into health districts, each of which contains at least one primary health clinic. There are now 74 health clinics around the island, including in Reykjavík, which after lengthy deliberation (having to do with the opposition of many urban private practice physicians in the capital) finally adopted the health clinic model in 1986, after evidence of unmet needs in the municipal population was collected (Planning Committee, 1987, p. 117).

Staffing of these clinics ranges from those that have several doctors, nurses, and other staff, to rural centers which employ a nurse or midwife only and have a doctor's reception area. Staff are paid in full by the state, although the communities maintain the facilities. It is expected that the demands placed on the health clinic system will both increase and change in coming decades. From 1980 to 1990, health clinic physicians will have increased from 133 to about 196, lowering the population-clinic physician ratio from 1,690:1 to about 1,300:1, and contacts are expected to increase to about 5 per resident year. The clinics will continue to experience an increase in patients presenting with social and psychological problems, and the geriatric workload is expected to increase in earnest after the turn of the century. Much more of the work of the health clinics will be tied to health surveillance, screening, and prevention (Planning Committee, 1987, p. 118).

Institutional care in Iceland is of mixed ownership, as much of the early construction was undertaken by private citizens and religiously-affiliated and non-profit groups. Since the war, the central government has played a much more prominent role, such that currently only one-quarter of medical-surgical and psychiatric beds are owned and controlled by these groups. In 1970, Iceland maintained 25 general hospitals with 1,400 medical-surgical beds (with at least one hospital in each of the health districts as stipulated by law). By May 1982, operating acute beds were reduced to 1,237 (about 5.5 per thousand), but the total number of all institutional beds rose 34% due to the proliferation of long-term care services. The acute-bed ratio is somewhat higher than in the other Nordic countries, which is accounted for by some-what longer lengths-of-stay in Icelandic hospitals. Ministry studies have found that about 20 percent of short-stay medical beds, 25 percent of rehabilitation beds, and 2 - 4 percent of surgical beds are occupied by long-stay geriatric patients, with the problem being particularly acute in Reykjavík, where about half the elderly population resides. Together with nursing and other personnel shortages which have lowered capacity, bed blockage accounts for a present undersupply of acute-care beds in Iceland. Because elderly patients frequently require emergency and acute hospital admissions, bed-blockage represents a special access problem for older Icelanders. Although the bed-blockage problem has not been thoroughly explored, there are questions as to what extent the erstwhile unavailability of home care services, together with the co-payments necessary for home care, could result in acute-bed blockages. The number of applications on waiting lists for long-term institution admission are almost everywhere at least twice the number of operating beds.

In contrast to the hospitals, over half the 1105 long-term institutional care beds (1985) are owned and operated by non-profit and religiously-affiliated groups, under the regulatory control of the Ministry of Health and Social Security. Level-of-care designations are the service flats (full board-and care, and congregate housing receiving community-based services), "old people's homes" offering an intermediate level of nursing care, and skilled care facilities (both freestanding and hospital-based) providing 24-hour nursing and allied health services.[6] Because of the bed-blocking problem in the city, the paucity of institutional geriatric services around the country, and the late growth of the elderly population, the government has embarked upon expanding the long-term bed supply. Relative to the other Nordic countries, the trend is thus to increase the already high long-term bed availability (see Figure 6). Nevertheless, based on a needs assessment which took into account 1985 long-term institutional utilization, the back-up of long-stay patients on other services, and admissions waiting lists of patients in the community, the Ministry projected a 33 percent shortfall in 1985 skilled beds. Further, using the 8.4 long-term beds per 100 elderly inhabitants they derived as a standard of need, it was projected that the bed supply would have to double by 2000, and more than quadruple by 2030 (Planning Committee, 1987, pp. 121-123).

Certainly some (but not all) of this apparently great need for institutional geriatric care is due to the erstwhile underdevelopment of formal home care services for elderly Icelanders. Until recently, the central government paid for institutional stays, but payment for home care was left to the local funds. Municipal and voluntary agencies, particularly in Reykjavík, took the early lead in extending these services. Still, Iceland is several decades behind the more mature Nordic states in extending community-based services. As is true elsewhere, rural and small-town elderly Icelanders must be more reliant

FIGURE 6

Long-Term Beds per Population Greater than 65 and
Greater than 80, Nordic Countries, 1965 - 1985

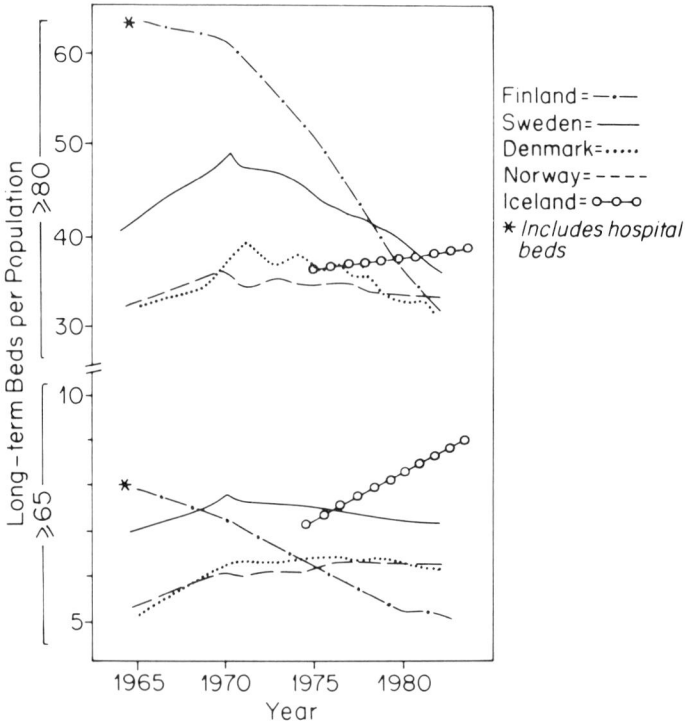

on the informal and familial support services that may continue to become
less available. The difficulty of transportation and communication in many
areas make the compensatory development of home care services particularly
challenging.

The 1983 Aging Act

In 1983, the *althing* (Iceland's parliament) passed legislation to promote comprehensive care and to integrate services which would enable
elderly Icelanders to live independently as long as possible and to receive
appropriate formal institutional and community services (Government of
Iceland, 1982/1984). This was Iceland's first governmental effort to coordinate medical and social services for older citizens, although governmental
involvement with the affairs of the aged in particular began with the earlier
social security legislation. Implementation of the new legislation stressed

linking geriatric services with extant institutions and agencies, i.e., the district health clinics and municipal community services.

The 1983 legislation also established within the Ministry of Health and Social Security a department on matters of the elderly, and a Commission on Aging. Statutorily, the commission is composed of members from the Icelandic Council of the Aged (a consumer organization), the Ministry of Social Affairs (bearing ultimate responsibility for municipal and local social services), and the Ministry of Health and Social Security (for health services). The director of the Department on Matters of the Elderly serves as commission secretary. The mandate of the commission is broad, and includes management as well as planning and advisory responsibilities. Its numerous tasks include: 1) initiation of policy-making concerning elderly Icelanders; 2) national-level planning of geriatric services; 3) acting as an intergovernmental communications center and information clearing-house for concerned individuals; 4) advising the Minister of Health and the government on geriatric affairs and the distribution of annual grants; 5) management of a construction for expanding physical capacity to deliver geriatric services; 6) making administrative rulings toward resolving conflicts arising from enforcing the legislation; and 7) proposing to the Minister regulations concerning institutionalization of the elderly and related issues (Pálsdóttir, 1986, p. 32).

For purposes of regional geriatric services planning and oversight, the legislation required formal cooperation between the boards of the district health clinics and the district social services councils. Each health clinic has its own clinical service group for elderly residents. The service group is an interdisciplinary team composed of health clinic and social services staff, and is "responsible for the supervision of the well-being of the elderly in its district" (Pálsdóttir, 1986, p. 33). Specifically, the group assesses patients' needs for institutional care, screens and refers clients to other clinicians with care recommendations, and may provide primary care. One of its basic functions is surveillance of the elderly population in its catchment, contacting elderly residents who have not utilized clinic or social services over given intervals. The activities of this community-based assessment team are similar to those described for Denmark (Schroll, 1989).

As suggested in the foregoing, a number of problems have developed in the system of geriatric care, some of which have been addressed by the recent aging legislation, if not yet resolved. The Aging Act itself has encountered several implementation and enforcement problems. First, as the new services initiative originated in and gave a certain amount of power to the Health Ministry, it has encountered some initial resistance in the social service bureaucracy. In 1983, the Division for Matters of the Elderly contacted the district clinic boards and social services councils and requested appointments of the district geriatric services teams. The local authorities were slow to act, and by 1986 only half the districts had formal, named services teams. In fact, the Ministry and the Division cannot directly enforce compliance, however, given their control over the services construction fund and licensure powers, the local districts are gradually being brought into line. In practice, many districts had close cooperation between social services and health clinics in geriatric matters prior to the act, and were able to exercise many of the mandated team functions without named geriatric teams—these were largely the sparsely-populated rural districts in which close contacts existed between professionals and clients. The real targets of the legislation were the urban districts in which geriatric team care and case management were thought to be most needed. This aspect of the legislation has been largely implemented in these critical districts (Pálsdóttir, 1986, pp. 43-44).

The relatively high institutionalization rate in Iceland remains to be affected by the legislative provisions. There is no reason to believe that the rate is an indicator of poor health or functional status relative to Iceland's Nordic neighbors. A number of factors seem to have contributed to this problem. Certainly, with population aging and modernization, decreasing availability of familial and other informal care resources (see below) increases the demand for institutional care in Iceland as elsewhere. Second, the underdevelopment of formal home care service in many areas of Iceland has played a role in the prominence of institutional care, although since 1984 more favorable state financing has stimulated growth in home services. Third, flaws in the process of financing construction and operation of geriatric facilities have led perimeter municipalities to operate sheltered flats as old-age homes, effectively raising the designated service level for a number of institutional beds (Pálsdóttir, 1986, pp. 81-85). Fourth, institutional care is generally of high quality—comparable to that in other Nordic countries (Beverfelt, 1980)—and has a good reputation in the community; thus, public concerns with care quality do not in themselves deter utilization. Fifth, perhaps the biggest culprit is the perverse economic incentives to enter institutions given to elderly living in the community (Pálsdóttir, 1986, pp. 60-61). People without private income receive pension supplements to meet the cost of old-age home care, plus spending money. For skilled care, people with private incomes need not spend personal income for that care (unlike home care), as it is fully paid by the health insurance system. The Aging Act addressed this flaw by covering both old age and nursing home beds by health insurance payments, and establishing a sliding fee schedule for co-payments based on income, but enforcement (at least by mid-1986) had been postponed indefinitely. One feature of the legislation may have contributed to the problem, namely, the few adult day care facilities prior to the Act were paid entirely by the national health insurance, but were subsequently required to collect co-payments, perhaps making the day care option less feasible for providers and clients (Pálsdóttir, 1986, p. 88). Finally, the important provision that admissions to institutions must be certified by the geriatric service teams has not been enforced due to the fact that many teams have not been (or only recently been) named, and the fact that a loophole exists whereby boards of institutions may overrule team recommendations in admitting elderly applicants (Planning Committee, 1987, p. 124).

A third problem area concerns the equitable public distribution and subsidization of services in the so-called pensioners' flats. (These are of two types: the "service" flats offer space for a caretaker, while the "sheltered" flats add 24-hour staffing, security devices, homemaker and meal services.) The Aging Act stimulated the proliferation of pensioners' flats through its construction matching financing of municipal/district construction funds for elderly. The *Althing*'s intention was that the municipalities or other bodies would rent these flats and charge service co-payments to community elderly who most needed this sort of community-based care on the basis of "health and social factors" (Pálsdóttir, 1986, p. 88). But, as outlined above, the costs of living in the community pose disincentives to the more financially needy who may instead be attracted to entering old-age homes. The trend concerning the service and particularly the sheltered flats has been toward self-ownership. For example, of the roughly 200 flats planned for Reykjavík in 1986, most were to be built or bought by the intended occupant. Thus, elderly Icelanders of financial means appear to be gaining disproportionate access to this publicly-financed level of service. Well-off elderly needing some practical assistance would seem to be attracted to the service and sheltered flat options, and municipalities have seen occupant-ownership of flats as a way of shifting construction costs from the municipal coffers while taking advantage of the national matching in building up local geriatric housing capacity. While the Aging Act did not stipulate that occupants of pensioners' flats be cleared for admission by the geriatric assessment teams, the Ministry has of late been moving to assure that applicants for publicly-subsidized flats and related services are admitted based on overall need, and that sheltered housing operating on an ability-to-pay basis is privately financed.

The Outlook for Equity and Uniformity in Resource Allocation

The development of public geriatric services in Iceland—and indeed the bulk of the welfare state apparatus—has heretofore been driven by a variety of centripetal social processes that have operated through Iceland's concurrent demographic and socioeconomic transitions. Iceland's economic development, considered above, was certainly a necessary condition. While it is difficult to demonstrate precisely how a widely-held principle of social equality among people of a common culture leads to development of a welfare state, there is little doubt that the commonality and content of Icelandic culture and religion have played a role. The standard by which most Icelanders judge their public services is whether these services are acceptable to themselves as users or potential users. There is little public expression of the attitude commonly encountered in certain developed multi-ethnic, class-stratified societies, which holds that an acceptable standard exists for, say, public-financed long-term care, beneath one's personal standard of acceptability.

In addition to its egalitarianism, the still small scale of Icelandic social life has supported efforts to extend equitably formal geriatric services. Commentators continue to remark on the relative importance of extended kinship networks, personal relationships, and individual capacities and initiative in achieving mobility in Icelandic social life and limiting social distance created by class stratification (e.g., Rich, 1976; 1980). One might also add the observation that there has been little in the way of public intergenerational-equity debates or age-based political action committees that have been ascendant in the U.S. and elsewhere. Modern Icelandic society in many ways extends the traditional social structure which emphasized cognitive kinship and the concept and importance of the individual. With a population of a quarter-million interrelated people, kinship principles continue to be important in social organization and in defining the bonds and mutual moral obligations of Icelanders.

The development of formal geriatric services has also been abetted by declining total population dependency—a function of the demographic transition in Iceland. As can be seen in Figure 7, the increasing ratio of the elderly population relative to the "working age" population will continue into the twenty-first century to be more-than-offset by the declining child dependency ratio. While there are various pitfalls in forecasting social needs, problems, and policy choices from arbitrary construction and simple-minded analysis of dependency ratios (Calasanti and Bonanno, 1986), one can observe that a "golden period" (with total dependency < 50) is in store for Icelanders in their public and private support of child and elderly dependents through first two decades of the next century. Assuming that the Icelandic birth rate remains at the replacement level, the gross overall dependency ratio will rise sharply in 2020 due to increasing elderly dependency, levelling off in the middle of the next century when population growth stops (with birth and death rates stable at 13) [Baldursson, 1987].

It is when one starts dissecting the implications of increasing elder dependency and relating it to current and projected changes in the Icelandic economy and family life that the centrifugal elements of population aging become apparent. These processes may be regarded as harbingers of Iceland's

FIGURE 7

Population Dependency, 1960-2050

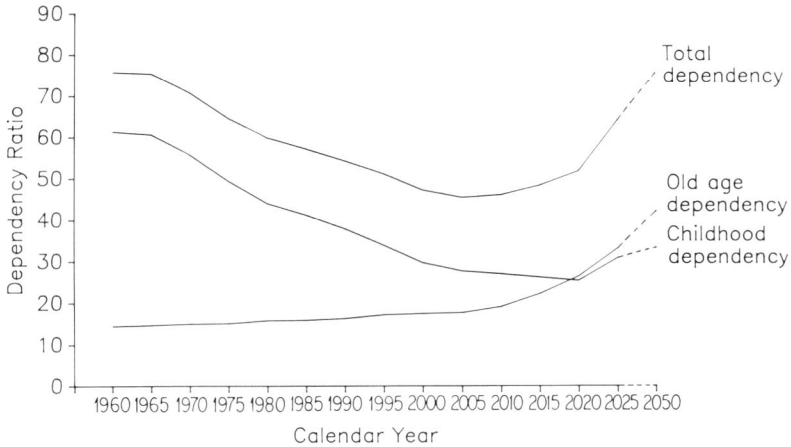

arrival at a post-transitional stage in which both demographic and socio-economic stratification are being simultaneously completed. It remains to be seen how these developments will play out, and to what extent they will be balanced by other, mitigating social forces such as those attested above. Nevertheless, one can anticipate and begin to observe the following trends.

There is concern with the viability of the various pension funds as aged beneficiaries and thus indexed pay-outs become proportionately greater, and Icelandic economic policy rides precariously along on relatively high foreign debt and inflation. In fact, the solvency of the pension funds has recently become a public issue and has emerged as a widespread concern. However, a larger economic issue remains in the background. After years of trying, Iceland has largely failed to diversify its economy and remains heavily dependent on its fisheries, such that real economic growth is expected to be half that of the other OECD nations into the next century, while its cost of living will remain high. This suggests that the Icelanders' living standard, among the highest in the world in the 1960s and early 1970s, may further erode. In addition to impacting elderly Icelanders directly, the perception of economic difficulties may hasten politicization of aging policy.

Rural-urban allocation issues have become a general problem in Iceland and are politicized to the extent that both a Regional Equality Party (part of a leftist ruling coalition in late 1988) and a capitalist-conservative, urban-based party have recently formed. The growth of Reykjavík as the dominant urban center has tended to limit the diversity of industrial, cultural, and social/health service sectors elsewhere. Some of the problems this has posed for elderly Icelanders and the equitable delivery of geriatric services have been discussed above, and were considered at greater length in the earlier paper (Wieland and Pálsdóttir, 1986).

One must consider in reviewing the replacement of childhood with old-age dependency the aging of the old population (> 65) itself. The burden of supporting geriatric services will not rise monotonically with the ratio of persons aged 65 and over to the "productive," working-age population. There will be an increasing shift away from actual economic productivity toward actual functional and economic dependency in the elderly population from the turn of the century. Demographically, the elderly population will not only age, but single, widowed, and unmarried women (i.e., a group lacking informal spousal support) will become even more characteristic. Epidemiologically, the aging and feminization of the old will increase the burden of functional dependency and demands on the health care system as well as long-term caregivers.

One critical issue in looking forward to the form and quality of geriatric services is the position and role of women in the workforce, the family, and as informal caregivers to aging parents and grandparents. The social transformation of Iceland has been accompanied by a great increase in women's participation in the formal, extra-domestic workforce, and by change in the pattern of fertility and the size of sibling and domestic groups. Figure 8 demonstrates an increase in women's workforce participation from 30% to 70% overall between 1960 and 1983. Of interest is the age pattern of this increase—it is greatest throughout the child-bearing years, and of course this increase is correlated with the decline in fertility. In 1960, women were bearing an average of five children between the ages of 15 and 44; by 1985, the mean number was 1.9 children (Planning Committee, 1987, p. 18). This decline is not due to an increase in the number and proportion of childless women, but rather to a fairly regular drop in the number of children born to all mothers. This and other factors (e.g., the increasing divorce rate and number of single-parent households, the absence of family members for reasons of work and education) have led to a considerable decrease in average household size (and a great increase in number) even in the last 25 years; the average size of two-generation households (containing at least one parent and one child) has decreased from 3.6 in 1964 to 3.0 in 1985 (Planning Committee, 1987, p. 185). Women generally tend to have their children earlier in their fertile years than was the case up to the inter-war period of the first half of this century. It is possible to view the initial shift as a response to the new prosperity that allowed a proliferation of conjugal groups and households (driving down the ages at which different stages of the moral career were achieved). In the modern context, the timing and limitations on childbearing are perceived as being controlled by the desire and/or need of mothers to work to help maintain an acceptable family living standard.

FIGURE 8

Workforce Participation of Women in 1960 and 1984 by Age

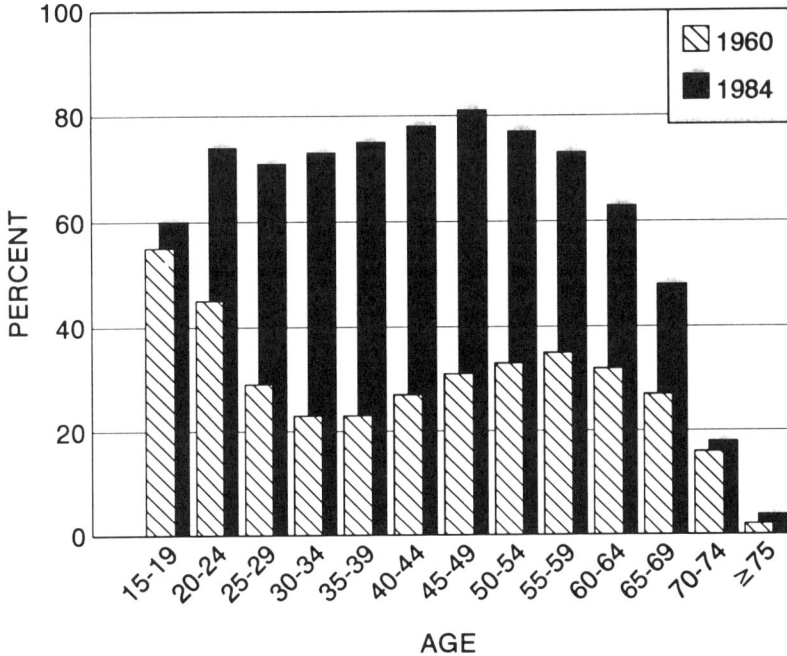

These various changes and trends in the status of women have led some Icelanders to observe and lament a decline in the strength and importance of the family as a social unit. The "traditional" role of the family to tend to children, the sick, and the elderly was a role of women in the family, and, to the extent that women have become occupied with other, extra-domestic roles, caregiving responsibility has to a great extent been increasingly shifted to male family members and formal social institutions. The question of whether this shift—and indeed the social emergence of women—is a beneficial development, has (like regional equity issues) become highly politicized, leading to the formation of a Women's Party that enjoys both considerable support and opposition (Kristmundsdóttir, 1989). Despite this division of opinion, there is an acknowledgement that Icelandic society has yet to deal with these changing conditions of domestic support, and that failure to do so will lead to an erosion of the condition of children and aged Icelanders alike.

A final divisive trend is introduced by the increasing class stratification of elderly Icelanders themselves. Now dying off are those cohorts that subscribed to the aforementioned Icelandic work ethic and social egalitarianism, and for whom acceptance of public support (i.e., *ad fara á hreppinn*, "going on the district") was abhorrent. Now aging are those cohorts socialized into the welfare state, whose members include many having different views concerning personal entitlement to public resources. But the problem goes beyond rising expectations for support. Elderly Icelanders will increasingly arrive at old age and frailty with more and different "class histories" and differing sets of private familial and financial resources than during Iceland's transition. Thus, questions will arise concerning equitable distributions among the elderly, such as that regarding government-financed flats for elderly in Reykjavík. The concept of a homogeneous elderly set may become more difficult to maintain while real allocations affecting older Icelanders are defined by class politics. In fact, class politics may begin to be couched in the internationally fashionable idiom of generational equity, as the communitarian idea of a unitary life course terminating in a dependent old age becomes less effective both as a means of perceiving social realities and as a principle for mobilizing social programs (Cole, 1989).

It is unclear what direction Icelandic policy will take into the next century given the aging of the population and the old, a declining or stagnant economic base, increasing demands from the elderly population, growing unavailability of family caregivers, and an increasing disparity of private resources held by elderly Icelanders. What is clear is that none of the imaginable remedies are without considerable social costs, whether born by the governmental sector or by "the community" (Walker, 1981). Governmental action is being projected on various fronts. An immediate task in the view of governmental officials is the elimination of incentives to use geriatric institutional care, although it is questionable whether this will ultimately be cost-sparing or merely cost-shifting. As mentioned above, Iceland is endeavoring to expand formal home-care services, and some municipalities have without fanfare begun to compensate family members for undertaking various home support services in lieu of formal geriatric services (national legislation to reimburse informal caregivers has not yet been contemplated). Respite care programs have been established on an *ad hoc* basis and may be expanded and formalized; here again, no national policy exists regarding respite care. A final measure being considered is the creation of a tax credit approach for the reinforcement of domestic caregiving (no bills are pending). It is unknown to what extent any of these programs will be means tested or subjected to cost-sharing or eligibility criteria.

Conclusion

The present chapter has provided a detailed perspective on the current and projected extension of health and social services to elderly Icelanders and their families, as well as an accounting of the current health and social condition of elderly Icelanders. As in other developed countries, the aging of the population is presenting new and increasing challenges to various members of the society as they struggle to adapt and modify formal and informal institutions for geriatric care. State-administered support institutions have grown very prominent in rendering geriatric services in Iceland, and continue to be widely viewed as the most viable means of concerted action in a variety of domains of social life. Future limitations on the growth or maintenance of state-administered and funded geriatric services appear to be tied more directly to economic constraints than to anti-statist political developments or any ascendancy of age politics. However, regional and gender equality issues have become an important part of social discourse, and will invariably affect future elderly Icelanders.

Notes

1. While procreativity in Iceland is certainly also changing, it continues to be bound up with preindustrial ideas and practices relating to "legitimacy" of offspring to betrothal (in lieu of marriage) [see Björnsson, 1971; Rich, 1978; also, Tomasson, 1980]

2. All 1985 data (Nordic Council of Ministers, 1987).

3. It is unclear whether in Iceland's post-modern development the high mobility characteristic of the prior period is continuing, or whether stratification along parentofilial lines is becoming more dominant.

4. With social stratification, symbols of class (e.g., linguistic, educational, and those pertaining to belief) are increasingly but subtly manipulated by some Icelanders to emphasize class differences (Pálsson, 1989; Wieland, 1989).

5. The exception is the comprehensive health and disability survey of almost one-third of the population mounted by the Ministry of Health and Social Security in the late 1960s (Gúdnason, 1969).

6. In practice, service levels are difficult to infer from facility type, as detailed level-of-care regulations for the sundry types have yet to be promulgated.

References

Baldursson G: Population. In Nordal J, Kristinsson V (eds): *Iceland 1986.* Reykjavík: The Central Bank of Iceland, 1987.

Beverfelt E: Norway. In Palmore E (ed), *International Handbook on Aging: Contemporary Developments and Research.* Westport: Greenwood Press, 1980.

Bjarnar V: The Laki eruption and the Famine of the Mist. In Bayerschmidt CF, Friis EJ (eds), *Scandinavian Studies.* Seattle: University of Washington Press, 1965.

Björnsson B: *The Lutheran Doctrine of Marriage in Modern Icelandic Society.* Oslo: Universitetsforlaget, 1971.

Blöndal J: *Félagsmál á Islandi* [Politics in Iceland]. Reykjavík: Almennabókafélagid, 1973.

Broddason Th, Webb K: On the myth of social equality in Iceland. *Acta Sociologica* 1; 49-61, 1975.

Calasanti TM, Bonanno A: The social creation of dependency, dependency ratios, and the elderly in the United States: a critical analysis. *Social Science and Medicine* 23 (12);1229-1236, 1986.

Cole TR: Generational equity in America: A cultural historian's perspective. *Social Science and Medicine* 29 (3); 377-383, 1989.

Davies AM: Epidemiology and the challenge of aging. *International Journal of Epidemiology* 14 (1); 9-19, 1985.

Eggertsson Th: The labour market. In Nordal J, Kristinsson V (eds), *Iceland 1986.* Reykjavík: Central Bank of Iceland, 1987.

Government of Iceland: Lög um málefni aldrada [Legislation on matters of the elderly]. Stjórnartídindi A, no. 91/982, with amendments no. 114/1984.

Gúdnason S: *Disability in Iceland.* Reykjavík: Prentsmidja Jóns Helgasonar, 1969.

Hagstofa Islands: *Tölfrædihandbók 1984* [Statistical Abstract of Iceland]. Reykjavík, 1985.

Hansen G: Social security. In Nordal J, Kristinsson V (eds), *Iceland 1986.* Reykjavík: Central Bank of Iceland, 1987.

Johnsen SG: The Increase in the Number of Elderly Citizens in Reykjavík. Report to the Central Committee for Health Services. Reykjavík, 1979.

Jónsson A, Halldórsson Th: Domiciliary assessment for geriatric patients in Reykjavík. *Gerontology* 27; 89-93, 1981.

Jónsson S: *Sóttarfar og sjúkdomar á Islandi, 1400 - 1800* [Epidemic and disease in Iceland, 1400 - 1800]. Reykjavík: Hid íslenzka bókmenntafélag, 1944.

Kristinsson V: Housing. In Nordal J, Kristinsson V (eds), *Iceland 874-1974.* Reykjavík: Central Bank of Iceland, 1975.

Kristmundsdóttir S: Outside, muted, and different: Icelandic women's movements and their notions of authority and separateness. In Pálsson G, Durrenburger P (eds), *The Anthropology of Iceland.* Iowa City: University of Iowa Press, 1989.

Lipset SM: *The First New Nation: The United States in Comparative and Historical Perspective.* New York: Basic Books, 1963.

Magnússon F: The hidden class: The emergence of a maritime working class in Iceland. *Ethnologia Scandinavica*; 84-100, 1986.

Magnússon F: Work and the identity of the poor: work-load, work-discipline, and self-respect. In Pálsson G, Durrenburger P (eds), *The Anthropology of Iceland.* Iowa City: University of Iowa Press, 1989.

Ministry of Health and Social Security: Aging in Iceland.   Report to the World Assembly on Aging. Reykjavík, 1982.

Nordal J, Kristinsson V. (eds): *Iceland 1986.* Reykjavík: Central Bank of Iceland, 1987.

Nordic Council of Ministers: *Yearbook of Nordic Statistics* [Nordisk statistisk arsbok, v. 25]. Stockholm, 1987.

Organisation for Economic Co-Operation and Development: *Financing and Delivering Health Care: A Comparative Analysis of OECD Countries.* OECD Social Policy Studies No. 4. Paris: OECD, 1987.

Pálsdóttir D: *Elderly in Iceland.* Reykjavík: Heilbrigdis- og tryggingamálaráduneytisins, 1986.

[Planning Committee] Framkvæmdanefnd um framtídarkönnun: *Gróandi thjódlíf: Island 2010* [Social Growth: Iceland in 2010]. Reykjavík: Forsætisráduneytid, 1987.

Research Working Group, Sir Douglas Black, Chair: *Inequalities in Health: The "Black" Report.* Hammondsworth: Penguin Press, 1982.

Rich G: Changing Icelandic kinship. *Ethnology* 15; 1-20, 1976.

Rich G: The domestic cycle in modern Iceland. *Journal of Marriage and the Family* 40: 173-188, 1978.

Rich G: Kinship and friendship in Iceland. *Ethnology* 22; 475-493, 1980.

Schroll M: Cooperation between hospital-based and community-based geriatric assessment. In Brocklehurst JC, Williams TF (eds): Multidisciplinary Health Assessment of the Elderly. *Danish Medical Bulletin,* Special Gerontology Supplement Series, No. 7, 1989.

Thorleifsson H: *Frá Einveldi til Lydveldis* [From Monarchy to Republic]. Reykjavik: Almennabókafélagid, 1973.

Tomasson RF: A millennium of misery: the demography of the Icelanders. *Population Studies* 31; 405-427, 1977.

Tomasson RF: *Iceland: The First New Society.* Minneapolis: University of Minnesota Press, 1980.

Walker A: Community care and the elderly in Great Britain: theory and practice. *International Journal of Health Services* 11 (4); 541-557, 1981.

Wieland GD, Pálsdóttir D: The development of health and social services for the elderly in Iceland: an overview. *Social Science and Medicine* 23 (12); 1333-1346, 1986.

Wieland GD: The idea of mystical power in Iceland. In Pálsson G, Durrenburger P (eds), *The Anthropology of Iceland.* Iowa City: University of Iowa Press, 1989.

World Health Organization: *The Uses of Epidemiology in the Study of the Elderly.* Technical Report Series No. 706. Geneva, 1984.

5

Switzerland: Social Policy and the Welfare State Crisis

Jean-Pierre Fragnière

Switzerland, whose economic and social conditions have been very similar to those of other industrialized nations, has nonetheless had a very particular rate of development of its social policy.[1] In some sectors Switzerland has pioneered; yet other problems were not resolved satisfactorily for many years and still delays persist (Tschudi, 1982). For example, the canton of Glaris was the first, as early as 1846, to limit the working hours for adults. In contrast to other European legislation of the same period, the 1877 Swiss federal law on factories was the one that protected workers best. Moreover, with the 1911 code of obligations, Switzerland was the first European state to make substantial juridical contribution to union contracts.

Yet social security developed very slowly, and the first half of the twentieth century was marked by a succession of setbacks for the various proposals made in this area. Almost all the existing social legislation was adopted after World War II. It might even be said that it was the result of the constraints of the War, and in the context of the plenary powers given to the Federal Council during this period. Thus, the conditions that arose allowed for the development of social legislation. With the exception of the Law on Health and Accident Insurance (LAMA) which was voted in before World War I, all of today's important social insurance laws date back to the period after 1945. Although the Old Age and Survivors Insurance Law was adopted in 1947, it was not until 1985 that the "Second Pillar" of old age insurance went into effect, within the framework of laws regulating the creation of insurance protection schemes for various occupations.

It was only at the end of the 1970s that the debate on health policy exploded in Switzerland, at which time it became a major focus of discussion and political activity. One can speak of a sudden reversal of the pre-existing situation and the sudden irruption onto the political scene of the health issue. In fact, the situation is very recent, as Gerhard Kocher does not hesitate to write: "Not many years ago, medicine and public health were autonomous, as it were, cut off from the external world, almost completely isolated. Medicine was the province of doctors; those 'foreign' to this domain were not supposed to become involved in the organization of public health but to accept with closed eyes what the 'specialists' recommended and did" (Rentchnick and Kocher, 1979).

With respect to housing policy, the Confederation intervened only belatedly, and this despite crises in this sector. It is only since 1972 that housing has been considered a permanent task of the Confederation.

As far as family policy is concerned, while it is widely advocated in rhetoric by political groups, its realization is infinitely more cautious.[2] Constitutional provisions adopted in 1945 for establishing maternity insurance have still not been carried out in legislation; and this is but one example.

These few examples show that, in essence, Swiss social policy is recent but that, while remaining limited in extent, it does cover most of the areas generally taken into consideration by the industrialized countries.

Juridical and Political Factors

In order to understand the structure and dynamics of Swiss social policy, it is necessary to take into account many factors which determine its evolution and functioning. It would be inaccurate to speak of a system and still less of a model. In fact, a certain number of specific characteristics exert considerable influence. We shall examine them.[3]

Federalism

In Switzerland, state functions are divided between the Confederation and the member cantons. Article 3 of the Constitution stipulates: "The cantons are sovereign insofar as their sovereignty is not limited by the federal Constitution and, as such, they exercise all the rights which are not delegated to fhe federal government." Over the last several decades, which is the period in which social policy has developed, the attribution of competence to the Confederation has accelerated and has generally been accepted without too much difficulty. There are, nonetheless, very important sectorial differences. If health and education remain essentially the competence of the cantons, social security depends greatly on the Confederation. Moreover, the federalist structure of the state exerts a determining influence on the creation of federal laws. These laws often set forth general principles and rules and give the cantons major responsibility for their execution. Important differences both in the pace and the effectiveness of their implementation do result. For example, the social insurance expenditure statistics by canton show differences which reflect variations in political orientation and in economic resources. The intercantonal system of financial equalization only partially corrects this situation.

Multiple-level Pluralism

This liberal trend, which is important in Switzerland, exerts considerable influence in the domain of social policy. The resistance to what is referred to as centralization or even direct government control is enduring. It manifests itself first at the level of organizations. The implementation of the social insurance laws occurs almost invariably at the lower administrative level. It affects numerous organizations, often private and of varying importance which carry out their tasks in territories of variable size. Thus, the administration of health insurance occurs through more than 400 different funds, some with less than 100 members. The administration of old age and survivors' insurance, disability insurance, and of payments for loss of income is accomplished through 115 compensation funds (two federal, 26 cantonal, and 87 professional). Suggesting an international comparison, Guy Perrin notes pertinently: "Switzerland represents an original exception, to the extent that the official conception of social protection deliberately assigned the domain of private charity to charitable organizations, encouraged and funded by public funds, integrating it into a global conception of the responsibilities of the society" (Perrin, 1986).

The force of pluralism is also expressed at the level of the insurance obligation. The tendency to refuse to submit to the compulsory insurance is clear, and is evident in many domains, particularly health insurance. The federal authorities explicitly recognize it when they state: "In requiring mandatory insurance at the federal level, one is heavily mortgaging the planned reform politically, even if this insurance would enhance the delivery of group benefits" (Révision partielle., 1978).

Nationalism

Switzerland's resources depend in large part on its export capacity and on the activity of its banking sector. This is well-known. Yet on the political level the opening toward the world is definitely more 'limited.' Pragmatism and the consciousness of being a very particular 'small state' do not encourage international collaboration but rather foster a certain mistrust of models likely to be imported. For example, Switzerland has ratified less than a third of the agreements of the International Labour Office. However, it is worth mentioning that generally these ratifications only take place when the application of the underlying principles can be assured.

Under these conditions, the argument that holds that Switzerland is lagging behind when compared with other countries in the area of social policy leaves the majority of the population rather indifferent.

Democracy

The institutions of direct democracy as they are organized in Switzerland indeed explain largely the characteristics of the social policies practiced. We have in mind the federal popular initiative and the referendum. The former is the power given to any 100,000 citizens to demand a modification of the federal Constitution. In framing a specific proposition, the signatories compel the authorities to call for popular and cantonal elections. The legislative referendum enables 50,000 citizens to demand that a federal law (or a federal ruling of general application) voted by Parliament be also submitted to a vote by the electorate.

The initiative has no direct effect; no initiative concerning social security has been accepted by the people and the cantons. Yet it makes pressure possible, orients legislators, gives rise to legislation. The referendum works in a more complex way. Of course it makes it possible to reject laws voted by Parliament. Moreover, the mere threat of holding a referendum exerts strong pressure on those authorities who have the task of preparing legislation. It encourages the adoption of substantial compromises to legitimate delays which can be very lengthy.

The existence of the referendum makes the implementation of a global system of social insurance difficult (and the same observation holds true for the other legal domains). Indeed, on a question of principle, a simple one, opponents generally vote 'No' for the same reason. When a more complex system is under discussion, implying a broader range of choices, the reasons for voting 'No' increase. This in turn gives rise to the famous 'No cartels,' i.e., a series of disparate groups which reject the law for various reasons but which altogether constitute a majority. We can add to that, that the alliance consists of a conservative Right which finds that the state goes too far, and an extreme Left which finds it too timid (this occurred in 1900 for the law on health and accident insurance, and in 1931 for old age and survivors' insurance). Thus one can better assess the near impossibility of a more coherent system of social security being realized (Bois, 1980).

No Overall Plan: The Example of Social Security

It would be useless to look for an overall coherent plan or the essence of a system in the different areas of Swiss social policy. Alfred Maurer notes in this regard: "The Confederation has not worked out a system of social insurance founded on an overall plan. Rather it proceeded in a pragmatic fashion, adopting specific laws in successive stages for those sectors which, given the spirit of the times, presented favorable arrangements. The setting-up and working-out of the system of social insurance constitutes a noteworthy example of the Confederation's attitude: instead of founding social policy on doctrines, one must do what appears feasible and realizable in a given situation, taking into account political and practical intelligence" (Maurer, 1983).

Observing the evolution of Swiss social security over the past ten years, Pierre-Yves Greber (1986) detects six significant trends.

1. First, he notes that there were earlier plans relating to the development of social security.
2. At the same time he observes a second trend, contrary to the previous one, but of more limited intensity. While there was no tendency to dismantle accepted administrative and policy approaches, there was an attempt to both consolidate gains and halt new initiatives.
3. A shift from private law toward public law induces a third trend. If the desire to guarantee contractual liberty remains strong, it is also true that the reinforcement of public law makes it possible to avoid a shift towards adverse selection of risks and, thereby reinforce the principle of solidarity.
4. Under these conditions the complexity of the system becomes more apparent. The absence of an overall concept and the multiplicity of intentionally pragmatic approaches only add to this complexity. A real social game develops. The user gets lost in the complexities of rulings and administrative directives.
5. But a fifth tendency can be observed also, one characterized by efforts to tighten, through coordination and harmonization of the various social security schemes. Concrete measures are taken, more or less grandiose plans emerge. These attempt to reinforce the coordination and harmonization of the various schemes across Switzerland.
6. Finally, at the conceptual level, he notes a rapprochement toward international law. It can be observed in many sectors of social secutiry law. One exception is, of course, health insurance law in Switzerland.

We agree that all these developments have left their mark on the development of social policy. Do they give rise to a particular reaction in the crisis situation of the last quarter of this century? Let us look at some facts.

Aspects of Swiss Social Policy

Let us examine first some aspects of the global picture that constitutes Swiss social policy, emphasizing five significant characteristics: its quantitative importance, its beneficiaries, its agents and promoters, its source of financing, and its qualitative functioning.

Scope

In order to appreciate the quantitative importance of Swiss social policy, we might make the following observations. The essential part of Swiss policy consists of transfer payments corresponding to the redistributive activity of the state and of social insurance organizations. The latter have increased markedly over the last two decades. A much more modest share is allocated for expenses of goods and services. Thus, social policy in Switzerland shows no tendency toward a more direct intervention or toward a policy of developing services. To those who affirm that the state-as-protector has reached its limits, one can reply that essentially policy limits are involved, as expressed by the taxpayers' refusal to accept a more equitable redistribution of income through taxes and social insurance contributions. In any case, no tendency of the state to claim a growing proportion of the national product to the detriment of private demand can be observed.

Social Policy Benefits

It can be estimated that in Switzerland the distribution of benefits through social policy is comparable on the whole to that observable in other countries of the European Community. Nonetheless a significantly greater weight of old age payments can be noted, while at the same time there are fewer family, maternity and employment benefits.

Agents of Social Policy

The activities concerned with social policy take place on the three levels of the federal state, except for health benefits, of which two thirds are the responsibility of the cantons and one third of the municipalities. Generally the Confederation takes charge of tasks concerning collective social security, while the cantons take over those regarding individual material welfare. Thus the cantons and municipalities are engaged in the construction of housing and social assistance, while the contributions to social insurance are assumed mainly by the Confederation.

Financing of Social Policy

A small portion of the social budget is taken over by the state and financed through taxes. Most expenditures represent the transfer of revenues financed through levies on both employers and the insured. Under these conditions, the principle of equivalent burdens (on both employer and the insured) takes precedence, in matters of social policy, over the principles of either solidarity or individual capacity. It should also be pointed out that for each franc of taxes, the Swiss pay more than sixty-six centimes to social insurance.

Qualitative Aspects

It is hardly possible to write a credible account of the qualitative aspects of Swiss social policy since the necessary indicators are not available and research is lacking in this particular domain. Nonetheless, efforts have been undertaken to put in place viable measuring instruments. In this regard, the delay to be made up is considerable. (Wagner, 1986)

Emerging Doubts

For nearly ten years Switzerland, like most Western industrialized countries experienced important developments often defined as "crises."

The Shock

Since 1974 Switzerland experienced the strongest recession of all the industrialized countries in terms of the decline both in production and employment. Unlike the recessions of the 1950s and the 1960s, recovery was slow and hesitant, except in 1977. It was not until 1979 however that the volume of per capita production reached its 1974 level, a fact which is unique among the industrialized countries. "The impact of this shock on employment was equally significant: from 1973 to 1976, the total active population declined from 3.1 million to 2.8 million (10% less overall employment). Two thirds of this reduction affected immigrant workers while, at the same time, 110,000 Swiss, women in particular, quit their jobs without however declaring themselves unemployed. The reduction in activity was quite widespread; it affected both private consumption and investment. Construction literally came to a halt as a result of the premature departure of many foreign workers. Public expenditures continued to increase during this crisis but less rapidly than previously, and therefore contributed very little to alleviate the depression. Ill equipped to fight against a brutal recession, poorly experienced in using government regulations over a long period of time, the monetary and budgetary authorities failed to acquit themselves of their multiple tasks with the desired efficacy" (Tschopp, 1983).

This diagnosis by Peter Tschopp indicates that Switzerland felt a real shock which affected mainly the immigrant workers and the more "silent" strata of the population. It was in this context that the offensive against the state and in particular against its social policies was launched, and that conservative trends found renewed vigor and efficacy.

The Role of the State

It was under the slogan "Less government, more liberties" that the initiatives challenging the dimensions of the federal state developed. The "state" extended to the entire public sector, including the cantonal and municipal levels. How should this situation be evaluated?

A State of Relatively Modest Proportions. In 1980, the federal council member, Georges-André Chevallaz, known for his close ties with the movement in favor of "less government," made the following assessment: "On the whole, our federalist regime with some 30% of the gross national product, including the cantons, municipalities and old age survivors', and disability insurance appears the least expensive of the European governments where the public budget accounts for anywhere from 35% to more than 50% of the gross national product. The Confederation alone, with some 11% of the gross national product is, by far, the least extravagant spender of the central powers. The German Federal Republic, the most federalist nation after our own, reaches 16%" (Chevallaz, 1980).

Despite the weakness of the available statistical data, some general observations confirm this judgment. If the growth of the public sector is undeniable, it is nonetheless relatively small in terms of an international comparison. Since 1960, of course, the Swiss state underwent a fundamental transformation. To the traditional duties of national defense, foreign policy and administration, others have been added, i.e.: infrastructure, water purification, aid to universities, and aid to research. This was in response to needs engendered by economic growth and the demand for an infrastructure; it also illustrated a long overdue catching-up in the social security sector. In this context, it is relevant to note the importance of the redistributive role of the state. In 1980, 63% of the Swiss Confederation's expenditures were transfer payments to third parties, to the cantons, to the municipalities and to the local governments. Only 37% of expenditures served to cover the Confederation's own needs. Thus the offensive launched against the state is essentially a political offensive using the multiple pretexts provided by the economic crisis (Rey, 1983).

Recent Tendencies, Reliable Safety Devices. This observation appears all the more plausible given that numerous structural barriers exist to prevent any attempt to promote an overly large state. Let us emphasize first the weight of the groups and professional organizations involved in all decision-making processes. The political history of Switzerland has evolved slowly.

This relates to the fact that a majority of the Parliament members believe in a system that one could call "corporatism of associations." This system allows for public duties to be the primary responsibility of various private groups and occupational organizations. It also tends to assign a monopoly on representation to certain associations; and although this is not written into law, it results in a de facto monopoly.

Federalism also curbs the extent of state involvement. Corporative federalism developed in order to satisfy new needs without encroaching excessively upon cantonal prerogatives. On the legislative level the federal state formulates the principles and the cantonal legislators implement them.

Popular rights, in particular, the rights of initiative and referendum, are also effective safety devices in preventing uncontrolled expansion of the role of the central state. Their effectiveness has been demonstrated on a number of occasions. Moreover the very liberal style of the Constitution, coupled with the principle of free enterprise for trade and industry, set strong limits on the scope of state intervention in the economic sphere.

Finally, the very small size of the federal administration considerably reduces the "risks" of legislative inflation and of state intervention in matters of everyday life.

Stability of Internal Structure with Loss of Municipal Autonomy. Within this context, nonetheless, important transformations are taking place. The Swiss social system appears to be structuring itself more and more along the center-periphery model characterized by uneven and dependent development. In particular, the main socio-economic activities may be found polarized in some urban trans-cantonal and border regions. These transformations are accompanied by a demographic movement which follows similar tendencies. On the fringes of these centers of growth intra-cantonal or inter-cantonal regions are emerging which, from a socioeconomic perspective, are considered stagnant or even regressive. Inside these regions, whether central or peripheral, relations of the same type exist between areas, municipalities and micro-regions. An undeniable political centralization is evolving despite strong resistances (Bassand and Fragnière, 1976)

These phenomena can be accompanied by significant areas of stability. Thus the sharing of public expenditures among the three levels—the Confederation, the cantons and the municipalities—has remained unchanged since 1938 despite the strong centralizing effect of World War II (which however quickly resolved itself). It is worth noting that if centralization is hardly noticeable at the level of public finances, it can however have an impact on the political level inasmuch as the central power imposes on the cantons and the municipalities norms which it does not necessarily support with financial contributions (Aprile, 1984).

On Four Fronts

It is in this structural context that a real questioning of the state-as-protector arose. It is true that, as pointed out above, new segments of the social security sector are being set up, in particular with regard to the implementation of decisions made previously for dealing with the economic crisis. However since 1975 one can observe a questioning of the social arena, even some frontal attacks. An official report on the situation and problems of the Swiss economy, published in 1978, stated: "For the future expansion of the Swiss social-state demographic and economic evolution will impose much narrower limits than in the past" (Bombach et al., 1979). This offensive is being deployed along four different fronts.

Reduction of Social Expenditures

In many of its fields of competence, the Confederation significantly limits its contribution to social expenditures. This phenomenon is especially spectacular in the field of health insurance. Jean-Noël Rey (1983) estimates that "since 1975 the Confederation has economized, overall, five billion francs in the social sphere."

Limiting the Numbers of Civil Servants

At the federal level, the freeze on hiring new personnel was introduced in 1974. Since then it has been applied in a relatively rigid manner. It has resulted not only in financial savings but also in a real slowdown of the activities of the state. Certain tasks are no longer performed, others are postponed. These consequences are even more serious because many cantons followed suit. The various sectors of social policy are affected by this general trend.

Economizing Measures

Since October 1974, federal authorities have taken many steps to reduce public expenditure. These affected most of the activity spheres of the Confederation; at the legal level, Parliament accepted a linear reduction of 10% in state subsidies. A genuine attempt to economize was fostered, often provoking a phenomenon of "auto-reduction" or self-limiting as far as demands were concerned, while at the same time legitimating the status quo.

Privatization Proposals

At the same time proposals were made at both the federal and cantonal levels to entrust the private sector with duties which are normally carried out by public entities. The list of sectors in question comprises in particular public health, housing, social services, and social insurance, all provided beyond the vital minimum guaranteed by the state. In fact, the privatization decisions actually made were very limited. Nonetheless these pressures markedly curbed the public sector's initiative. Today, innovation seems to have become the privilege of the private sector.

It is in this context and with these constraints in mind that one must interpret the evolution of social policy over the past ten years. Loss of legitimacy, multiple constraints, mistrust which is sometimes explicit, and maneuvers for postponing decisions—these are some of the contextual elements. Working class milieux and the political groups which want to represent them, as well as the trade-union organizations, all have unquestionably been caught unprepared by the virulence of the Right's offensive. Did they have analyses of the situation at hand and did they have firm policies enabling them to organize a credible response? This is doubtful.

Today support for the 'preservation of gains' made so far is being organized. It is important to maintain reasonable flexibility and not to succumb to dogmatic slogans. Guy Perrin recalls this with some strong statements: "If nothing prevents us from assuming that an institution considered as the 'legitimate daughter of industrial society' can disappear within this society, it would be illusory to assume that our desires and fears are the reality. When considering the following: the evolution of social protection systems since their inception, the scope of unfulfilled needs by even the most advanced of these systems, the unrestrained growth of mandatory social contributions even during the economic crisis, and the irrepressible progression toward common aspirations, the impartial observer …is tempted to conclude that both the age-old trend toward the public extension of social protection and the fading-away of the tutelary function of the state are not yet in sight. And this, in spite of the unrelenting effort of some doctrinaire individuals seeking the way of the future by relying on liberal models of a bygone past" (Perrin, 1986).

Future Prospects

Switzerland is facing a new challenge. In times of prosperity the compromise easiest to achieve is to make the state responsible for certain services, in particular in the social sphere. Generating the necessary subsidies for financing these services is not an overly difficult task. In a period of recession, on the contrary, individuals and social groups are concerned with a decline in their income, or the shrinkage of ecomonic growth rates which might be induced by an increase in taxation.

In the period of economic stagnation which followed a period of growth, one notes that it was not only the highest institutional echelons that found themselves in an unfavorable position, but also that the compromise between various social forces was made difficult. In this phase, we are witnessing then not only a restructuring of the distribution of duties within the public sector, but also a challenging of the growth of services provided by public collectivities. On the political level, in this phase, it is rather the other aspect of federalism which is emphasized, i.e., the independence of the various institutional echelons. Upper echelons are therefore freed of certain duties which are then relegated to lower echelons (Aprile and Rossi, 1980).

This tendency to discharge obligations onto local collectivities often has the effect of reinforcing inequalities with respect to the access to goods and services. All these initiatives proposed for limiting, or even reducing social policies do not correspond to what some have called a 'dismantling' procedure. Slowly nonetheless they tend to change the rules of the game. They encourage attitudes of resignation or evasion…and it is by no accident that even in Switzerland the debate focusing on the 'new poor' has recently escalated. Not without reason, alas.

It would certainly appear that the last ten years of social policy in Switzerland have been characterized by a shift from a climate of 'social conquests' to that of the 'preservation of existing gains.' Yet already it seems that the terms of the equation have changed: a number of recent studies point to the importance and the soundness of that which has already been achieved and implemented. They also reveal gaps and regressive tendencies, as well as a penchant for procrastination. They also show that the future cannot be conceived in terms of a mere re-deployment of already existing models.

All these considerations allow us to appreciate what constitutes the strength and the weakness of Swiss social security. One thing is certain: past achievements in the field of social security, albeit slow, are resting on a solid basis. Yet preparing for the future requires a vigorous effort in order to overcome existing gaps and improve on a system which appears increasingly difficult to manage.

Notes

1. For a general approach to Swiss social policy, see Pierre Gilliand, *Politique sociale en Suisse: Introduction,* Réalitiés sociales, Lausanne, 1988; and Jean-Pierre Fragnière, Gio Christen, *Sécurité sociale en Suisse:Introduction,* Réalitiés sociales, Lausanne, 1988.

2. On this issue see Pierre Gilliand's edited volume, *Famille en rupture. pensions alimemtaires et politique sociale,* Réalitiés sociales, Lausanne,1984.

3. On these various issues, see Philippe Bois, "Spécificités de la politique sociale en Suisse", in: Patrick de Laubier and Jean-Pierre Fragnière, *Droit et politique sociale,* Vevey, 1980. See also: Wolf Linder, *La décision politique en Suisse,* Réalités sociales, Lausanne, 1987.

References

Aprile, Gianni. *Les dépenses publiques en Suisse*, Geneva, Paris: Librairie Droz, 1984.

Aprile, Gianni, Angelo Rossi, "L' imbrication de la gestion financière des différents échelons des pouvoirs publics en Suisse", in: *Schweizerisches Jahresbuch für politische Wissenschaft,* 1980.

Bassand, Michel, Jean-Pierre Fragnière, *Les ambiguïtés de la démocratie locale*, Georgi, St-Saphorin, 1976.

Bombach, G., H. Kleinewefers, L. Weber, "Problèmes économiques de la politique sociale en Suisse", in: *Rapport du groupe d'experts "Situation économique"*, 1978-1979, Berne, 1979.

Bois, Phillippe "Spécifités de la politique sociale en Suisse", in Patrick de Laubier and Jean-Pierre Fragnière (eds), *Droit et politique sociale*, Vevey, 1980.

Chevallaz, Georges-André, "Particularités du régime politique suisse", *Documenta*, Berne, 4/1980.

Fragnière, Jean-Pierre, Gio Christen, *Sécurité sociale en Suisse*, Réalités sociales, Lausanne, 1988.

Gilliand, Pierre. *Politique sociale en Suisse,* Réalités sociales, Lausanne, 1988.

Gilliand, Pierre (ed), *Famille en rupture, pensions alimemtaires et politique sociale*, Réalités sociales, Lausanne, 1984.

Linder, Wolf. *La décision politique en Suisse*, Réalités sociales, Lausanne, 1987.

Greber, Pierre-Yves. "L'évolution de la sécurité sociale en Suisse, 1974-1984", in Jean-Pierre Fragnière (ed), *Dix ans de politique sociale en Suisse*, Réalités sociales, Lausanne, 1986.

Maurer, Alfred. "Traits fondamentaux et caractéristiques de la législation sociale en Suisse," in: *Un siècle de sécurité sociale. 1881-1981*, Réalités sociales, Lausanne, 1986.

Perrin, Guy. "La fin de l'Etat-Providence en Europe? Du mythe aux réalités," in Charles Ricq (ed), *Droits sociaux et politique sociale en Suisse et en Europe*, Réalités sociales, Lausanne, 1986.

Rentchnick, Pierre and Gerhard Kocher. *Chère Médecine*, Lausanne, 1979.

"Révision partielle de l'assurance maladies, Rapport et avant projet," Berne, 1978.

Rey, Jean-Noël, *Trop d'état?*, Réalités sociales, Lausanne, 1983.

Tschopp, Peter, "De la conquête de la prospérité à la gestion collective de ses effets," *Manuel système politique de la Suisse,* Volume 1, Haupt, Berne, 1983.

Tschudi, Hans-Peter. "La politique sociale suisse depuis 1950," in Roger Giod and Patrick de Laubier (eds), *La politique sociale dans les pays occidentaux*, Réalités sociales, Lausanne, 1982.

Wagner, Antonin "L'évolution du budget social de la Suisse," in: Jean-Pierre Fragnière (ed), *Dix ans de politique sociale en Suisse*, Réalités sociales, Lausanne, 1986.

6

Distributive Justice, Contradictions, and Rationality in Mature Capitalism: The Case of Health Care and Social Services for the Aged in Italy

Allessandro Bonanno and Toni M. Calasanti

In Memory of Danilo Giori

Introduction

Discussions of policies for the aged and distributive justice have often been couched in terms of "young" versus "old." In the past, the elderly were depicted as a forgotten group, neglected by the younger generation. More recently, the emphasis has changed and concepts such as "intergenerational inequality" have been developed to refer to the possibility that the aged benefit from social programs at the expense of younger generations (Kingson, Hirshorn and Cornman, 1986). However, these positions ignore two fundamental issues. First, public expenditures for the elderly also serve younger populations as the latter would otherwise bear the full burden of any financial assistance to their older relatives (Myles, 1984). Second, the development of welfare states in advanced western capitalist societies is shaped by differences in power at social and political levels. Indeed, historical analyses reveal class distinctions within generations are more crucial than age in explaining both policy formation and the political context of fiscal crises of the State (Bonanno and Calasanti, 1988; Calasanti and Bonanno, 1986).

As one ages, many needs become more important, such as health care. At the same time, social structural changes can lead to "problems" for the elderly where none previously existed. Examination of the formation of policies for the aged reveals the elderly do not become vulnerable because of "the ravages of age" or the actual process of maturation. Rather, the vulnerability of the elderly lies in the way aging is shaped by political and economic forces in society (Myles, 1984: 169). It is the interrelations between these forces which shape policy formation and the realization of distributive justice.

In the following chapter, this position is employed to examine welfare policies for the aged in relation to distributive justice concerns in Italy. It is argued that the present barriers to equal access to health care and social services result from the class nature of policy formation. Similarly, the fragmentation of health and social programs, which leads to both overlapping services and large gaps where needs are untended, is the outcome of conflicting interests in the political arena.

Beginning with post-unification Italy in 1860, and through the analysis of the Fascist and post-World War II periods, the characteristics of health care and social service development are discussed. Due to political, economic and social changes occurring from 1860-1920, these services became a part of the public sphere. The legislation of 1888 set a precedent for health care delivery to the poor despite its restricted implementation. With the new century, the working class was able to exert pressure to enact mandatory health insurance. As structural changes made it more difficult for families to provide care for the aged, the Socialist party also successfully lobbied for the passage of public assistance for the elderly.

These public programs for the population as a whole and for the aged in particular deteriorated under the Fascist regime. During the 1920-1945 period, much of the past legislation was revoked or weakened. Health care became privatized and Mutual Assistance Funds were created. Inefficient State bureaucracy led to waste and duplication in remaining public services as clientelism became an important legitimation strategy. The aged suffered from the actions of the Fascist government as quality health care became the privilege of the well-to-do and gaps in social services became the norm.

With the new Constitution of modern democratic Italy in 1946, health care and social services for the aged became a reality. At the same time, the State's democratic objectives concerning distributive justice and welfare were contradicted by the actual implementation of public programs and the historical development of capitalism. These contradictions are readily apparent in the effects of both the fiscal crisis and recent economic expansion on policies for the elderly. The avowed goal of providing a comprehensive system of services to the Italian elderly generally has failed.

The development of health care and social services for the aged is further discussed in terms of contradictions which emerged from policy implementation. We argue that health care and social assistance policies have been formed in accordance with the unique historical configuration of class tensions. As these tensions were themselves enacted within the sphere of health care, equal access and availability of health care and social services to the elderly have been negated.

Two pervasive themes emerge in our investigation of the development of the Italian welfare state. First, the inability of the market to provide adequate health care has meant that the State increasingly has had to intervene. Second, health and social service policies are not merely imposed from above but also result from pressures exerted by the working class. These historical forces have not moved smoothly or evenly, resulting in the present piecemeal system characterized by waste and duplication on the one hand and lack of needed services on the other.

In the final section of the chapter, we discuss both our findings and our reflections on what constitutes distributive justice. From this vantage, it is apparent that the present form of capitalism in Italy, together with the political nature of social programs, contradict the progressive goals of distributive justice present in the ideological underpinnings of modern Italian society.

Health Care, Social Services and the Elderly in Post-Unification Italy (1860-1920)

The 19th century was a particularly important period in Italian history. Politically, the country was unified for the first time since the collapse of the Roman Empire more than one thousand years before. Economically, the bases for establishing an industrial-capitalist productive system were created through accumulation of capital and the generation of a modern work force. Socially, advanced, nationwide institutions addressing the growing needs of a modernizing country began to be constructed. These institutions included a unified educational system controlled by the central government, a relatively sophisticated transportation system and organizations emerging to represent the interests of the working class.

Health care and social service systems were parts of this process of transformation. It was during this century that these services left behind their purely "ethical" characteristics and entered the economic sphere. Health care and social services based on payments of fees and oriented toward profit generation became prevalent. These services also increasingly became associated with the political issue of distributive justice. For the first time numerous segments of the population undertook political action to demand access to health care and social services. The "potential availability" of such services was contradicted by their "actual unavailability" to those who could not afford them. Simultaneously, the inability of market forces to reconcile the supply and demand for health care and social services required growing State intervention. The response of the nineteenth century Italian State was to repress and contain the popular demand for health care and social services, however (Piperno, 1985:155).

Despite the overall progress, post-unification Italy still contained lagging economic and social elements, particularly in the South (Graziani, 1979; Podblieski, 1974) where prevalent rural conditions and the outflow of capital and human resources greatly retarded economic development. Transcontinental migration and impoverishment were the fate of most Southern Italians[1] (Gerschenkron, 1962; Mutti and Poli, 1975). This economic situation contributed to a growing gap in health status between North and South.

Measurements of nation-wide health status indicate a poor situation overall. In the last four decades of the century the general mortality rate averaged 25 per thousand, and the infant mortality rate averaged 195 per thousand. Epidemics were a constant threat, as exemplified by the cholera outbreak of 1884. Other contagious diseases such as pellagra and tuberculosis were quite widespread due to poor sanitary conditions at home and in the work place (Del Panta: 1980).

Despite the frequency of disease, examinations by doctors were infrequent. Ill individuals were either cured by healers or according to traditional remedies and usually at home. Hospitalization occurred in extreme cases and only when the condition of the patient was a serious threat to family or community. In most cases hospitalization involved institutions which had little resemblance to present-day hospitals. During this period the practice of hospitalization reflected a process of segregation from society more than an actual intent to cure the patient (David, 1985:186; Cherubini, 1977:81).

Assistance for the elderly usually was provided by the family. In the event that the family could not function as caregiver, the Roman Catholic Church and its institutions constituted the only viable alternative. These institutions were sponsored by charitable contributions and were not under State control. Despite attempts to secularize assistance for the elderly in the 1850s and 1860s, it was not until the latter part of the century that the Italian State took concrete action in this direction (Giori, 1983:188). This movement, however, concentrated more on health care than on social assistance. Despite legislation in 1890 which nationalized the major system of charitable organizations (Opere Pie), social assistance remained under private and religious control until the post-World War I period.

Economic growth and parallel increases in industrialization, urbanization and education, became critical in shaping new trends. In terms of health care, the number of hospital admissions increased. By 1898 the hospitalization rate stood at 15.9 per thousand inhabitants. A decade later, 1908, the figure rose to 18 per thousand inhabitants. In absolute terms, between 1891 and 1907 the number of hospitalized Italians almost doubled from 372,965 to 607,804. Simultaneously, the characteristics of hospitals changed. From their historical function as detention centers (Foucault, 1976), hospitals became diagnostic and therapeutic places. It was in this period that hospitals were divided into departments according to specializations (Piperno, 1985:159).

For the elderly these changes in health care meant receiving professional medical assistance was possible. It also meant, however, that the aid provided was increasingly medical rather than social in nature, with little regard for the actual needs of the aged individual. In essence, the rise in hospitalization signified wider availability of care but also an expanded ability of the system to exercise control over marginal segments of society, such as the aged, pregnant women, the disabled and the poor. In fact, health care institutions in Italy during this period have been characterized as performing a "policing function." (David,1985:188).

The role of physicians in the Italian health system was also changing. Prior to the turn of the century, unemployment among medical doctors was relatively high (Cherubini, 1977). This situation was due to the rapid increase in number of medical school graduates at a time of limited development of health facilities (Piperno and Guazzini, 1982). Physicians also faced the competition of healers who enjoyed a notable popularity among the working class and peasant strata.

This situation changed in the late 1800s. First, physicians obtained control of the medical occupation through the establishment of a professional order (ordine dei medici). Successful completion of a public nationwide examination was one of the fundamental conditions for membership in the order and for the legal practice of medicine (Giori, 1978). The creation of the "order" also allowed physicians to monopolize medical education as the order certified both teachers and the content of the national exam. Second, "collective bargaining" actions against the State[2], which controlled the majority of medical jobs available, also lowered unemployment. State-sponsored medical positions had been generated through legislation creating new hospitals. Implementation of this legislation did not occur for over two decades, however, leaving numerous medical positions unfilled (Piperno, 1985:167). The collective bargaining actions of physicians succeeded in forcing the State to fill the vacancies. Third, "Fraternal Occupational Orders" (Società di Mutuo Soccorso) also began hiring physicians to attend workers who had acquired health insurance (Pullan, 1978).

State intervention in health matters included the 1888 legislation of free sanitary, medical and surgical assistance to poor individuals. Expenses were to be borne by local administrative units (Giori, 1983:191). Despite the progressive character of this legislation, however, implementation was restricted (Cherubini, 1977:86; Piperno, 1985:157). Free assistance was reserved only for the extremely poor whose names were recorded on a special list renewed every year. In addition to the social stigma and consequent discrimination associated with membership, the list penalized the "new poor," who had to wait an entire year to qualify for assistance. As the list was compiled at the county level, it also discriminated against migrant poor.

In 1890 the first act regulating the functioning of hospitals was passed (Giori, 1983:188). The economic reliance of the health sector on charitable organizations had culminated in a fiscal crisis (Piperno, 1985). The 1890 legislation sought to generate additional monies through the reorganization of the entire hospital administration. Rationalizing and improving the bureaucratic apparatus of hospitals both at the regional and unit levels, but not State economic intervention, were thus mandated.

While the elderly population as such did not receive specific attention from the State during this period (David, 1985:188), the State's overall posture damaged rather than enhanced their position. Though legislation was passed in 1859 concerning pensions and monetary assistance for aged individuals in need of care (the Life Annuity Fund for Old Age), the Italian government failed to implement it because of technicalities. More importantly, the State maintained a position adverse to any new programs or increase in medical expenses for the working class, including the elderly.

State action during this time was dominated by conservative bourgeois groups whose objective was to increase accumulation of capital with the State's assistance. At the same time, State intervention in other socioeconomic spheres was strongly opposed (Mutti and Poli, 1975). Consequently, there emerged a tendency toward health care and social service privatization at the expense of the lower strata of society. The State's conservative actions were not unopposed, but it took until the new century for countervailing forces to exert strong political pressure.

Changes in the New Century

The turn of the century was characterized by increased social tension. The government's austere political economic strategy and the severe tax measures imposed on the proletariat and petty bourgeoisie created an environment for working class unrest. Strikes and demonstrations led by members of the newly formed Italian Socialist Party (PSI) were common. Demands for more social equality and for social programs became fundamental objectives of the Italian working class movement. Together with a reduction in the working day, increased wages and recognition of the right to strike, improved health system and social assistance legislation were requested (Manacorda, 1972). Simultaneously, structural changes occurring at the social level further motivated the struggle of the working class. Among those deserving mention are family and community changes. Industrialization, migration and urbanization initiated a breakdown of the extended family[3] and the integrated community, that is, gemeinschaft. The network of care and services that these social institutions once provided was therefore less available. In the newly formed urban dwellings the re-creation of the same family or communal ties was difficult. Consequently, the unfulfilled demand for care was directed toward municipal and regional institutions which were largely inadequate for the task (Barbagli, 1977). The ultimate outcome of this process was decreased quality and availability of services.

The collapse of the extended family and community was particularly devastating to the elderly. As a result, old age and pauperism became synonyms for members of the working class. Traditionally, assistance to them had been provided by charitable institutions organized by the Church (Compagnia di Misericordia) (Giori, 1983:190-191). The rapid increase in demand for care, however, underscored the inadequacy of religious organizations and pressure was exercised for the secularization of assistance. In 1898, following a strong campaign by socialist representatives in the Parliament, the National Social Assistance Fund for Disability and Old Age was finally passed. This act involved economic assistance to elderly and disabled individuals who had either occasional or stable manual jobs. Participation in this program was optional and discriminated against those who did not have a job or could not demonstrate periodic employment.

The inadequate character of the National Social Assistance Fund led to calls for the creation of mandatory insurance against sickness and for old age. These proposals were opposed by entrepreneurial segments which viewed them as restrictions on professional and economic freedom. More specifically, these groups rejected the idea of providing mandatory contributions for the creation of pension funds on the grounds that they would increase the cost of labor (Giori, 1977:86). Further resistance was provided by State officialdom which rejected direct and restrictive interference in the "affairs" of the industrial bourgeoisie (Piperno, 1985:160). The State's resistance to the proposed legislation was motivated by concerns that the establishment of a mandatory insurance would permanently extend the role of the State to the sphere of old age and health care services (Cherubini, 1973). These various poles of resistance and a division in the political representation of the working class contributed to a temporary defeat of the legislation (Giori, 1983:191).

Further industrialization and the social, political and economic changes associated with World War I finally led to the establishment of mandatory old age and sickness insurance (David, 1985: 185). In 1917 mandatory insurance for all workers 17 and older was instituted. This legislation, however, established insurance solely for those workers involved in war production and mandated that the payment of insurance premiums be shared equally by employers and employees. It was only in 1920 that similar legislation was extended to workers in all productive sectors. While this legislation was possible largely due to the action of working class groups (specifically the PSI and the national trade unions [Confederazione Generale Italiana del Lavoro or CGIL]), it was clearly limited to those who were employed. Unemployment became not only a condition of economic destitution, but also of discrimination in public assistance availability.

Welfare and Dictatorship: Health and Service Systems
During the Fascist Regime (1920-1945)[4]

The State's increased involvement in health care and social assistance for the elderly was drastically halted during the Fascist regime. Democratic organizations of the working class were eliminated. Both the Socialist Party and the CGIL were outlawed as were any political organizations which did not belong to the Fascist party. The CGIL and other unions were replaced with corporative unions. Based on a principle of co-existence, representatives of both managerial and working classes were in the same organization. It was assumed that, through cooperation, differences and disagreements would be negotiated and equitable social arrangements would be obtained. Actually, this corporative system deprived the working class of any real power. Unions were left in the hands of management which exercised harsh control over labor. During the Fascist period management was able to reduce wages to pre-World War I levels, increase control in the work place and eliminate any expression of dissent to its economic strategy (Castronovo, 1975).

In terms of health care and assistance for the elderly, the Fascist regime's strategy involved reduction and eventual elimination of State expenditures so as to relocate these services in the private sphere. Put differently, the goal was the reprivatization of all services related to health care and assistance for the aged that had become State-sponsored in the preceding period (Piperno, 1985:162-163).

In 1929, the 1917 legislation instituting mandatory insurance was summarily dismissed. The Fascist "Superior Council of the Economy" declared the program too costly and unsuitable to the economic conditions of the country and the priorities of the government (Preti, 1980). Similarly, the

State denied additional economic support to hospitals, who turned to private payment in an attempt to solve their fiscal problems. Such funds were insufficient, and services deteriorated rapidly in contrast to a general improvement in the other advanced countries in Europe. Under these conditions, the public assistance mandated by the 1888 legislation was reduced to a bare minimum. Coupled with declining economic conditions of the working class, health care and geriatric services became a *de facto* privilege of the upper classes (Serrani, 1978).

The decline of public health care was paralleled by the development of privately managed hospitals which multiplied in the 1920s and 1930s. In these hospitals members of the upper classes could find the quality care missing in public hospitals and institutions. Influential members of the medical profession also saw the private hospitals as a source of lucrative gains. Further, physicians were not affected by the State's disengagement from public hospitals as these facilities were now open not only to publicly assisted patients but also to paying customers. The medical profession therefore did not resist the privatization of health care (Cherubini, 1977).

The Fascist regime attempted to legitimize its action against the majority interest through two distinct strategies. The first involved building new hospitals in major Italian cities. In the late twenties two major hospitals were built in Rome, while others were erected in Milan, Florence and Turin. These constructions were widely publicized through carefully planned propaganda stressing the regime's commitment to health assistance. The availability of these new hospitals, however, stood in stark contrast to the large number of people who could not afford their services.

The second strategy was the creation of "Mutual Insurance Funds" (Casse Mutue). These Funds were established to provide financial assistance to workers in the absence of publicly supported health insurance. Mutual Insurance Funds were mandatory, sponsored jointly by employers and employees and were based on a correspondence between contributions paid in and the amount of assistance provided. Though these institutions were legally a part of the public apparatus (Istituti di Diritto Pubblico), their regulation was exclusively entrusted to the private realm. The Funds were considered private agreements between workers and management. The transfer of regulation to the private sphere can be seen in the trade union laws of 1926, 1927 and 1928 which mandated that labor contracts were not legally valid if a provision concerning illness was not included. By connecting health care to labor contracts the State had further relinquished control of medical assistance to the industrial relations sphere. Health care once again became a matter of agreement between management and labor in a social context in which labor was virtually deprived of power and management's failure to pay contributions was a daily practice (Piperno, 1985).

The private nature of Mutual Insurance Funds also limited their use. Management was reluctant to implement them and the legal system's bias toward the entrepreneurial position made enforcement of the law virtually nonexistent. During the Fascist regime Mutual Insurance Funds were supported almost exclusively by workers' contributions and limited to sickness compensation (partial payment of daily wages). Workers were forced either to forfeit health care altogether or to qualify as indigent and be hospitalized according to the 1888 welfare legislation. Because participation in Mutual Insurance Funds was voluntary, not many workers were covered. Enrollment trends reveal the inequities in health care and social assistance. By the end of the 1920s there were 1,000 Mutual Insurance Funds in the industrial sector, 34 in the service sector and only 7 in agriculture. The total number of workers covered was less than 700,000. Ten years later, while over 2 million workers were benefitting from mutual health assistance, most were still left out. Even in the industrial sector, where the highest proportion would be expected, less than half—46%—of workers were covered. Only one in four agricultural employees participated even though the majority of the population was engaged in farming. 17% of those occupied in the service sectors benefitted. As late as 1940 only 35% of all workers were enrolled in Mutual Insurance programs (Piperno, 1985:166).

The privatization of health care and social assistance was paralleled by a decrease in State bureaucratic efficiency. The bureaucratic apparatus charged with providing health care and social services deteriorated as there was both rampant duplication of agencies and lack of coordination among agencies. The waste of both economic and human resources, and the inability of these institutions to function properly were among the principal consequences (David, 1985; Giori, 1978: Piperno, 1985). The major cause of this process was the 1934 abolition of the "General Headquarters of Health," (Direzione Generale della Sanitá) which had been in charge of coordinating all health service activities. This institution was never replaced and activities involving health care were delegated to other governmental departments. For example, the Department of Agriculture was assigned the task of directing the health campaign against malaria without the power to coordinate action with the Health Department or other health authorities. The control of sanitary conditions in the work place and the health status of workers was assigned to the Department of Labor (Ministero delle Corporazioni), which was exclusively under the control of entrepreneurs. Not coincidentally, sanitary conditions and workers' health progressively deteriorated during this period (Piperno, 1985:163).

The duplication of services decreased power for local administrations whose financial resources were greatly cut. Further, service redundancy caused local institutions to engage in conflicts over jurisdiction of health matters. Accordingly, county and regional institutions fought one another, to the overall detriment of service (Piperno, 1985:163).

Duplications within social assistance and health care institutions were not just an "error" of the Fascist administration. Rather, redundancy was a specific legitimative strategy to redistribute power among local political leaders and it was a clientelist[5] response to the lack of jobs. Specifically, administration of these institutions became a source of power to Fascist leaders who, by controlling the funding and the functioning of the institutions, maintained and increased their local economic and political power. At the same time, these institutions became employment sources for people who maintained allegiance to Fascism and local leaders in particular (David, 1985:189). This clientelist aspect also extended to the sphere of dispensation of services. Membership in the Fascist Party as well as loyalty or favors performed for the local leaders were considered fundamental prerequisites to obtain such services.

The duplication of structures was publicized by the regime as a strategy to improve and accelerate service. In reality, however, it decreased the already limited availability to the general population of services and crippled both health care and social assistance delivery.

The withdrawal of State intervention and the privatization of services both magnified inequality among regions. The development of health and service structures was more pronounced in the economically advanced North than in the largely rural South (Piperno, 1985:168). The concentration of economic resources and the higher incomes in the North were fundamental conditions for the growth of private health institutions. Urbanization was also more rapid in the North, creating the conditions for a sustainable demand for health and social services. In the impoverished South the process of privatization of health care and social services took place, but at a slower pace. Along with the lack of public intervention, this led to a deterioration of the overall system of services available in that region.

An additional consequence of this process was the expansion of the urban-rural gap. In the absence of a coordinated policy orchestrated by the public authority, rural areas were left behind in both the South and the North. Unfortunately, the consequences of both these north-south / urban-rural disparities are still present in today's Italy and continue to characterize the development of the health care and service systems of the last four decades.

In general, then, this period culminated in diminishing the previous tentative strides made in fostering public access to health care. The case could be made that not only the majority of elderly but the population as a whole were worse off than before the Fascist regime. So many inequities abounded that many aged, workers, rural persons and Southern residents could not afford health care and, due to duplication and inefficiency, found their particular needs unmet. Despite legitimacy claims of the Fascist regime, fewer could partake of public or private health and social services.

Modern Italy: From the Reconstruction to the Welfare State

The post-war era witnessed the expansion of the Italian welfare system and the development of Italy's health care and social services for the elderly. These changes were prompted by a democratic political system which emphasized equality and freedom. The new Constitution approved in 1946 stressed a principle of State intervention, hoping to remove social and economic inequities. This stance recognized the existence of socio-economic factors which create inequality among citizens and impair the right of all citizens to obtain assistance (Gianolio, 1980). The growth of the labor movement and the creation of a civic consciousness in the Italian population gave further impetus to the development of a modern welfare system. Simultaneously, it was realized that assistance and services for the elderly were separate from issues of general health care. Some groups acknowledged that the elderly were an active portion of the population and not one merely in need of constant medical assistance (Burgalassi, 1983).

The progressive nature of the Italian constitution and the growth of the welfare system, however, did not bring exhaustive solutions to the problems of aging. Indeed, health care and social assistance for the elderly still constitute important problems for the social and political agenda of the country (Paci, 1985). The contradiction between the objectives of the Italian democratic welfare system and its actual development will be discussed in the remainder of the chapter.

The Post War Reconstruction

The State adopted a progressive stance in the immediate post World War II period. This posture was greatly influenced by leftist parties in the governmental coalition and was also a reaction to the years of stagnant and reactionary social policies of the Fascist regime (Graziani, 1979). The progressive intentions of the administration were, however, countered by a social and economic situation which did not allow introduction of rapid or broad reforms. The destruction caused by the war, the precarious economic conditions of the country and the imperative to rebuild the productive apparatus demoted issues of the aged and the health system to a subordinate position.

The implementation of reforms was further delayed by political changes in 1947. The governmental coalition was dissolved in favor of the constitution of a more conservative cabinet. The Christian Democratic Party (DC), a Catholic political formation, obtained the relative majority in the parliament and formed an administration which included only center and right parties. In this political framework the realization of a modern and progressive welfare system became more an ideological objective than a concrete political project.

Despite the political change, some legislation was passed to improve assistance for the elderly. The State took direct control of health care administration. Accordingly, all the services provided by the Mutual Insurance Funds became State managed, as were their finances. This change improved the situation considerably as it partially relieved hospitals from the serious and chronic lack of funds they had experienced during Fascism. At the same time, the problems of service duplication and inefficient organization of hospitals and agencies were not tackled. In fact, most of the health care agencies of the Fascist period were maintained in the new political system. The clientelist relationship between political power and service dispensation also was reproduced. The provision of welfare assistance remained in the hands of the political groups in control of the hospitals. Individuals tied to the DC and other minor political parties of the governmental coalition simply replaced Fascist leaders on the boards and middle-level management of hospitals (David, 1985:199; Piperno, 1985:169).

In 1952, in response to workers' demands, the retirement age was lowered, making retirement benefits accessible to more citizens. The State-sponsored retirement and disability pension systems also were extended not only to all hired workers but also to petty commodity producers such as farmers (1957), craftsmen (1962) and shop-keepers (1966). Finally, the total amount of State expenditure for the elderly increased constantly (Giori, 1983:192).

The Economic Expansion and the Crisis

Fueled by a renewed emphasis on social policies, expenditures for social and health services for the elderly continued to grow during the sixties and seventies to a total of $10 billion (Bonanno and Calasanti, 1988:250; David, 1985:192). Overall State intervention in the welfare sphere increased substantially from 29.3% of the GNP in 1954 to 45.4 % in 1970. Despite the direct sponsorship of health care and social assistance institutions, the Italian State's intent was to develop a welfare system based on monetary transfers to families, which were considered fundamental to providing care (Bonanno and Calasanti, 1988:250; David, 1985:198; Paci, 1985:789). The goal was to establish a complementary relationship between the family and care providing institutions. The family was viewed as the primary caregiver, while hospitals, retirement centers and the like were to be employed only if the family as caretaker failed.

The State's ability to increase expenditures for social services also was made possible by the rapid economic expansion through the early 1970's. In this period the economic growth rate was higher than those of other advanced Western states. This growth was fueled by the low costs of domestic labor and imported raw materials (Graziani, 1979; Podblieski, 1974).

Political equilibria and existing structural constraints, such as the developmental gap between North and South, sharply influenced the allocation of resources and welfare spending. The South only marginally benefitted from the economic growth of the rest of the country. It still lagged behind in terms of per-capita income, employment rate, social service availability and other important indicators of social wellbeing (Boccella, 1983; Graziani, 1978; Podblieski, 1974). State action, conditioned by the political strategy of the ruling party (DC), further increased regional differences. Of particular relevance for this study is the State's clientelist posture regarding assistance. The allocation of welfare funds for the elderly was tied to the development and maintenance of electoral support for the DC. In return, State officials committed themselves to policies and/or personal favors which led to granting pensions and other benefits to individual clients. This was particularly the case in the South (Bonanno and Calasanti, 1988:249). Economically, clientelist intervention limited the effectiveness of welfare expenditures as resources were divided among a growing number of clients regardless of specific needs. Simultaneously, the creation of an economically dependent clientele made withdrawal or reallocation of State intervention problematic. Specifically, welfare benefits were provided to indigent individuals who did not necessarily qualify for the particular program. For example, compensation for unemployed farm workers was also given to elderly who had not worked in agriculture for years and did not qualify for support. Similarly, individuals were granted fraudulent disability pensions. In return for this magnanimous interpretation of welfare regulations, electoral votes were cast in favor of the ruling political party (Bonanno, 1987; Bonanno and Calasanti, 1988).

To be sure, the State clientele was composed of people who actually occupied marginal positions in the productive apparatus, often unemployed or underemployed. Given the lack of job opportunities and truly in need of assistance, they identified the State as the principal source of economic sustenance (Pugliese, 1983). Unfortunately, State assistance was provided in a clientelist and arbitrary manner, creating the conditions for inefficiency and waste.

The clientelist and particularized character of Italian assistance was also fostered by the irrational development of assistance and health care expenditures from 1945 to the mid-seventies. In 1969, the lower chamber of the Italian Parliament (Camera dei Deputati) released a study which provided a panorama of the welfare situation:

> welfare assistance is characterized by legislation which does not correspond to the real needs of the collectivity...Furthermore, inefficiency, waste, lack of services and duplication of tasks best describe the situation of the sector. The legislation for social programs has been developed in a fragmented manner, lacking any coordination which addresses the fundamental objectives to be reached by a well developed welfare system. Assistance has not been targeted toward the individual in his/her family and social networks and toward his/her needs. Rather, it has been aimed at sets of particular categories of citizens, creating clients legally authorized to receive specific services (Camera dei Deputati, 1972 [1969]: 11-25).

In the mid-1970s actions were taken to correct this situation. First, jurisdictions were decentralized and delegated to local Regions (autonomous local administrative entities comparable to States in the United States). Second, legislation was enacted to dismantle a large number of organizations providing assistance. Unfortunately, the decentralization process has been hampered by a lack of available finances at the local level. The operating funds for maintenance of these bureaucracies alone averaged 40 percent of the institutions' budget[6] (David, 1985:199). Accordingly, local administrations have been largely unable to carry out many of their assigned functions. Dismantling redundant welfare organizations also has been difficult to implement. The resistance of powerful groups associated with these organizations has often delayed or prevented dissolution. The 1977 legislation mandated the elimination of 74 redundant welfare organizations. Later this number was reduced to 69, then to 62; presently it is not certain how many of the remaining targeted organizations will actually be dissolved (Bassanini et al., 1977:216; David, 1985:197-199).

In summary, during the first three decades of the post war period two State activities marked the expansion of the health care and service sectors for the general public, including the elderly. On the one hand, the State increased its economic intervention, expanding the spectrum of assistance. On the other, its clientelist posture limited the effectiveness of intervention, as it was aimed at the creation of political and electoral support for State officialdom.

The economic situation changed drastically in the early seventies. Increases in the cost of raw materials, particularly of imported oil, diminished Italy's ability to maintain high rates of economic growth. At the same time, trade unions were successful in establishing higher levels of compensation for workers in key sectors of the productive apparatus. Increased costs of both labor and raw materials severely limited Italy's ability to compete in the international market (Graziani, 1979). The consequent economic crisis diminished the State's ability to maintain current levels of social expenditures. Accordingly, the State sought to curtail social program expenses and redirect such services to the private sphere.

The State's strategy was met with significant opposition by the working class. Politically, this was indicated by the action taken in parliament by representatives of the PSI and the Italian Communist Party (PCI). Economically, trade unions organized strikes and demonstrations in protest. Simultaneously, the State had its own difficulties restructuring the welfare system due to its clientelist nature and the importance of clientelism in the maintenance of political support.

The End of the Crisis and the New Welfare

The State's inability to maintain high levels of welfare expenditure without incurring a fiscal crisis was not eliminated by the new economic expansion of the 1980s. Referred to as decentralized and informal activities[7], the recent growth of the Italian economy has been fueled by a multiplication of small firms which maintain low labor costs by paying low wages and/or avoiding fringe benefits payments. These flexible production strategies and labor organization differ sharply from the rigid developmental model adopted immediately after World War II.

In the three postwar decades, capital accumulation was based on the establishment and growth of large centralized industrial productive units. The labor force was largely male, aged 25 to 45, highly unionized and highly paid. Production strategies were rigid and employment was stable. Core economic sector employment was virtually guaranteed in return for reduced anti-management union activity and for increased union work toward high productivity and international competition levels. Politically, a stringent separation between core and peripheral workers was maintained as working class organizations concentrated on the enhancement of the socio-economic conditions of core workers and core sector development. Little attention was paid to marginal workers in peripheral enterprises (Bonanno, 1987; Mingione, 1985).

In contrast, in the 1980s it has been the decentralized and informal enterprises which were able to generate high rates of accumulation of capital and pull the entire Italian economy out of the recession and into a period of growth. Based on this new economic pattern, however, the State experienced additional difficulties and limitations in its ability to tax. Due to the unrecorded and covert nature of many of the informal and decentralized enterprises, tax payments were escaped (Mingione, 1985; Bonanno, 1987, 1988).

Additionally, two different avenues of limitations developed. First, legislation favoring the development of small decentralized productive units was introduced. This legislation included measures providing tax and other economic incentives to enterprises employing less than 15 workers (Lazerson, 1988:335-336). Second, the restructuring of the core sector led to fiscal constraints on the State. Reduced employment levels and limited economic growth in some core industries have served to curb tax revenues. Furthermore, additional taxation of core workers has been resisted by strong trade union action. In essence, the State's inability to adequately tax informal and decentralized activities and the resistance of traditional economic sectors to further taxation have precluded the adoption of effective solutions to the State's fiscal crisis.

Health Care and Social Services for the Elderly: Present Trends

Economic growth patterns, demographic trends and policy directions constitute serious obstacles to the development of an efficient and comprehensive welfare system for the aged. As a result, the post-war contradiction still remains between a constitutional mandate to create public assistance and the reality of the social service situation.

At the economic level, the pattern of expansion described earlier does not allow for a sufficient increase in the State's financial resources. Further, the maintenance of a substantial segment of marginal, low paid workers represents a violation of the constitutional mandate of economic and social equality.

At the demographic level, trends indicate an increase in the actual and relative numbers of elderly. The proportion of aged increased from 13.1% in 1951 to 17.1% in 1980 and is projected to exceed 20% by the year 1990. This pattern alone portends a simultaneous decrease in potential tax revenues and an increase in demand for care.

At the welfare policy level, a contradictory situation is also evident. On the one hand, reform attempts have been enacted. On the other, implementation has been influenced by the clientelist, particularized and irrational character of the overall welfare posture adopted by the Italian administration.

In 1978 changes in the health care system were sought. The aim of the reform was to dismantle the old Mutual Fund Insurance System and replace it with one providing free health care to all Italians. The Mutual Funds and related legislation had meant that free public health assistance in Italy until 1978 was available only to those who could demonstrate indigence and to the employed. All others were excluded, including temporarily unemployed workers who did not qualify for welfare relief but were unable to pay for private care. Troubled by an increasing budgetary deficit, however, the

Italian State has been forced to review the extent of the reform and to introduce measures involving out-of-pocket payments for health care, including medicinal purchases. The goal of free care for everyone has yet to be achieved (Piperno, 1985:180).

The reform was also aimed at restructuring the health care provision system to improve the human and structural resources available. In Italy there is one physician for every 301 inhabitants[8]. This ratio is better than in other European countries such as West Germany, Switzerland and Great Britain, where the comparable figures are 1 to 374, 1 to 421, and 1 to 600, respectively. The availability of physicians and hospitals has not been used to its full potential, however, as the reform's cost control of public health institutions has been problematic, causing much public distrust[9] (CENSIS, 1982; Piperno, 1985:178). Moreover, the entire reform has been accompanied by a timid financial commitment. Though public expenditures for health in Italy are higher than in the United States (6.1 percent of the Gross Domestic Product versus 4.4%), they are not as high as in other countries, such as West Germany (11.5%), Sweden (8.6%), France (7.5%) and the Netherlands (6.8%). These European nations have made stronger commitments to the development of public welfare systems (U.S. Bureau of the Census, 1987: 804; Burgalassi, 1983:365).

As to the quality of care, the orientation toward hospitalization has remained. Despite the administration's objective of creating welfare institutions to address both the "social and medical needs of the population," the result has been quite different (David, 1985:203). The entire reform has fostered a "medicalization" mentality so that problems are defined and solutions sought in terms of strict medical assistance. What this means is that a whole host of social conditions, such as loneliness or job-related frustration, are medically treated.

This situation is evident within the overall welfare system for the elderly. As previously mentioned, the goal of State welfare spending for the aged has been to transfer monies to families[10] as part of a complementary system. However, the family's role as primary caregiver has not been accompanied by the creation of supportive structures. "Light" flexible structures such as day-care centers, home assistance and neighborhood recreational programs would assist families and allow the elderly to remain in their social environment. Unfortunately, these supports generally have not been created. On the contrary, expenditures for the generation of "rigid" structures have been prevalent (Paci, 1985). These are institutions which provide centralized, total services and tend to sever the aged from their social and human networks[11]. The elderly are subject to "generalized and useless hospitalizations, rather than careful assistance based on their needs" (Burgalassi, 1983:367). In many cases, the social becomes medical, as symptoms and not causes are the focus. The status quo is maintained while socially-induced problems of the aged recur.

Distributive Justice and Contradictions in the Welfare State

In the foregoing, the historical roots of the present policy situation for the Italian aged were described. This has shown the importance of examining the socio-historical context of policy formation. At the same time, other advanced capitalist societies also fall short of the distributive justice ideal in their health care and social policies for the elderly. For example, in the United States, the classic notion of distributive justice "has not well served the health or medical care needs of the population" (Gill and Ingman, 1986:1214). Indeed, a year after the enactment of Medicare and Medicaid legislation, cost containment concerns began to override the original notions of equity (Brown, 1984). In our examination of social provisions for the Italian aged, similar points could be made despite the more highly developed Italian welfare system.

This final section, therefore, has two goals. On the one hand, the primary focus is on the most important contradictions which impede the realization of distributive justice in Italy. While these contradictions are interrelated, they can be analytically separated. Thus, present problems in the modern Italian system will be discussed as an outcome of the tension between the movement of capitalism and the goals of distributive justice. Our second goal is to indicate a more general application of some of these contradictions to other mature capitalist societies.

Contradictions

First, the State's role in mature capitalism contradicts the achievement of distributive justice. That is, within advanced capitalism there is conflict between the State's need to both foster accumulation and to maintain legitimation. On the side of accumulation, the bourgeoisie pressures the State for actions which will increase profits. The State also has a vested interest here as it relies on accumulation to finance its existence. At the same time, legitimation, popular support, is necessary either in material or ideological form (Offe and Ronge, 1987; Bonanno and Calasanti, 1986). Welfare spending is one material legitimative strategy. These social expenditures are resisted by the bourgeoisie, however, as they are contradictory to accumulation. As the State must also be concerned with accumulation, legitimation through expenditures is carried out only if a strong push from below exists.

The tendency of the State to establish welfare programs only as needed to preserve legitimacy means there is no general plan for their development. Struggles between the bourgeoisie and working class further fragment policies over time. This is clearly evident in Italy. The uneven coverage of welfare policies for the Italian aged is an outgrowth of the State's reluctant and contradictory intervention. Pressure from the working class, for example, led to the passage of mandatory health insurance in 1917. Yet, when the bourgeoisie was strong, as during Fascism, this legislation was revoked. Similarly, when the working class is weak or cannot fight back, as during the fiscal crisis of the State, social expenditures are reduced or rejected. Under these conditions, a comprehensive welfare plan is never developed, and distributive justice cannot be achieved.

A second contradiction rests on the fact that social policies were developed in a clientelist manner. This refers to the development of networks in which favors are given in exchange for electoral support and, ultimately, in exchange for legitimation. Individuals who support the group in power are rewarded accordingly.

Clientelism exists because State power structures are engaged in legitimative actions. That is, instead of tackling the issues, State governments are trying to reproduce themselves. This translates into the provision of social services and health care based on loyalty rather than needs. Thus the goal of equal access to health care and social services—distributive justice—is denied. Clientelism also works against quality care even for those with access because monetary redistribution and program formation are based on politics.

In Italy, clientelism became an established mode of legitimation during the Fascist regime. It has continued into modern day Italy as subsequent governments have used this system to garner electoral support. At the same time, the maintenance of clientele networks contradicts the contemporary State's efforts to end duplication and waste. Thus, resistance to this system exists but efforts to reform cannot succeed.

The third contradiction to distributive justice is more broad and can be seen beyond the Italian example. This contradiction might be termed the "disorganized development" of social programs. As discussed above, there is no comprehensive plan for the creation and implementation of health care and social services due to clientelism and the contradiction between accumulation and legitimation. In addition, power differentials between groups plays an important role. Programs were not developed in a proactive manner, with the needs of all in mind. Rather, they have been a response to pressure from particular groups with power at given points in time and thus have been formed in a particularized, reactive manner. Attempts to reform the welfare system are thus doomed as the bases upon which policies were enacted are so varied.

Specific groups, such as core workers, historically have pressured the Italian State to provide medical and social services. At the same time, such groups agitate only for specific populations or for particular legislation. This occurred, for example, when unions fought for stable jobs for core workers leaving less privileged workers behind. Subsequent legislation was then piecemeal rather than comprehensive as groups lobbied to have their needs met. Hence the present situation for the Italian aged, described earlier. Not only are some elderly denied access to services, but the care available does not address their needs. For example, monetary transfers are given to families, yet a network of supportive social services is not available. This means families cannot effectively deal with problems which accompany aging. At the same time, rigid structures exist which further medicalize the problems of the aged and ignore the individual's and family's needs and input. Disorganized development of welfare programs has thus contradicted the establishment of distributive justice.

The fourth contradiction also has broad applicability as it results from the "irrationality" of welfare under advanced capitalism. That is, two different types of rationality, instrumental and substantive, are put together, creating an irrational system. This leads to waste of human, economic and structural resources.

Within the instrumental rationality of capitalism, actions are geared to profit accumulation. This logic mandates that all services remain in the private sector so that they are produced and consumed—commodified. Thus, provision of services would be based on demand. Totally commodified health care and social services would be consistent with instrumental rationality, although provision would be unequal, open only to those who could afford it.

Within substantive rationality, actions are based upon a notion of ethics. The fulfillment of human needs, including preservation of human dignity, is the goal. This logic mandates that services not be commodified. In this instance, need becomes the basis for service creation and provision, not supply and demand. Service providers and recipients are identified by the State rather than according to laws of the market.

Distributive justice, based upon substantive rationality, has come about because of the capitalist State's need to legitimate. But it is introduced into a system dominated by instrumental rationality, based on capitalism's need to accumulate. This leads to irrationality, wherein the social system cannot operate effectively according to either logic and hence operates in a manner which contradicts both. In such a mixed system, in which the two logics are combined, neither can adequately respond. Such is the case in Italy where some services have become decommodified but not all. Health care, for example, is provided through State welfare expenditures, yet the services themselves are provided by the private health care industry which operates according to instrumental rationality. As a result, inefficiency and duplication characterize present health and social service assistance. Under these conditions, distributive justice cannot be achieved.

The final contradiction, medicalization, refers to the process by which problems which are social in nature are considered medical. Care is defined only in terms of medical science. The social bases of problems, and hence social solutions, are denied. The medical process is pre-ordained; everything is administered from above by "experts"—medical personnel.

The goal of distributive justice is to provide human dignity, yet the process of medicalization denies individual variation or even individual agency. Within the medical science framework, participation of the aged, as well as participation of family, friends and neighborhoods is precluded. The elderly are subjugated by a codified behavioral system, the medical treatment:

> when medicalization ends in confinement to a "total institution," the patient is exposed to a closed and rigidly administered life-style that reduces the individual to the symbolic antithesis of what is presumed to constitute "adulthood" [Goffman, 1961] . Self-determination and freedom of action disappear as options, and for all practical purposes the old person drops through to the bottom of the age-grading system.

> As confining as age norms can be for the elderly, being treated as a child at the age of seventy-five facilitates a complete degradation of self. (Evans and Williamson, 1984:61)

Thus, even if access to health care were equal, the goals of distributive justice would still be contradicted as the type of care delivered would negate the individual. The aged person would become the object of care rather than a subject engaged in seeking services.

In Italy, the local sanitary units (USL) were created to integrate health care and social service provision with families, neighborhoods, and communities. Medicalization prevents the USLs from performing this function, however. Aspects of care which are not commodified are replaced by those which generate profit. This means, for example, that the care or services provided by intimates is subordinated to medical treatments, often drugs. The input to be provided by the local areas and persons has become secondary to medical treatment and authority.

Taking all these contradictions together, it appears the very nature of the welfare system prevents distributive justice for the elderly. Welfare policies for the general population are incomplete as the State resists social expenditures. When they do occur, they are put forward by particularized interests and are fraught with clientelist practices. The subsequent fragmentation and duplication of services in turn means existent policies do not meet social needs and may leave the individual in a worse position. This is especially true of welfare policies for the aged in Italy and other countries, where these programs have created dependence as a way of maintaining the status quo (Bonanno and Calasanti, 1988; Calasanti and Bonanno, 1986).

Distributive Justice and Policies for the Aged: A Matter of Political Choice

The contradictions outlined above demand a scrutiny of the basic assumptions of distributive justice as they clearly establish its impossibility in mature capitalism. If capitalism and distributive justice are incompatible at this point in time, what do we do? What are our alternatives?

Of course, one possibility is to formulate a particularized notion of justice based on instrumental rationality. From this perspective, access to social services would be unequal, but this would not contradict accumulation. Thus, our idea of justice would be based on the particular mode of production and profit maximization.

Another alternative is to create a justice which transcends historically contingent situations, such as accumulation of capital. Such universality would rest on the satisfaction of needs which ensure the continuation of life and the dignified existence of human beings. Accordingly, we call for the formulation of a need-based concept of justice in which the satisfaction of class-based "wants," which are relative, is replaced with the objective satisfaction of "needs." This requires that we forsake instrumental rationality, in which needs are defined in terms of economic utility, for the establishment of a system based upon substantive rationality, in which ethics and humanity are central.

The process of establishing such a system is, of course, a political one. It is "just" as it favors all human beings by depending upon the satisfaction of human needs and dignity. Though this proposal may appear Utopian to skeptics, our analysis has clearly demonstrated that without altering the logic of instrumental rationality, social justice cannot be achieved. Accordingly, a transformation in the logic with which society operates is required *if and only if* justice is the goal.

Notes

The authors would like to thank Peter H. Law for his editorial suggestions on an earlier draft of this chapter.

1. Conversely, other regions of the country and particularly the North benefited from the drain of resources from the South financing their economic development. It was this unequal process of growth that made possible the creation of an advanced capitalist system in Italy. It was also this process that generated a situation of internal

socio-economic disequilibrium between North and South still typical of present Italy, however.

2. The term State is employed here to indicate the governmental apparatus of the country, including central and peripheral governments and their agencies. This term is not to be confused with the concept of the territorial entity as commonly employed in American English.

3. The breakdown of the extended family through industrialization and urbanization should not be understood as causing the birth of the nuclear family. Nuclear families existed even before this period and were dominant in some regions of the country. However, extended families were a common trait of Italian society in the last century.

4. The Fascist rule of Italy began on October 21, 1922, with the so-called "March on Rome," a bloodless coup d'état orchestrated by Benito Mussolini. The end of The Fascist dictatorship occurred on July 25, 1943 in the midst of WWII and shortly after the Allied troops began the invasion of Italy. However, North Italy remained under Fascist rule until the end of the War in Italy on April 25, 1945. For heuristic purposes the period discussed in this section goes from 1920 to 1945.

5. The term "clientelism" refers to the process through which a dependent relationship between political leaders and social constituencies is established. This relationship is paternalistic in substance and involves the control over a group of individuals by providing financial and in-kind assistance in return for political support. This term is used here and throughout our discussion as there are no other English synonyms which convey all the nuances of clientelism. "Constituency" is not the same as "clientele" as the former refers to a situation in which votes are exchanged for political actions. While this is also true of clientelislm, the latter involves an even greater power imbalance and involvement in individuals' lives.

6. The seriousness of this situation can be better described by examples. In 1976 ANMIL, an organization assigned to provide welfare assistance to the handicapped, spent only 20 percent of its budget on this task. The same institution in 1977 purchased a new building for the total cost of several million dollars. Also in 1976 another institution, ENAGM, had a $500,000 operating fund. It spent $261,800: $238,700 of this sum for administrative costs and only $23,100 for actual assistance.

7. For a discussion of the characteristics of the Italian economic growth in the 1980s and the processes of decentralization and informalization, see Bonanno and Calasanti, 1988 and Bonanno, 1987.

8. This ratio is even lower in large cities such as Milan and Rome (1 to 180 and 1 to 178 respectively) where there is an even larger concentration of physicians.

9. As there was no public control over costs, doctors and hospitals were charging very large fees. At the same time, the public felt that quality of care did not equal the money expended.

10. In financial terms, monetary transfers to families account for 70% of total expenditures in services for the elderly (Flora, 1988).

11. The overall situation has been aggravated by the increasing participation of weak segments of the labor force (particularly women) in the productive process. This phenomenon has further reduced the availability of family time and human resources for the care of the elderly (see Bonanno and Calasanti, 1988:250-253).

Bibliography

Barbagli, M. 1977. *Famiglia e Mutamento Sociale.* Bologna: Il Mulino.

Bassanini, M.C., C. Lucioni, P. Pietroboni and E. Ranci-Ortigosa. 1977. *Servizi Sociali: Realtá e Riforma.* Bologna: Il Mulino.

Boccella, N.M. 1982. Il *Mezzogiorno Sussidiato.* Milan: Franco Angeli.

Bonanno, A. 1988. "Economia Informale e Sviluppo Regionale." *Economia e Lavoro* (3):103-112.

Bonanno, A. 1987. *Small Farms.* Boulder, CO: Westview Press.

Bonanno, A. and T.M. Calasanti. 1988. "Laissez-Faire Strategies and the Crisis of the Welfare State: A Comparative Analysis of the Status of the Elderly in Italy and in the United States." *Sociological Focus* (3):245-263.

Brown, E.R. 1984. "Medicare and Medicaid: The Process, Value, and Limits of Health Care Reforms." In M. Minkler and C.L. Estes (eds.), Readings in *The Political Economy of Aging.* Farmingdale, NY.: Baywood Publishing Company, Inc.

Burgalassi, S. 1983. "La Condizione Anziana: Problemi e Prospettive." *Studi di Sociologia* (4):356-369.

Calasanti, T.M. and A. Bonanno. 1986. "The Social Creation of Dependence, Dependency Ratios, and the Elderly in the United States: A Critical Analysis." *Social Science and Medicine* (12):1229-1236.

Camera Dei Deputati. 1972. *Stato e Prospettive dell'Assistenza Pubblica e Privata in Italia.* Rome: Camera dei Deputati.

Castronovo, V. 1975. *La Storia Economica.* In Storia D'Italia. Vol. 4.1. Turin: Einaudi.

CENSIS. 1982. *XVI Rapporto sulla Situazione Sociale del Paese.* Milan: Franco Angeli.

Cherubini, A. 1977. *Storia della Previdenza Sociale.* Rome: Editori Riuniti.

Cherubini, A. 1973. "Note Sulle Assicurazioni Sociali di Malattia nel Periodo 1923-43." *Previdenza Sociale* (5-6):17-43.

David, P. 1985. "Il Sistema Assistenziale in Italia." In U. Ascoli (ed.) *Welfare State all'Italiana*. Bari: La Terza.

Del Panta, L. 1980. *Le Epidemie nella Storia Demografica Italiana*. Turin: Loescher.

Evans, L. and J. B. Williamson. 1984. "Social Control of the Elderly." In M. Minkler and C.L. Estes (eds.), *Readings in The Political Economy of Aging*. Farmingdale, NY.: Baywood Publishing Company, Inc.

Flora, P. 1988. *Growth to Limits*. New York: Walter de Gruyter.

Foucault, M. 1975. *The Birth of the Clinic*. New York: Vintage Books.

Gerschenkron, A. 1962. *Economic Backwardness in Historical Perspective*. Cambridge, MA.: Belknapp Press of Harvard University Press.

Gianolio, R. 1980. Assistenza Sanitaria e Assistenza Sociale: Una Difficile Riforma. Relazione di Sintesi. In R. Gianolio, L. Guerzoni and L. Strorchi (eds.), *Assistenza e Beneficenza tra "Pubblico" e "Privato."* Milan: Franco Angeli.

Gill, D.G and S.R. Ingman, 1986. "Geriatric Care and Distributive Justice: Problems and Perspectives." *Social Science and Medicine* (12):1205-1215.

Giori, D. 1983. Old People, Public Expenditure and the System of Social Services: The Italian Case. In A. Guillemard (ed.), *Old Age and the Welfare State*. Beverly Hills, CA.: Sage Publications.

Giori, D. 1978. *Essere Vecchi*. Venice: Marsilio.

Goffman, E. 1961. *Asylums*. Garden City, NY.: Anchor/Doubleday.

Graziani, A. 1979. *L'Economia Italiana dal 1945 ad Oggi*. Bologna: Il Mulino.

Kingson, E., B. Hirshorn and J. Cornman. 1986. *Ties that Bind: The Interdependence of Generations*. Washington, DC: Seven Locks Press.

Lazerson, M. 1988. "Small Firm Growth." *American Sociological Review* (3):330-342.

Manacorda, G. 1972. *Storia dei Movimenti Sindacali*. Rome: Editori Riuniti.

Mingione, E. 1985. Social Reproduction of the Surplus Labor Force: The Case of Southern Italy. In N. Redclift and E. Mingione, *Beyond Employment*. New York: Basil Blackwell.

Mutti, A. and I. Poli. 1975. *Sottosviluppo e Meridione*. Milan: Mazzotta.

Myles, J.F. 1984. Conflict, Crisis, and the Future of Old Age Security. In M. Minkler and C.L. Estes (eds.), Readings in *The Political Economy of Aging*. Farmingdale, NY.: Baywood Publishing Company, Inc.

Offe, C. and V. Ronge. 1979. Theses on the Theory of the State. In J.W. Freiberg (ed.), *Critical Sociology*. New York: Irvington Publishers.

Paci, M. 1985. "Approfondire L'Analisi sui Confini Fra Assistenza, Previdenza e Solidarietá." *Conoscere e Partecipare* (30):785-791.

Piperno, A. 1979. La Politica Sanitaria. In U. Ascoli (ed.), *Welfare State all'Italiana*. Bari: La Terza.

Piperno, A. and G. Guazzini. 1982. *La Crescita della Domanda Sanitaria*. Progress Report, Mimeo.

Podblieski, C. 1974. *Italy: Development and Crisis in Post-War Economy*. Oxford: Claredon Press.

Preti, D. 1980. *Contributo allo Studio dell'Organizzazione Sanitaria Italiana in Periodo Fascista: L'Ospedale Come Istituzione Pubblica di Assistenza e Beneficienza*. Rome: Editori Riuniti.

Pugliese, E. 1983. *I Braccianti Agricoli in Italia*. Milan: Franco Angeli.

Pullan, B. 1978. *Poveri, Mendicanti e Vagabondi*. In Annuali Storia *D'Italia: Dal Feudalesimo al Capitalismo*. Turin: Einaudi.

Serrani, D. 1978. *Il Potere per Enti: Enti Pubblici e Sistema Politico In Italia*. Bologna: Il Mulino.

U.S. Bureau of Census. 1987. *Statistical Abstract of the United States:1988* (108th edition). Washington, DC.

7

The Elderly and the Social Policy in Poland: Stereotyping, Uncoordinated, and Over-Bureaucratic

Jozefina Hrynkiewicz, Joanna Starega-Piasek, and Jolanta Supinska

Introduction

Before World War II, Poland had an extensive network of public, private, local, and cooperative institutions. These institutions provided the web of social life for a rapidly industrializing society. After World War II, the government decided to encourage rapid industrialization. This policy encouraged the creation of a monolithic political structure, and the destruction of the pre-war pluralistic social order. The political crises of 1956 disrupted the process and two enclaves of the former social order remained—small/private farms and marginal craftsmen. Indirectly, agriculture and the Catholic Church were forced to bear some of the costs of industrial development. However, the Church could not serve any official public function.

The new policy after 1956 accepted the existence of these enclaves as permanent, and even widened the scope of their activities, but any public actions were precisely limited. After a short hiatus, however, the strategy of heavy industrial development at the cost of consumption and working conditions was adopted again. In practice, but not in theory, a person's worth was described in terms of production needs; considering him to be one of the production factors. The tendency to maximize investments was cyclically corrected as a result of social protests, but was quickly revived again.

During this period the monolithic social order slowly deteriorated, both because of internal processes, e.g., the disintegrating role of the heavy industry lobby, the anti-reform attitude of lower administrative personnel,

lower management personnel becoming dependent upon informal con-
nections and secondary economy, and because of external processes, e.g., the
gradual autonomy of cultural life and communications, the revival of the
Polish Church after the election of Pope John Paul II, the unconventional and
illegal, as well as political and social initiatives of trade unions. In the 1980s
"Solidarity" made an unsuccessful attempt to introduce pluralism into the
social system. Recent changes in the international and domestic distribution
of political power allow for another attempt in this direction. The success of
this attempt will also determine the fate of particular fields such as care for
the elderly.

Demographic Characteristics of the Old People in Poland

In Poland at the "threshold of old age," we have women of sixty and
men of sixty-five, that is, people who have reached retirement age. Poland
still belongs to the countries with a considerably high ratio of children and
adolescents, and a relatively low ratio of old people. The figures of the post-
war censuses show a systematic increase of the number and proportion of the
old people. The numbers were as follows: 1950 -1.8 m people, 1960 - 2.4 m,
1970 - 3.5m, 1980 - 4.3 m, 1988 - 5 m.

The proportion of the old people in the population has been rising
steadily (12% in 1988). Additionally, the old people population ages, i.e.,
the proportion of persons who are 80 and older (in 1985 - 18.6%) is rising
also. In that same year the structure of the old people was as follows, 65-69
years - 28.6%, 70-74 years - 29.5%, 79-70 years - 23.3%. The sex and family
status structure was characterized by the dominance of women (about 70%)
and widows (61%). Among old men the majority are married (almost 80%).
The sex structure of the old people in Poland is the result of the war losses,
the growing tendency of "excessive mortality" of men and shortening of the
average life expectancy for men (Polish women on average live 75.2 years,
whereas men on average live 66.8 years - 1987). Every fourth woman and
every tenth man forms an individual household.

The increase in the numbers of old people after World War II was associated with a number of factors. The most important among them are the so-
called waves of demographic infusions and contractions, the fall of the
average life expectancy observed for men since the mid-seventies and for
women since the beginning of the eighties, the increasing occurrence of
mortality among males in the productive years and the escalation of youth
migration abroad.

The social and economic character of the aged in Poland was formed
under the influence of numerous factors of an historical nature which are

particularly characteristic of Poland. The age groups which have lately reached retirement age are burdened by the highest ever losses in Polish history. These losses were due to the impact of World War II, domestic struggles to secure communist rule, mass deportation to concentration camps and to compulsory labor programs, often forced emigration and finally to the process of scattering the population. According to estimates there were 6 million Poles who died between the years 1939 and 1945. The number of casualties in Poland amounted to 220 per every 1000 (whereas in France it was 13, in Great Britain 8, in the USA 1.4). The war and the post-war losses have had a serious effect on the condition and structure of the Polish population. Additionally, it is important to note that the victims were mostly males and educated people. The occupying powers assumed that by liquidating the educated citizens they could destroy the nation. Furthermore, the victims of the post-war struggle to secure communist rule in Poland were also mostly educated persons, as was the majority of post-war emigrants.

In present day Poland it is the old people who experienced the severest consequences of war and occupation. They lost their closest family members and friends as well as social, family or territorial ties. The devastation of both the physical and mental health of people deprived of life's necessities and subjected to constant stress escapes statistics. The biological and social losses caused by war and occupation are considerably more painful than statistical data can show and should be taken into account when analyzing the position and the condition of the old people in Poland.

The generation of people who were professionally active during the post-war period of intensive industrialization have also reached retirement age. Their health is especially precarious, because of the harsh working and living conditions they experienced. Most devastating was the way of living of the so-called "farmer–blue-collar workers," a strange creation of the economic policy of that time. They lived in the country where they ran a tiny farm and commuted every day to their work in the city. Among these groups of excessively exploited people in their productive age, one should include women employed in a three-shift system in industry (Poland has not yet ratified the 1919 convention of ILO forbidding women to work at night).

The elderly in Poland are generally poorly educated: about 88% have either not completed or have only completed elementary education (in the rural areas as many as 98% of women and 94% of men, and in the city 60% of men and almost 80% of women). Such a low level of education is the result of war losses which made it impossible to attend school during the war. The low level of education of the elderly influences their needs, way of life, aspirations, and social, cultural and political activity.

The majority of people with post-elementary education live in big cities; they constitute 41.6% in Krakow, 11.4% in Warsaw, 38% in Poznan,

31.5% in Wroclaw, and 20.8% in Lodz of the overall population of old people living in those cities.

The aging of the Polish population is more advanced in rural areas. Its rate is 2.5 times faster than in the cities. This is the result of the intensified migration to the cities during the last 45 years; the majority of the migrators are young people who are usually well educated. The old people constitute about 11% of the total city population, but 14% in rural areas. The differences in the demographic structure become even more apparent when we take into account various regions of the country or even separate districts of large towns. In the rural areas there is a higher concentration of needs, if old people in the regions with traditional and backward agriculture, as well as poorly developed services, are considered (old people constitute over 15%). As far as cities are concerned the major cities have the largest share of old people, e.g., in Lodz—nearly 18% or Warsaw—nearly 17%. Old people living in cities are concentrated mostly in the old districts, e.g., in the old district of Katowice the proportion of old people reached over 35%, similarly in Lodz, Warsaw, and Krakow. In the same districts the number of old-old (aged 80 and more) also increases. They are mostly women and more than half of them operate independent households. The concentration of old people in the oldest city districts results in their homes having, on average, lower standards. Not only are their apartments poorly equipped but often (as in industrial cities) they are situated close to factories, and in environments degraded by industry and having poor public transportation.

In the country the old people concentrate mostly in villages far removed from any city transportation, health centers, or many other facilities. Their housing is worse than that of the majority of villagers. Most of the older rural people occupy apartments without modern conveniences. Many pensioners'—former employees—dwellings (situated mostly in the cities) do not have running water (15.5%), a flush toilet (57.9%), a telephone (84%). The corresponding figures for retired farmers (mostly living in villages) are respectively 60.1%, 80.4%, and 99%.

The situation of the old people living in the rural areas worsens systematically. They lose prestige. They occupy a lower position in the family hierarchy. Their income declines. They dispose of their land. They are deprived of the care of their children who still migrate to the cities in large numbers. Many old rural people who live on their own farms are in the worst situation.

The majority of the old people from rural Poland are still professionally active. Among male farm owners who are over 70 years old, 97% still work (87% of the women). The corresponding figures for the city are 5% and 1.3%, respectively. The occupations of both country and city older inhabitants are extremely diversified. It is mostly individual farm owners who work in the country. The high proportion of individual farm owners who are aged is a result of the ineffective system of pensions (a farmer's pension is about 30% lower than an average pension of any other worker). Almost 20% of farmers cannot meet the economic criteria determined as necessary for pension eligibility.

A level of work can be observed in the cities among many old people other than blue-collar workers. While among blue-collar workers they are in the majority, the proportion of the old people who continue in an occupation is very low.

In Poland a male who reaches his 60th birthday has on average 15.1 years to live (15% of his lifespan), whereas a woman lives on average another 19.7 years (that is 25% of her lifespan). How should the conditions and quality of such a life be evaluated? Both the picture of a "poor, neglected, old man" and the picture of a "rich, fit, old man" would be false. The worst off are those who worked hard physically; who are the least educated; who lived in the rural areas; who were alone; who no longer have a family; and who are female. Old people are in a better situation if they are educated, if they were white-collar workers, and if they have a family.

Policy Making Institutions

The first question one should ask is which institutions or social groups in Poland are concerned with the problems of the elderly. The customary procedure is that the State sector organizes the majority of such actions. It assigns to the Polish Red Cross and the Polish Social Welfare Committee the more troublesome tasks. These two social organizations practically limit themselves to those assignments and they have not chosen to take on other responsibilities. Consequently, they can be regarded as constituting an integral part of the State sector.

There are many indications that the State performs the duty of supporting the elderly without great enthusiasm. They consider the so-called "burden of the post-productive citizens" as limiting the policy of national income distribution. The political changes of the last decade are slowly compelling the party and State officials to change their attitude towards the oldest citizens. The political system had become seriously destabilized, both because of the revolts of the 30-year-olds at the beginning of the 1980s and the recent threats of the near-anarchist mutiny of the 20-year-olds.

Old people tend to be conservative. They not only fear chaos and changes in their life styles, but also physical disability and material poverty. It was the old people who constituted the largest segment supporting martial law and who remained loyal to the communist party trade unions. However, with the more democratic electoral law (negotiated at the "round table"), and with the perspective of earlier elections in June, 1989, it became worthwhile to try to win over the votes of the older electorate. Traditionally regarded as economically useless, they suddenly became treated as politically useful. It remains to be seen if this change will result in greater generosity from the State treasury.

Ogolnopolskie Porozumienie Zwiazkow Zawodowych (All Polish Agreement of Trade Unions - OPZZ) is an organization which used to be dominated and steered by state agencies, but for the last one to two years has assumed a role of the "workers' communist opposition." The organization was established during the period of martial law. In the years 1982-89 it was guaranteed by law that OPZZ was the sole representative of the employees. Initially, the pensioners seemed most eager to join trade unions affiliated with OPZZ. Having been made into paupers, the elderly regarded this membership as a way of getting access to the funds and welfare provisions provided by their previous employers. Confronted with the unavoidable transfer of a sizable number of its members to "Solidarity," OPZZ began to formulate very radical and boisterous demands. The requests were also made on behalf of the so-called "work veterans" who are regarded as the most reliable. Thus, OPZZ struggles to keep retirees in its ranks, e.g., by organizing the first legal anti-government demonstration in April, 1989 held in post-war Poland. Therefore, it is mostly advancing claims from the State sector and not undertaking actions to satisfy the needs of the pensioners, even though such actions exist.

The *social sector* was traditionally led by the Catholic Church in its policy towards the elderly. This tradition originated a long time ago, but was discontinued in 1950 when the Church's dependent "Caritas" was dissolved. The shelters of Caritas were transferred to the state dependent organizations and these organizations were at odds with the episcopate association of the secular "Caritas". Since that time and up to 1981 charity, in general and also on behalf of the elderly, was of marginal interest to the Church. It was reactivated on a larger scale when help had to be organized for the internees and prisoners once active in "Solidarity." Furthermore the distribution of gifts sent from various countries in these difficult times for Poland had to be arranged. By comparison with western Europe, the Polish Church recently made a rather belated attempt at modernizing its operations. The fact that the Church is now open to the parish community, and has lifted the blockade imposed upon sacral constructions seems very helpful. It appears that the new procedures and parish facilities serve the "more difficult" parishioners, e.g., adolescents or families with children. At one level the older generation is simply offered the right to participate in religious rites. In addition, there can be found single indications of broader changes, e.g., in one of the small towns in the Przemvsl Voivedeship, the Church has begun to operate a small parish social welfare home for old people.

The majority of the violent and independent social initiatives found shelter in "Solidarity" during its first period of legal activity in 1980-81. This mass social movement was a multifunctional "omnibus" exploding movement that suddenly set free multidirectional and miscellaneous actions. It was an "engine" pulling smaller social movements together and providing these movements with a place to "incubate," before they established deep roots. Also the pensioners could voice their demands for a more advantageous retirement law. The social workers employed in social welfare in turn presented their reform ideas. None of these initiatives, however, attracted the attention of the majority of "Solidarity" members and its observers. In the new legal period—which "Solidarity" entered in April, 1989—the union in the role of an incubator is no longer of such vital importance even to the less conventional initiatives. When the liberal Law on Associations was enforced, it brought with it a more favorable social attitude towards associations as well as a better legal framework. If we were to compare how much the old people contribute to associations, and how much they are assisted by these associations then the result would be that the elderly contribute more than they receive. First of all, they constitute the core of the activists of many "old" associations (pre-Solidarity associations that were integrated with the State sector). Secondly, the elderly are also noticeable in some of the recently formed associations. However in the field of aging services, there are few initiatives. Therefore, with regard to aid for the elderly the State will find collaborators, controllers or competitors even less often than in the spheres of environmental protection, children's aid or the struggle with addiction.

The non-formalized *"private and family"* sector, too, could be characterized by the asymmetric relationship of the services transferred between generations. Old people in Poland often help their grown-up children financially, even after retirement. They share their apartments with young couples and generally take care of their grandchildren and great-grandchildren. They do this regardless of their poverty and lack of physical strength. Nevertheless, for an important majority of old people, the family is the main institution taking care of their needs, i.e., performing a social and protective role in the cities, and until recently, also taking care of material needs in the villages.

The *commercial sector* delivering goods and services especially to the elderly is practically non-existent. First, the elderly's purchasing power is limited. Second, state manufacturers, in the face of permanent instability of the market, do not take into consideration any special categories of buyers. The more flexible, though still marginal, private sector focuses on young consumers and production of prestigious gadgets. Here, the services offered on the market are especially deficient. Since 1981 and up to now, the government has been announcing successive stages of economic reform which are to redirect the economy, yet so far without success in the manufacture of consumer goods. Since the end of 1988, the new government has propagated the notion of limitless possibilities for the development of private enterprises. The new Law on undertaking economic actions guarantees equal rights for the private and the state agencies. Rapid and drastic changes in these sectors are to be expected, but it is difficult to say if and how these changes will affect the oldest consumers.

Programs of Reforms and Evolution of Services
Influencing Living Standards of the Elderly

In this section, we will concentrate on the long history of modernization of the Retirement Law and the laws regulating the functioning of social welfare in Poland. They bear the most direct influence on the living standards of the elderly. The history of these decision making processes portrays the attitude of the central government towards the elderly as well as the social atmosphere around them. They designate the shape of the two subsystems of the state sector—the sphere of obligatory services and the sphere of optional services which are managed according to different rules and values. If Polish social policy is dominated by the state agencies then the "public welfare mix," that is, the relationship between social insurance and optional help, is of the utmost importance.

The history and the state of the *pension system* in Poland can be evaluated in regard to: (1) its *efficiency* in securing decent material standards for people in the post-productive age; (2) its ability to assure the old people of their *safety*; (3) its commitment towards *egalitarianism* in relations between the elderly and the rest of the society, as well as between various groups of the elderly; and finally, (4) its *burden with side functions*, e.g., motivating political or economic behavior desired by the State.

The introduction in 1946 of retirement pensions constituted a fraction of the necessary costs of living at the beginning, and in 1955 they still did not exceed 20% of an average salary. A rapid increase of the pensions—never again to be repeated—made it possible in 1960 to reach 40% of an average salary. Convention No. 102 of the ILO regarded this as a minimum; however, Poland has not yet ratified this convention. This ratio improved in the next decades, but frequent steps backwards could also be observed. In 1970 an average pension amounted to 65% of an average salary, 1980 - 54%, 1987 - 64%. In the first two months of 1989 the ratio of pensions to salaries in the so-called productive sphere of the economy (excluding the service sphere) amounted to 50%. These indicators place Poland in a favorable position among other socialist countries. The situation of the elderly farmers seems a lot worse. The pensions for farmers date back to the beginning of the 60s, but only in 1980 did a relatively satisfactory pension plan come into effect. Up to now farmers' pensions are considerably lower than other workers' (1970 - 30.6% of average salary and 47% of worker's pension; 1987 - 39.4% of salary and 61% of pension). In 1987, 57% of old farmers received retirement and disability pensions.

A worker's pension insures only very modest living standards, e.g., in 1987 as much as 47% of the pensioners' total budget was spent on groceries. In households with an income visibly lower than the one calculated by the State Labor Institute for a single pensioner, the so-called "crisis pension's" minimum income, the money spent on groceries amounted to almost 56%. In every fifth household, the pensioners live below the minimum. In 1985 many families responding to the Central Statistical Office Poll indicate that "there is not enough money even for the cheapest food and clothing." The poorest families comprise households of the oldest pensioners and of those especially where the woman has never worked professionally (these women are entitled only to family bonuses of a minimum value).

Manufactured goods are relatively expensive in Poland. For an average monthly pension in 1987 one could buy, e.g., 12 men's flannel shirts (1970-7.5, 1980-18), 2.4 pairs of women's winter boots (1980-2.3), 1.36 women's winter coats (1970-1.0, 1980-1.26), 0.28 of an automatic washing machine (1970-0.14, 1980-0.31), half of a black-and-white TV (1970-0.19, 1980-0.49). Obviously, these ratios would be compounded if the economic surplus remaining after paying for groceries was taken into consideration. To draw a more complete picture of the pensioner's buying power, one should add that the Polish market is constantly fluctuating, and that during the previous year another phase of intensified shortages occurred. It is estimated that 10% of people's income comes from the "second economy." It results in polarization of the Polish society—also of pensioners. Those who "get" the desired goods acquire large profits, especially if they decide to resell them; their real income rises. Whereas, those forced to shop on the well-developed black market weaken the buying power of their nominal income. For example, in the first three months of 1988 people reselling a furniture set demanded a 20% higher price than the original price (in the last three months it was already 30%). Parallel figures for other goods were: - iron-34% (40% in the last three months), -automatic washing machine-20% (27%), - color TV-21% (25%). A pensioner who had enough time, health and the necessary con-nections to secure a color TV, and then resell the color TV could earn at "one go" an equivalent of 2.5 times the average monthly pension. Pensioners are predominant among people who profit from the illegal trade of alcohol when it is unavailable in the stores (they sometimes also manufacture alcohol). They benefit from the gaps in the administrative program for fighting alcoholism. For others the chance of buying many articles—

especially household appliances, becomes illusory. The elderly have the privilege of buying primary articles without having to stand in line. Everyday these privileges cause rage among the people who must stand in line, and some express a gerontophobic attitude in response. The suspicions of these privileges being abused are often legitimate. One of the more important functions that the elderly serve in the families of their children, is the help they provide with shopping.

The above digression concerning the situation of the market leads to the following conclusion: the obligatory payments for the elderly are still too low. But even a considerable rise will not bring the desired effect if a "pro-market" and a "pro-consumer" move is not brought about in the Polish economy. For more than 30 years, successive attempts at economic reform have been made. The reforms of the 1980s, more radical in design, have already been to a withdrawal phase on three separate occasions and still the government proclaims new reformatory actions ahead. The state still cannot resolve the conflict between political rationality (striving towards maximum control of the economy and the society) and economic rationality.

Social welfare stimulates *the feeling of security* if it is obligatory, if its real value is guaranteed, if the regulations determining its assignments are clear, and if the necessary formalities to receive welfare are not troublesome.

In Poland the first of these tasks has been realized fully, even though it was greatly delayed in regard to needs. Obligatory pensions for a rising percentage of old people, together with the free health service (since 1973 also available for the farmers) and free drugs for pensioners, stimulated real and psychic security among the elderly.

Up to 1986, though, pensioners were deprived of the automatic mechanism for maintaining the value of their incomes. For several years the scientists have indicated—by preparing concrete projects—that automatic adjustments based upon inflation guaranteed by law would not require much more than the "ad hoc" increases; but would spare the elderly their concerns about the future. The central government, however, counted on the possibility to save on budget spending. They must have also measured the prospects of using consecutive increases for propaganda purposes and depicting them as acts of generosity and care to legitimate the state. The way in which these raises were administered resulted in part in the improvement of the standards of some groups and the deterioration of others. In some periods a considerable part of the pensioners found themselves among those with minimal incomes, e.g., in 1981, it was more than half the pensioners because the minimal pension was often raised.

Up to the end of the 1970s both prices and living costs changed little. Nevertheless, any increase was painful for the old people who struggled to satisfy their primary needs. They also felt threatened. Towards the end of the 70s there appeared a new phenomenon—more and more open inflation which reached two digit numbers in the 1980s. It shattered one of the stereotypes of social economy. The old people were especially prone to inflation panic and particularly defenseless in regard to price rises. In the years 1981-82 the cost of living rose almost 60% annually, between 1983-86 it rose about 20% annually to reach about 60% again in 1988. In this situation the government finally introduced automatic indexing of pensions (in relation to an average salary) to occur once a year. However, they also established maximum increases that could occur and added other ways to limit the impact on the budget, and thus the pension system remained defective. As the result of the agreement negotiated by the government and the opposition at the "round table" in April, 1989, the indexing or valorization of pensions will be more frequent and will take place every three months. One could add that, regardless of all the events occurring in the last few years, the pensioners benefited from the pension system for it did secure their buying power; whereas workers were left with strikes, and started the so-called "wild indexation" of salaries to protect their buying power.

Finally, we must mention the extremely complex pension system as well as the generally criticized institutions managing the pensions. It is an additional source of fear, especially for the least educated and the least physically fit people.

The pension system in Poland guarantees the elderly a constant income, but it maintains *income differences* between the pensioners and the salaried. The pensioners themselves are not equal. Although the number of various pension plans has been reduced from 16 in the 1970s to 7 in the 1980s, many of the differences still exist. For instance the very high pensions for State Government members together with special family pensions for their offspring were eliminated, but the more profitable pensions for police and military employees as well as for miners (to compensate for their harsh working conditions) were preserved; and new privileges for war veterans were introduced. It would seem that the veterans should include the declining handful of the oldest pensioners. The definition however appeared very flexible and encompassed also the so called "participants in the struggle to secure the people's rule" of the post-war period. In effect, the number of veterans (in this sense) constantly increased. They benefit from various privileges designed for the most wealthy, with the best housing facilities such as telephone and central heating discounts, price reductions for apartments bought from the state, and for small plots of land used for recreation. The other systems created for those who did not work for state sectors are characterized by higher dues and lower pensions. On account of complying with the principles of digression, though, the basic group of pensioners are more egalitarian at the onset of retirement than they were at the time of their professional activity. In subsequent years of retirement this equality—among the same age group—increased. This levelling off, however, was downward just as the above-mentioned shortcomings indicated. As the influence of salary structure on the pensions' diversity decreases, the influence of age, and particularly of the year of retirement, increases. The older the pensioners, the poorer they are.

What also should be criticized is *burdening the pension system with functions which have no connection with the idea of social security*, especially economic functions. This is most apparent in the subsequent versions of the regulations regarding pensions for old farmers. At the beginning in 1962 only those who had ceded their farms to the government free-of-charge were entitled to a pension (an extremely low pension). In 1978 retirement laws also included those who ceded their farms to members of their closest family, and who sold their produce to state institutions. These social security policies were to stimulate economically deteriorating farms (at the end of the 1970s every third farm was managed by farmers who had reached retirement age). Free land trade was prohibited, however, because it was feared that large plots of land would be accumulated by private owners. Therefore, the first endeavors concentrated on land transfer to the state sector, and then on retaining the smallest family farms (in 1987 57% of farms had less than 5 hectares). At the same time old farmers were regarded as potential obstacles to boosting agricultural production. Yet it must be remembered that the farmer's pension was twice as low as that paid to other workers.

A pensioner's work was also regarded in a similar way. If the salary of a pensioner reached a rather low limit, then the pension was suspended. Some occupational categories, *those in highest demand*, acquired the right to a higher limit for additional earnings. The tendency then was to allow these people to work, not those who had strength and motivation, but those who were recognized as politically useful to the administration.

After having discussed the obligatory services we now turn to the optional services. They are granted mostly by the state sector, and only to a small extent, by the trade unions and social or church organizations.

The very nature of *optional services* implies that they should stimulate the service providers to individualize the analysis of the situation of the needy. At the same time it means that the type of service, its character and quality should fit the needs of the service beneficiaries. In Poland this idea practically amounts to the State not having an obligation to assist the needy, but only the *capability* to help if considered appropriate and if there are satisfactory means. Though the forms of assistance are very stereotypical, such practice deformed the original sense of the optional character of services. Additionally, State social welfare has a tendency to retain information concerning its aims and obligations; so that the expectations of society will not exceed the state's power to deliver services.

Social welfare in Poland functions on the basis of the 1923 Law and a number of operating provisions prepared by appropriate departments without any consideration for its being consistent with the spirit of the Law and its execution. The Law itself, in its solutions, is not compatible with the organizational and political structures. The departments' regulations are also characterized by a lack of coherence. They are drawn under the influence of immediate needs or under the pressure of social problems or spectacular actions. This explains why the elderly constitute 90% of social welfare recipients, even though only 3% of the elderly are clients of social welfare.

There appears to be an easily noticeable and seemingly uniform category for which institutions should be created that would help the aged. The existence of social welfare and directing it stubbornly toward old people justifies the shortcomings of the social policy on their behalf. There is always the claim that social programs exist to help care for those who are too poor, too sick, or too lonely to take care of themselves, or who remain under family care.

The history of the post-war attempts which were made to pass a new Law on Social Welfare is a good illustration of the attitude of the State sector towards the needs of the old people—and of people in general. The announcements for the preparation of a new law are always made by the government when there is danger of an economic crisis or recession. Social Welfare is still understood by the government as financial aid. The government announcements are to certify that the State is ready to undertake a number of actions protecting the most vulnerable groups (old people constitute a large percentage of them).

Despite these prerequisites a new law has not been passed yet, because the project makes it necessary to answer a number of fundamental questions. Ideology demands that the government answer them in the positive, while organizations and financial issues demand that government answer them in the negative. One of the unsolved problems is the matter of the social pensions for persons without any income. The hesitancy of the government resulted in rejecting 15 proposals for reform. The last proposal was created in consultation with social politicians, sociologists, lawyers and economists. The opinions of the experts were delivered to the Ministry of Health and Social Welfare. It looked as if there was a chance to pass a law worthy of the 21st century until the ministry clerks worked out their *own* proposal under existing law, which codified the status quo.

A new chance appeared at the round table talks between the opposition and the government in the Spring of 1989. As a result of these talks, the government was made responsible for delivering a new revised proposal to the Polish Parliament before the end of 1989. With this mandate to hold social consultation, a new round of negotiations began.

The position of the old people in Poland is characterized by weak human rights and very few responsibilities. Their situation also has an effect on the status of social aid and other institutions concerned with the elderly. Poland is one of the few countries where there is no research center involved with geriatrics and gerontology. Gerontologists in Poland must view it as a hobby; they have other specialties (psychology, social politics, or medicine). It is generally known how such institutions are organized worldwide. But old people and their problems do not exert any pressure in either a moral or an immediate sense, and that is why there is such backwardness in the theory and in the practice of gerontology in Poland. Problems of the elderly are solved in a highly public, spectacular way and they themselves are treated in an ancillary way. For example, in 1982 people approaching retirement age obtained the right to retire earlier. The Polish Gerontology Association had fought for this very law in their reports directed to the government and since the mid 1960s to Seym (similar to the U.S. House of Representatives, the second chamber of the Polish parliament). There was no reaction from the Government for years. The government responded only when there supposedly was a danger of unemployment in 1982. To secure work places, people were asked to retire earlier. The motivation used, however, was the concern about the retirees and the postulates of gerontologists.

The knowledge of the needs of the elderly, acquired from empirical research in Poland and in other countries, allows for designing a variety of services for them. There is much to be desired; however, reform and expansion of the delivery system has not typically been realized. This happens due to a number of reasons, and it is worthwhile to list and analyze some of them:

- the matters of the elderly are divided between *various State institutions* (departments of health, labor and social politics, housing, etc.), and their coordination is unsatisfactory,
- the large diversity of the elderly is not taken into consideration and various needs are not accommodated,
- there is a constant lack of financial resources,
- syndromes of the difficult life situation faced by the poor elderly which are hard to break into isolated actions.

In practice the variety of services provided for the old people seems to be large as described in the following analysis of the optional services.

Special Geriatric Health Care

In Poland experts argue that geriatric care has three stages—prevention, treatment and rehabilitation and that these three stages are equally important. In Poland geriatric *prevention* develops mostly during seminars and conferences. There is a lack of geriatrics, a lack of routine check-ups, both because of technical and economic reasons and due to the low level of health awareness of the society. In the mid 70s there were about 10 Voivodeship Geriatric Centers. Their function was to help the general practitioners in the health service. At the end of the 80s there are only two such centers left. *Treatment* of the elderly seldom takes into consideration the impact of illness and pharmacotherapy in old age. This results from the low level of geriatric instruction in medical schools. *Rehabilitation* constitutes a separate problem, it hardly has a place throughout medical practice. As far as the elderly are concerned only a small percentage benefit from it. Geriatric rehabilitation to stop disabilities is performed in social welfare homes both for its inhabitants and for people living in the community. Such solutions are not the rule, however, and they occur in pensioners' homes where it is in the interest of the personnel that the pensioners remain physically fit for as long as possible.

Terminal care is provided in homes for chronically ill, in hospitals and in hospices. Naturally difficult terminal care brings various additional problems in Poland, because of the lack of disposables, personnel and accommodations with proper technical and sanitary equipment. Formal terminal care is partly assisted by the Polish Red Cross nurses, and thus it is provided in the home of the ill, often with the aid of the family. Low wages and difficult working conditions create many problems in finding a satisfactory number of nurses. In 1981, an Association for Aiding the Sick "Hospicjum" (Hospice) was created. It is inspired by the Church and trains people to care for the terminally ill. It was not possible to build any hospices yet, even though the financial means have been secured. It is potentially the most important social initiative for the old people, although the association devotes much of its attention to people with cancer. Nowadays, dying old people are mostly directed to the overcrowded hospitals where they stay to the end. According to numerous accounts of physicians working for "Hospice," they are usually treated as the worst category of patient, taking places away from the other sick patients; "they are very demanding and disturbing; and they destroy statistics."

Residential Help

People in their retirement years are directed to pensioners' homes (women of 60 and more, and men of 65 and more). These retirees are considerably physically fit, independent, and not demanding any special care or nursing, but are no longer self-reliant in everyday life.

It should be stressed that the definition applies to applicants for a place in such homes. Naturally their health deteriorates while waiting for a free place and subsequently during their stay in the homes of pensioners.

The worse the care found at their place of residence, the bigger the need for pensioners' homes. For years, however, the number of pensioners' homes kept dwindling. The pensioners were transferred into homes for chronically ill without changing the name. The Ministry of Health and Social Welfare has long since abandoned transfers from pensioners' homes to homes for chronically ill of those whose health has seriously deteriorated. Such transfers are made only in special cases.

Pensioners' homes are usually located in the cities; only a few exist in small towns and in rural areas. The majority of them are placed in buildings built especially for this purpose after World War II, although only those built in the last decade comply with appropriate standards (single or double rooms, with the majority being the former, bathrooms in every room, spacious living area and a satisfactory number of communal rooms).

Apart from the generally accessible pensioners' homes there are also the so-called departmental homes (in Warsaw the Home for the Health Care Service Employees, the Home for the Workers' Movement Veterans, the Home for Builders; in other cities 3 Homes for the Meritorious Teachers and 14 Veterans' Homes). In general there are 109 pensioners' homes in Poland with 10 thousand places. These facilities cover 65% of the need.

There is, however, a gap between home and residential care. From the moment of granting the right to residential help to the time when there is a vacancy in an appropriate home, the old person may wait for years, and during this time he or she is often deprived of any social aid.

Homes for the chronically ill are designed for those adults who have chronic somatic diseases or some serious handicap and do not require hospital treatment but constant and attentive care. Homes for the chronically ill accept people who are at least 18, though 80% of the patients have reached retirement age. Very significant is the number of bedridden persons who often cannot control their physiological functions, and are totally dependent. Medical rehabilitation seems to be of special importance among the activities of these homes. It is adjusted to the needs and possibilities; and it aims at impeding the pathogenetic processes or at restoring the lost functions, even if only partially. Among homes of all types there is the highest number of places in homes for the chronically ill, and the highest number of applicants. There are 184 such homes with 25 thousand places. They cover 61% of the demand.

Additionally, it is unclear how many old people are found in four other types of social welfare houses. 1. *Homes for the mentally ill* are homes for people who are either moderately, considerably or deeply mentally retarded and because of various reasons cannot live in society—independently or under family care. Rarely, slightly retarded people are accepted to these homes if the combination of the handicap and the sickness make independent living impossible. Task and work therapy (paid work in a protected environment) as well as social rehabilitation are especially stressed in homes for the mentally ill. There are 93 such homes with 11 thousand places. This covers 24% of the need.

2. *Homes for the chronically ill with nervous system deficiencies* are homes for adults who do not require hospital treatment, but whose senility, chronic somatic disease, central or peripheral nervous system deficiency, or serious handicap made it necessary to provide them with—apart from doctors' and nurses' care—psychiatric and neurologic care. There are 82 homes for the chronically ill with nervous system deficiencies, with 9 thousand places, covering about 25% of the need.

3. *Homes for alcohol addicts* are designed for adults who are incapable of work and independent living as a result of permanent health changes caused by alcohol addiction, but who do not require treatment. It is a totally new type of social aid home, introduced by the Law on encouraging sobriety and alcohol addiction prevention passed on October 26, 1982. As of now there is only one such home in the country.

4. *Homes for the blind* admit people either totally or partially blind, incapable of leading an independent life and not adapted through appropriate rehabilitation to life in society. Four such homes exist in Poland, and this is sufficient since the results of rehabilitation of the blind in Poland are very good and the blind people with severely damaged health are admitted to the homes for the chronically ill.

Among the above-named homes there are some which carry the label of "Caritas," yet they practically function according to the same rules operating the State homes.

Under the Constitution the services in the social welfare homes—constituting a part of the free health care—are formally provided free of charge. The pensioners have been coaxed, though, to pay voluntary fees for years.

There is a lack of private pensioners' homes for the elderly in Poland. The cooperative building societies, however, tried to build cooperative homes for the elderly; an initiative not very significant in numbers but important in further perspective. The history of one such home in Gdansk was very instructive. After some time this home was transformed into a home for the chronically ill. The state social welfare did not want to take care of it for a very long time (considering it a matter for the cooperative) and the cooperative did not know how to take care of it and also did not wish to solve this problem of care.

Service Help

Assuming that it is most important to keep old people in their own homes, and viewing institutionalization as an extreme measure, the help in everyday life is considered most crucial. It is mostly provided by state social assistance and the network of caregivers from the Polish Social Welfare Committee (PSWC). PSWC is basically a social organization, but it is subsidized by the government, which changes its character considerably. Social welfare provides services such as: housekeeping (cleaning, cooking, shopping, bringing meals from a cafeteria, coal from the cellar, lighting the stove, gardening), arranging washing services, bathing, hygiene, sewing, facilitating transportation (arranging transport to doctors, to the club), etc. They are organized in a variety of ways throughout the country and cover the needs in various degrees. Additionally, because of the difficulties in finding people willing to work in the Polish Red Cross or PSWC, both organizations pay the neighbors to do it. This form of aid develops fairly quickly. It has a number of positive features: a natural social bond between neighbors develops and the service benefits both parties. A special form of aid occurs when an old person subleases a part of the apartment in return for everyday help. Housing shortages made this form of aid quite attractive, especially for young women who are mostly students.

We can say almost nothing about paid social care. In at least two cities (Warsaw, Lodz) private nursing agencies were established during the last two years. The scope of their activities is very small, however, and the prices rather high. A nurse's charges for one night's care are higher than the monthly, so-called "nursing care allowance" granted to pensioners who require constant care. One could also locate a housekeeper through an ad in the paper. At the beginning of the 60s even families with average income could afford such help, but today it is a luxury, affordable only to the wealthiest, and there are fewer and fewer volunteers.

Warsaw Charity Association which was reactivated in 1981, after 60 years, tried to implement the innovative idea of organizing paid services for those old people who need care and have the means to pay for it. The accumulated sums were to be used for financial aid for the poor, and also for old people. These activities had a limited scope, mainly because of the difficulties in finding people willing to work in this capacity, even though it was quite well paid.

Often the transition between residential care and home care is the *day care center*. These require special attention. They provide all-day stay, three meals, various forms of recreation, often a possibility of physical therapy, constant medical care, and at the same time they do not remove the elderly from their social environment. In the years 1970-1987 the number of such homes rose from 5 to 180 and the number of places from 150 to more than 6,000.

Free Time and Activities

The most general form of organized free time for the elderly are the so-called *"seniors' clubs."* Several times a week social gatherings and cultural events are scheduled, usually on the premises of some institution or a housing estate. There exist more than 1,700 such clubs. More intensive and more attractive programs are offered by the Universities of the Third Age that operate according to western patterns. The first one was established in Poland in the 1970s. Today, almost 20 such centers are operating. Old people living in the cities are offered special activity areas to visit (without night accommodations). There are small plots of land in the garden area that are divided into 300 meter gardens situated within city limits, and with a common club room (a phenomenon unknown in other countries). It appears that the most local, social initiatives, not necessarily of an innovative character, are found here.

Most educated people try to avoid the "ghettos" created especially for the elderly; and they use what is generally accessible in the community. In the presence of commercialization of cultural goods and services they are often left with taking part in less attractive but free events. These events represent remnants of the abandoned programs created under policies of the late 1950s which attempted to popularize culture. The elderly also often constitute the core of groups such as marginal social associations and local self-governing bodies with no authority left. In this way—against their will—they find themselves again in an old people's ghetto, because younger people are not interested in such forms of activity.

Self-organization of the elderly takes on many forms. The most common is membership in the Polish Pensioners' and Disabled Persons' Association, often purely formal. The organization which has greatly influenced Polish political life is the Freedom and Democracy Fighters Association (FDFA). It was formed in 1949 out of a merger of 11 different veterans' associations, and today has more than 800 thousand members. For years this organization gave shelter to veterans who fought during the war and who were later negatively assessed by the communist rulers. The FDFA was able to help financially and verified the rights of veterans' pensions. For some, the FDFA was a feature of "national agreement" within the generation of the 70-year-olds, once severely divided by political hatred. For others, the FDAF is an organization influenced or directed by the government, an artificial merger, an obligatory union of the torturers and their victims from the period of domestic struggle and Stalinist terror. Recently, some citizens demanded that the veterans' organization become once again pluralistic. Parallel with the wave of new initiatives at the end of the 1980s, old people are among the initiators of associations directed towards the past; these associations bring together lovers of the lost eastern lands, and former political prisoners or former Siberian exiles.

The emotions and actions described above are controlled by an elite. A sizable majority of the old people concentrate on family life (where they play difficult roles), on religious practices and on passive watching of TV (99% of pensioners' households in 1987 had a TV, whereas in 1975 only 60%). In 1979, 78% of pensioners had not attended a cinema and 59% had not read any books. It does not appear that there will be any improvement. This situation is mostly a result of the low level of education among this generation.

Conclusions

Research has indicated that the stereotype of an old person in Polish society includes many negative features. An elderly person is often stereotyped as sick, poor, badly dressed, untidy, alone, sad, without perspectives or as a person living in poor housing, for example. Especially now, at the time of crises, when negative assessments of the past are generally voiced, the old people are unconsciously blamed for all that is bad. The attitude towards the elderly is also influenced by the fact that charity occupies an ever lower position in the value system of the society.

Social policy towards the old people in Poland is constituted by a number of uncoordinated actions bringing both intended and unintended consequences. The major outcome of this policy is the strengthening of negative consequences for the aging process, through:

- poverty of the old people,
- creating in various spheres a number of obstacles making the life of an old person more difficult,
- creating a constant fear of danger and uncertainty in old people,
- supporting the lack of trust towards institutionalized services,
- a substantial lowering of the position of the elderly in society,
- transfer of old people under care of social welfare (as if old age was some fact difficult to anticipate).

The above thesis should be even sharper when formulated in regards to the old people living in rural areas.

The situation of old people in Poland is mostly influenced by two sectors: the State sector (together with a couple of social organizations controlled by the State sector) and the informal sector. The *State sector* represents the type of rationality common to other bureaucratic organizations. With declaration of servitude towards such values as safety and equality, the State often sins against these values. It is financed from the State budget. Only recently, attempts were made at creating guarantees of automatic influx of financial resources from the budget for social purposes, but support for non-routine decisions dominates. The most common shortcomings of these decisions are that they are arbitrary and unsystematic.

Managers and executives are poorly paid, tightly controlled and wield little power. Their institutions do not stimulate community activity. Individual services recipients are sometimes treated as unwanted customers. On the other hand, the *informal sector*—family and neighbor help, self-aid in the "black economy"—tries to fill the enormous gaps left by institutionalized public welfare. Its role is determined more by the absence of other institutions than by a critical evaluation of these institutions themselves. Extensive political, social and economic changes that have taken place recently on the national level can soon destabilize the two-sector model and infuse it with new elements and probably new conflicts as well.

Our critical stance towards social policy in regard to the elderly comes from a belief that a better policy is feasible, and that there are countries which have better policies, (which come from more pluralism, in general). In contrast to this last statement we will cite the results of a representative poll of Polish public opinion (carried out twice—in 1979 and in 1983). A vast majority of Poles thought that social welfare for the elderly and for the disabled was better in socialist rather than capitalist countries (1979-73%, 1983-67%). This aid, then, was considered one of the major advantages of the socialist system (together with full employment, free education, care for mother and child, free health services and social equality), while the capitalist system's advantages were: high living standards, an abundance of consumer goods, democratic liberties, well managed organizations and efficiency in the workplace. Such convictions of scientists and stereotypes of the public are worth verifying by international comparative research.

Note

1. Another version of this chapter was published in the following booklet: A. Evers and I. Svetlik (eds.). 1991 *Welfare Systems in Care for the Elderly - Shifting Mixes of Public and Private Responsibilities* (3 Volumes). Volume 1: Czechoslovakia, Hungary, Poland, and Yugoslavia (Slovenia). Vienna: European Centre for Social Welfare Policy and Research.

8

The Provision of Primary Health Care to the Elderly in the USSR: Problems and Their Solutions

Rustam R. Muzafarov and Ernest M. Kurleutov

Introduction

One of the main goals of mankind throughout history has always been to combat premature aging and to promote long and happy life for all. The English scholars, Thompson and Welpton, calculated in 1933 that by 1988 the proportion of persons aged 64 and over would make up 12-13% of the population of industrialized nations which would generate problems concerning current earning capacity unless "the socioeconomic structure provides an appropriate employment for them" and issues of employment and geriatric care would arise soon afterwards as social policy concerns. Their prognosis was correct, for in the early 1950s, in most developed countries, the proportion of the population aged 65 and over had reached 8-12%.

Currently, the USSR has 58.1 million pensioners, which represents some 20% of the general population. There were 37 pensioners per 100 working population. It is estimated that by the year 2000 pensioners will make up 19% of the population. Public policy will determine how many pensioners will be re-employed in the year 2000.

When attempting to understand a social phenomenon it is necessary, in the first instance, to provide a sound definition of the phenomenon and then to provide past and present causes of that phenomenon. The assessment of consequences will make it possible to formulate relevant theories, and if necessary, to develop social policies that relate to new demographic realities.

Old Age, Needs, and Provisions

Opinions vary as to when the process of aging starts. Some people look old at age 45 while others look young at 75. This issue is not as simplistic as it first might appear. It deals with how chronological aging is used in statistical reports on old age. For example, it is important to create a common definition of old age that allows one to deal with the social and economic, as well as biological complexity of old age. The majority of people over 65 are still able to keep their home and care for themselves, despite the gradual loss of functional capacity. Yet, some elderly persons are quite helpless and require the care commonly provided for young people who are physically or mentally handicapped. It is often suggested that old age is geared to the loss of occupational capacity, yet research findings in the USSR suggest that during the initial years after retirement most pensioners retain their capacity to work. But this is not to say they do not have needs and demands typical for their age. Old people as a social group have needs which should not be ignored by the community even if they continue as productive members of the labor force.

What tasks need to be addressed by a society whose population is aging? Evidently, such a society should guarantee the satisfaction of needs of people who are not active at present but who have formerly created the material wealth as well as the social and cultural environment that younger generations enjoy. On the one hand, the elder generations have needs and demands common to all people: the need to be recognized as persons and to enjoy the respect of their fellowmen. On the other hand, old people have the needs specific to their age, i.e., needs related to reduced income, declining work capacity, health losses and fading physical power. Compensation for these losses is essential if an appropriate moral and ethical context is to be created wherein the elderly will continue to play a respected part in the life of the community.

It should be noted that the issues of medico-social care for the veterans of war and labor and the elderly citizens have always been the focus of attention of governmental authorities, and in recent years they have become matters of priority.

The state provides care for the elderly in many ways: the payment of pensions and grants, health care provision, and accommodations in old people's homes. An integrated program for the provision of social care for the disabled and socially isolated has been developed and implemented. A range of services provided by Red Cross charities enjoy great popularity. The executive committees of local Soviets which consist of people's deputies have special commissions dealing with the elderly; they coordinate the activities of public and voluntary organizations providing care for elderly citizens.

Accounts of the social life of old people require reference to the All-Union Council of Veterans which has departments in all republics and regions of the USSR. Veterans are honorable guests at all public gatherings and are truly respected for their sacrifices and past services in World War II. Nevertheless, their daily life often consists of coping with illness, drug taking, and housework which is sometimes burdensome. Yet it would be unrealistic to believe that the elderly person needs only social care and medical care. Even for those who live in families with loving and caring children and grandchildren, communication with others on a routine basis is quite essential as well.

Our research findings are fully consistent with the reports of other researchers: people should be prepared for retirement in advance and this preparation should be rationally grounded. The range of issues in creating a sound social science should encompass all aspects of living: domestic life, leisure, cultural interests, health and social life. These are multifaceted issues to be addressed by the society as a whole.

When considering community health projects in the field of social care, we would like to focus upon the projects aimed at the solution of one urgent problem, that is, the problem of the lonely aged requiring outside help.

Declaration of Alma-Ata and the
Development of Social Justice Concepts

The International Conference on Primary Health Care organized by WHO/UNICEF, took place in Alma-Ata, USSR, in 1978. The intergovernmental conference was attended by delegations from 134 governments and by representatives of 67 United Nations organizations, specialized agencies and non-governmental organizations. The first document and other related materials of the Conference were distributed among the participants at the 33rd Session of the UN General Assembly in New York. These documents were the center of attention at subsequent sessions of WHO Regional Committees which continued the discussion on the necessity to reorient health systems in most countries, and to pursue the relevant activities of WHO started in Alma-Ata. The WHO Program Committee in November 1978 joined the main statements of the Alma-Ata Conference with new proposals and ideas on the development of the strategy for the attainment by the year 2000 of a level of health which will enable the "people to lead a socially and economically productive life."

The "Health for All Strategy" demands great changes and a real social revolution in the provision of health care. It is aimed at altering the outlook of people, introducing necessary changes to the structure of health care systems and to reorient the work of health personnel. The approaches taken to realize these changes will determine whether justice and equity is the cornerstone of health care delivery. Progress in the health field is not only associated with the development of education and agriculture but also with such factors as reduced international and social tension, employment for all and comprehensive protection of the environment. The Global Strategy rests on five major principles formulated in Alma-Ata: 1. equitable distribution of health services and their accessibility; 2. extensive community involvement in the development of health systems; 3. health promotion and disease prevention; 4. technologies which are scientifically grounded and socially and economically acceptable; 5. taking into account mutual and direct influence of all spheres of human activity on health and health systems.

The progress in the development of the Alma-Ata concepts was on the agenda at the WHO International Meeting entitled: "From Alma-Ata to the year 2000—a midpoint perspective." This conference took place in Riga, USSR, in 1988. At this meeting it was noted that both a significant improvement in the health status of populations as well as in the availability of health care had been achieved since the 1978 Alma-Ata conference. Now, it was felt that it was necessary to identify the spheres needing similar development and to uncover the barriers to reform.

The Global Health for All (HFA) strategy implies a close and complex interlinking of health and development. The attainment of health is in large measure dependent on factors outside the health care system; one of which is sufficient income. Nevertheless income is not a sufficient guarantee of health but must be associated with the ability to make wise decisions. Therefore, primary health care services identify the developmental factors which have both negative and positive effects on health, and incorporate such priorities in the delivery of primary health care (PHC).

Accelerated progress in technology has led to deep changes in human living. People are provided with better housing, clothes and foodstuffs; standards of education and health services have risen and new agricultural and industrial technologies are improving human existence. However, grave social consequences resulting from environmental pollution, inadvertent release of radiation from atomic power stations and increasing resource depletion run counter to these positive achievements.

Evidently it is necessary to pay greater attention to the factors affecting industrial production and the development of technologies as they impact upon the health status of populations. Technology, itself, will not resolve the problems of development pertaining to the demographic, economic and social conditions.

The commitment of WHO member-states to achieve health for all by the year 2000 rests on a fundamental principle of social justice: all people have an equal right to health. The major problem encountered by the majority of countries consists in the lack of resources for the development of the health sector. Tables 1 and 2 present the proportion of the Gross National Product that is allocated for health and primary health care in WHO member-states.

The proportions of funds targeted toward primary care resources in different societies vary from under 20% to over 80%, and there is no

TABLE 1

Share of Gross National Product (GNP) Alloted to Health (in the Regions of WHO)

| Share of GNP in % | Number of Countries | | | | | | |
	AFRO	AMRO	SEARO	EURO	EMRO	WPRO	Total
Under 5%	21	13	9	9	15	5	72
5% and over	3	24	1	2	5	8	57
Total	24	27	10	35	20	13	129
Information unavailable	20	7	1	–	2	7	37
Overall	44	34	11	35	22	20	166

AFRO Regional Office of Africa
AMRO Regional Office of the Americas
SEARO Regional Office of Southeast Asia
EURO Regional Office of Europe
EMRO Regional Office of Eastern Mediterranean
WPRO Regional Office of Western Pacific

TABLE 2

Share of Resources Alloted to Health and Used for Primary Health Care (in Regions of WHO)

| Share in % | Number of Countries | | | | | | |
	AFRO	AMRO	SEARO	EURO	EMRO	WPRO	Total
Under 20%	4	6	–	3	2	4	19
20, 0-29, 9%	4	–	1	5	4	3	17
30, 0-39, 9%	3	–	3	2	3	1	12
40, 0-49, 9%	5	–	1	3	3	1	13
50, 0-59, 9%	3	1	1	1	1	5	12
60, 0-69, 9%	2	–	2	–	1	–	5
70, 0-79, 9%	–	–	–	–	–	–	–
80 and over	–	1	1	1	1	–	4
Total	21	8	9	15	15	14	82
Information unavailable	23	26	2	20	7	6	84
Overall	44	34	11	35	22	20	166

correlation with economic development levels. However, nations from the American Region (AMR) are more likely to devote less to primary care than all other regions.

To make progress toward the achievement of social equity the populations should be provided ample opportunity to improve their basic needs: nutrition, health education, safe water supply, adequate housing, employment and income.

As formulated in Alma-Ata, one of the main prerequisites for the implementation of required measures is the political will to allocate sufficient resources to primary care. The manner by which social and economic support will be provided depends on social and cultural values and on the political system of the country concerned. Measures should be taken to solicit support from social leaders, tradeunions and influential public and religious organizations. It is necessary to look for ways in involving health professionals and members of other social groups and organizations seeking to achieve health for all. Mass campaigns need to be organized in order to provide public support to the movement. These principles from the Alma-Ata Conference have been important for the development of aging policies and their implementation locally.

The Elderly in the USSR

One of the basic laws in society is the law of increasing demands. This law reflects the trend toward the sophistication of demands as expressed by society, individuals and social groups, a set of demands primarily stemming from the evolution of productive forces and culture. Demands already satisfied make way for the other more complex and sophisticated demands. It should be noted that the official acceptance of various societal demands and their satisfaction are stipulated by the USSR Constitution. However, their satisfaction seems unattainable for various reasons discussed below.

On the whole, USSR's aging population is increasing. In 1987 the proportion of males over 60 and females over 55 reached 16.8%. In 1951 it was only about 10.29%. As in other industrialized societies the primary reason for this increase is the reduced birth rate. Thus the percentage of children and teenagers under 16 declined from 32% in 1951 to 26.3% in 1981. Improvements in the average life expectancy in the country have also contributed to this demographic shift. Figure 1 and tables 3 and 4 provide an overview of the age structure of the population as well as the percentage receiving pensions in the society.

The above proportion takes into account *only* the population category whose main income depends on old age pensions. This group includes women over 55 and men over 60. Moreover both the former and the latter

FIGURE 1

Dynamics of Old Age (Min. of People)

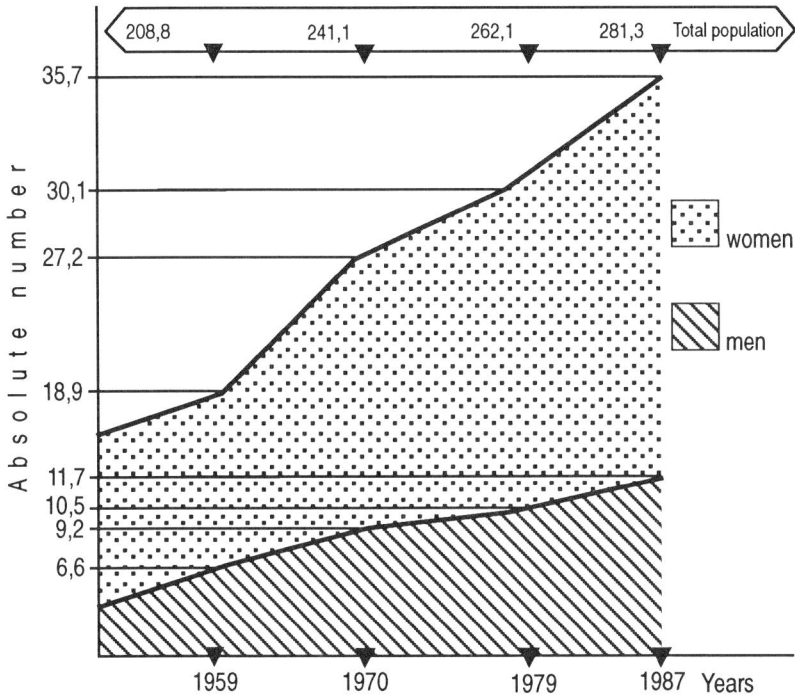

may receive old age pensions on favorable terms. Yet many people entitled to become pensioners still continue to work and do not register their status officially.

Throughout the country there is a general trend toward a smaller family. This trend affects the process of aging in the population; it is also noticeable in the rural areas of various Asian republics. The process is almost complete in Moldavia and is underway in Armenia, Azerbaijan and Kazakhstan. Eventually there will be a decline in the birth rate, and as a corollary, an increase in the number of elderly. It should be noted that a shift towards a lower birth rate and a smaller family size is inescapable for the total population and especially for the regions where the birth rate is still high. (See Table 3)

This phenomenon is a consequence of social equity which has been translated into reality. It has enabled the woman to abandon the traditional

TABLE 3

Age Structure of the Population in 1987 (Percentage of Total) (4)

	Total population			Rural population		
Males	0-16	17-59	60 and over	0-16	17-59	60 and over
Females	0-16	17-54	55 and over	0-16	17-54	55 and over
USSR	27,0	56,2	16,8	31,1	49,3	19,6
RSFSR	23,9	57,8	18,3	26,2	50,6	23,2
Ukraine	23,4	56,1	20,5	23,2	49,4	27,7
Byelorussia	25,0	57,0	18,0	22,5	48,8	28,7
Uzbekistan	42,9	49,1	8,1	48,3	44,7	7,0
Kazakhstan	33,3	54,9	11,8	38,1	49,5	12,4
Georgia	26,6	56,4	17,0	27,5	53,7	18,8
Azerbaijan	34,5	56,0	9,5	37,8	53,2	9,0
Lithuania	24,5	57,0	18,5	24,2	49,4	26,4
Moldavia	30,1	55,6	14,3	32,7	50,5	16,8
Latvia	22,7	57,1	20,2	24,4	52,5	23,1
Kirghizia	39,6	50,5	9,9			
Tadzhikistan	44,7	47,3	8,0	48,4	44,3	7,3
Armenia	31,5	57,1	11,4	34,1	53,2	12,7
Turkmenia	42,7	19,9	7,7	47,1	45,8	7,1
Estonia	23,3	57,0	19,7	23,7	52,8	23,5

TABLE 4

Age Distribution of Pensioners (Percentage as of 01.01.1988) (4)

		Granting of pensions for		
Age	Old age	Length of service	Invalidity	Loss of breadwinner
under 16				34,9
16-19			0,2	13,3
20-29			4,7	0,5
30-39		1,5	9,9	0,7
40-49	0,4	16,4	15,9	1,3
50-54	3,5	41,8	14,1	0,7
55-59	20,6	25,8	17,5	1,1
60-64	27,7	6,8	14,0	2,3
65-69	16,4	3,7	7,3	3,9
70 and upwards	31,4	4,0	16,4	41,3

role of mother and housewife and to adopt a new social role. This shift contributed to a decline in the birth rate. Over the last quarter of this century total birth rates in this country dropped by about 25%. This trend is still continuing. Asian republics and Azerbaijan are not necessarily an exception to this trend. Here the birth rate started to decline in the middle 70s, but still remains high. If the impact of younger age structures in Asian republics and Azerbaijan were excluded from the overall population distribution, the proportion of aged in the total population would exceed the existing level by 15%.

Undoubtedly, the basis for decision-making on meeting the needs of the elderly involves a complex comprehensive evaluation of their health and welfare. The physical, mental, social and economic well-being of the elderly as well as their health status are closely connected. However, difficulties in developing comprehensive evaluation methods arose due to the tendency to give consideration to separate aspects of health and welfare (morbidity, economic support, mental health, social support, etc.). As a first step toward a complex evaluation we are proposing a "hierarchy of demands" (see Figure 2) which is based upon four aspects: daily living activities; physical and mental health; health status; economic status.

Daily Living Activities

Modern living and the avoidance of everyday aggravations seem impossible without the universal availability of support services, such as transportation, trips to the beauty parlor, public catering, etc. The elderly have their specific needs which demand special attention on the part of society. These problems are especially acute for the socially isolated elderly. At present, the country has 10 million of the lonely isolated elderly, many of whom are disabled. Over 700,000 persons need everyday care (of them 320,000 are residing in old people's homes and nursing homes). Services to provide assistance to support ADL include personal care, prosthetic care, the provision of special medical appliances, the provision of foodstuffs and meal preparation, and the provision of housekeeping services.

Physical and Mental Health

As a rule, aging is accompanied by health disorders and chronic diseases typical of old age. Old age is characterized by the abrupt reduction in the main physiological functions, reduction in adaptation and the increasing threat of death. In the USSR it is acknowledged that the assessments of health status and morbidity prevalence rates are most suitable for comparing the results of specialist physicians with the level of health care need. Figures 3 and 4 allow for assessing the prevalence of major chronic diseases among the elderly residing in urban and rural areas.

During 1980-1988, in accordance with the Plan of Collaboration with the WHO's Regional Office for Europe, the WHO Collaboration Center for PHC in Alma-Ata was conducting research into intersectorial collaboration

FIGURE 2

Welfare of the Elderly—The Need in Services

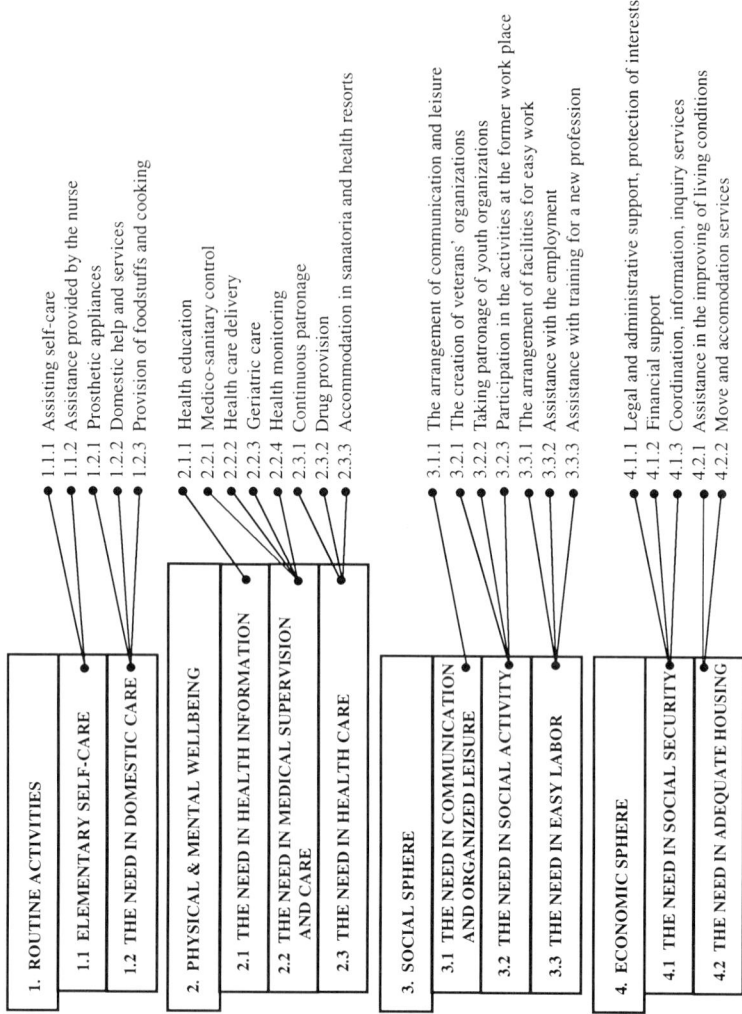

1. ROUTINE ACTIVITIES

1.1 ELEMENTARY SELF-CARE
- 1.1.1 Assisting self-care
- 1.1.2 Assistance provided by the nurse

1.2 THE NEED IN DOMESTIC CARE
- 1.2.1 Prosthetic appliances
- 1.2.2 Domestic help and services
- 1.2.3 Provision of foodstuffs and cooking

2. PHYSICAL & MENTAL WELLBEING

2.1 THE NEED IN HEALTH INFORMATION
- 2.1.1 Health education
- 2.2.1 Medico-sanitary control

2.2 THE NEED IN MEDICAL SUPERVISION AND CARE
- 2.2.2 Health care delivery
- 2.2.3 Geriatric care
- 2.2.4 Health monitoring

2.3 THE NEED IN HEALTH CARE
- 2.3.1 Continuous patronage
- 2.3.2 Drug provision
- 2.3.3 Accommodation in sanatoria and health resorts

3. SOCIAL SPHERE

3.1 THE NEED IN COMMUNICATION AND ORGANIZED LEISURE
- 3.1.1 The arrangement of communication and leisure
- 3.2.1 The creation of veterans' organizations

3.2 THE NEED IN SOCIAL ACTIVITY
- 3.2.2 Taking patronage of youth organizations
- 3.2.3 Participation in the activities at the former work place

3.3 THE NEED IN EASY LABOR
- 3.3.1 The arrangement of facilities for easy work
- 3.3.2 Assistance with the employment
- 3.3.3 Assistance with training for a new profession

4. ECONOMIC SPHERE

4.1 THE NEED IN SOCIAL SECURITY
- 4.1.1 Legal and administrative support, protection of interests
- 4.1.2 Financial support
- 4.1.3 Coordination, information, inquiry services

4.2 THE NEED IN ADEQUATE HOUSING
- 4.2.1 Assistance in the improving of living conditions
- 4.2.2 Move and accomodation services

and community involvement in the provision of primary health care to various population groups. The investigators (Dr. V. M. Konukhov and staff) studied the work capacity and morbidity of pensioners residing in Alma-Ata (n=3,000). The morbidity of pensioners is mainly chronic.

FIGURE 3

Prevalance of Major Chronic Diseases among the Working and Retired Elderly Population According to the Data of Three Years' Recourse to Health Care and Medical Examinations (5)

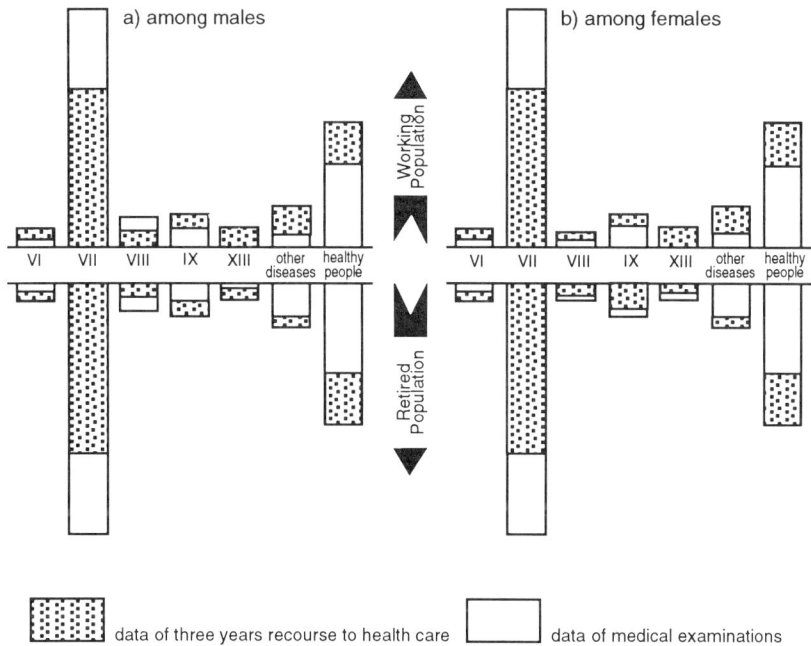

The leading disorders were blood circulatory disorders (42.5% of all pathology), respiratory diseases (14.6%), diseases of musculo-skeletal system and connective tissues (11.15%), diseases of the nervous system and sense organs (10.4%), and gastro-intestinal diseases (9.7%). These disease classifications represent 88.3% of the total morbidity of the populations studied. By means of expert assessment the elderly contingent was divided into five functional capacity groups and four health status groups (Tables 5 and 6).

Generally assessments of morbidity, functional capacity and health status of the elderly are undertaken in order to measure the health promotion of this contingent. Thus, we have made an attempt to compare the objective

FIGURE 4

Prevalence Rate and Structure of Chronic Diseases in Pensioners
Residing in Rural Areas According to the Data on Recourse Rate (n=2100)
and the Data of Complex Medical Examinations (n=650) (5)

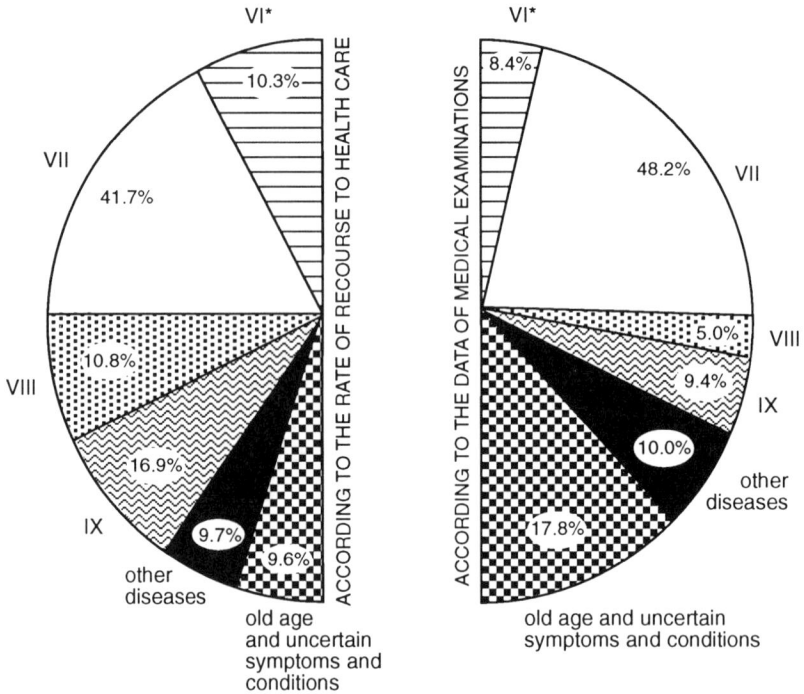

TABLE 5

Assessment of Working Capacity of the Elderly

Group	Health status	% of persons examined
I	Fully incapacitated, needs constant care	1.8
II	Fully incapacitated, capable of self-care	18.5
III	Reduced work capacity	28.1
IV	Working capacity preserved but under favourable working conditions	40.1
V	Working capacity fully preserved	13.5

TABLE 6

Assessment of Health Status of the Elderly

Group	Health status	% of persons examined
I	Health without chronic diseases	1.4
II	Minor functional disorders	9.9
III	Chronic disease without serious functional impairment	48.3
IV	Chronic disease with marked functional impairment	40.4

and the subjective assessments of individual health. All pensioners of groups I and II characterized their health as "good" and "satisfactory," as well as 3.4% of group III and 0.7% of group IV. "Unsatisfactory" and "poor" health was reported by 84.6%, all of those in groups III and IV. Only 4.1% of individuals entering these two groups were more optimistic about their health than their physicians. Thus, we found a correlation between subjective and objective assessments of individual health.

The research of Dr. Kurlevtov and his staff have enabled us to identify the need for medical and other services provision if the protection of the mental and physical health of the elderly is to be assured. These needs are as follows: health information, medical supervision and services, and chronic care. Further specification of needs is outlined in figure 2.

Social Status

The level of maturity and social participation arouse in the elder generation the need for self-respect as they retire. Retirement fundamentally alters the pattern of life; in the long run a break in the rhythm of lives is detrimental to health. One's social routine is affected and alienation is increased.

The new set of attitudes a pensioner has to face, may affect his psychological well-being. Elderly people crave for communication, especially those who live isolated from relatives. Thus the society is confronting the problem of how to restore the social status of retirees. Sociological studies of the elderly suggest that the elderly are aware of two ways of solving the problem: to resume work, and to maintain a social life. Our research found that 13.5% of the pensioners were working and 40.1% could work under favorable conditions. The interview survey of pensioners has shown that 37.6% of retired pensioners might easily resume work. At the Constituent Assembly of the All-Union Organization of War and Labor Veterans (1986) it was stressed that millions of retired people could, in fact, re-enter the work force and also that they expressed a desire to do so. The lack of social interaction has led to the creation of hobby clubs as well as veterans' clubs set up either at their former work place or at their place of residence. And, naturally, in order to provide employment for pensioners the society has to make arrangements for suitable work settings and also set up centers for training these "new" workers.

Well-Being

The material needs of the elderly are associated with the actual or perceived loss of sufficient income. In addition, many of these persons never worked or only worked a short amount of time prior to retirement (mostly women). The USSR Constitution acknowledges the right of every citizen to material support in old age. The available source of income—a pension, as a rule—should guarantee the satisfaction of not only everyday needs, but also of social needs which are in line with the existing social standards. Until now pensions had been calculated on the basis of one's salary. At present, maximal pensions constitute 70-75% of former salaries. The breakdown of pensioners according to the size of the pension is presented in Table 7.

TABLE 7

Breakdown of Pensioners According to the Size of Pension (6)

	All pensioners		Old age pensioners	
	1983	1987	1983	1987
	In accordance with the Law on Pensions Granted by the State			
Total (Mi people) with monthly pensions	43,2	48,4	28	33
up to 60 roubles	49,5	31,4	40,2	20,2
from 60 to 100 roubles	29,3	33,9	32,9	38,3
100 roubles and over	21,2	34,7	26,9	41,5
	In accordance with the Law on Pensions granted to the members of collective farms			
Total (Mi people) with monthly pensions	10,4	9,7	9,2	8,8
up to 60 roubles	92,4	84,7	93,0	85,6
from 60 to 100 roubles	6,4	11,8	6,0	10,8
100 roubles and over	1,2	3,5	1,0	3,6

Thus, average pensions granted to workers and office employees in old age amount to 89.4 roubles per month. In order, to identify ways for raising the elderly's material well-being Goskomstat of the USSR conducted a survey of budgets of pensioners' families whose pensions constitute their only source of income. The data collected show that a pensioner residing in Moscow spends 52% of his income for food, 21% for other consumer goods, 6% for clothing, footwear and textiles, 2.6% for medications, and 0.5% for books and newspapers. Transportation makes up 2.3%, rent 7%, phone bills 2.3%, everyday services 0.5%, entertainment 1%, and State's subsidies for the accommodation of pensioners at sanatoria and rest homes make up 1%.

To be equitable with regard to the needy, the system should assure that the disabled, children who have lost their breadwinner, and the elderly are able to satisfy their most urgent needs. According to research data provided by the Research Institute of Labor, 52% of elderly pensioners, 71% of disabled and 68% of persons who have lost their breadwinner are not able to fully satisfy their needs. It should be noted that the elderly are not in a position to modify their needs all of a sudden. Formerly they had been able to satisfy the needs completely. For example, it has been shown that those people who used to have high earnings are more prone to continue working because they are not able to adjust to the abrupt loss of income. Another important factor is that specific needs of the elderly include the procurement of drugs, a healthy diet with adequate fresh produce, and increased need for everyday services associated with the degradation of their physical capacity, for example.

The study of the needs of the elderly suggest that it is necessary to design a system for social security and primary health care which is balanced and which also offers good prospects for implementation. Under the existing medico-demographic conditions the development of services provided in this system is one of the important indicators of social justice.

Trends in Social Policy and the Elderly

Demographic aging urges the society, that is, its social, economic, political, legal and cultural institutions, to respond in various ways to the growth of the absolute number and proportion of old people. Communities should adjust through developing new standards, criteria and attitudes with respect to the aged, e.g., by redefining the role and status of the aged within the social structure. Meeting the needs of the elderly within the context of other age groups is becoming one of the major trends in social policies of most countries. Population aging alters the attitudes toward aging, both on the part of the entire society, as well as on the part of various social groups and communities.

Social policies as they affect the aged—their goals, their status within society and the whole range of their relationships to social environments—

are a kind of litmus test of social equity and justice under various socio-economic systems. The nature of the State system determines the prevalent attitudes toward such important life events as retirement. The State system determines the scope of work and leisure in old age, in general. The system predetermines the roles and functions of old people who have retired, expanding or limiting, supporting or hampering their activity levels in various spheres.

The realization of socioeconomic rights with a view to raising the standards of life and gradually eradicating social inequities means the satisfaction of a fundamental human need: social justice. This is an important basis for social satisfaction. Life satisfaction within the context of social justice can be achieved only through integrative social policies based on realistic perceptions and reflecting the real state of affairs and attitudes found in the society. In the first instance, the objective evaluation of the efficiency and effectiveness of social security and health systems should be implied. Namely these systems are designed to satisfy the needs of the elderly. They are to ensure that the elderly enjoy a status, lifestyles and life standards comparable to those of other people. This is achieved through a complex of measures provided by the socialist society which are aiming at the satisfaction of two major fundamental needs—labor and material well-being.

In the USSR social security performs a vast number of functions. The prominent are: (1) distribution of material wealth which affects the availability and distribution of public funds; (2) social rehabilitation which has an impact on the satisfaction of specific needs of the elderly and the disabled; (3) provision of care with an attention to the needs of the above population groups, and (4) the promotion and protection of their rights. Social security comprises a vast range of services. Only a few types of services will be discussed here: (1) material well-being and social rehabilitation; (2) medical rehabilitation and socio-cultural services.

These services enable the equalizing of the material well-being of various population strata, because under socialism such differences continue to exist. Such equalization can be achieved through free health care, education and other services paid by public funds. Because of the increasing role of social services in the patterns of consumption the necessity arises to assess the costs of services with respect to both the real incomes of the population and the assessment of the overall consumption. Such assessment is especially important when services are provided free-of-charge and when they are consumed by the disabled who are granted both public payments directly (pensions and grants) and free or partly paid services.

The attainment of an optimal balance between separate types of social security makes it possible to pay greater attention to both the needs and demands of the disabled in a socialist society as well as all-round satisfaction

of the aged. The issue here is the development of such services as employment and professional training of partly disabled persons, the provision of
medical services enabling such individuals to restore their social status.
The types of social security services are geared to specific forms of rehabilitation: 1) material and socio-domestic, 2) socio-occupational or professional,
and 3) medical and socio-cultural. Functionally, each of these types may
correspond not only to a single form, but to other forms of social rehabilitation as well. Each type comprises the services provided by the overall
public system of services, but on terms especially appropriate for the
disabled, and a range of social services exclusively targeted.
The breakdown of social services might be as follows:

1. Services concerned with the provision of material well-being and socio-
    occupational rehabilitations: a) a complex of specialized services,
    (e.g.,institutionalized care, the supervision of the disabled residing at
    home and care by boarding houses for the disabled); b) services provided
    by the overall public system (housing and domestic services, public
    transportation, communications, shopping assistance, public catering).
2. Socio-occupational (professional) rehabilitation services: a) a complex of
    specialized services (employment and professional training for new
    occupations in special environments); b) services provided by the overall
    public system (employment and professional training for usual work
    environments).
3. Medical rehabilitation services: a) a complex of specialized services
    (certification of a disability status, for prosthetics, and for special medical
    appliances); b) services provided by the overall public system (curative-
    preventive care, sanatoria resort treatment, medical certification of
    temporary disability, drug therapy).
4. Socio-cultural services: a) a complex of specialized services (e.g.,
    services provided by the blind/deaf societies); b) services provided by the
    overall public system (e.g., access to places of entertainment).

Such people should live at home, in their normal environment. They
require not only treatment, but also good care which can be provided by their
relatives under the supervision of skilled out-patient physicians and nursing
personnel. Yet this care is problematic because the children and relatives of
the elderly are busy during the day. Hence, in order to provide such care it is
necessary to solve a whole range of socio-economic problems associated with
non-material matters, e.g., need to develop and implement a system of
material incentives to stimulate those who take care of their elderly parents
and relatives. Specifically, caregivers need more flexible working schedules
and the opportunity to work at home.

The needs of the elderly are covered by the public consumption funds (Figures 5 and 6). Public consumption funds cover such things as the allocation of pensions and grants and costs of medical services, accommodations in old people's homes and boarding houses.

FIGURE 5

Dynamics of Payments and Grants to the Population Provided at the Expense of Public Funds of Consumption of the USSR (6)

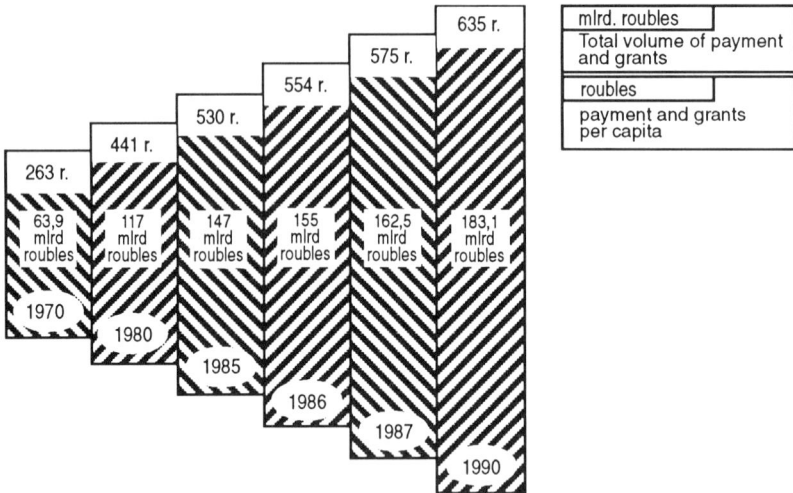

Many aspects of social security are closely related to former employment and income, e.g., the allocation of pensions. Sizes of pensions depend on the length of service as well as the nature, intensity and complexity of one's previous work. Evidently, since the pension does not constitute a simple repayment system, the pension amount depends upon social factors. The social status of pensioners depends on their contributions to social labor. At the same time, part of the resources of the public consumption fund is distributed irrespective of absolute labor contributions (figure 7).

Government policy pertaining to the distribution of income is based on the fact that salaries and wages constitute its main source. Great attention is given to direct payments from the public consumption funds whose amount is expected to increase more rapidly than the wage fund. It is worth noting that for a rather long time a balance has been maintained between monetary payments on the one hand and free services and incentives made available from public consumption funds on the other.

FIGURE 6

Sources of Public Funds of Consumption of the USSR and Their Distribution

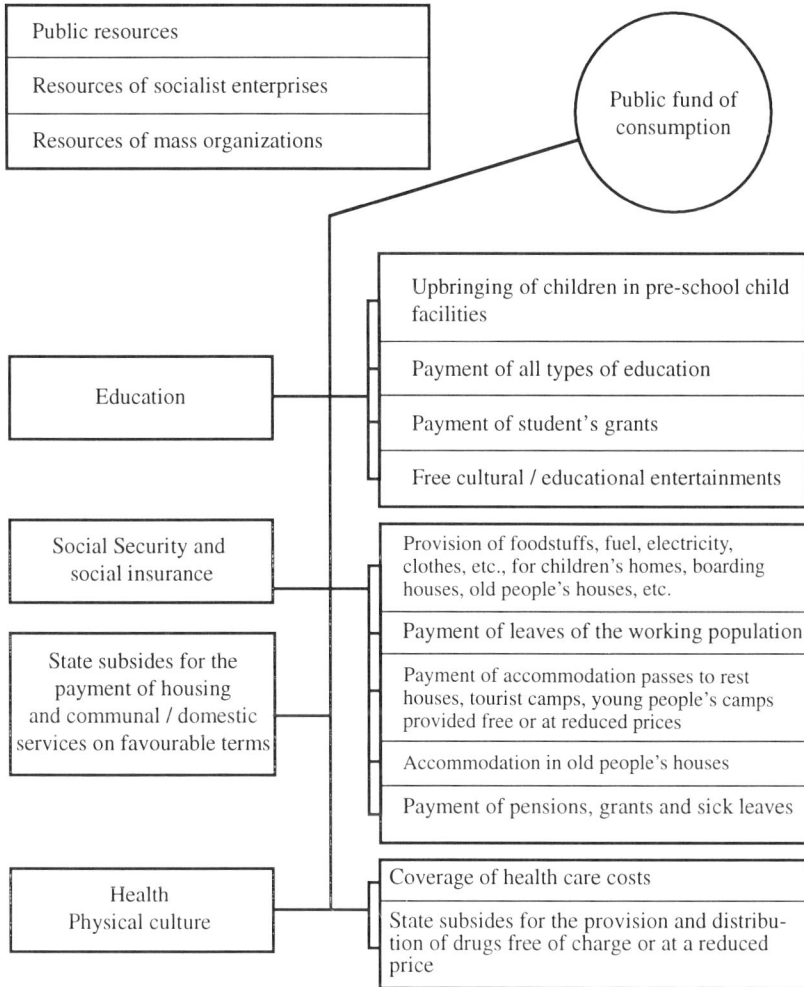

The differences between monetary payments lie not only in their forms and outcomes but also in the patterns of provision. The allocation of payments depends on the quantity and quality of labor; it is carried out in accordance with the socialist distributive principle, i.e, according to labor input. The provision of services does not depend on these; in some cases

FIGURE 7

Patterns of Distribution of the Resources of Public Funds
of Consumption among the Elderly

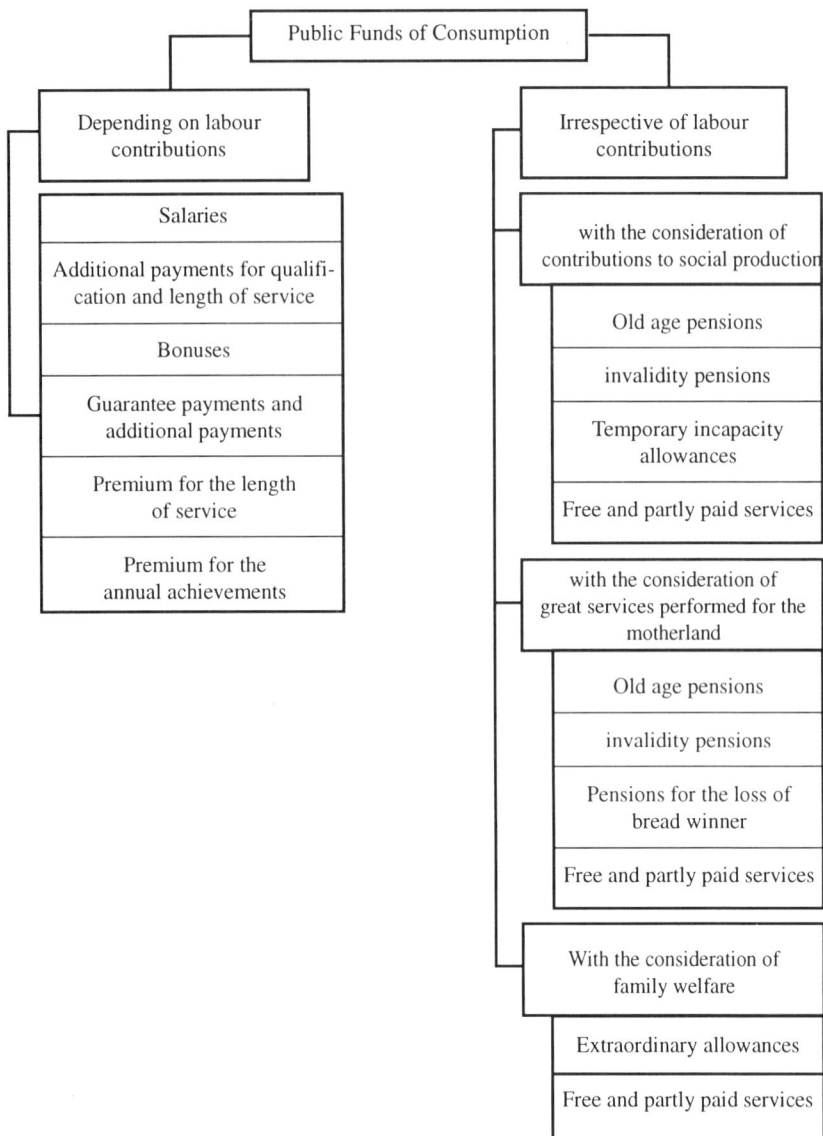

services are provided as the need arises (e.g., health care), in other instances,
the available resources and opportunities are taken into account.

The basis of this distributional approach is an absolute recognition by the state of the variety of needs and the granting of equal opportunity for all citizens to satisfy them. In this case social justice is expressed in the acknowledgement of the dignity and value of each individual. Thus in a situation where it is not yet possible to guarantee full satisfaction of needs and demands to all people, the preference is given to those individuals who worked most for the benefit of society, who have created the material values and the national wealth for the benefit of future generations. It has been proven that each person over his active period of life produces much more than he or she consumes. If the average age for entering the work force is 19, and the average age for retiring is 62, by 28 years of age a person fully covers all costs for his upbringing in early age, even including the cost of education, housing and social care in old age. In the years past their 28th year a person creates a net profit for the society. Thus, the elderly person who has been working for many years has already paid in advance for his living in old age. It would therefore be in accordance with the principles of social justice to meet his needs.

When discussing the role that public consumption plays in the realization of the principle of justice, M. Gorbachev, General Secretary of the CPSU Central Committee, Chairman of the Presidium of the Supreme Soviet of the USSR, was quoted as saying:

> ...We are basing our argument on the assumption that these funds are not charity funds. They are playing an important role in providing all citizens with equal access to education and culture, in equalizing the conditions for child rearing, and in facilitating life for those who for this or that reason require continuous assistance or extraordinary allowances. At the same time, this is a means to encourage and stimulate qualified and skilled labor.

In accordance with the provision of the "law on state industrial enterprise," the working collectives are to show constant solicitude to workers, war veterans and the disabled. They are responsible for providing suitable work settings for pensioners who are still able to work and for involving them in social activities. In addition, the industrial enterprises take part in the construction of old people's homes and facilities for the disabled, as well as sponsor them and provide the necessary material and financial support for them. As a corollary, the granting of equal rights to all citizens is in no way contradicting the principle of social justice. Naturally, the principle of social justice should not be oversimplified. According to the USSR Constitution all citizens of the country have the right to material support in old age. However more substantial pensions are allocated to those who lost their health defending the motherland.

In line with the reforms currently underway in the country the government is planning to improve fundamentally the nation's well-being. At present the improvement of the pension system represents one of the most urgent social policy issues to be addressed. The employment of pensioners also remains a problem to be solved. The precarious state of the health system and the quality of care are causing public concern. The scholar E.I. Tchazov, USSR's Public Health Minister, believes that the deficiencies in the public health system are primarily having an adverse effect on geriatric care. A nationwide system of geriatric care needs to be established. The problem of social care for the elderly, i.e., the provision of various specific services corresponding to the needs of the elderly also demands close attention. The urgency of the problem of housing for senior citizens consists not merely in providing a comfortable apartment for each family. Old people should have separate apartments but in the neighborhood with younger people so as to make their distribution more natural. The artificial concentration of the old, sick and infirm in one place violates the law of nature: young shoots are growing under the canopy of mature trees; and when becoming older and stronger young trees in turn prolong the lives of century-old trees. Lonely trees wither in the wind and eventually fall.

Community Involvement in the Implementation of Target Programs of Medico-Social Care

The International Conference on Primary Health Care (Alma-Ata, 1978) emphasized the fact that although health services will always receive priority attention, they alone will not protect people from illness. Health, which is a state of complete physical, mental and social well-being, and not merely the absence of disease or infirmity, is attainable only through the concerted effort of many other social and economic sectors, in addition to the health sector. This effort must be supported by extensive community involvement.

The resources allocated by the health and social security services are, of course, not unlimited, and the reason for the ineffectiveness of medico-social care lies in poor community support. Our research findings help reveal the two main tendencies responsible for this ineffectiveness.

On the one hand, formal mechanisms of community involvement in health care provision and centralized management of community involvement have created a situation where both the community leaders and the health professionals believe that it is up to the various bodies of government to address these needs. Furthermore the centralization of management has resulted in brushing aside "community involvement" as a managerial "branch," thereby denying it relevancy for the planning and administration of services. This was reflected in the limited evaluation criteria used traditionally, e.g., the number of new members and the sum total of financial resources that have been collected. These criteria and indicators are unable to characterize efficiency and effectiveness. The output of the staffs are de-emphasized. We continue to observe that community involvement in solving health problems is demphasized.

With regard to health issues, the medical training programs lack a clear conception of equal responsibility to be shared between the community and the health sector. Consequently the importance of public support for the detection and resolution of health problems is somewhat neglected. The population therefore is often left uninformed about problems that are arising.

Meanwhile, community involvement implies the responsibility for one's own health and for the health of others, coupled with the deliberate effort to improve the health of the community. The importance of community involvement in the provision of medico-social care consists not only in the allocation of additional financial and manpower resources, but also in fostering humaneness in young people.

We have conducted a study of target programs of medico-social care provision for the elderly. Presently there exist three types of such programs: (1) Charity Society programs, (2) Red Cross programs, and (3) the integrated, intersectorial target program "Care." The study was concerned with the general focus of the programs (objectives, target groups, and structure) as well as the sources of support (financial subsidies, professional support, and legal mandate and organizational context). We will discuss these three programs below.

Medico-Social Care Provided by the "Charity" Societies

The members of these societies are seeking to provide social care for the lonely elderly people. As a rule outside expertise is not requested and the supervision by authorities and/or voluntary organizations is not practiced.

The "Charity" Societies' involvement is prompted by a feeling of compassion and charity. The forms and methods of work and the lists of persons needing medico-social care are discussed at the society's meetings. The main types of services offered are: publicity about charity at various meetings and through mass media; communication with the elderly, domestic help, delivery of books and magazines, and reading aloud to those requesting it. In other words, the society provides individualized services.

Initially, the "Charity" Society was backed up by the donations and contributions from sponsoring organizations. Moreover these societies were set up by people with charitable inclinations who were declining the help of official authorities and voluntary organizations.

Yet when confronted with the whole range of problems needing immediate attention the societies' organizers became acutely aware of the lack of financial support. Financial support is essential for supplying prosthetic devices for the disabled. At present, the majority of "Charity" societies are sponsored by large industrial enterprises. They also receive subsidies from various cooperative movements which are increasing in this country.

One of the "Charity" organizers commented recently:

> Because we do not have as yet a well developed system, a sound strategy and the necessary facilities, we cannot depend upon public enthusiasm in support of our cause. That is why our first leaders could be characterized as somewhat extravagant idealists with strong charitable inclinations, yet devoid of organizational skills and the ability to concentrate on major tasks. We have attained our preliminary goal, that is, drawing the public's attention to the problems of need. To continue like this would mean exploiting public enthusiasm.

The "Charity" Society is presently operating within the framework of the Soviet Fund for Health and Charity. This is an amateur voluntary organization which has its own organizers and sponsors. Its activities are regulated by the Charter of the Fund, as stipulated in the USSR Constitution. In addition, its activities are not subject to taxation. In order to stimulate charitable actions, the profits of sponsors transferred to the societies' bank accounts are not subject to taxation either. A society's organization operating within a community has the right to make a profit.

As a rule the societies are created under the aegis of one of the founding organizations which provides all essential assistance. For example, in Alma-Ata, the "Charity" Society is sponsored by the City Komsomol Committee, whereas in Riga, it is sponsored by the Hotel Department and the Tramways and Trolleybus Depot.

The importance of the "Charity" Society consists in the fact that it draws the attention of wide population strata to the problems of medico-social care. The projects that will be discussed later show that in spite of the existing programs, the problems relating to medico-social care still remain. Essentially "Charity" societies are instrumental in helping publicize the issues by making the public aware that the social problems are everyone's concern and that no one should be excluded. At the same time, these programs cannot be viewed as independent. They require financial and material support, adequate facilities, managerial consultation and personnel training. Yet according to a motivations study involving community members and a public opinion poll, social goals and objectives can be achieved along with the generation of donations within a given community, that is, the actual programs, enables the people to see the tangible outcome of their charitable actions.

Programs Implemented by Red Cross Charity Societies

These programs have existed for many years. In our country the Red Cross is a voluntary organization reaching a significant portion of the population. Its medico-social activity is directed primarily at the lonely elderly in need of health care. The work is organized by the Society's Regional Committee. Direct organizers are health visitors who are staff members of the Red Cross Charity Service. They perform the treatment procedures—prescribed by the local health services physicians— and coordinate the delivery of social care. Red Cross active members, called activists, work under the supervision of charity nurses. They receive training through a special medico-social care program. Young activists—members of Red Cross medical clubs who are also supervised by charity nurses—are recruited among school children. Recently a new form of organizing the activists became widely popular: nursing students join the units of community nurses who deliver medico-social care to the elderly within the framework of the Red Cross Charity Service.

Activists and community nurses work on a voluntary basis in their spare time. Salaries of both teachers and instructors, as well as the cost of equipment (such as badges, certificates, bags, first aid kits and outfits) are covered by the Red Cross. The Red Cross also pays the staff members of the Charity Service. The financial resources of the Red Cross are derived from membership dues and donations. Because medico-social care is one of the aspects of material support provided by the Soviet Red Cross to the needy, the organization of charitable thrift stores as well as benefit auctions and concerts are becoming increasingly popular.

The activity of the Red Cross Society is regulated by its Statutes and is defined by a number of articles in the USSR Constitution. Suffice it to say that in addition to being the organizer and sponsor of the Soviet Fund for Health and Charity, the Red Cross is one of the main voluntary organizations whose primary functions are health promotion and charity. But its facilities and resources are centralized and the powers of providing financial and material aid are delegated to various large regional departments of the Red Cross Society.

The Red Cross Society has its own methodological units whose responsibility it is to summarize the existing expertise and make practical recommendations. The Society has a number of contracts with scientific research institutes. Specifically, the WHO Collaborating Center for PHC is cooperating with the Red Cross in studying the effectiveness of community involvement in PHCs. Postgraduate training of the Society's officers is provided by the Central Institute for Advanced Medical Studies in Alma-Ata.

The impact of this project consists in the direct provision of medico-social care for the lonely elderly in need of assistance. Moreover the involvement of school children and nursing students is helping to develop a humanistic outlook in young people and to orient them as to their future occupational choices. Yet the fact that this project functions within the Red Cross Charity Service, i.e, its relative autonomy, is a disadvantage. Specifically, the scantiness of financial and material resources has resulted in limiting the number of persons under care.

The "Care" Medico-Social Program

The "Care" program is not a national governmental community-oriented program. Program coordination and management are performed by local authorities, specifically the AD HOC commission of the Soviets of peoples' deputies. In its initial phase the program attempted to detect those individuals in need of care. This first phase was implemented in 1987 during the All-Union campaign at a time when the essential needs of the aged were uncovered. Based on these findings, the activities of a number of organizations were subsequently coordinated. The most important ones are:

1. The Department of Social Security—the main local body responsible for the welfare of the elderly. At present, this department establishes social care units staffed by social workers who have undergone specialized training. The network of the old people's homes is expanding. Additional residential centers are being built providing the lonely elderly (singles or couples) with a full range of domestic and social services, the opportunity for light work, as well as recreational facilities.
2. The Board of Health, which is responsible for the management of geriatric care.
3. Organizations and enterprises, i.e., former work settings of the pensioners. Their sponsorship consists in making arrangements for providing employment to the pensioners based on the latter's physical abilities. They also offer passes for accommodations at various sanatoria based upon trade union membership and organize festivities on holidays and birthdays. Youth organizations, such as the Komsomol and the Pioneers, also support pensioners. Their activities also involve minor domestic tasks such as delivering drugs, magazines, books and food. Medical units of students are active in providing health care for the aged, and the student construction teams help build and remodel residential facilities. Communication problems are also addressed. The integration of the elderly into the social life is effected under the supervision of the local department of the Council of Veterans.

Financial support for the "Care" program is more easily available than it is for the first two sectors because the budget is managed by the local Soviets of people's deputies. Moreover, they have in their account the money from local enterprises which is to be allotted for social development.

According to the USSR Constitution and as a result of broad public discussion at the l9th Party Conference the Soviets of people's deputies—the local bodies of authority—are delegated all necessary powers. They have the right (1) to finance programs and to utilize for this purpose the funds of all the various enterprises and institutions; (2) to coordinate program implementation, and (3) to earmark special subsidies as well as deal with taxation issues.

Summary

The three community health projects (CHP) in the field of medical and social care presented above allow us to draw the following conclusions. Because community health and social welfare policies are affecting primarily the members of the community, community involvement in the implementation of these projects is crucial. Based on the results of sociological surveys and analyses we must stress the necessity of the above CHPs and all other projects which are to emerge in the future. These projects facilitate the involvement of the population in health issues, for community involvement is one of the goals we hope to achieve. As far as the mechanisms of community support and autonomy are concerned, we feel that in our country's present context, the most appropriate ones are programs such as "Care" which are supported by the government on a permanent basis and which take into account the opinions of all interested organizations.

Yet this variant of the program is far from ideal. In our opinion, such a program should coordinate the implementation of all projects and programs dealing with this problem in communal settings. The emphasis should be placed on a scientific study of the needs of the elderly. Upon priority selection, comprehensive programming should follow, which should be based on the experience of all social groups and voluntary organizations. Such programming should be performed directly by the organizations' co-leaders. This would stimulate local initiative and help reduce the overly bureaucratic orientation of community involvement. Program budgeting should also be implemented taking into consideration the measures to be financed and the skills of the people in charge of implementing them. The power for allocating material and financial resources should be delegated more extensively.

We feel that in this manner the community will perform its duty to the persons of the "third age." We must not only add years to life, but add life to years. To reach this goal legal provisions and guarantees are not sufficient. The care of the aged cannot be viewed in terms of "measures." It is not only an honorable right, it is everyone's duty. And not only because old age is the fate of every human being. It is the indicator of a society's moral state. As Stefan Zweig put it: "True compassion demands action, not sentimentality; this is the only way to help."

References

Gorbachev. Political Report of the Central Committee of the 27th Congress of the Communist Party of the Soviet Union. M., 1986.-128 c.

9

The Political Economy Perspective of Health and Medical Care Policies for the Aged in Japan: Centering on the Decade of Free Medical Care Program for the Aged

Yasuhito Kinoshita

Introduction

With accumulating knowledge of the aging process and living situations of the aged, it is fairly well understood today that provision of quality health and medical care services is essential for the well-being of the aged, but this is indeed a very difficult task to accomplish for any nation since this should be done cost effectively at the same time. It also requires reconsideration of the still dominant concept of the "medical model" and reorganization of cure-oriented health and medical care systems. Japan is no exception.

The decade of 1973-1982 was quite unique in the Japanese history of health and medical care for the aged. The decade was known, and is now remembered with nostalgia, by the Japanese as the period of the free medical care program for the aged (*rojin iryo muryoka*), and it was true that those over 70 years old and the "bedridden" between the ages of 65 and 69 were entitled to receive both ambulatory and hospital care services free of charge.

This policy was unique in several important points. For instance, the process of its establishment was unusual compared with previous examples of policy revisions in Japan. The impact of the program was dramatic, as seen in a rapid increase of medical expenditures for the aged and in higher rates of their receiving medical care. Opinions on its effectiveness varied a great deal within the government circles, the opposition parties in the parliament, interest groups such as the Japanese Medical Doctors' Association, and the public generally represented by the mass media, triggering emotional rather than rational controversies. Furthermore, discontinuation of the free medical care program paved the way toward a more fundamental and long-range policy in provision of health and medical care for the aged, unfortunately, however, without gaining a consensus as to what would be the quality of geriatric services, how the medical care costs for the aged should be generationally shared, what measures should be taken in order to control the ever growing expenditures, and so forth.

While structurally more solid and more comprehensive in scope, it remains to be seen whether or not the new system established after the free medical care program is working in the way it was intended by the government. A trial and error approach continues.

The vicissitudes of the free medical care program were direct outcomes from interactions between prevailing political situations and changing economic conditions in Japan when the nation was preparing for a social system to cope with aging problems. Therefore, a focus on the decade of the free medical care program for the aged provides us with a strategic perspective to understand how Japan is approaching the societal problems of aging in general, and health and medical care issues for the aged in particular.

Major Characteristics of Japan's Aging Population

Although much is known about Japan's aging population, it may be necessary to present its major characteristics as it provides a general background for our discussion.

The demographic characteristics may be summarized in the following four points: First, life expectancies for both men and women have been the highest in the world since around 1985. In 1989 that of men was 75.91 years and for women it was 81.77 years, both only closely matched by such countries as Iceland, Sweden, Switzerland and France. Regarding life expectancies at the age of 65 in 1989, it was 16.22 years for men and 19.95 years for women, respectively.

Second, as Figure 1 illustrates, the proportion of the aged (65 and older) in the total population is estimated to reach a level higher than in other countries. For instance, while the aged accounted for only 4.9% of the total population in 1950, two decades later in 1970 it jumped to 7.1%. And, in 1990, it reached 12%. According to government predictions, it will be 16.3% in 2000 and will reach the all-time high of 23.6% in 2021.

Third, the speed of population aging is much faster in Japan than in other industrialized nations. Figure 2 compares the speed in terms of two indicators commonly used by the Japanese government: the number of years it will take for a given nation to reach 14% from 7%, as well as actual years recorded in both percentages. As shown, it takes France 130 years from the early 1860s to the early 1990s. As to the number of years, it was 85 years for

FIGURE 1

Trends of the Ration of the Aged (65 years and over) to the Total Population

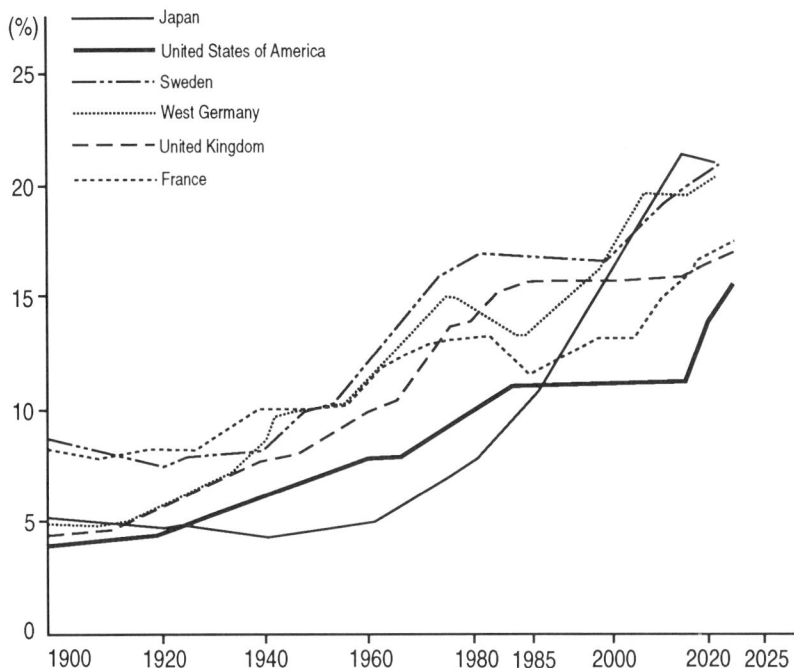

Source: For Japan, Statistics and Information Department, Institute of Population Problems, Ministry of Health and Welfare for other countries, from UN.

Sweden and 45 years for the United Kingdom and West Germany, respectively, and will be 70 years for the United States. In contrast, it will be only 25 years for Japan, corresponding roughly to the period from 1970 to the mid-1990s.

Fourth, as an inevitable consequence, the portion of the old-old (75 and older), the segment which is at higher risk for health and medical care, including long-term care, is expected to increase steadily. In 1985 the old-old accounted for 3.9% of the total national population, and in 2000 the portion will become 6.4%. In addition, in 2025 it will reach the level of 12.9%; in other words, in that year the old-old will account for more than one half of the aged population and the actual number will be approximately 17 million.

Moreover, these demographic changes are taking place when Japanese society is undergoing various social changes typical of highly industrialized

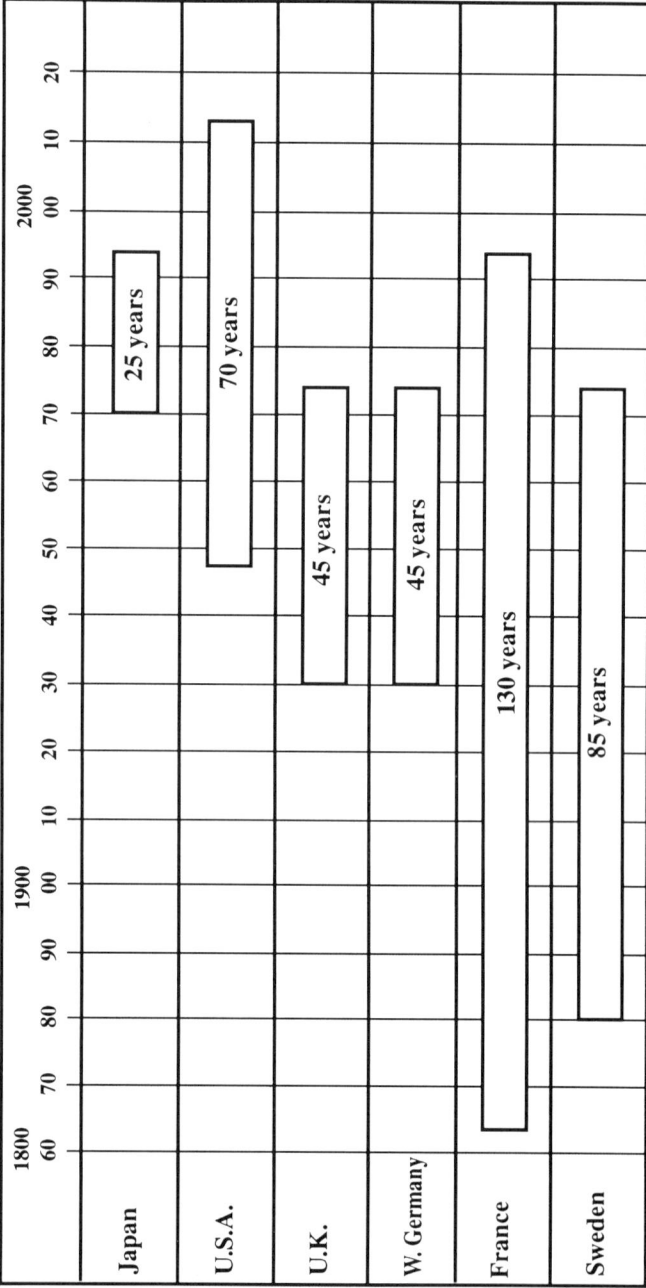

FIGURE 2

International Comparison of the Speed of Population Aging

societies, e.g., smaller size of family, women's participation in gainful employment, geographical dispersion of aged parents and their adult children, and stronger individualistic orientation in life-styles and consciousnesses, just to name a few. Taken together, this means dwindling family responsibility and capability for dependent aged parents and greater roles of public as well as private sectors when it comes to health, medical and social services for the aged.

Of course, these changes are relatively recent ones, but they should be interpreted in the larger social context of drastic social changes that Japan has experienced since the end of World War II, most notably with regard to changes in family systems. Before 1945 Japan had an institutionalized patriarchal family system in which the status of aged parents was secured and filial responsibility was strictly prescribed. In those days, co-living (*dokyo*) was virtually the only way for the aged to live in later life with a realistic assumption that necessary care was to be provided by the daughter-in-law, and since adoption was common for childless couples, those aged without supporting family members were stigmatized as social failures. Following Japan's defeat in the war, a massive wave of democratization set in and the family system was officially abolished, as it was said to be feudalistic.

Although democratic, this has created a kind of normative vacuum regarding which, and to what extent, adult children should be responsible for aged parents since under the present Constitution and Civil Code, adult children are required to cooperate with one another for the well-being of their parents. And, this vacuum has not yet been filled by new sets of norms.

Let us take a look at changing living arrangements of the aged in the post-war period. As pointed out, the traditional arrangement of co-living was practically the only alternative before the war. Even in 1960, 87.3% of the aged were living together with families of their adult children, mostly those of the eldest sons. The proportion was 83.2% in 1970, then it dropped to 73.9% in 1980 and further down to 69.7% in 1985. In addition, there are distinct tendencies for younger cohorts of the aged to live separately from their children more than older cohorts of the aged. Traditional living arrangements are more prevalent in rural regions than in urban areas. These proportions may still look high to Westerners, but to the Japanese, especially for older people, they mean uncertainty and anxiety because the society has not yet developed the necessary service systems.

On the other side of the coin, households of single aged and those of aged couples have been increasing rapidly and will continue to do so for the coming three decades or so. Figure 3 illustrates this trend and other significant trends pertinent to living arrangements and family size in 1970-2020.

To summarize, Japan is presently in the midst of preparation for its version of the welfare state and it must do so before time runs out, which is

FIGURE 3

Future Estimates for the Number of Elderly Households, etc.

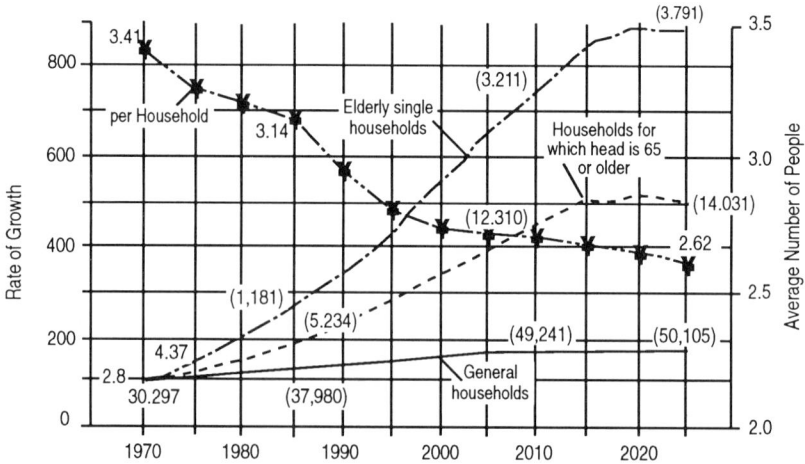

N.B.: In the case of the number of households, it is the growth rate with 1970 as 100. The figures in parenthesis are units of 1,000 households.

Source: Up to 1985 from "State of the Nation Survey" produced by the Statistics Bureau of the General Affairs Agency, 1990 and after from "Future Estimates of the Number of Households in Japan" produced by the MHW Institute of Population Problems.

after all not such a remote possibility. Although Japan is the first non-Western nation experiencing the aging of its population, it is not certain whether or not, or in what way its unique socio-cultural characteristics may help the nation cope with aging problems [1].

Genesis of the Free Medical Care Program for the Aged

The free medical care program for the aged started in January, 1973. However, the Japanese government was not enthusiastic about it and adopted this policy most reluctantly.

Here it is necessary to discuss briefly health insurance systems in Japan. Although the nation is moving toward a simple, standardized health insurance system, current systems are very complex and, therefore, only those characteristics that are relevant to our discussion will be explained. There are six major systems: Government-managed Health Insurance,

Society-managed Health Insurance, National Public Service Employees Mutual Aid Associations, Local Public Service Employees Mutual Aid Associations, Private School Teachers and Employees Mutual Aid Associations, and National Health Insurance. These are all public in nature: membership is mandatory and the insured pay a health insurance tax which is automatically withheld from their salaries or paid directly to operating entities, usually municipal governments, in the case of the self-employed. Also employers must contribute to the systems, as does the national government in the form of a subsidy.

General characteristics of health insurance systems in Japan are shown in Figure 4 which also includes those for day laborers and seamen; today less significant than before.

Private health insurance policies are not necessary to receive medical care; it is purchased not to pay medical bills, but for supplemental purposes. It is not yet popular, but as this chapter indicates, there may be a larger market for it in the near future. Particularly for long-term care of the aged, private insurance is beginning to be sold, and the government is encouraging the industry to expand its role by providing actual services in addition to cash benefits.

Put another way, Japan has health insurance systems to cover all residents and membership is determined according to the working status; non-working family members are covered as dependents of the household head. And, each system is financially managed independently. What is important to note here is the role of National Health Insurance that has been established to cover those who are not qualified for other insurance systems, such as farmers, the self-employed, employees of small corporations (less than six employees), students over 18 years of age and retirees. Thus, unless the aged are covered by one of the major systems, or become dependents of their working adult children, the only health insurance system available to them is National Health Insurance. National Health Insurance is, as it were, a bottom-line safety net system whose contribution rate is also lower than the others, and public support of this system is the largest of all.

The benefit rate for the insured under National Health Insurance is 70% of the cost and the remaining 30% is to be paid directly by the insured at the time they receive medical care. This ratio is the same both for ambulatory care and hospital care, as well as for the insured and their dependents.

For the other major systems, the insured had been entitled to receive a 100% benefit, but since 1984 a 10% cost-sharing requirement has been introduced as part of overall cost sharing measures to reduce national medical costs. Today, the insured are covered for 90% of their medical costs both for ambulatory care and hospital care, but for their dependents coverage is reduced to 70% for ambulatory care and 80% in the case of hospitalization.

FIGURE 4

Outline of Health Insurance Systems in Japan

(at April 1, 1989)

Kind of scheme	Health Insurance (Nat'l Government)	Health Insurance (Health insurance societies)	Day-laborers' health insurance	Seamen's insurance	National health insurance (General citizens / Cities towns & villages, Special Wards)	National health insurance (Nat'l health insurance societies)	National health insurance (Retired Persons / Cities & villages)	Nat'l public service Mutual Assoc.	Local public service M.A.A.	Private school teachers' & employees' M.A.A.
Basic Act	Act No. 70, 1922	Act No. 70, 1922	Act No. 70, 1922	Act No. 73, 1939	Act No. 192, 1958	Act No. 192, 1958	Act No. 192, 1958	Act No. 82, 1983	Act No. 152, 1962	Act No. 245, 1953
Coverage	General employees	General employees	Day Laborers	Seamen	General citizens except employees (i.e. farmers, self-employed persons, etc.)	General citizens except employees	Retired Persons	Employees of nat'l government and executives and employees of the former public corps. (JR,JT,NTT)	Employees of local governments	Private school teachers' & employees'
Responsible body	Nat'l Government	Health insurance societies (1 800)	National Government	National Government	Cities towns & villages (Special Wards) (3 262)	Nat'l health insurance societies (167)	Cities towns & villages	Nat'l public service M.A.A. (27)	Local public service M.A.A. (54)	Private school teachers' & employees' M.A.A.
Injured person (in thousand) (Dependant)	15 863 (17 356)	13 322 (17 223)	139 (72)	162 (844)	41 560	3 778	recount 2 321 (1 176)	1 689 (2 648)	2 965 (3 987)	373 (350)
Contribution rate — Insured person	4.15%	3.500%	1st–11th class ¥55–¥755 per day	4.15%	Annually ¥132 855 per household			2.64–4.98%	3.50–6.99%	3.65%
Contribution rate — Employer	4.15%	4.603%	1st–11th class ¥85–¥1215 per day	4.15%				2.64–4.98%	3.50–6.99%	3.65%
Contribution rate — Total	8.3%	8.137%	1st–11th class ¥140–¥1970 per day	8.3%				5.28–9.96%	7.00–13.98%	7.30%
National subsidy — Administrative expenses	The Whole cost	The Whole cost	The Whole cost	The Whole cost	The Whole cost	The Whole cost	The Whole cost	The Whole cost	The Whole cost	A part of cost
National subsidy — Benefits	Nat'l Subsidy for Health Insurance managed by Government .. 16.4% of benefits	Nat'l Subsidy for Health Insurance managed by Government ... 16.4% of benefits	Medical care benefit ¥3 000 million		50% of benefits	32–52% of benefits	*1 None	None	None	None

Financial resources (Contribution rate, National subsidy)

* There are contributions from schemes for employees instead of national subsidy

*1 There are contributions from schemes for employees instead of national subsidy.

Hereafter, we will consider only National Health Insurance because the majority of the aged belong to this system, and accordingly National Health Insurance has experienced the problems in providing health and medical care to the aged. Funding for the free medical care program for the aged was such that the national and local governments paid directly to National Health Insurance 30% of the costs on behalf of the aged patients, thereby enabling them to receive both types of medical care with no out-of-pocket payments. In other words, if the system had provided 100% coverage, the free medical care program would not have been necessary. This is why the program was regarded by the Japanese as a "welfare" program rather than a health and medical care program: it was added to the existing health insurance systems and as such it had nothing to do with the quality of geriatric services.

Of course, the insured aged paid the health insurance tax to the system if he/she was the household head, or else it was paid by the adult child to whose household they belonged as dependents. However, when their incomes were below a certain level, the tax was much smaller or there was none at all. Because of the basic characteristics of National Health Insurance, the amount of this tax per household was fairly reasonable.

The free medical care program for the aged was not an invention of the national government. Before the program began nationwide in 1973, many prefectural (roughly equivalent to states) and municipal governments (cities, town and villages) had already initiated similar programs of their own as part of their welfare policies for the aged. I stress similar because while the financial mechanism for free medical services was the same, contents of the benefit package were variable; for instance, some only for ambulatory care while others were for both ambulatory and hospital care, and the eligible ages ranged from as high as 80 to 70, 65 or as low as 60 depending on the programs. In addition, many had income restrictions for eligibility.

The first local government to initiate a free medical care program was a small, impoverished farming village in northern Japan, Sawauchi Village, now a legendary place for its innovative preventive and primary care programs; a village plagued with one of the highest infant mortality rates and many stroke cases among the aged. It first started a free medical care program for infants and later expanded it to all residents of the village, with intensive health education programs. The results were miraculous in that the once plagued village soon became a model municipality in health and medical care services[2].

Sawauchi Village started a free medical care program for those over 65 for ambulatory care in 1960 and in 1961 the program was expanded to include hospital care while lowering the eligibility age to 60 years.

However, it was in the late 1960s and the early 1970s that this kind of program became widely adopted in many prefectures and municipalities. For instance, by April 1972, forty-four out of forty-seven prefectures had developed similar programs. This means that such programs were in effect a national policy since all municipalities in that prefecture were covered by the same program, if not by better ones of their own.

In other words, the free medical care program for the aged began as a kind of grassroots movement in smaller municipalities, and was subsequently adopted by prefectures, which eventually forced the national government to impose it on a national scale in a standardized way. In this process, the program developed and implemented by the Tokyo Metropolitan Government played a decisive role since it was one of the most comprehensive programs and as will be discussed, there was a good political reason for that.

The development of the free medical care program as a national policy was virtually unique. In Japan major policies in any field are traditionally formulated by the national government and passed down to local levels to be implemented, as policy making is done in a centralized way. Rarely can either prefectural or municipal governments exercise initiative in formulating or influencing national policies.

Why then did the national government decide to enforce the free medical care program nationwide despite its rational forecast that under a general reimbursement system based on the fee-for-service principle, such a program would increase the cost of medical care for the aged and despite its previous efforts to discourage local governments from adopting or continuing such programs? The answer is found in the contemporary political situation in Japan.

Although Japanese politics have been quite stable since 1945 under the dominance of the conservative Liberal Democratic Party, the political climate in the late 1960s and the early 1970s was characterized by a strong wave of socialists and socialist-coalition candidates sweeping the governorships and mayoralities. The trend was particularly evident in major prefectures and large urban municipalities. At the peak, the Tokyo Metropolitan Government had a socialist governor and the Osaka Prefectural Government, the western center of Japan, was led by a communist governor. In particular, the socialist governor in Tokyo was regarded as the symbol and the Tokyo Metropolitan Government was a stronghold of this new political wave. The governor, by criticizing the backwardness of the national government's welfare policies, advocated and actually introduced many innovative programs in welfare service, among which the free medical care program for the aged was given a top priority. Thus, it became a very distinct political issue.

During this period, continuation and/or expansion of the free medical program was a dominant campaign issue as if it were a symbol of advancement of welfare services. Gubernatorial and mayoral candidates, socialists/communists and conservatives alike made escalating promises to continue or expand the program. This explains why the Tokyo Metropolitan Government, among others, adopted the most comprehensive program.

It is a question for political scientists to analyze why the socialist wave emerged in Japan during that time. For us, it suffices to mention several points. Japan was in transition from the post-World War II reconstruction and industrialization to the stage of stabilization, with people's attention focused on issues relating to their own living conditions. For instance, worsening environmental pollution was a serious problem in that period. The wave was most characteristic of urban regions; however, the conservative Liberal Democratic Party based in rural regions could still maintain its dominance in national politics. In short, the urban residents, many of whom had migrated from rural areas or local cities after the war, expressed their frustrations by supporting socialist or socialist-coalition governors and mayors, not so much because they believed in socialist ideology but as a criticism against the national government.

Given the prevailing political climate in which it was feared that the socialist wave might penetrate into national politics, and given the circumstances in which virtually all prefectures adopted free medical care programs for the aged in one way or another, the national government had little choice but to approve and nationally enforce the standardized program. For, even if it had opposed such programs, local governments would likely have continued their programs with their own budgets.

What was unfortunate, however, was that the Japanese people were too preoccupied with the free-or-not aspect of the program. The politicians emphasized this aspect because it became a big political issue; the opposition parties in parliament strongly demanded its continuation. And the mass media, which was generally anti-government in the post war period, emphasized this particular aspect. Thus, none of them presented the more fundamental issues convincingly, issues such as quality of health and medical care services for the aged, cost sharing, cost containment, reorganization of medical institutions and preparing for long-term care facilities, and so forth.

Of course, it may be said that the Japanese were misled, but half the blame should be theirs. Their obsession with petty cash payments, along with the ask-then-be-given attitude vis-à-vis the government, signified their lack of political maturity. As will be discussed later, the free-or-not issue was very insignificant compared to the issue of coping with the increasing total cost of medical care for the aged. Metaphorically speaking, the Japanese only saw a tree just in front of them but failed to notice the vast forest behind, to which they had to send nourishment in the form of a health insurance tax.

On the other hand, since the Japanese system of health and medical care services is very complex, it was difficult for anyone to present the whole picture with its inherent problems. In addition, since drastic structural change was necessary to deal with the fundamental issues, such a proposal was politically too risky at that time. To anticipate the conclusion of this chapter, it was, ironically, the free medical care program for the aged that later helped the national government to challenge the system and to facilitate its abolition.

The year 1973 marked a turning point in the Japanese health, medical and welfare (social services) policies in general and those for the aged in particular. However, this was not so much because the free medical care program for the aged became a national policy, but more importantly because of major improvements in pension systems and health insurance benefits. For instance, in addition to the free medical care program, an automatic adjustment to inflation rates was introduced to the pension systems, and so was a new program for high-cost medical care[3].

Subsequently, the national government proposed a package of improvements in health, medical and welfare policies, and the overall social security budget in that year was increased by as much as 30% over the previous year.

Those forces which had demanded that the government adopt the free medical care program for the aged as a national policy rejoiced at these improvements since they thought that the emphasis on the program successfully pushed the government to expand the social security services. That is, the issue of the free medical care program for the aged was in fact an effective political issue.

On the other hand, with this package and the new budget, the government proudly proclaimed the year of 1973 as the first year for the Japanese Welfare State (*fukushi gannen*), not anticipating, of course, the Oil Shock which would occur in autumn of the same year, and the subsequent economic recession. Yet it may be obvious that when the government made such a proclamation at the end of the fiscal year 1972, this was a shrewd political maneuver. At the expense of fiscal growth in overall social security expenditures, including health and medical costs for the aged, it tried to regain the political upperhand from the socialist-dominated local politics. And, as it might be anticipated by the government, the free medical care program was no longer a political issue since the program was incorporated into the broader social security legislation.

Impacts of the Free Medical Care Program for the Aged

Table 1 shows annual trends of national medical care costs for thirty years from 1955-1985[4]. This Table is important for our discussion because it presents information on the cost increase. The total amount of national medical care costs has increased consistently by about sixty-seven times in the three decades and it appears to do so continuously. In the same period, per capita national medical care costs have increased by forty-nine times. The ratios of national medical care cost vis-à-vis Gross National Product and National Income are also shown in the Table.

Needless to say, it is the increase in the aged population that is the most significant contributing factor to the growth of national medical care costs. But a couple of other factors should also be pointed out, including prevalent use of high-tech medical equipment for patients of all ages and the increasing cost of drugs. The latter is peculiar to Japan where nearly all hospitals operate their own pharmacy service divisions inside the hospitals.

Information on medical care costs for the aged is shown in 1973 and thereafter. As mentioned earlier, the free medical care program for the aged started in January, 1973 and ended in January, 1983. In 1973, for instance, when the aged accounted for about 7% of the total population, the costs of medical care for the aged were 10.9% of national medical care costs. Ten years later in 1982, while about 9% of the population was the aged, the ratio in medical care costs was nearly doubled to 19.8% of national medical care costs. Per capita medical care costs for the aged increased by a little more than four times.

After discontinuation of the free medical care program, while the actual costs of medical care for the aged and the proportion of medical costs for the aged in national medical costs kept increasing, the ratio to the previous year dropped sharply, as typically shown in 1984 and 1985. This was largely due to a new system of health and medical care for the aged, which will be discussed later.

In any case, as of 1985, roughly speaking, the aged, 10.3% of the population, were responsible for 25.4% of national medical care costs.

The impact of the free medical care program may also be seen in terms of a dramatic increase in rates of receiving medical care (both ambulatory and hospital) by the aged. Figure 5 illustrates trends in this rate by age groups in selected years. As shown, while there is not much change in the younger age groups, a noticeable increase is observed in the older groups, especially the group 70 and older, the eligible age bracket for the free medical care program. Even before the program was nationally enforced in 1973, there was a tendency for older people to receive more medical care, which may be attributed to local versions of free medical care programs. Yet the sudden rise in the rate in 1975 and its stabilizations in 1980 and 1984 were undoubtedly caused by the nationally adopted program. Moreover, what should not be overlooked is the trend in the old-old group: the rates were going up in successive years, reflecting increased hospitalization.

Another impact of the free medical care program was the fact that soon after the program started, there appeared a large number of hospitals which

TABLE 1

Annual Trends for National Medical Care Costs

	National Medical Care Costs			Ratio of National Medical Care Cost		Medical Care Costs for the Elderly		Per Capita Medical Care Costs for the Elderly (1,000 yen)	Ratio of Medical Care Costs for the Elderly to National Medical Care Cost (%)
	Total (100 million yen)	Ratio to Previous (%)	Per Capita National Medical Care Costs (1,000 yen)	To Gross National Product (%)	To National Income (%)	Total (100 million yen)	Ratio to Previous (%)		
1955	2,388	11.0	2.7	2.7	3.3				
1960	4,095	13.0	1.4	2.5	3.1				
1965	11,224	19.5	11.4	3.3	4.3				
1970	24,962	20.1	24.1	3.3	4.1				
1971	27,962	9.2	25.9	3.3	4.1				
1972	33,994	24.7	31.6	3.5	4.4				
1973	39,496	16.2	36.2	3.4	4.1	4,289		101	10.9
1974	53,786	36.2	48.6	3.9	4.8	6,652	55.1	148	12.4
1975	64,779	20.4	57.9	4.3	5.2	8,666	30.3	184	13.4
1976	76,884	18.4	67.8	4.5	5.5	10,780	24.4	220	14.1
1977	85,686	11.7	75.1	4.5	5.5	12,872	19.4	250	15.0
1978	100,042	16.8	86.9	4.8	5.9	15,948	23.9	295	15.9
1979	109,510	9.5	94.3	4.9	6.0	18,503	16.0	326	16.9
1980	119,805	9.4	102.3	4.9	6.0	21,269	14.9	360	17.8
1981	128,709	7.4	109.2	5.0	6.2	24,281	14.2	394	18.9
1982	138,659	7.7	116.8	5.1	6.4	27,487	13.2	425	19.8
1983	145,438	4.9	121.7	5.1	6.4	33,185	20.7	443	22.8
1984	150,932	3.8	125.5	5.0	6.3	36,098	8.8	461	23.9
1985	160,159	6.1	132.3	5.0	6.3	40,673	2.7	499	25.4

N.B. Medical care costs for the elderly up to the end of January 1983 are those for persons subject to the old medical care cost supply system for the elderly, while those from the beginning of February 1983 are for persons eligible for medical care in accordance with the Health and Medical Services Act for the Elderly. Because of the increase in eligible persons pursuant to the establishment of the health and medical services system for the elderly, no simple comparison can be made between 1981 and 1982, and 1982 and 1983

Source: Ministry of Health and Welfare

FIGURE 5

Trends in the Rates for Receiving Medical Care for Different Age Groups

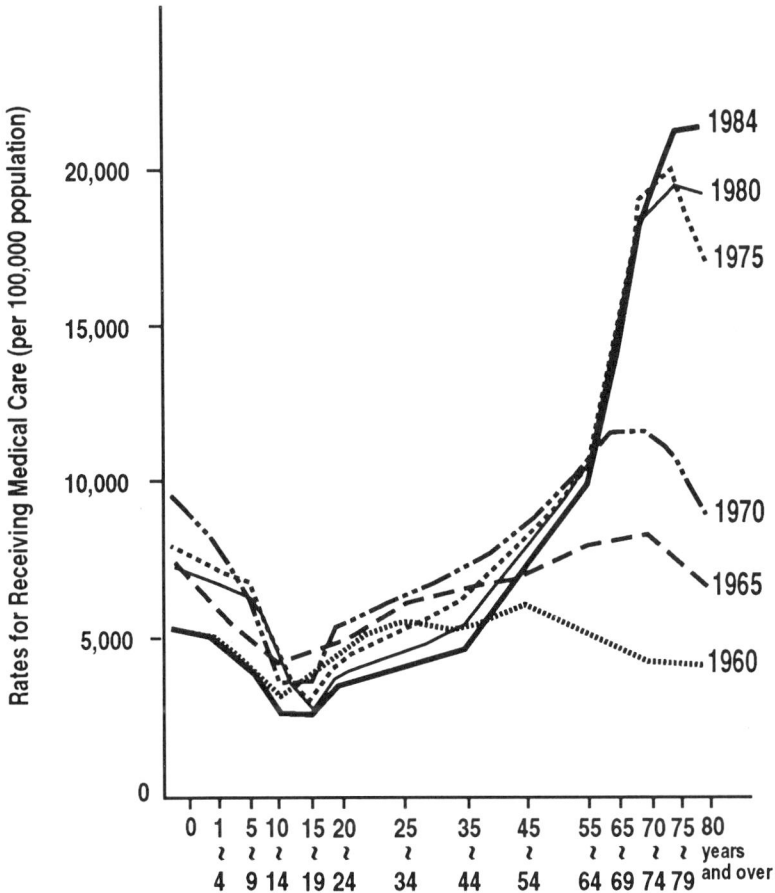

Source: "Patient Survey", Statistic and Information Department, MHW.

had many aged inpatients. So many in fact that the Japanese mass media coined a term, *rojin byoin*, literally hospitals for the aged. However, they were not geriatric hospitals officially categorized as such—there was no such category in Japan until 1983 when a new health and medical care system for the aged was established, replacing the free medical care program, but it was a spontaneously emergent social phenomenon.

This was indeed a unique phenomenon for which the free medical care program definitely played the role of midwife. There were several underlying social conditions. First, the number of frail aged had been increasing. Second, as pointed out in the first section of this chapter, the traditional arrangement of family care for the aged was becoming increasingly problematic. Third, there was a shortage of long-term care facilities for the aged: the Japanese government had built since 1963 welfare homes for physically and/or mentally dependent aged quite extensively, but they were still small in number and at inconvenient locations. Admission to these homes carried social stigma both for the aged and their adult chidren because the Japanese welfare system was/is still based on an assumption that the aged would be taken care of by their families. Hospitalization was not only a face-saving way for them but also economical, as it was free of charge; whereas even the aged who were institutionalized in welfare homes were required to pay some fees for their care depending on their income including pensions. Fourth, since the free medical care program operated within the general reimbursement system based upon the fee-for-service principle, it was profitable for hospitals to have as many inpatients as possible and to provide various

FIGURE 6

Trends in Hospitalization by Age Groups in Selected Years

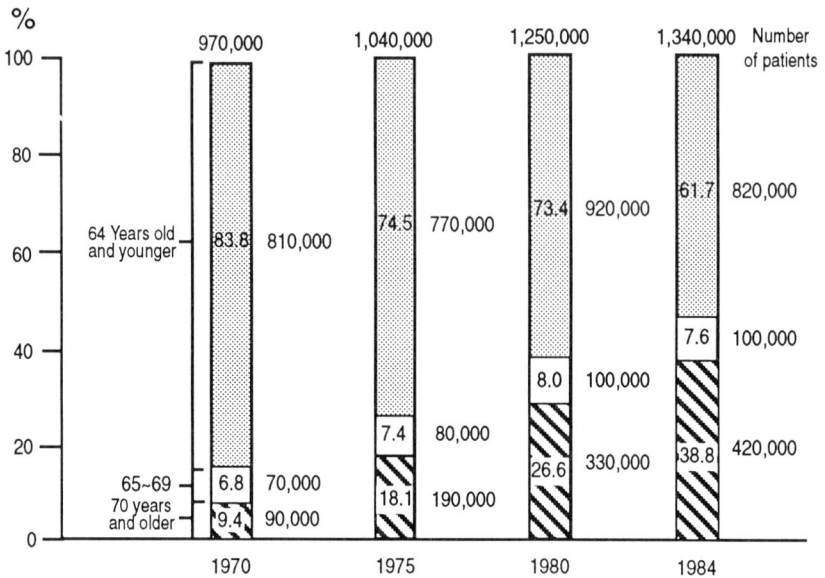

Source: "Patient Survey" Ministry of Health and Welfare

treatments and prescribe many medications. I do not mean that all hospitals took advantage of and outmaneuvered the system to generate profits, but just point out that if intended, such actions were possible under the system. Also, it should be added that generally speaking, hospital management is getting very difficult and there are many private hospitals in Japan, many of which are small in terms of the number of beds. Therefore, the free medical care program for the aged pulled a trigger, as it were, in a potentially explosive situation, whereby the interests of the frail aged and their families and those of hospitals coincided beautifully with each other.

Trends in hospitalization are shown in Figure 6 by three age groups (less than 64; 65-69; and older than 70) in terms of the actual numbers as well as proportional breakdowns in selected years of 1970, 1975, 1980 and 1984. The number of inpatients as a whole steadily increased from 970,000 in 1970 to 1,340,000 in 1984. More salient, however, is the increase in the over 70 years bracket: the number of inpatients grew from 90,000 in 1970, to 420,000 in 1984, and the proportion has risen from 9.4% in 1970 to 18.1% in 1975, then to 26.6% in 1980, and further to as high as 38.8% in 1984. Meanwhile, there was not a big increase both in the number of inpatients and the proportion among the 65-69 age group even though the "bedridden" in this age group were covered by the program. Therefore, in 1984, 46.4% of all inpatients were those over 65 years old.

With regard to length of hospitalization among the 70 and older group in 1984, as Figure 7 indicates, more than half of them stayed at hospitals for longer than six months with the actual number being 220,000 patients.

For the national government, the most immediate and serious impact of the free medical care program for the aged was a fiscal crisis in National Health Insurance. We have already discussed the major characteristics of this insurance system along with those of other systems. As a bottom-line safety-net system, even before the free medical care program began, National Health Insurance had suffered from chronic financial problems due to its shaky revenue basis and the higher proportion of at-risk members than other systems, so that the government had to provide direct subsidies to the system in order to keep it solvent.

Recall that each health insurance system operates independently without inter-system mutual help mechanisms. Thus, when one has financial problems, there are essentially two ways to adjust, either cutting down the benefit rates or raising the health insurance tax, and the latter is more likely. However, National Health Insurance has been plagued with two interrelated, inherent problems. Unlike other systems, it could not count on a higher tax from the insured. It is important to notice in this context that because of the structural change in the industry, farmers, the group whose tax was a most stable revenue source for the National Health Insurance, decreased from 40%

FIGURE 7

Duration of Hospitalization among 70 Years Old and Over in 1984

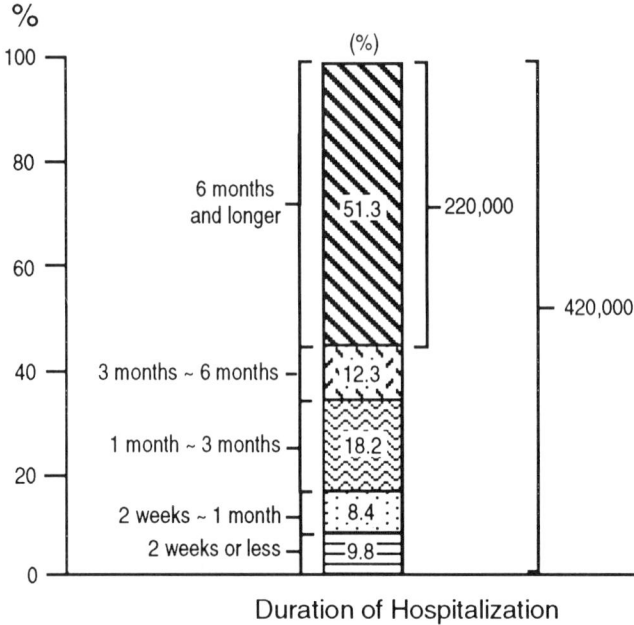

Duration of Hospitalization

Source: "Patient Survey" Ministry of Health and Welfare

of the total insured in 1965 to only 10% or so in the late 1980s, according to the most recent report. On the other hand, the number of the insured older than 70 years has been increasing, so that the system has to pay more to hospitals. For instance, this age group accounted for only 5.3% of those insured by National Health Insurance in 1966, but it became 12.5% in 1986. Recently, the jobless insured, among whom the pension-dependent people are included, accounted for nearly 30% of its members. In contrast, in 1986 the portion of the insured over 70 was 4.3% in Government-managed Health Insurance and only 2.9% in Society-managed Health Insurance, three to four times less than National Health Insurance.

Under the free medical care program, both the national and local governments paid 30% of individual costs for the eligible aged. Of course, this expenditure became quite significant. However, from the standpoint of the national government, what was more serious was the growth of its subsidies to National Health Insurance. The subsidies were less visible to the public; one needs to be familiar with the complexities of the health insurance systems in Japan in order to understand its seriousness. Partly because of this, the mass media focused only on the free-or-not aspect of the program, and the government did not try very energetically to make the public aware of this problem, lest it might be criticized for lack of proper management skills.

The operating entities of National Health Insurance are municipalities (cities, towns and villages) and each of them operates independently. Thus, depending on their performance, the national government provided subsidies from 32% to 52% of the total expenditures. It is understandable that the government feared that unless some measures were taken for cost sharing and cost containment, its expenditures would skyrocket. The situation was getting explosive, as the nation's overall financial condition turned worse, generating pressure for drastic reforms.

Different Views on Effectiveness of the Free Medical Care Program

Around the late 1970s, it became apparent that with the continuation of the free medical care program for the aged, medical care costs for the aged would increase at an alarming rate, and the government began working out reform plans.

The political economy situation was also changing favorably for the government. The political climate, once dominated by socialist governors and mayors, shifted to a low ebb, which was symbolically marked by the defeat of the socialist governor in Tokyo, whose administration had left the financial situation of the Metropolitan Government rather chaotic. He expanded various "welfare" programs without solid financial planning, and the fiscal crisis of the Metropolitan Government made the public aware of the necessity of cost effectiveness.

More importantly, the Japanese economy itself was in a serious state throughout the 1970s and the early 1980s: it went into a long recession period, triggered by the Oil Shock of 1973 and worsened by the second one in 1977. For the first time since 1945, Japan was faced with a problem of slow economic growth and the need to reorganize the industrial structure to be less dependent on fossil fuel. One example is the subsequent growth of the electronics industry which does not require so much energy in the production process. With decreasing tax revenues, the government was forced to operate with extremely tight budgets. In subsequent years, no growth was approved in the national budgets vis-à-vis the previous year. The government coined a peculiar Japanese-English term, "minus ceiling," to advocate its budgetary policy. Naturally, wide-ranging cuts were made across the Ministries, and bureaucratic organizations were requested to eliminate excess fat.

Meanwhile, medical care costs for the aged were growing alarmingly.

This was the social context in which the free medical care program was to be reviewed. The government, with the help of reforms recommended by several advisory councils, tried to discontinue the program and to establish a more comprehensive system for health and medical care services for the aged.

Interestingly, although the law proposed by the government was generally rational, the rationale given by the government did not really focus on financial and structural problems of the existing systems, nor did it call for the necessity of cost-sharing and cost-containment measures. Instead it argued that under the free medical care program, some aged were receiving medical care beyond their legitimate medical needs because the services were free of charge, suggesting that the aged and the program itself were responsible for the growth of medical costs. The government suggested that costs might be reduced through the introduction of disincentives for medical utilization by the reintroduction of a system of co-payments.

Against this contention, different views were raised with regard to the effectiveness of the program. For instance, the opposition parties in the parliament strongly opposed the re-introduction of partial payments because of the symbolic nature of the free medical care program and partly because it was a good political issue with which to attack the government, or perhaps, as they claimed, because they feared that discontinuation of the program might cause a chain reaction of cost containment in other welfare programs.

The Japanese Medical Doctors' Association, which traditionally supports the conservative government, opposed discontinuation of the free program since it would hurt private hospitals the most. It launched a series of one-page opinion advertisements in major newspapers, maintaining that it was important to continue the program in order to provide proper health and medical care for the aged.

The position of the mass media was more ambivalent. On the one hand, they reported articles about seemingly excessive use of medical care by the aged, while on the other, they criticized the government's proposal to discontinue the program and to reintroduce partial payments.

Since it was again the issue of free or not, it generated wide public debate, centering on arguments for and against the government's claim that the aged were abusing the program. Sociologically speaking, this situation is characterized as competing attempts in social construction of realities.

Around 1980, observations appeared which supported the government's interpretation. The following three examples appeared in one of Japan's major newspapers, *Asahi Shinbun*. A nurse wrote:

> Although families of elderly patients are generally grateful to us when these patients are hospitalized, it occurs not infrequently that the same

families complain about their own lack of ability to care for elderly relatives and ask us for longer hospitalization of their aged parents when we suggest their discharge. This hospital is not a nursing home, and the elderly patients cannot stay as long as they are alive. Please think of really ailing people who are waiting for necessary hospitalization (March 26, 1980).

And, a hospital owner wrote:

My hospital has 150 beds and most of them have been occupied by the elderly. At least one third of them can be, medically speaking, discharged. Their families complain that they cannot take them back home because their houses are too small. If medical care were not completely free for these patients, this could not take place (March 26, 1980).

A high school girl who visited a hospital for a cold made this observation:

The other day I went to a hospital early in the morning, and I was surprised to find that the waiting room had already filled with the elderly. While waiting for my turn, I was stunned by the following conversation between two elderly women: "Nothing wrong with my health. But you know, it's free. I wouldn't come here if I had to pay." "Yeah, yeah, indeed." I wondered how the really sick people waiting in the room would feel about their conversation. I heard that our government spends very much for welfare of the elderly. But I felt sad to realize the public money was spent even for such elderly people as the women I met at the hospital (February 18, 1981).

As indicated by these observations and implied by the discussion in the previous section, the view of excessive use or abuse of the program by the aged was based upon two contentions. One was that the aged patients occupied many hospital beds without legitimate medical reasons, thereby making it difficult for younger sick people to gain access to hospital care. Although its origin is not known, the mass media began using a term, *sha-kaiteki nvuin*, literally social hospitalization, meaning non-medical hospitalization, to describe such dischargeable patients. The other was that the ambulatory aged flooded waiting rooms of hospitals turning the latter into their "saloons," that is, their social gathering places, so that younger people had to endure much inconvenience.

It is difficult to either prove or disprove the government's interpretation since any version of social construction of reality is based on partial truth. Rather, the question was wrongly presented, or presented in a political way which demands an either/or answer. It seems obvious that there were some cases of excessive use or abuse of the program by the aged, but certainly not all of them.

Similarly, there should be some truth apart from the perspectives of particular interest groups in counter-interpretations of the government's position. The opinions emphasizing effectiveness of the free medical care program for the aged are summarized as follows: the program only provided the needed opportunities for the aged to receive necessary medical care, for they could not afford doing so when/if they were required to pay 30% of costs each time out of their pockets. Many of them were living on limited incomes and this partial payment meant too much for them to bear, so that they would not seek medical care until they were really very sick. The higher rates of medical care are evidence of the success of the program because the aged tend to suffer from multiple chronic illnesses and need constant examinations and medications for health management. Since preventive and primary care are essential, it is beneficial not only for the aged but also for the insurance systems and the government in the long run. That is, the rapid growth of medical care costs for the aged was only a transitional, short-time incident and the free medical care program would eventually have been cost-effective.

This view is supported by the fact that although since 1963 free medical checkups had been available annually for all aged, utilization rates were consistently very low at around 20% because, it was argued, even if some illnesses or chronic health problems were diagnosed during the checkups, they had to pay 30% of their medical care costs in order to receive treatments and medications.

As for longer hospitalization of the aged, it was pointed out that it was the unbalanced local density of hospital beds that was the most important factor; the regions with larger numbers of beds in proportion to the number of residents of all ages tended to record hospitalization of the aged higher in proportion and longer in duration than other regions. This was a failure of the government's policy for hospital planning. In addition, the government was criticized for the serious shortage of long-term care facilities for the aged, an underlying condition.

In the end, however, the government's view became stronger, not so much because it was widely supported but probably because of the general political, economic and social atmosphere favoring fiscal constraint at that time, as discussed earlier. What was significant in the process was a report prepared by a watchdog agency on governmental administration, which investigated actual performance of the free medical care program on a national scale. The report came out in 1981, concluding that at least 10% of the hospitalized aged could be discharged, and that the reasons cited for non-medical hospitalization were: refusal of families to care for their elders, refusal of patients to return home, no caretaker at home due to employment, no relatives, or kept waiting for admission to welfare home for the aged.

Health and Medical Services for the Aged—a New System

Since February, 1983 partial payments by the aged have been reintroduced. However, this does not mean that they are required to share 30% of medical care costs as before the free medical care program started, but they now need to pay set amounts, instead of a proportion—Y400 (about $3) at each visit per month and Y300 (about $2) per day in case of hospitalization up to the first two months only. These amounts were raised somewhat in 1987 but are still small compared with early co-payment requirements at almost a third of the cost of treatments and yet still generated anger among the opposition political parties. Of course, those sides which opposed the government's proposal thought that it was their intensive efforts that reduced the co-payments to a low level. Yet, there is more to it than that, as will be explained shortly.

As a revenue source, the partial payment accounts for roughly 1.6% of the total medical care costs for the aged. This portion is quite insignificant, which in turn makes one wonder about the intentions behind this policy change.

There may be four major intentions on the part of the government. First, it focused on the reintroduction of partial payments as a way of distracting attention away from those basic characteristics of the system which will require the working people to pay higher health insurance taxes.

Second, by requiring the aged to make small payments for their own medical care, it tried to discourage excessive use of both ambulatory and hospital care. When rates of medical utilization drop, overall medical costs would naturally fall.

Third, by sending to the public a no-free-lunch message, it hoped to eliminate the free-or-not issue once and for all as a troublesome, emotion-laden political issue.

Lastly, it may have assumed that partial payment would make the aged and their families more cost conscious, which in turn might improve their levels of awareness that self-responsibility is important for proper management of health conditions. This was in fact an official government explanation.

What was most important was not discontinuation of the free medical care program, but the very fact that for the first time in Japanese history a new system called Health and Medical Service System for the Aged (HMSSA) was established independently of the existing health insurance systems to cover those over 70 years of age. Thus, a new framework was created, which would function through necessary adjustments, i.e., adjusting tax rates, in the foreseeable future.

Four major characteristics of HMSSA are to be discussed[5].

1. *Cost-Sharing Measures.* The financial basis of HMSSA has three groups of contributors: aged patients themselves, the national and local governments, and the existing health insurance systems. Since the proportion that the aged can contribute to HMSSA is estimated to be 1-2% of the total medical care costs for the aged, we will ignore this portion hereafter when we discuss the cost-sharing rates between the government's and the other health insurance systems. It suffices to mention that even though HMSSA allows the national government to raise the set amounts for individual partial payments, politicians are understandably reluctant to invoke this mechanism; fees may be raised slightly but not to a level at which they would become a significant revenue source for the new system.

The governments contribute to HMSSA 30% of the total costs, with the national government responsible for 20% and the prefectural and municipal governments for 5%, respectively.

The remaining 70% is now to be jointly shared by the existing major health insurance systems. This is the essence of cost-sharing measures in HMSSA. Recall that before HMSSA, each health insurance system operated independently as far as financial management was concerned, regardless of the actual number of, or the proportion of, members over 70 years of age, or of the free medical care program for that matter. Consequently, as discussed earlier, National Health Insurance which had an unevenly large number of such aged insured but whose revenue base was very unstable, plunged into a serious fiscal crisis. In other words, the medical care costs for the aged were not evenly shared among the insurance systems.

Under HMSSA, each health insurance system, including National Health Insurance, shares the costs evenly. This means that Government-managed Health Insurance, Society-managed Health Insurance, two Mutual Aid Associations for National Public Service Employees and for Local Public Service Employees, and others, which have strong financial foundations but with fewer aged members, contribute more than before to HMSSA for medical care costs for the aged. Therefore, this will directly affect the health insurance tax rate among the working people. To ease this impact, the government has set a transitional period during which this cost sharing will be gradually introduced.

Put another way, National Health Insurance is the one that is saved by HMSSA. Furthermore, despite the commitment to 20% cost sharing, the national government will be able to reduce its direct subsidies to the existing systems, especially to National Health Insurance, when the aged population is growing.

The impact is already noticeable. For instance, Society-managed Health Insurance, one of the largest systems, and which previously maintained a sound financial balance, suffered from deficits in two consecutive years of 1987 and 1988 due to its increased contributions to HMSSA.

2. *Cost-containment Measures.* While a general reimbursement system based on the fee-for-service principle is kept intact for the other health insurance systems, a new reimbursement system is introduced to HMSSA, setting limitations on various tests, treatments, and length of hospitalization. In a way, this is very similar to, for instance, Diagnosis Related Groups (DRG) in the United States in the sense that it restricts certain types of people in their access to medical care. But HMSSA does so not in terms of types of illnesses but by the age of 70 or older. This measure is subsequently criticized as a kind of age discrimination, and it is truly so.

As the regulations concerning reimbursement limitations are so detailed and complex, it may be sufficient to take the basic rate for hospital care as an example. The basic rate is to reimburse the service of physician's examination and the rates are determined per day in terms of length of hospitalization. It is Y2,350 (about $16) for the first month; Y1,920 (About $13) for longer than one month but shorter than three months; Y1,330 (about $9) for more than three months but less than six months; Y1,130 (about $7.50) for more than six months but less than one year: and Y820 (about $5.50) for longer than one year. For a comparative purpose, the rates in general reimbursement are also presented. Note that periodic breakdowns are more detailed than HMSSA: Y4,200 (about $28) for less than one week: Y4,060 (about $27) for more than one week but less than two weeks: Y2,700 (about $18) for more than two weeks but less than one month; Y2,020 (about $13.50) for more than one month but less than two months; Y1,880 (about $12.50) for more than two months but less than three months; Y1,340 (about $9) for more than three months but less than six months; Y1,100 (about $7.33) for more than six months but less than one year; Y910 (about $6) for more than one year but less than one year and a half; Y870 (about $5.80) for more than a year and a half but less than two years; and Y840 (about $5.60) for longer than two years.

The point is that the reimbursement system of HMSSA functions in such a way that unless hospitals are managed within the limitations, they have to absorb the exceeded costs themselves. In particular, if aged patients stay at hospitals very long it becomes less profitable for the hospitals than before HMSSA.

Soon an expected phenomenon began appearing. Many hospitals were putting stronger pressures on the long-hospitalized patients to be discharged. However, where could they go now? They were hospitalized in the first place because they had few places but hospitals to go to and receive the necessary care.

3. *Preparing for Long-Term Care Facilities for the Aged.* In 1987, four years after the establishment of HMSSA, the government took two steps to address the problem of long-term care. First, it officially classified *rojin byoin*, the spontaneously emergent general hospitals with large numbers of aged inpatients, as geriatric hospitals. This was *ex postfacto* logic, but nonetheless a sensible decision. The official definition of geriatric hospitals is hospitals which provide medical care services for patients over 65 years of age, who suffer from chronic, not acute, conditions and which have more than 70% of inpatients aged 65 or older. The geriatric hospitals are covered by HMSSA.

Although the reimbursement rates are lower for them, the regulations are also loosened: for instance, with a geriatric hospital of 100 beds, the number of physicians is three, as opposed to six if the same size hospital is to be categorized as a general hospital. Similarly, the number of nurses is 17 for the geriatric hospital whereas 25 nurses are required for a general hospital. But thirteen nursing aides are also required for the geriatric hospital. No such regulation applies to general hospitals. In 1990, roughly 12% of hospitals in Japan were classified as geriatric hospitals, accounting all together for about 9% of all beds, with the actual number being 148,177 beds.

Secondly, the government set up a new type of intermediate care facility for the aged, called *rojin hoken shisetsu*, Health and Medical Care Facility for the Aged. With an emphasis on rehabilitation programs, these facilities are expected to facilitate smooth transition from general hospitals to living at home. The length of stay is thought to be approximately three months. The staffing requirements for a facility of 100 beds are one physician, eight nurses and twenty nursing aides. Also, the aged at this type of facility are required to pay a set amount of Y50,000 (about $333) per month. The government has set a goal to build an increasing number of this type of facilities in the coming years.

4. *Emphasis on Home Care Services.* Generally speaking, the Japanese are becoming convinced that the handicapped, aged or otherwise, should be able to live at home, instead of being institutionalized, with the help of organized care services. HMSSA reimburses home visits by physicians, nurses, physical and occupational therapists, and the reimbursement rates for these services will be expanded in the near future. Particularly noteworthy in this regard is a government proposal to establish a new system of home nursing within HMSSA.

Although not being covered by HMSSA, it should be mentioned that the number of home helpers has been increased, as shown in Figure 8. It is

FIGURE 8

The Number of Home Helpers

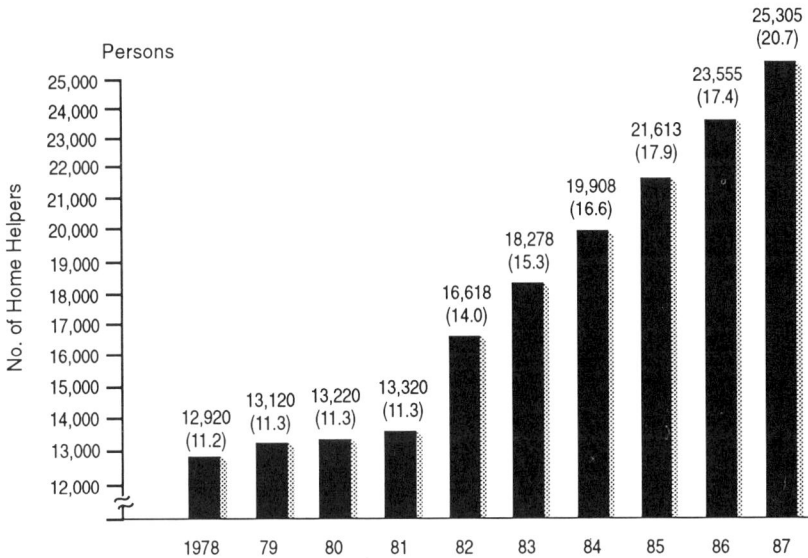

N.B. 1. Home helpers are also dispatched to the physically disabled and mentally and physically handicapped children, as well as to the elderly.

2. Figures in brackets show the ratio to 100,000 population

Source: Social Welfare Bureau, MHW.

clear that efforts have been made since 1982 to increase the number. Yet, using a ratio of the number of home helpers per 100,000 population, Japan is still far behind other industrialized nations such as Denmark and Sweden. The government has publicly stated that it will increase the number of home helpers by four times the number available in 1987, before the turn of the century.

Conclusion

Focusing on the decade of the free medical care program for the aged in 1973-1982 from a political-economy perspective, we have seen how Japan has struggled with one of the most difficult problems in an aging society, namely how to provide the aged with quality health and medical care services in a cost-effective manner.

The free medical care program for the aged was in a sense an "enfant terrible" in its ironic role of provoking debate and dispute. It was born at least with good intentions but ended up in amplifying problems and contradictions inherent in the existing systems, and with its eradication helped the government establish a new, and more comprehensive system, HMSSA.

In June, 1990, the Japanese parliament amended a group of laws pertinent to health, medical and welfare (social) services, including those for the aged, as proposed by the government. One major amendment was to require prefectural and municipal governments to formulate coordinated plans in these service areas. The national government finally realized its limitations in policy making in these areas and the need for a greater involvement of local government. The irony is clear; the free medical care program was imposed upon the national government against the wishes of the conservative politicians who controlled parliament. When circumstances combined to impose restrictions upon free medical care, national government had to concede the rights to local government to exercise considerable policy-making power.

Yet, how local government can exercise this power is unclear, which has far more implications for the Japanese people than the quality of human services for the aged. What is now at stake is their political maturity and their ability to establish local control. Historically, these tasks have been very difficult for the Japanese to accomplish.

The Japanese experience with the so-called free medical care for the aged underscores one common theme recurrent in various nations. Pressures from either consumers (e.g.aged and labor) or providers force a national government to create benefits for a particular group, which then leads to high utilization of services and high inflation of costs, especially of charges.

Providers, that is, physicians and hospitals, demand that prices not be controlled when these plans are designed under the ideology: "we are honorable men and women who should be trusted to not charge excessive amounts". However, the ideology does not operate or temper provider behavior and the inflation of medical care costs becomes extreme. The state then attempts to introduce some controls after the system has been established, and after some failed attempts to control providers, the state and media blame the consumers for overutilization and cost inflation. Yet, various studies typically show that providers control both supply and demand for medical services and together with the technological imperative cause most of the medical care inflation.

This scenario roughly describes the politics of health economics that have operated for the last 30 years in Japan. Great Britain with its National Health Service is one society where health care inflation has been best controlled, and is an exception to the "golden rule" of medical care inflation found in many nations where a national health insurance model is the dominant organizational approach to health care financing.

Notes

1. For more detailed discussion on various characteristics of Japanese aging, see Kinoshita and Kiefer (in press).

2. A comprehensive study of an approach taken by Sawauchi Village was done by Nobuo Maeda (1983), who has been studying the village for nearly thirty years.

3. A relief program for high cost medical care was introduced. When the partial payment of the insured or his/her dependents exceeds Y50,000 (about $333) per month, the excess amount is to be reimbursed to the insured by the insurance system to which he/she belongs. The amount has been raised since then and was Y57,000 ($380) in 1989. Note that these amounts, and those appearing in this chapter, are converted at a rate of $1 = Y150, even though exchange rates tend to fluctuate.

4. Since ratios and proportions are important for our discussion, the amounts are not converted into U.S. currency.

5. With the establishment of HMSSA, a sub-system for retirees in the age bracket of 60-69 and their dependents was also newly created within National Health Insurance, as shown in Figure 4. Since HMSSA is for those over 70 years of age but the retirees and their dependents have to belong to National Health Insurance with lower rates of benefit, i.e., 70% coverage by the insurance compared with 90% when they were working, this sub-system is expected to ease this gap by providing the retirees with 80% coverage in both ambulatory and hospital care and their dependents with 80% in hospital care and 70% in ambulatory care. Financial support to the sub-system is shared among major insurance systems.

References

Estes, Carroll L. *The Aging Enterprise: A Critical Examination of Social Policies and Services for the Aged.* San Francisco, CA: Joosey-Bass Publishers, 1980.

Kinoshita, Yasuhito and Christie W. Kiefer. *Refuge of the Honored: Social Organization at a Japanese Retirement Community.* Berkeley: University of California Press, In print.

Maeda, Nobuo. *Medical Service of Sawauchi Village in Iwate Prefecture (Iwateken Sawauchimura no Iryo).* Japan: Nihon Hyoronsha, 1983. In Japanese.

Ministry of Health and Welfare. *Health and Welfare Services in Japan.* Tokyo: Japan International Corporation of Welfare Services, 1988.

Ministry of Health and Welfare. *Health and Welfare Statistics in Japan.* Tokyo: Health and Welfare Statistics Association, 1990.

10

Health Care in Canada

Neena L. Chappell

Introduction

This paper focuses on health care in Canada, beginning with a brief demographic profile and some health statistics for the elderly population. The remainder of the paper discusses the health care system available to elderly persons. The medical care system in Canada has universal access to physician services and acute care hospitals. Community services, however, were established later and are less universalistic, more fragmented. The issues of equity, appropriateness and accountability of the Canadian system are then discussed. It is argued that greater equity, appropriateness, and accountability within the Canadian system, particularly in terms of community services, is warranted.

A Demographic Profile

Like other industrialized nations, the proportion of elderly persons (those aged 65 and over) in Canada has been increasing gradually but steadily throughout the century. The proportion of elderly in Canada was slightly below that of the United States in 1986 (10.7% vs. 12.1%). This, however, is less than some European countries such as the United Kingdom (15.5%). Indeed, even at the turn of the century it is estimated that only 11.9% of Canada's population will be elderly. It will not be until around 2031 that approximately 20% of the population will be aged 65 and over. In that year approximately 45% of elders will be age 75 and older (Statistics Canada, 1987; U.S. Bureau of the Census, 1988; Chappell, 1989; United Nations, 1990). In other words, the population now considered elderly is itself aging; the proportion of those who are old old is increasing.

Canada, however, is a country comprised of ten provinces and two vast northern territories. The proportion of elderly varies from province to province, from a low of 8.1% in Alberta to a high of 12.7% in Prince Edward Island in 1986. The territories have fewer elderly, 3.7% in the Yukon and 2.8% in the Northwest Territories (Statistics Canada, 1987, see Table 1).

TABLE 1

Percent of Elderly by Province and Territories, 1986

	Total Population	Number Age 65+	Percentage Age 65+
Canada:	25,309,330	2,697,580	10.7
Rank Order - Highest to Lowest:			
Prince Edward Island	126,645	16,085	12.7
Saskatchewan	1,009,615	128,600	12.7
Manitoba	1,063,015	133,885	12.6
British Columbia	2,883,370	349,480	12.1
Nova Scotia	873,180	103,835	11.9
New Brunswick	709,445	78,740	11.1
Ontario	9,101,695	992,700	10.9
Quebec	6,532,460	650,635	10.0
Newfoundland	568,350	49,950	8.8
Alberta	2,365,825	191,325	8.1
Yukon	23,505	860	3.7
N.W.T.	52,240	1,475	2.8

Source: Statistics Canada, Age, Sex and Marital Status, 1986 Census. Ottawa: Minister of Supply and Services, September, 1987, Catalogue 93-101, Table 1, pp. 1-1 to 1-13.

The percentage of elderly females compared with males has been increasing and has stabilized around 57%. Demographic projections suggest that the proportion of female elderly will continue to outnumber the proportion of male elderly. The gap between them is projected to stabilize, not increase, when the baby boom generation reaches old age (Statistics Canada, 1984; Chappell, 1989). Approximately half of elderly individuals are married. This has remained more or less stable throughout the century. One-third of elderly persons are widowed. There is great gender variation by marital status, with women much more likely to be widowed compared to men (48% of women but only 14% of men were widowed in 1986). Elderly men are much more likely to be married (75% of men compared with 40% of women were married in 1986). This difference is accounted for both by the greater life expectancy experienced by women together with the fact that Canadian women tend to marry men a few years older than themselves.

A major concern of old age, both individually and societally, is deteriorating health; more characteristic of this phase of the life cycle than of earlier phases. Generally, health status of elders has focused on the presence or absence of disease or the degree of functional incapacity or disability. Increasing age in Canada, as elsewhere, is associated with a greater likelihood of experiencing chronic conditions and functional disability. Over 80% of elderly persons report at least one chronic condition. Importantly, however, chronic conditions need not translate into functional disability or limitations on activity.

In the Canada Health Survey, approximately half of all elders reported some limitations to their activities. However, if one examines functional disability with basic activities of daily living or severe limitations compared to those experiencing disability with instrumental activities of daily living or less severe limitations, the figure drops to approximately 10% (Chappell et al., 1986; Health and Welfare Canada and Statistics Canada, 1981). In other words, while both the number of chronic conditions experienced and the extent of functional disability tend to increase with age, these chronic conditions do not necessarily translate into functional disability. Furthermore, while approximately half of all elderly individuals experience some functional difficulty, only a small proportion have functioning problems with basic activities of daily living such as eating, personal mobility, and toileting.

The five most common chronic illnesses among elderly Canadians are: arthritis and rheumatism (experienced by 55%), hypertension (39%), heart trouble (26%), respiratory problems (24%), and diabetes (9%). The percentages do not total 100% because people can have more than one condition (Statistics Canada, 1987). However the most common chronic conditions are not synonymous with the leading causes of death. The leading causes of death among elderly persons are: cardiovascular disease (45%), cancer (26%), respiratory diseases (7%), accidents (5%), and diseases of the digestive system (4%) (Statistics Canada, 1988).

To understand the formal health care system which is available for treating diseases and coping with functional disabilities requires an understanding of the decentralized provincial responsibility for health care in this country. The next section describes this system.

A Medical Care System

In health matters, Canada has a decentralized system of provincial responsibility. At the time of confederation in 1867, the British North American Act made no mention of welfare measures, either income security or social services. Responsibility for quarantine centres, marine hospitals, and "special" groups such as the Armed Forces and Veterans, were assigned to the federal government. Responsibility for other hospitals, asylums, charities and charitable institutions was assigned to the provinces. Any jurisdiction not assigned federal responsibility was to be within provincial jurisdiction if it arose later (Sirois, 1940). Provincial responsibility for health was confirmed in the patriated Canadian Constitution in the 1980s.

Nevertheless, the federal government has played an important role in shaping Canada's health care system through its command of monetary resources and its ability to set national standards and priorities. The beginnings of the national health care system which is available in Canada today were first evident in the federal government's initial entrance into this area. After the Depression of the 1930s, a research and training program in medicine and assistance in hospital construction were implemented. This was begun in 1945 (Marsh, 1975). These two measures encouraged more personnel into medicine and ensured hospital construction throughout the country. In 1957 the Hospital Insurance and Diagnostic Services Act ensured hospital care for the entire population. This Act established cost sharing between the federal and provincial governments for hospitals. Care institutions such as nursing homes and homes for the aged were excluded. With hospitals insured they became a major arena for practicing medicine. The Medical Care Act was implemented in 1968, providing national insurance for physician services.

By 1972 all 10 provinces and the two territories belonged to the cost-shared medical insurance program. Cost sharing started with the federal government matching every dollar the provinces spent on approved services. To be eligible for federal cost sharing, a provincial plan had to include universal coverage, reasonable access to services, portability of benefits, comprehensive services, and non-profit administration by a public agency. Hospitals and medical care delivery systems contract with the public insurance plans to provide care at specified rates of reimbursement. Payment from the government sector is analogous to that of group insurers such as Blue Cross and Blue Shield in the United States. Provincial governments and medical associations negotiate fee schedules. Most physicians are paid on a fee-for-service basis. In other words, the provinces controlled overall health expenditures, but the federal government controlled service eligibility.

The 1970s saw considerable concern over the escalating health care dollar on the part of the federal government and charges of interference in a jurisdiction of provincial responsibility by the provinces. As a result, a system of cash grants (a type of block funding) from the federal to the provincial governments was instituted in 1977. This effectively limited the rate of growth of federal costs by divorcing funds from specific expenditures. It gave the provinces more control over health expenditures because transfers were no longer tied to specific services. It is important to note, however, that this took place only after a very expensive medical/industrial/pharmaceutical complex was already in place.

The national insurance schemes established a medical (physician) and an institutional (hospital) focus within the Canadian health care system. As Schwenger and Gross (1980) point out, these are the two most expensive forms of care. Community-based programs were not covered by any comprehensive national insurance. The lack of a national insurance scheme for home care services in Canada is reflected in the lack of uniformity from province to province in these services.

In 1966 the Canada Assistance Plan Act provided payment for some health care services not covered by hospital insurance and Medicare. However, unlike the latter, the Canada Assistance Plan incorporated a means test. Furthermore, each province administers its social assistance program with no uniformity among the provinces (Lee, 1974; LeClair, 1975). In some provinces, homes for the aged come under this provision but other provinces do not have similar institutions and those that might be considered similar are not uniformly covered. The Canada Assistance Plan does not provide national or comprehensive coverage for non-hospital, non-physician related services.

Involvement of the federal government has ensured a health care delivery system with a medical emphasis. This is perhaps best demonstrated by the role played by physicians within the system. Evans (1976a; 1976b; 1984) has estimated that physicians control approximately 80% of insured health care costs. Only about 19% of total health care expenditures go directly to physicians but they control or influence hospital admissions, prescribing of drugs, ordering of tests, and recommending return visits. By and large it is physicians who make the decision to use expensive health services, not the client or patient. That is, the system is provider driven, not user driven.

Disentangling physician practice from hospital utilization is impossible but clearly physicians play a major role in the use of these institutions. Patients usually have access to hospitals only if admitted by a physician. The very name of the health care system, Medicare, reflects the central role of physicians. For 1987, 49% of insured health care costs went to hospitals and nursing homes, that is, acute care and institutional care. Twenty-three percent went to salaries for professional services, including but not exclusive to physician services, and 14% went to drugs and appliances. Only 14% went to all other costs (Statistics Canada, 1991). Utilization figures confirm these cost comparisons. One or more visits are paid to the physician by 83% of elderly persons in a year (Statistics Canada, 1985). Although figures for community care are much more difficult to obtain it is estimated that in 1981 .8% of elderly persons received meals-on-wheels, 3.5% transportation services, 4.3% homemaker or home help services, 4.3% assistance with shopping and banking, and 2.7% nursing or other medical skills at home (Statistics Canada, 1983).

Adding Community Services

One of the major shortcomings of the formal Canadian care system is its failure to meet the needs of the chronically ill elderly (Chappell et al., 1986). A small proportion of elders are in long-term care at any one time. In 1986, 8.9% of elderly individuals lived in long-term care institutions in Canada (nursing homes and institutions for elderly and chronically ill persons). However, fully 17% of those 75 and over lived in long-term care institutions in that year (Statistics Canada, 1987). While the proportion in facilities at any one time is small, one-quarter of elderly persons can expect to spend some time in long-term care institutions before they die.

Community care, however, is a relatively neglected aspect of the system. It was not until the 1970s that there was substantial growth of home health services. It was recognized that residential services were best able to meet the needs of the very sick (nursing homes) and the very well (housing units). Meeting the needs of those who were intermediate between these two extremes had not been given priority. Early home care programs tended to offer medically oriented services as a means of shortening hospital stays. They were not considered a means of treating and maintaining people needing chronic or long-term care in the community. In the late 1970s, it was documented that almost half (45%) of the residents in nursing homes were in self-sufficient or Level 1 care and that most of these people could remain in the community with proper supports (Dulude, 1978). In addition, intermediate levels of community support were considered less expensive than institutional care (Lalonde, 1974). The search for alternatives was fueled by the increasing aging of the population which raised concerns that greater demands would "bankrupt" the health care system.

Even though the Department of National Health and Welfare had established a committee for developing pilot home care programs as early as 1957, there were only 26 programs operating in six provinces one decade later in 1967. A federal/provincial working group on home care was established in 1974. In the next year it reported that the number and variety of home care programs was growing but there was little consistency in objectives, eligibility criteria, services offered, staffing, terminology, or funding. The report (National Health and Welfare, 1975) argued for federal/provincial initiatives to correct this lack of uniformity. At that time Manitoba was the only province providing a universal home care program, one which was part of the provincial health care system but not dependent on medical authorization.

It was during the mid to late 1970s that home care programs developed more rapidly and a broad definition of services evolved. Home care was viewed as a service in its own right rather than primarily as a means of shortening hospital stays. This is reflected in the broad definition accepted by the working group as the guideline for home care programs:

Home care should be regarded as a basic mode of health care that coordinates and/or provides the variety of personal health and supportive services required to maintain or to help function adequately in the home, those persons with health and/or social needs related to physical or mental disability, personal or family crises or to illness of an acute or chronic nature. A prerequisite is that the home is judged to be a viable place where treatment or care can be provided. Supportive services include social services and other services to assist such persons and their families. (National Health and Welfare, 1975:13)

The types of needs that can be met through home care are frequently classified as: basic (necessary for the maintenance of the person and include assistance, for example, with preparing food or bathing), supportive (helping the individual to cope with the indirect effects of illness such as providing personal attention, company, or reassurance), and remedial or therapeutic (requiring professional intervention and treatment such as medical, nursing, or family counselling) (Shapiro, 1979). In the recent past, basic and supportive needs have usually been met by the individual or by family and friends, while remedial needs have been provided by professionals.

An example of a community-based program is the Manitoba home care program which has a coordinated entry point and offers a range of services available after an initial assessment by a nurse and/or a social worker. There is no unilateral restriction by medical, nursing, social, or financial condition. Services are provided at no cost to the recipient. Home care in Canada, as in other industrialized countries, has been accepted as a necessary component within a continuum of care (Kammerman, 1976). Social services are considered necessary in addition to medical services and the need for coordination with other health care services accepted.

Despite increasing awareness of the importance of community services, the decentralized Canadian system and the lack of national coordination makes the compilation of utilization statistics difficult. The independent jurisdiction of the provinces relative to health matters makes generalization to the entire country problematic. At the current time, the provinces and territories offer some services but vary in terms of the services offered, the need for physician certification, age restrictions, and user fees. That is, interprovincial diversity in both availability of and access to services is evident.

Support for community services is evident in the recent federal document, *Achieving Health for All* (Minister of Supply and Services Canada,
1987). This document embraces the World Health Organization definition of
health which includes social, psychological, economic, and environmental
aspects in addition to medical aspects of health. It recognizes the role of
societal structural constraints to individual action as well as the individual's
responsibility in choosing among various lifestyles. It recognizes the role of
community support. The importance of this report is the further acceptance of
a broad definition of health which is not restricted only to medical intervention.
Current discussions to implement such a health promotion framework are
laudable and far-reaching. They are, however, primarily discussed as add ons
to the existing medical care system with little discussion of changing the
current medical care system. How that system becomes changed has
implications for distributive justice, the topic to which we now turn.

Equity Within the Canadian Health Care System

Physician and hospital care in Canada, that is, medical and institutional
acute care, are covered by public, not private insurance. Public insurance
spreads the economic burden of care more equitably and lowers barriers to
"needed" care. The Canadian system has been successful in removing the
income barrier to care (Evans, 1984:58,59). Before public insurance in
Canada, poor people were sicker but they received less care. After public
insurance poor people are still sicker but they now receive more care. The
greater use is attributed to the fact that they are sicker and not to a misuse or
abuse of the system.

The system is equitable to the extent that most communities have
hospitals and physicians available. It is up to the individual to seek the first
contact with the physician. That is, social class differences in utilization
patterns related to lifestyles (rather than income) are still operating. Further,
availability of hospital facilities and physician services is not uniform across
the country, rural areas and particularly remote areas have more difficulty
locating physicians within their areas. Not unlike other industrialized
nations, expensive technology and a greater variety of medical services tend
to be available in the large urban centres.

Hospitals in Canada can be classified somewhere between public and
private firms. They (and other medical care delivery systems) contract with
the public insurance program to provide care at specified rates of reimbursement. They share their entrepreneurial decision-making power with
governments and private physicians. However, they must be non-profit to be
eligible for federal dollars. Physicians act more like private entrepreneurs in
that they are paid a fee-for-service negotiated by their provincial organi-

zations with provincial governments. As long as they provide the service, their income is guaranteed. During the early 1980s there was much concern and debate surrounding extra billing by physicians (additional charges to patients over and above the payment schedule) and hospital user fees to help finance the provinces' share of health insurance costs. Concern that reasonable access was threatened resulted in the Canada Health Act (federal legislation) which provided for a reduction in federal financial contributions to provincial health plans by the amount of extra billing and user charges implemented in the province. Current action by the federal government is reducing the transfer payments to the provinces to nil over a specified period of time in exchange for increasing the province's taxing powers. This course removes the power within the Canada Health Act to penalize provinces who charge user fees. It also removes much of the national power to ensure more or less comparable services across the country. Despite objections from across the country, the federal government is maintaining this course.

There are also accusations of a two-tier system developing because of waiting lists as governments limit the supply of hospital beds and equipment. Those who can afford to, can go elsewhere and receive services immediately. The extent to which this is having an adverse effect on the health of Canadians has not been established. Canadians have a high physician to population ratio, higher than that considered necessary for good health of the nation (Evans, 1984). It is not yet clear whether this will become a problem. If a second tier develops it could be convenient for those who can afford it but may not be detrimental to the health of those who have to wait. At the present time it is not at all certain that such a second tier will develop.

In sum, medical and hospital services are universally available to those in need, irrespective of ability to pay. This does not ensure availability of these services irrespective of where the individual lives within the country. However a spend down system, as is evident in the United States, is not part of Canada's health care system. One does not have to become poor in order to receive medical care from the province.

Such an equitable system, however, does not exist for either long-term institutional care or for chronic care within the community. I have argued elsewhere that a major shortcoming of the formal health care system in Canada is its failure to meet the needs of the chronically ill elderly (Chappell et al., 1986; Chappell, 1988). With Canada's decentralized provincial system for health, a lack of national insurance makes the coordination of uniform programs particularly problematic.

Which services are available varies by province. Nova Scotia, for example, offers no respiratory therapy within their home care program but Manitoba does; New Brunswick offers no transportation but Alberta does. Some provinces, such as Newfoundland, Prince Edward Island, and Ontario, still require physician certification, referral, and/or supervision to some aspects of their home care programs. For example, in Prince Edward Island a physician referral is needed for home care nursing services but not for visiting homemaker services. Other provinces no longer require medical participation in this way. Some programs have age restrictions (in New Brunswick recipients of the chronic home care program must be 65 or over, in Ontario recipients of the home support program must be 65 or over), some have income restrictions and some implement user fees. For example, in Prince Edward Island there are user fees for medical supplies, in Quebec for medication, and in Ontario for visiting nurse services. In terms of support services, Prince Edward Island charges user fees for visiting homemaker services, Nova Scotia charges them for all support services, Quebec for meals, Manitoba for meals and transportation, Saskatchewan for all services, British Columbia for homemaker services and adult day care services, etc.

It is obvious from these few examples that the provision of community services is not equitable. Services are subject, depending on the province, to restrictions by age, income, and medical referral. Similarly, long-term institutional care is administered by each province through its social assistance program with no uniformity among the various provinces (Lee, 1974; LeClair, 1975).

In sum, the Canadian health care system is well-established in terms of physician and acute care services. Indeed the most equitable aspects of Canada's health care system are its medical and hospital services, those aspects which Schwenger and Gross (1980) note are the most expensive. In a time of economic constraint it is imperative to ask whether these types of services are the most appropriate for an aging society. If care for elders calls for a different focus, for long-term social care within the community, then additional dollars and efforts directed towards improving the medical/ institutional system currently in place may not be the most efficient or efficacious use of health care dollars. More energy and more money directed towards redistributing physicians or building more long-term institutional beds will not meet the needs of an aging society. This leads to a discussion of the appropriateness of the Canadian health care system, the topic of the next section.

Appropriateness

Services can be equitable or accessible but if they are not appropriate they will not lead to a healthy society. The major illnesses of old age are chronic conditions or acute flair-ups of chronic conditions. That is, the greatest need among elderly persons is for services to help them cope with chronic conditions and functional disability. Yet community care programs have tended to develop as add ons to existing institutional and medical care services in Canada. New monies have to be found in order to fund community services. They have not been implemented in a fashion whereby dollars from existing physician and acute care services are being transferred over. This detracts from their desirability when viewed through government eyes.

While there is an increasing recognition of the importance of community and social services for an aging population, this is occurring when a powerful, expensive and complex medical/pharmaceutical/industrial system is already in place. That basic system in Canada has not undergone major transformation even though McKeown and Lowe (1966), McKeown et al., (1975), Dubos (1963), and McKinlay and McKinlay (1977) have demonstrated that medical intervention is not the primary cause of declines in mortality in this century; Maxwell (1975) and Weller and Manga (1982) have shown that the major diseases of old age are chronic not acute illnesses and health care expenditures are not necessarily correlated with health outcomes; Syme and Berkman (1981) and Grant (1984) have shown that social class and poverty are significantly correlated with health; and others (Coddington et al., 1990) report estimates anywhere from 25% to 60% of physician services to seniors are unnecessary or inappropriate.

Amid such established findings questioning the value of extending medical care, there is recent Canadian evidence that medical treatment of the elderly is increasing at a faster rate than the proportion of elderly within the society. Evans (1988) and Barer et al. (1986) argue convincingly that the aging of the Canadian population will not place a significant strain on the health care system. There will be a slow and steady increase with certain sectors increasing more than others, such as long-term care, home care, etc. but that society can handle that gradual increase. Nor is there any evidence to suggest that changing morbidity patterns among elders will lead to drastically increased utilization.

However, there is evidence of dramatic increases in the utilization patterns of health care services (including medical, acute/rehabilitation hospital care, and long-term care) by elderly persons (in the province of British Columbia where the data are collected). There is an increased servicing which is rising faster than the increase in the proportion of elderly. The increased utilization is not due to the demographic change by itself nor does it appear to be due to changing morbidity patterns. Rather, the relative intensity with which the health care system is treating elders is rising dramatically.

As Gill and Ingman (1986) have pointed out, with the explosion in biomedical knowledge it is hardly surprising to see such an increase in service provision. However, since this can continue indefinitely and given the growing opportunities for intervention during old age, there has been growing doubt about the effectiveness and ultimate value of these treatments. Given the biomedical focus of physicians, and the chronic and disability needs of old age, together with a recognition that the system is provider driven and not patient driven, it is a distinct possibility that increased medical servicing is escalating in an unwarranted fashion. As others have pointed out, the medical care system is driven primarily by physicians, not patients (see for example Walker, 1986). Other than the initial visit, patients return to the physician on the physician's advice. Physicians and only physicians have admitting privileges to hospitals, physicians control the tests that will be ordered, the drugs that will be prescribed, the services that will be received, and when the patient will be released from the hospital. These decisions are by and large out of the control of the patient.

The power and strength of the medical/industrial complex is reflected in society's acceptance of those services as more important than social services. Community and social services tend to be equated with tasks normally done for oneself or by family or friends. These tasks, such as homemaker, handyman, and meal services, are seldom thought of in terms of formal agencies. When they are provided formally there is an historical tendency to equate them with welfare and to make them means tested, stigmatizing recipients (Tenhoor, 1982). As economic constraints tighten, Estes and Wood (1986) note that the United States is turning to a medicalization of community care as a result of their medically oriented reimbursement policies.

This has not been the tendency in Canada to date. Indeed the move has been away from home care programs requiring physician certification to those accepting any referral source. However the report of the Canadian Medical Association (1987) on health care for the elderly recommends that while there be both a medical and a social component to assessment prior to entry into the system, the "physician should play a central role" in subsequent coordination of health care. If community care develops under medical dominance, either to receive legitimacy earlier or to tap into the existing national health insurance system, it will not provide a necessary broadening of the medical system to a health care system. By definition, a physician dominated community care program will be medical rather than health-oriented. It is only by embracing a broad definition of health, which includes social, economic, psychological, and environmental aspects of health, in addition to the medical, that the health care needs of Canadians will be met.

There is little research on the demand for community services should they be offered as add ons to the existing system. Kane (1985) reports that in British Columbia the demand curve for community services plateaued after two years. He argues that the key to control is a universal system administered from a single entry point with a fixed budget. The experiences in

British Columbia, Manitoba and Ontario all suggest that services can be provided within a fixed budget. With about 10% of the nursing home budget, these provincial governments have offered a desirable package of home care services (Kane and Kane, 1985).

Part of the rationale for establishing these services is that they will reduce the use of more expensive forms of care, i.e., physician services, hospital and long-term institutional care. Kane and Kane (1985) did not find evidence of institutional care displacement in the aggregate. However they do argue that the presence of an alternative system of care makes it more feasible to implement a policy to restrict building more institutional beds. Havens (1985) notes that savings in a mature system occur primarily in less use of acute care hospital beds by long-term care patients. Supporting this argument are data from Manitoba adult day care users (Chappell and Blandford, 1983). Furthermore, Levin (1985) points out that while there has been a continued growth in long-term care beds, it has been less than expected by the increase in the number of elderly. The continued increase of 2% per year of elderly individuals and the fact that they use the bulk of long-term care mean that large decreases in the use of other sectors cannot be expected. If the system continues without major re-organization, limited supplies of community services with low overall budgets can be expected.

There is also a growing acceptance that funding for long-term community care should come from a redistribution of health dollars from the acute care sector. The recent federal report of the Standing Committee on Health and Welfare, Social Affairs, Seniors and the Status of Women (Porter, 1991) recommended that a framework be developed for the gradual shift of resources from the institutional sector to community home care, and social support services. National expenditure on hospitals did decrease slightly from 44.4% in 1975 to 39.2% in 1987 with expenditure on home care increasing slightly from .3% to .8% in the same period. The Ontario government (Ministry of Community and Social Services, Ministry of Health, and Ministry of Citizenship, 1991) has just proposed transferring 37.6 million annually into long-term care and support services. This constitutes less than 1% of hospital expenditures.

It is evident from this discussion that while Canada offers a universal and reasonably equitable medical care system, it falls short in terms of a health care system for elderly persons. A system can be equitable but not appropriate. Many of these problems of appropriateness are tied to the issue of accountability.

Public Accountability

The universal aspect of Canada's health care system (physician and hospital services) has had neither cost accountability nor intervention evaluation (does a particular treatment work?). Despite the fact that Canada's rate of increase in the cost of health care services has been somewhat less than other industrialized countries (Bennett and Krasny, 1981; Weller and Manga, 1982), there is much concern over the continually escalating costs of the health care dollar. Indeed, Canada's combination of self-regulation by the medical profession plus public insurance coverage has led to price escalation (the introduction of public insurance resulted in a high rise in provider incomes and health expenditures initially with less of an increase in the long run) (Evans, 1984).

Physicians receive a negotiated fee for service and their incomes are one of the highest of occupational groups in the country. While the fee-for-service principle has been defended as preserving the autonomy and professional standing of the physician and the doctor-patient relationship, the argument does not withstand scrutiny. The implication is that physicians who are salaried do not have the same autonomy of diagnosis and treatment or the same status or the same integrity within their professional relationship as those working within a fee-for-service system. However, other professionals who are in salaried positions, including university professors and salaried lawyers, have no such problems. Salaried physicians could receive a wage which is sufficient for a comfortable standard of living. A trend to salary physicians is not yet evident in Canada, despite the profit-motive obvious within a fee-for-service system. The latter provides an economic incentive both to see more patients (thereby spending less time per patient) and to diagnose and treat particular illnesses (those which have higher reimbursement levels). However, recent reports are calling for more salaried options and an end to fee-for-service (for example, the Report of the British Columbia Royal Commission on Health Care and Costs, Province of British Columbia, 1991; and the special report commissioned for the Ministers of Health, Barer and Stoddart, 1991).

By and large the Canadian strategy for controlling costs has been to limit overall supply, to stop building hospitals, hospital additions, decreasing the acquisition of new technology, etc. In recent years there has also been some effort to restrict enrollment in medical schools, thereby limiting the future supply of physicians. While hospital space has been relatively stable since 1971 (Evans, 1984:176), the number of physicians has grown more rapidly. The result has been physicians' access to hospital space has been reduced, limiting his or her billing capacity and increasing pressure on hospitals. Hospitals in Canada are not under any institutionalized pressure to provide the least costly care. Indeed Walker's (1986) description of the genuine customers of hospitals as physicians, not patients, and hospitals competing for these customers by offering extensive technology, favourable working conditions, less bureaucratic regulation and control over production is as applicable to Canada as to the United States.

The issue of cost accountability is receiving attention in Canada as health care costs continue to rise. How it will ultimately be dealt with, if at all, is not yet clear. The issue of cost accountability is tied to the issue of intervention evaluation, for which there is no overall mechanism in the Canadian system. While intervention which is clearly harmful will be quickly discontinued when it comes to the attention of the public and professionals (such as adverse effects of drugs such as thalidomide), interventions which do not do any apparent harm remain within the system. While individual citizens and citizen coalitions can challenge physician decisions (both within their offices and through the courts), the specialized expertise of the medical profession calls for a mechanism which has equivalent expertise. The extensive and pervasive nature of the profession calls for a national mechanism for public accountability, as Gill and Ingman (1986) note, through the body politic to the general population.

Part of the problem is adequate funds for research. In 1982 over three hundred billion dollars were being spent annually to improve the health of Canadians (Evans, 1984:21) but there was no systematic effort to measure the results. Canada does not even conduct periodic systematic national health surveys as does the United States. Rigorous testing of the maximum amount of days for patients to remain in hospital is not well studied, potentially harmful or indiscriminate use of antibiotics or excessive diagnostic radiography are potential problems within the system. When new interventions or programs become implemented, seldom do their less effective counterparts become phased out. The result is a large and growing system which is incoherent.

Because capacity has been demonstrated to influence use (a built bed is a filled bed) (Roemer, 1961), one cannot add to the system without correspondingly removing something from the system if cost containment is to become a reality. If adult day care programs are implemented based on the rationale that they will permit early discharge from hospital, then early discharges from hospital and bed closures must also be implemented. If home care programs are implemented to reduce long-term institutionalization, long-term beds must also be reduced. Otherwise if adult day care programs and home care programs are simply added, these programs will become filled and the existing supply of hospital beds and long-term institutional beds will remained filled, so the end result will be added costs to the system.

The issue of intervention is also related to the issue of patient autonomy. While it is accepted that health care professionals, in particular physicians, are in possession of a specialized body of knowledge which few if any of their patients share, this specialized knowledge does not necessarily mean they are in a position to make all decisions for the patient. A qualified physician may be able to tell the patient that a specific operation will save his/her life, but will leave the patient handicapped. It is the patient's decision as to whether he or she chooses to live a shorter life of higher quality or a longer life with reduced quality. Indeed it is not uncommon for physicians to recommend an elderly person be institutionalized because they are becoming frail and they are at increased risk of falling and fracturing bones if they remain in their own home. However the elderly individual may prefer to take that risk, fully cognizant of those risks, rather than go to a long-term institution earlier than what they perceive is necessary and perhaps not at all.

Canadian society, not unlike other industrial societies, has yet to come to terms with old age as a natural process, distinct from medical intervention. When is it appropriate for medicine to intervene in the inevitable decline of bio-medical function which is part of the usual experience in the later stages of life? Some attention has been directed to the issue of prolonging life in the face of death but most of this discussion has centered around euthanasia and life saving measures. Collective decision-making concerning medical intervention to the very end, taking into account the issues of distributive justice and the best allocation of scarce resources, is only just beginning. It is argued here that it is necessary if we are to ensure health care in place of the medical care that is available today.

With discussions of medical intervention at the very end of life have come the hospice movement for dying with dignity outside of the medical hospital setting. While the hospice setting has been more popular in the United States than in Canada, it is beginning to be evidenced here as well. If this is any indication, extensive discussions of the role (or reduced role) of the medical profession during old age could perhaps lead to the same results, that is, to less of a role for medicine during the last decades of life. However, if the recommendation of the Canadian Medical Association that the physician be central to any collaborative medical and social assessment, the other direction will be more likely, that is, the medicalization of community services.

Non-physician control, of course, does not guarantee cost containment. Indeed, the current discussion in Canada (and Britain) to privatize home care services will not necessarily lead to cost containment either. In both countries private home care firms are growing. Individuals who have been assessed as eligible for particular services (for example, sitter attendant services) from the province or a national program, but where that program cannot provide the services due to unavailability of personnel, are authorized to utilize a private firm and the provincial or national program reimburses that private firm. Such a trend can lead to cost escalation since private firms are more likely to engage in aggressive marketing to increase demand for their services than are those provided through government auspices. According to Davies (1989), the future for Britain is one which sees the private health care sector dominating in the delivery of community care. This individual sees the role of government as one of setting standards and of subsidizing low income individuals who cannot afford to pay for these services themselves. Such a system, of course, is non-universalistic and has all the disadvantages of means tested programs. In Canada, the willingness to reimburse private firms is a step in this direction. It is taking place even in a province such as Manitoba, which is known for its universal government home care program.

It is clear that if the system continues without reorganization, the provision of community services is unlikely to take a central place within the health care system in this country. The escalating nature of medical servicing for the increasing elderly population is simply too expensive to allow for the provision of comprehensive community services. Similarly, if the medical profession becomes central to the provision of community services within the existing system, this will escalate the cost of health care to an even greater extent. The establishment of a broad health care system for elders in Canada, while maintaining the laudable universal nature of the medical care system, is possible within cost containment only through adequate cost and intervention evaluation.

It is suggested here that such accountability will point to a wholesale reorganization of the medical care system to one which provides more of an equal footing for community care services. It is only through cost accounting and intervention that the value (and lack thereof) of medical intervention for the health of elders, that is, for their quality of life, can be demonstrated. Once it is demonstrated, it will require a strong political will to implement a truly reorganized health care system. The possibility is there; whether it will become reality is not known.

Conclusions

In reflecting on Canada's health care system, it is instructive to remember the country's different historical roots, especially in contrast to those of the United States. Lipset (1985) reminds us that, in the late 18th century, Canadian elite saw the need for state protection of minority cultures, of English Canadians against the Yankees, of French Canadians against the Anglophones. Americans, by contrast, saw the Atlantic Ocean as an effective barrier for maintaining a weak state which did not require extensive military maintenance. Canada's founding fathers emphasized "Peace, Order, and Good Government," whereas Americans stressed "Life, Liberty, and the Pursuit of Happiness," portraying the same distinction between a strong state and individualism. Canada's respect for the state, Lipset argues, has resulted in much greater support for social, democratic, redistributive and welfare policies. The dominant laissez-faire tradition in the United States has been more opposed to such policies.

Canada shows greater redistributive justice than the United States. Even though there has never been serious consideration of replacing her public insurance system with a free competitive market, there has been and continues to be conflict over who will direct the power of the state in regulating the health care market. Currently, physicians exercise much of that power. However, the medical care system has come under heavy criticism, both because of its cost inefficiencies and its health outcomes. The combination of rising costs, together with increased questioning of the effectiveness of medical care, can provide the opportunity for greater provision of community care within the health care system. This opportunity for improvement can maintain the values of universal health care while ensuring more appropriate services to an aging society. Whether Canada possesses the political will to reorganize its health care system remains to be seen.

References

Barer, M.L. and Stoddart, G.L. (1991). *Toward Integrated Medical Resource Policies for Canada: Background Document.* Vancouver, B.C.: Centre for Health Services and Policy Research, University of British Columbia.

Barer, M.L., Evans, R.G., Hertzman, C. and Lomas, J. (1986). "Toward Effective Aging: Rhetoric and Evidence," paper presented at the 3rd Canadian Conference on Health Economics, Winnipeg, Manitoba, May.

Bennett, J.E. and Krasny, J. (1981). "Health Care in Canada." In D. Coburn, C. D'Arcy, P. New and G. Torrance (Eds.), *Health and Canadian Society: Sociological Perspectives.* Don Mills, Ontario: Fitzhenry and Whiteside, 40-66.

Canadian Medical Association. (1987). *Health Care for the Elderly: Today's Challenges, Tomorrow's Options.* Ottawa, Ontario: Department of Communications and Government Relations, Canadian Medical Association.

Chappell, N.L. (1988). "Long-Term Care in Canada." In E. Rathbone-McCuan and B. Havens (Eds.), *North American Elders: United States and Canadian Comparisons.* Westport, CT: Greenwood Press, 73-88.

Chappell, N.L. (1989). "Aging and the Family." In G.N. Ramu (Ed.), *Courtship, Marriage and the Family in Canada.* Toronto, Ontario: Prentice-Hall of Canada, forthcoming.

Chappell, N.L. and Blandford, A.A. (1983). *Adult Day Care: Its Impact on the Utilization of Other Health Care Services and on Quality of Life.* Ottawa, Ontario: NHRDP, Health and Welfare Canada.

Chappell, N.L., Strain, L.A. and Blandford, A.A. (1986). *Aging and Health Care: A Social Perspective.* Toronto, Ontario: Holt, Rinehart & Winston.

Coddington, D.C. et al. (1990). *The Crisis in Health Care.* San Francisco, CA: Jossey-Bass Publishers.

Davies, B. (1989). Personal communication.

Dubos, R.J. (1963). "Infection into Disease." In D.J. Ingle (Ed.), *Life and Disease,* New York, NY: Basic Books.

Dulude, L. (1978). *Women and Aging: A Report on the Rest of Our Lives.* Ottawa: Advisory Council on the Status of Women.

Estes, C.L. and Wood, J.B. (1986). "The Non-Profit Sector and Community-Based Care for the Elderly in the U.S.: A Disappearing Resource?," *Social Science and Medicine,* 23(12):1261-1266.

Evans, R.G. (1976a). "Does Canada Have Too Many Doctors: Why Nobody Loves an Immigrant Physician," *Canadian Public Policy,* II:147-160.

Evans, R.G. (1976b). "Modelling the Economic Objectives of the Physician." In R.D. Fraser (Ed.), *Health Economics Symposium: Proceedings of the First Canadian Conference,* September 4-6, 1974. Kingston, Ontario: Queen's University Industrial Relations Centre, 33-46.

Evans, R.G. (1984). *Strained Mercy: The Economics of Canadian Health Care.* Toronto, Ontario: Butterworths.

Evans, R.G. (1988). "Plenary Address." Paper presented at Connections '88, International Symposium on *Research and Public Policy on Aging and Health,* Saskatoon, Saskatchewan, February.

Gill, D.G. and Ingman, S.R. (1986). "Geriatric Care and Distributive Justice: Problems and Prospects," *Social Science and Medicine,* 23(12):1205-1215.

Grant, K.R. (1984). "The Inverse Care Law in the Context of Universal Free Health Insurance in Canada: Toward Meeting Health Needs Through Social Policy," *Sociological Focus,* 17:137-155.

Havens, B. (1985). "A Long-Term Care System: A Canadian Perspective." In *The Feasibility of a Long-Term Care System: Lessons from Canada.* Tampa, FL: International Exchange Center on Gerontology, 19-27.

Health and Welfare Canada and Statistics Canada. (1981). *Canada Health Survey.* Ottawa, Ontario: Minister of Supply and Services.

Kammerman, S.B. (1976). "Community Services for the Aged: The View from Eight Countries," *The Gerontologist,* 16:529-537.

Kane, R.L. (1985). *The Feasibility of a Long-Term Care System: Lessons from Canada.* Tampa, FL: International Exchange Center on Gerontology, 1-19.

Kane, R.A. and Kane, R.L. (1985). "The Feasibility of Universal Long-Term Care Benefits," *New England Journal of Medicine*, 312:1357-1364.

Lalonde, M. (1974). *A New Perspective on the Health of Canadians*. Ottawa, Ontario: Health and Welfare Canada.

LeClair, M. (1975). "The Canadian Health Care System." In S. Andreopoulos (Ed.), *National Health Insurance: Can We Learn from Canada?* New York, NY: John Wiley and Sons, 11-93.

Lee, S.S. (1974). "Health Insurance in Canada—An Overview and Commentary," *New England Journal of Medicine*, 290:713.

Levin, P.J. (1985). "A Comparison, from a Hospital Administrator's Viewpoint, Between Three Canadian Provinces' Long-Term Care Programs and the U.S. Non-System." In *The Feasibility of a Long-Term Care System: Lessons from Canada*. Tampa, FL: International Exchange Center on Gerontology, 28-36.

Lipset, S.M. (1985). "Canada and the United States: The Cultural Dimension." In C.F. Doran and J.H. Sigler (Eds.), *Canada and the United States: Enduring Friendship, Persistent Stress*. The American Assembly and Council on Foreign Relations, 109-160.

Marsh, L. (1975). *Report on Social Security for Canada*. Toronto, Ontario: University of Toronto Press.

Maxwell, R. (1975). *Health Care: The Growing Dilemma*. New York, NY: McKinsey & Company.

McKeown, T. and Lowe, C.R. (1966). *An Introduction to Social Medicine*. Philadelphia, PA: F.A. Davis.

McKeown, T., Record, R.G. and Turner, R.D. (1975). "An Interpretation of the Decline of Mortality in England and Wales During the Twentieth Century," *Population Studies*, 29:391-422.

McKinlay, J.B. and McKinlay, S.M. (1977). "The Questionable Contribution of Medical Measures to the Decline of Mortality in the United States in the Twentieth Century," *Milbank Memorial Fund Quarterly*, summer.

Minister of Supply and Services Canada. (1987). *Active Health Report*. Ottawa, Ontario: Minister of Supply and Services, Catalogue H-39-106/1987E.

Ministry of Community and Social Services, Ministry of Health and Ministry of Citizenship. (1991). *Redirection of Long-Term Care and Support Services in Ontario: A Public Consultation Paper*. Ontario: Community Support Services Area Offices.

National Health and Welfare. (1975). *Report on the Federal-Provincial Working Group on Home Care Programs to the Advisory Committee on Community Health*. Ottawa, Ontario: National Health and Welfare.

Porter, B. (1991). *The Health Care System in Canada and Its Funding: No Easy Solutions* (First Standing Report of the Standing Committee on Health and Welfare, Social Affairs, Seniors and the Status of Women). Ottawa, Ontario: Canada Communication Group—Publishing, Supply and Services Canada.

Province of British Columbia. (1991). *Closer to Home: Summary of the Report of the British Columbia Royal Commission on Health Care and Costs.* Victoria, B.C.: Crown Publications Inc.

Roemer, M.I. (1961). "Bed Supply and Utilization: A Natural Experiment," *Hospitals: Journal of the American Hospital Association,* 35:35-42.

Schwenger, C.W. and Gross, J.M. (1980). "Institutional Care and Institutionalization of the Elderly in Canada." In V.W. Marshall (Ed.), *Aging in Canada: Social Perspectives.* Don Mills, Ontario: Fitzhenry & Whiteside, 248-256.

Shapiro, E. (1979). *Home Care: A Comprehensive Overview.* Ottawa, Ontario: Policy, Planning and Information Branch, Health and Welfare Canada.

Sirois, J. (1940). *Report of the Royal Commission of Dominion-Provincial Relations,* Vol. 2.

Statistics Canada. (1983). *Fact Book on Aging in Canada.* Ottawa, Ontario: Minister of Supply and Services.

Statistics Canada. (1984). *The Elderly in Canada.* Ottawa, Ontario: Minister of Supply and Services.

Statistics Canada. (1985). *General Social Survey Public Use Tape.* Ottawa, Ontario: Minister of Supply and Services.

Statistics Canada. (1987). *The Daily.* Ottawa, Ontario: Minister of Supply and Services.

Statistics Canada. (1988). *Causes of Death, 1986.* Ottawa, Ontario: Minister of Supply and Services, Catalogue 84-203.

Statistics Canada. (1991). *Canada's 125th Anniversary Year Book (1992 edition).* Ottawa, Ontario: Minister of Supply and Services.

Syme, S.L. and Berkman, L.F. (1981). "Social Class, Susceptibility and Sickness." In P. Conrad and R. Kern (Eds.), *The Sociology of Health and Illness: Critical Perspectives.* New York, NY: St. Martin's Press, 35-44.

Tenhoor, W.J. (1982). "United States: Health and Personal Social Services." In M.C. Hokenstad and R.A. Ritvo (Eds.), *Linking Health Care and Social Services.* Beverly Hills, CA: Sage Publications, 25-59.

United Nations. (1990). *1988 Demographic Year Book.* New York, NY: Publishing Division, United Nations.

U.S. Bureau of the Census. (1988). *Statistical Abstract of the United States: 1986 (108th edition).* Washington, DC: U.S. Summary.

Walker, G.K. (1986). "Reforming Medicare: The Limited Framework of Political Discourse on Equity and Economy," *Social Science and Medicine,* 23(12):1237-1250.

Weller, G.R. and Manga, P. (1982). "The Reprivatization of Hospital and Medical Care Services: A Comparative Analysis of Canada, Britain and the United States." Revised version of the paper presented at the 10th World Congress of Sociology, Mexico City, Mexico.

11

Governmental Responsibility:
Adequacy or Dependency for the USA Aged

Jon Hendricks

Introduction

Any number of advanced industrial societies are facing fiscal crises due to mounting expenditures by federal and local governments. The United States is not alone in this regard. We entered the 1970s astride a bubble long inflated by our ascendancy in the world's economy, plentiful energy resources, and the advantaged position of the dollar. When the bubble burst it was heard around the world, and up and down the social ladder at home—perhaps no place louder than on the lower rungs. As the 1980s drew to a close, the aftermath had become rather grim for those relying on public programs to provide for their fundamental well-being. To say the economic picture for the country as a whole or for the less advantaged social categories is still less than rosy is to miss the poignancy of events.

This chapter provides an overview of how shifts in selected federal policies affect the well-being of older persons. It is not an exaggeration to say governmental policies are crucial to the quality of life of those under their sway. If those policies provide for adequacy in terms of lifestyle, they have one effect. If, in spite of governmental intervention, recipients continue in a status of structured dependency and destitution, the outcome will be quite dissimilar (Townsend, 1981). At last count there were over 100 federal programs affecting the daily lives of the elderly. The focus here will be primarily on two. We start by looking at the nature of inequality. The discussion then moves from a critical, historical summary of Social Security to a discussion of current issues. Next, we examine how adequacy or dependency in the realm of medical care is shaped. As with the discussion of the fiscal picture, we critically examine the notion of maintenance of a market economy as an organizing framework for medical benefits. Finally, we introduce alternatives whereby federal policies and service provisions could approach adequacy for those older persons dependent on them.

Social Policies and Inequality

Social class membership and hierarchical stratification are facts of life. With them come more than mere income differences, they spell major lifestyle inequalities as well. If other things were equal, income would be equally distributed across all segments of the population. Anything less than an equitable array indicates that some phenomena or processes are altering the way income is distributed. There has never been much doubt that the nation's wealth has been concentrated in the hands of a few at the top. What is now changing is the extent of the disparity in the distribution of income (Levy, 1987. We have long acknowledged disparities but passed them off as evidence of personal initiative or, at worst, as an unfortunate downside to normal costs of doing business. The gap between those whose finances provide relatively open access to life's opportunities and those who must queue-up to seek assistance with essentials has widened. Worse yet is the erosion nibbling away at the relative standing of the lower tiers while accelerated accumulation is occurring on the very highest levels. As Braun (1991) and others point out, growing inequalities imply more than just individual differences, they imperil the very foundation upon which the country rests.

Moving up from the very lowest rungs of the economic ladder the picture does not get any better. Differences in the standard of living between those whose incomes put them in the 75th percentile and those who are pegged at the 25th percentile or lower, have also grown shudderingly unequal. If real money income, before taxes but including transfers is used aggregate household income in 1986, the last full year for which information is available, was approximately as follows: the poorest quintile received a scant 3.8%; the next poorest 9.7%; the middle, 16.4%; the next, 24.1% and the richest quintile received 46.1%. As dramatic as these differences may appear on their face, what is most significant is that over the past 20 years they have been growing steadily.

Using a widely recognized measure of income inequality, the Gini index, relative dispersion can be highlighted. A value of 0 on a Gini index represents an equal distribution and 1.0 represents total inequality. The 1986 distribution above yields a Gini ratio of .420. If governmental transfers were taken away the disparities would be exacerbated even further. The poorest quintile would then receive 1.1%; the next poorest, 8.5%; the middle, 16.0%; the next richest quintile 25.6% and the richest quintile 49.2% for a Gini ratio of .473—a substantial worsening of inequality (U.S. Bureau of the Census, 1988). What the existing ratio means is that the richest five percent of the population have incomes three times greater than the poorest forty percent. As a nation we need to ask: Do both top and bottom get what they deserve?

For those who point to public outlays as a major culprit in stagnating economies the answer is clear. The solution is reduction of existing entitlement programs and redefinition of the relationship between the Federal government and the country's citizens. Those people on the bottom are simply using too many valuable resources and what were once held as sacred precepts should be questioned. From the New Deal to the Great Society, the citizenry developed expectations as to who would provide their safety net. A key component of the ideology of the United States has been that we aspire to egalitarianism—where there are not only equal rights under law, but equity of access. Such is the moral economy upon which the system was originally erected (Thompson, 1971; Rein, 1976: Hendricks and Leedham, 1990).

When discussing poverty and transfer statistics we must be mindful of some thorny issues and how statistics can be manipulated, depending on the goal. It is not easy to decide what is income and how it should be counted. We presently define Social Security as income, should we also count Medicare/Medicaid benefits? If they are classified as income, should they be included at full market or fungible value only? Should we do likewise with employer contributions for employee health insurance? Should housing subsidies and school lunch supports based on fair market value be included? If we do, should we also include or even tax the business lunch provided at no cost to the employees, or those meals for which employees are reimbursed? Should things like free trips from airline mileage plans be treated as income? Should capital gains be included or excluded? Questions about income are not straightforward, neither are questions about Social Security. Characterizing Social Security as a transfer program, like AFDC, is itself problematic as it ignores previous contributions and implies more of a settling of resources on the elderly than is the case.

The revisionist notions of appropriate moral economy that undergird stratification are also implicit in governmental social policies. This is not to say social welfare does not help, it does. Those who prefer the *status quo*, or even reductions in entitlement programs, maintain that egalitarianism has never been a premise of public policy. We are even hearing that old people are being greedy by asking that benefits be tied to inflation. Hardly a surprise, since there is no place in the ideological edifice upon which public policies are erected where it is contended that a principal goal of American public welfare should be to rearrange existing patterns of social stratification. Redistribution toward the poor is not seen as essential to the compact, despite pervasive norms of reciprocity.

Yet, a premise of entitlement policies is that they are intended to provide alternate routes to access to opportunities for those who would otherwise do without. It is exactly those policies propounded to be the "safety net" that have been placed under a microscope. No one claims to want to impose financial or physical destitution on any client population. Short of that point, however, we are beginning to see what had previously been cast as rights of citizenship being redefined as some of life's negotiables. What recipients and their advocates have hitherto regarded as irreversible policies are increasingly seen as conditional, predicated on priorities dictated by the United States' position in the world economy. In the view of some, sacrifices in domestic social welfare programs are necessary if we are to remain competitive. It is not merely rhetoric leveled at the presumed culprits but real evisceration of programs fueled by a real fiscal crisis.

While surpluses in Social Security that came to light late in the 1980s actually off-set part of the Federal deficit, we have long been accustomed to thinking of this and other benefit packages as costly drains on the economy. In point of fact, thus far in its history Social Security has not imposed any drag whatsoever on the Federal deficit. Actually it has been quite the opposite. Until 1991, Social Security reserves were factored into the total Federal budget, thereby reducing cutbacks mandated by Gramm-Rudman-Hollings by some $230 billion—the approximate size of the reserves that year. In 1991 the law changed, excluding Social Security monies from budget calculations yet still permitting the government to borrow from them rather than elsewhere.

Insofar as age benefits are perceived to account for a large portion of federal outlays, public policies will face greater scrutiny (Myles, 1984a). For many years redistribution programs for the elderly were celebrated for providing safety net support for the deserving poor. As these policies have come under attack, however, the thrust has been to examine expenditures. The welfare state, such as it is in the United States, is defined by formal entitlement legislation, rationalized in accord with perceived rights of citizenship and is at risk. There is no mistaking the case that some are making for a shift in resources away from the elderly to younger segments of the population or toward full-scale curtailment (Quinn, 1990). We are witnessing a fusillade aimed at programs previously claimed to be moral rights and the substitution of a variety of means-tested alternatives in their stead. For good or ill, the existence of these entitlements circumscribes life chances, occupation involvements and socially defined identities. With the exception of a handful of commentators (Myles. 1984b; Olson, 1982; Estes, 1979; 1983; 1986; Quadagno, 1989), the consensus has been that continued inequality among a minority of elderly is due not to inadequate state outlays or distribution programs, but rather to irrational and/or ineffective policy formation and implementation (Crystal, 1982; Kutza, 1981).

Laying the Groundwork for Economic Security

The Original Focus of Social Security

The fact that the model for much of the entitlement legislation in the United States came about during the 1930s is significant; unemployment was high, production had stalled and there were few avenues for occupational mobility (Hendricks and Hendricks, 1986). In a nutshell the economy was stagnant. Like much New Deal legislation, Social Security was designed to spur the accumulation process; the Keynesian goal explicitly to stimulate private enterprise through public spending. At the same time political pressures were such that universal cradle-to-grave protection was not seen as acceptable despite immediate crises. Instead, a closely targeted and delimited system which did not violate certain value positions was deemed apropos.

In the sense that Social Security was to provide the aged with funds which would then be spent in the marketplace, while simultaneously freeing business from economic responsibility for older persons, it undoubtedly seemed an optimal solution. The State would be seen as enhancing accumulation while at the same time those workers who bore the brunt of the economic crisis were provided for, and legitimation of the system and its values assured. The fact that an axiological assumption of the entire framework was that it was never intended to provide sole-source funds during the later years can be read as mute testimony to its being predicated on a particular set of values. The Federal provisions provided a safety net for individuals and an alternative to the private sector assuming responsibility for deferred wages. In the process of doing so, however, the State was precluded from unsettling established social hierarchies based on ideologies of competitive individualism. It is also testimony to the role of the State in circumscribing what are commonly called "life's chances," and thereby the social identities and biographies of those who come under its sway (Weber, 1922: Dowd, 1980).

Because Social Security was touted as an age-based issue, the working-class *per se* appears to have played a relatively minor role. Rather, the battle lines were drawn between monopoly and non-monopoly capitalists as well as Southern aristocrats each with their own agenda protective of their economic niche (Quadagno, 1984). Strong opinions were expressed. Ultimately, Social Security passed in a form proclaimed to be social insurance, rather than welfare, bolstering the ideology of free enterprise by tying benefit levels to past earnings. No apple carts were upset as the wages of retirement were based on the wages of work (Myles, 1984b). To borrow from Adam Smith; the "principal causes" of differential wages were replicated in assignment of retirement benefits. The rationale was straightforward: It is the only fair way. At the same time, Social Security effectively separated a significant number from the ranks of those seeking or holding employment, opening the way to younger workers more likely to make demands.

This ground-breaking legislation also served to enhance accumulation by removing barriers to profit-making while infusing money into the market-place. It was deemed palatable by preserving *marketplace ideology* and by simultaneously labeling Social Security an earned privilege, not a handout. It cast the State in a paternal role, preserving legitimacy but setting the Federal government in guardianship over individual rights and security by virtue of categorical legislation. Employers themselves were thereby excused from direct involvement in workers' old age security. Tying benefit levels to earnings further buttressed existing social stratification through what is called individual equity. It also preserved relative positions among marginal workers as well as those higher in the pecking order. By making Social Security a "funded" system supposedly based on monies on reserve, con-straints were automatic. The only benefit increases permissible were those predicated on changes in withholdings. At the same time unemployment rates were reduced by reclassifying a portion of the work force as "retired"— although it would take several years for the full effect of Social Security to be seen. It also "proved" the economy was back on track, bolstering business confidence. Social Security, abetted by other New Deal measures, success-fully stemmed worker unrest while simultaneously providing for increased capital accumulation.

It is important to note that the means-tested portion of the Social Security Act (Old Age Assistance), generally referred to as Title I, was kept distinct; the effect being a partitioning of the "needy" from the "deserving. " Further, each state was to establish its own criteria for determining adequate benefits for the "needy" and the conditions under which they would be provided. Title II, the earned benefits portion, covered approximately sixty percent of the labor force"—those in mainline commerce and industry—as marginal occupations not considered central to macroeconomic well-being were initially excluded (Hendricks and Hendricks, 1986). The effect was to circumscribe which groups would be assured of funded benefits versus those who might find themselves without assurances. In so doing it defined those whose retirement finances might approach adequacy, in contrast to those who would remain dependent on State determination of what constituted ade-quacy. By and large this latter category included those marginal laborers located in the competitive peripheral sector of the economy whose training was minimal, retention nominal and who were certainly not crucial to the economic well-being of employers. In fact, periodic worker turnover might even be instrumental in assuring profitability. Of course other explanations of the pattern of coverage have also been offered, administrative or constitu-tional hurdles being the most common. Regardless of the explanation, covered occupations clearly clustered around those jobs central to corporate economic interests and maintenance of the Gross National Product.

Revision in Welfare for the Aged: A Decade of Change

While the institution of Social Security came about in response to economic crises, the pension reforms of the late 1960s and early 1970s occurred during economic growth and low unemployment. Nor is it a mere happenstance that pension increases coincided with national elections. Focusing on politics, however, belies the struggles between various industrial factions and workers. Alterations in national social security and health care provisions were still an outgrowth of class distinctions, this time in a different economic context. Amendments to Social Security in 1972 indexed benefits to the Consumer Price Index, thereby enhancing the economic adequacy of those whose working lives had been marked by dependable wages (Quadagno and Meyer, 1990). In the absence of continuous or generous wages, subsequent financial hardship remained an unenviable prospect. For the first time, 1974 saw poverty rates among the elderly decline. The downside is that they were replaced in the dubious first place position by poverty among children— a condition that has worsened in the intervening two decades (Palmer, Smeedley, and Torry, 1988). What is usually missing from discussions of intergenerational issues like this is that poverty rates among the oldest and youngest segments of the U.S. population are among the highest in the industrialized world.

Some say modern economies have been transformed, bifurcated into distinctive sectors, and that the nature of class tensions within governmental sanctioned benefits reflect this change. By many accounts the nature of the growth in capitalism experienced in the United States from the end of World War II to the 1970s favored the interests of the middle and upper classes. One of the paradoxes of the economy is that low rates of joblessness or "full employment capitalism" may actually have been inimical to maximum profit-making (Myles, 1984a). Among the reasons this could be so is that workers in monopoly industries could lobby effectively for raises whenever the reserve labor pool was depleted in the face of a need for more workers. How could the issue be resolved? How could management and labor each achieve their goals?

As monopoly firms, almost by definition, typically contribute disproportionately to the GNP, their problems cannot be ignored if the State is to remain viable. To alleviate potential "profit squeeze," yet control labor's demands, the Federal government turned to retirement policies to facilitate resolution. Pension reforms were instituted. The Nixon administration stepped in to improve pension benefits as a "deferred wage"—instead of receiving immediate income, labor's demands were deferred to the future and turned over to the State in the form of promised retirement resources (Myles, 1984a). Foremost among the ameliorative changes was the indexing of Social Security to the Consumer Price Index rather than to real wages. Among other things, this resulted in cost-of-living adjustments increasing more rapidly than the taxable wage base. Accumulation was bolstered yet again, however, as management was spared immediate costs while being able to anticipate stable wage profiles. Simultaneously, legitimation of the whole pension reform effort was buttressed through effective resolution of labor disputes and the increased oversight role accorded the Federal government.

It is relevant to point out that not only did these reforms temporarily resolve the accumulation-legitimation debate, it was accomplished in a way that perpetuated life-long social class standing. That is, nothing was changed about benefits—they were pegged to past earnings. Nor did these changes substantially alter the position of marginal labor. While it is true that more categories of workers were covered, to the point where we now see approximately 94% of all workers included, benefit levels remain minimal for many workers recently incorporated. Still excluded were seasonal and domestic workers whose working lives reflect a lifetime of low wages. Furthermore, the provision of IRA and KEOGH plans was structured to provide maximum benefit to those in at least the 30 percent tax bracket. With the advent of IRAs the single largest pool of private capital ever came into existence. It is fairly accurate to say that over $334 billion is available through IRAs as loans to private enterprise to capitalize business ventures (Investment Company Institute, 1987). Ironically, workers in secondary labor markets are still penalized for their place in the economy. Working in areas characterized by job instability, they are caught in a double bind as availability and coverage of retirement incomes and health insurance are linked to continuous labor force participation—a near impossibility under conditions of their employment. In 1991, 45% of all full-time employees had no private pensions, and these were concentrated in the secondary sector of the economy.

The Current Status of the Elderly

To understand the effects brought on by recent retrenchments an incontrovertible point must be emphasized. While the fiscal crisis of the welfare state is sometimes attributed to elderly recipients of Social Security and/or Medicare, neither Social Security nor Part A of Medicare are financed from general revenues. To say the structuring of the nation's Social Security programs was originally class or market based probably prompts less disagreement than pointing out that current attacks on the aged are equally class based. Serious questions were raised as to the solvency of Social Security during the Reagan administration. Continual reference to overall budget deficits may serve scant purpose other then to legitimate attacks on the program. While cuts and/or realignments in Social Security and Medicare have resulted from the austerity rhetoric, confounding these programs with those financed solely by general revenues allowed deeper recisions to be made in programs designed for the needy aged and non-aged. As has been pointed out, up to the year 2030, surpluses will build to approximetely $11.8 trillion. Depending on new laws, these monies might still be utilized to underwrite existing Federal shortfalls or as a source of loans to the Federal government, or even as a way to spur economic development. One other alternative that has been floated is to cut current withholding rates so that no additional surpluses accrue—a move that appears short-sighted on its face but is defended as a means of precluding abuse of the funds. In fact, in 1991, Senator Moynihan (D-NY) and others focused attention on surpluses and how they were being used to mask the apparent size of the Federal deficit to the tune of nearly $230 billion. While many compromises were made, accounting procedures were at least revised to insure full disclosure.

Entitlement: A Two-Edged Sword

In 1991, over 40 million people received Social Security, roughly 62 percent of whom were over age 65. The average payment was $602 a month, and the typical age at which people began drawing benefits was 63. In 1991, regulations limited people between the ages of 65 and 69 to earned incomes of $10,440 annually. Above that level benefits are reduced by $1.00 for every $3.00 earned up to $20,000 after which no benefits are received as long as wages remain elevated or until the wage-earner turns age 70. The "retire-ment earnings test" clearly penalizes paid labor for those who must work. It says nothing, however, about incomes derived from non-earned sources. For those receiving dividends, interest, annuities, anything but wage income, the sky is the limit. Also, for those able to finagle wages in unreported cash, an underground economy has sprung-up.

Certainly reforms would remove disincentives to work or the necessity of violating the law, but will they also cease penalizing older persons earning above stipulated thresholds yet not affluent enough to get by without benefit of Social Security? By abolishing the earnings test, Social Security could face additional payouts estimated at the time to some $7 billion annually. In the context of monthly payouts of $20 billion, representatives of the Reagan administration acknowledged the sum was hardly exorbitant. On the flip side; it must be recognized that roughly 80 percent of the beneficiaries of Social Security receive no other income. For them the Social Security check is all there is. Another 10% earn something less than the allowable maximum and only about 10% earn in excess of $10,440. The distribution of sources of income among five categories of people is shown in Table 1. The table shows the overall average and sources of income among the lowest and highest income quintiles for the five categories. As can be seen, it is only for those persons with incomes that place them in the highest quintile that Social Security ceases to be a primary source of income. The implication is clear; as reductions in Social Security or other welfare programs are contemplated, they are unmistakably settled on the poorest among us.

Having said Social Security policies are class based insofar as they do not affect all elderly equally, we must also note that there are also gender

TABLE 1

Aggregate Share of Adjusted Family Income from Particular Sources, by Type of Beneficiary, and Income Level[1]

Family income sources	Retired worker	Disabled worker	Aged wife	Aged widow	Minor child
Total					
Total	100	100	100	100	100
Social Security	40	38	40	37	35
Property income	21	6	23	18	4
Earnings	20	37	18	33	52
Means-tested income	1	3	1	2	2
All other sources	19	16	18	11	7
Lowest quintile					
Total	100	100	100	100	100
Social Security	85	76	78	80	72
Property income	([2])	2	5	5	1
Earnings	3	4	4	3	15
Means-tested income	8	13	11	9	10
All other sources	4	5	2	3	2
Highest quintile					
Total	100	100	100	100	100
Social Security	24	17	22	14	14
Property income	29	9	33	25	5
Earnings	27	54	26	48	74
Means-tested income	([2])	1	([2])	([2])	([2])
All other sources	21	20	19	13	7

[1] Those with negative income are exluded
[2] Less than 0.5 percent

Source: Social Security Bulletin Reprint, "Income and Assets of Social Security Beneficiaries by Type of Benefit" 52.1 (January, 1986) P.6.

biases, What is too frequently overlooked when evaluating global income statistics is that two-thirds of the elderly poor are female. Though there have been many reforms, without exception these have reinforced the primacy of market ideology. Benefit levels will most likely remain tied to work histories and past earnings. Interrupted labor force participation, or reduced wages such as those of many women, are a "built-in" facet of benefit calculations. Quadagno and Meyer (1990) point to a gender gap in retirement income as one way of encapsulating the differential opportunity structures upon which Social Security is predicated. As a consequence of the way the system is set up, inequalities throughout the first half of life are replicated in the second. The paradox is that social justice or the very concept of what Thompson (1971), Kohli (1989), and others term moral economy, reflect the same market mentality—benefits based on narrowly defined contributions rather than need.

Proponents of a political economy perspective are adamant, welfare policies for the elderly are rife with examples of market driven social justice. For example: Numerous reports have surfaced which point to the "over-whelming" number of present and future elderly and warn of dire consequences of providing a safety net. The report of the President's Commission on Pension Policy, released a decade ago, became a focal point as it forecast a gloomy picture exacerbated by an aging population. The actuarial cost estimates were said to portend short and long-term crises for Social Security as outlays were predicted to outstrip collections. For the system itself to remain healthy, revenues must clearly exceed expenditures. According to many experts, the differential must exceed 50%, to allow for all contingencies. By 1989, the reserve ratio had reached 57% and was projected to climb to 77% by 1991, it should not fall significantly for the next four decades.

Short-run problems so conveniently highlighted early in the 1980s were actually ephemeral once tax ceilings were adjusted. Nonetheless, the specter of a *demographic iceberg* needs to be addressed. Certainly it is trotted out often enough to pose some nagging questions. Age-dependency ratios are frequently used in forecasts of hard times. Yet reliable estimates suggest that between now and 2010, the ratio of older people to working age people will not change appreciably; neither will the number of babies born. Consequently, the *net change* in the "dependent" portion of the population will be either nil or perhaps even slightly lower. It is only after the baby boomers reach retirement age that problems loom. Myers (1985) suggests that around 2035 the ratio will approach 39.5 and remain constant for some years thereafter. In real terms this means that the current 5.0 workers for every retired or disabled beneficiary will decline to about 2.2 by 2035, the most significant changes coming after 2010. Alternately, and as a way to include macro-economic transitions as a percentage of taxable payroll, projected outlays will increase by approximately one-third by the mid-21st century.

Beginning in 1990, and continuing until at least the year 2020, surpluses will build in the OASDI trust fund as a consequence of new tax ceilings implemented in 1988 and even higher rates which became effective in 1990 (15.3%). Still, beyond 2010 an imbalance is likely. The question is, what do these projections mean? Large surpluses may accumulate, up to $6.9 trillion in 1990 dollars by the year 2015 (Quadagno, 1989). Myers (1985) puts the differential at as much as five times over outlays. As is apparent in Figure 1, the Trust Fund balance will grow, surpluses will accumulate and deficit spending will not even begin to occur until we approach the third decade of the century.

To help put the figures in context, it is also relevant to point out that as we move into the 21st century retirement age will begin to rise. Age 67 will be the law by 2027 with penalties imposed on early claimants. To encourage additional surpluses, those who postpone retirement will be rewarded with increased benefits. By 2009, it is possible these bonuses for delayed exit from the labor force might range up to eight % over what individuals would otherwise have received.

Based on segmented age-dependency ratios, projections of Federal fiscal responsibilities may be misleading. Indeed, studies increasingly indicate that the present form of Social Security could remain viable for the next 50 years if inflation and unemployment remain low (Friedmann and Adamchak, 1983). However, projections have often been manipulated to curtail payouts and control demand for wage increases (Caplovitz, 1979). While the projection of "too many old people" may be specious (Myles and Boyd, 1982; Friedmann and Adamchak, 1983; Myles, 1984b: Calasanti and Bonanno, 1986), the ideology has taken hold and remains a credible argument for regressive policies and further disfranchisement.

Perhaps more effective than statistical slight of hand has been the conflation in the minds of the public of Social Security, Medicare and the general budget. Also, assets of the three primary trust funds could be pooled but are treated instead as distinct entities (OASI, Disability, Hospital) rather than as what they really are; accounts which receive *allocated proportions* of payroll taxes. Most of the population is unaware that Social Security and the majority of Medicare payments are not welfare transfers derived from general revenues; just as they are unaware that Social Security taxes account for greater withholdings from the paychecks of three-quarters of all wage earners than does income tax. In fact, only Part B of Medicare and Medicaid draw from general revenues. Still, it is easy to fall prey to the argument that the Federal deficit can be substantially reduced by limiting spending for the elderly. Neither are we aware that disabled workers may receive benefits, along with auxiliary benefits for eligible spouses or children, at any age. In short, the "problem," such as it is, is one created by regulations and by

FIGURE 1

Annual Surplus or Deficit and Balance in the OASDI Trust Funds
as a Percent of GNP, Selected Years, 1945-2045[a]

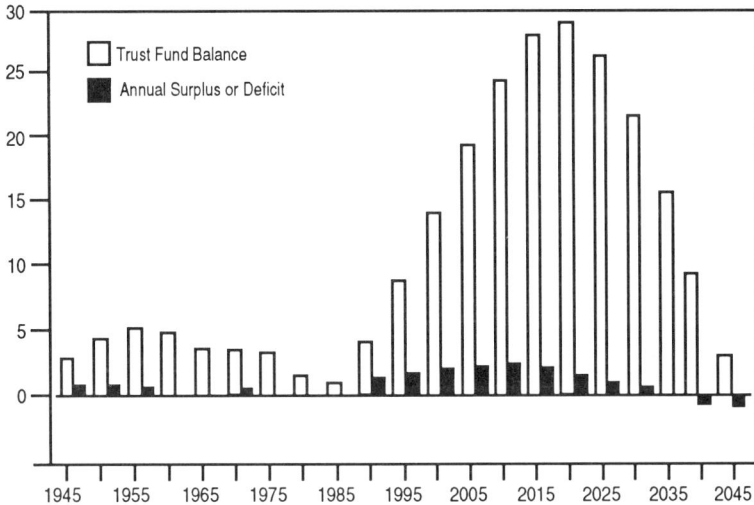

[a]Figures for 1945-1985 represent the average of the annual surplus or deficit and balance in the OASDI trust funds over the preceding five years. Figures for 1990-2045 are annual figures projected under alternative assumption II-B of the 1988 OASDI Trustees Report.

Sources: *Social Security Bulletin, Annual Statistical Supplement, 1987*, by the Social Security Administration, 1987, Tables 23 and 25, pp. 98 and 100; *1988 Annual Report of the Board of Trustees of the Federal Old-Age and Survivors Insurance and Disability Insurance Trust Funds* (1988), Tables G1 and G2, pp. 141-144.

Reprinted from: John R. Gist, "Social Security and Economic Well-Being Across Generations" Public Policy Institute, American Association of Retired Persons. Washington, D.C., 1988, p. 66.

accentuation of one-sided information. The attention directed to the surpluses as we began the decade prompted public recognition of the accumulation of huge reserves in the Social Security Trust. As a nation we began to see that the problem was not one of short-falls and that, in fact, Social Security funds were being commingled with general revenue accounts.

Using the aged as a lightening rod, administrations of the 1980s actually implemented a number of policies geared to redistributing income toward wealthier segments of the population. Tax laws were revised and spending reductions enacted to enhance accumulation, yet the blame for the Federal deficit was still placed at the feet of aging—and needy—population. In point of fact, from 1980 to 1985 the overall Federal deficit, as a percentage of GNP, increased by 1.6% while "...the net contribution of Social Security and Medicare to the deficit has remained the same (.5% of GNP)" (Storey, 1986).

A closer look suggests the deficit so lamented in the 1980s was a result of tax changes, defense spending, and interest payments on the national debt (Storey, 1986). It is important not to lose sight of how tax code revisions helped affluent elderly, while exacerbating dependency among their working class counterparts. Entering the 1990s, the repeal of Catastrophic Health Insurance illustrated the power of the affluent to shape policy. In fact, tax policies are routinely implicated in passing tens of billions of dollars in savings annually to the wealthiest segments of the population (Nelson, 1983). The irony is that we persist in pointing to the elderly as drains, underscoring the two-edged sword that is the very nature of entitlement. To intervene and seemingly adhere to our value framework we depict all recipients as down-trodden and indigent. The real plight comes not from growing old, but from the aging of economically disadvantaged persons. Despite our *benign ageism*, those who depend on public programs are far less numerous than the aged population as a whole.

Spurred by the "aged as burden" mentality, the present climate has yielded a number of cutbacks that primarily affect lower class elderly while tax breaks beneficial to higher income categories are unchallenged. The cuts of 1982-83 were partially offset by the Social Security Act Amendments of 1983, yet the net outcome for high income elderly was negligible. They were aided by favorable taxes and low inflation, at most experiencing minor adverse effects from the taxation of Social Security. On the other hand, middle class aged on fixed incomes did not gain from tax cuts and only somewhat from low inflation rates. The group most adversely affected were lower income elderly—that segment of the population relegated to a marginal labor pool earlier in life to service an expansionist economy and who in old age were again called upon to perform comparable roles. This segment depends most heavily on exactly those assistance programs that were the biggest losers in the budget struggles of the 1980s. Compared to their standing in 1981, social services (under Title XX), community services, health services and food stamps—programs targeted at all marginal laborers not just the aged—experienced the greatest cuts (in relation to other programs serving the elderly). Medicaid, also geared to low income persons, and Medicare were not far behind. For the aged as a group, the early years of the Reagan administration resulted in a five % decrease in cash and in-kind income but this was disproportionately cut from benefits drawn by the least affluent (Storey,1986).

Sufficient or not, Social Security and Supplemental Security Income represent important financial resources for most older people; their abolition would be disastrous. Approximately 13.6% of the general population was poor in 1986. If all transfer programs had magically been taken away, that rate would have increased to 20.8%. Contrast that to a poverty rate among those 65 or older of some 9.0% and on the face of it that does not sound too bad. But, if all governmental transfers had been excluded the resulting poverty rate would have climbed to 47.5%. By adding in Social Security, the rate drops back to 14.0%. By including Supplemental Security Income and the fungible value of both Medicare and Medicaid the rate declines to the 9.0% figure. It is apparent governmental transfers reduced what might otherwise have been the poverty rate by 81.1%—with Social Security accounting for the largest share (U.S. Bureau of the Census, 1988). Who would not agree that is a substantial reduction?

None of this addresses basic questions of appropriate focus or definition. Poverty, among old and young, is usually discussed in terms of human capital—what an individual brings to the marketplace—and not often enough in terms of widespread shifts in the economy beyond the control of individual workers. For example, the debate as it is narrowly construed sidesteps the fact that the country's wage structure is shifting as we move toward a service economy. With a greater number of lower paid positions, the taxable wage base shrinks just as it does during periods of high unemployment. One of the ironies of the whole economic question is that while the overall economy is losing jobs, the health-care industry is gaining positions at a 4.7% rate in the first half of 1991. Without those positions there would have been over 400,000 fewer jobs available.

By recognizing that the source of Social Security "revenue" is changing, and can be intentionally changed, the problem becomes one not simply of demand. The changing character of labor markets may provide insight into why poverty among certain categories is so common. Closer inspection reveals striking commonalities in the employment situation of single mothers of young children, minorities, female, and marginal elderly. In fact, recognizing the preponderance of new positions, something on the order of 80%, are being created in the service sector. This ought to alert us to what the nature of the problem is going to be as we move into the next century. The agenda is being set as the economy is taking shape.

Medical Coverage

The Federal government's role in health care is far more extensive than merely direct service provision. From its sponsorship of biomedical and other research, training of health care professionals, to the stipulation of protective provisions of the Occupational and Safety Health Administration, the Federal government is deeply involved. To keep the discussion manageable, this portion of the chapter will concentrate on Federal involvement in health care for older persons. While the ethical questions cannot be resolved, perhaps some of the nuances of the debate will be clarified.

In 1991, total health care costs amounted to $618 billion or over 13% of the Gross National Product, up from 6% in 1965. By the year 2000, this figure may climb to over 51.5 trillion or over 15% of the GNP. Seen in this light it is not too surprising that health spending is often described as a money magnet in a market economy. Whether it is disproportionate or not money spent on health care is still money spent.

Characteristically, the onus for reining-in cost-benefit ratios is being laid at the door of *consumers*. If something is wrong, surely it must be on the demand side. By advocating a short-term return on the health care dollar, proponents of rationing, based on ability to pay, lose sight of the long-run benefits stemming from having a healthy citizenry. In Germany where health spending is about nine % of the GNP, Canada where it is 8.5%, or Japan where it is 7%, more extensive employer responsibility brings additional funding and buttresses the priority claim accorded health care. It may not be purely altruistic either; a healthy workforce is a more productive workforce. While health may be cast in economic terms, care is available to all nonetheless.

For purposes of this discussion the issue is, are monies spent on older citizens likely to reap particular benefits or forestall particular expense? Navarro (1987) asserts that social class controversies are seldom acknowledged in the health care literature. The outcome is that while disparities and unequal claims exist they are infrequently explicated. In the realm of elder care the question of class is compounded but addressed even less frequently. There is another question that must also be asked: What will be the effect on current workers if a less than desirable future awaits them in retirement? The Older Americans Act, under which many current policies affecting older persons are formulated, has as its avowed goal the preservation of personal dignity, honor and health in the later years. Heretofore social justice has mandated adequate care for those unable to fend for themselves and is a promise imposed on the future. As has been said repeatedly, these values are being reformulated as medical care is redefined by market forces (Clark, 19851.

Challenging or criticizing Medicare does not gainsay the fact that it has been a major boon. Since its inception we have seen age-specific life expectancy increase by roughly 2.5 years for those already age 65. We have also seen the number of visits to physicians by older persons reach parity with those of younger persons as large numbers of people obtained medical attention previously beyond their reach. The list of benefits is extensive, no doubt about it, but new problems have arisen. Without forgetting the good Medicare/Medicaid have wrought, let us focus on a few details of the system and some of the criticisms being mounted.

Medicare Coverage. Medicare provides for at least minimal health coverage for acute and short-term care. In 1987, total health spending for the elderly reached $162 billion, $5,360 per capita, these amounts representing a 13.6% annual increase for the ten year period prior to 1987 (U. S. Senate, 1991). Total national health spending reached $539.9 billion the same year so monies spent for elder care amounted to over thirty % of the total (U. S. Senate 1991). By the mid-1990s these figures will have risen appreciably. Driven by emerging expensive technology, labor costs, and inflation, total health spending may reach $1.5 trillion, or almost 16.5% of the GNP before 1996. In 1991, the Federal government paid roughly 29.2% of the bill, or $157 billion, a rate that had remained flat for ten years. When all factors are taken into consideration, the fact remains that the elderly still pay as much out of pocket, 15%, as they did before Medicare. Least this appear to be the entire story, however, it is important to note there are hidden costs; spending for health not directly labeled as a health expenditure, tax subsidies for employer supported health plans, tax deductions for those spending a stipulated percentage of their adjusted gross income and, so on.

In light of cost-saving measures, Medicare is now thought to be fiscally secure through the end of the century (U.S. Senate, 1991). This despite the fact that gross outlays totalled $108.2 billion in 1990. The Federal payout was $11.6 billion less after beneficiary premiums were deducted. Just a word on the basics: After deductibles and co-payments, Part A, the Hospital Insurance Trust Fund, provides fixed amount reimbursements for approved charges in acute care hospitals based on average treatment costs in 477 DRGs. If costs are less, the facility retains the difference. If costs exceed stipulated rates the hospital has no recourse with Medicare nor are they permitted to bill patients. Part A is available to anyone eligible for Social Security, and others may buy in. With an annual growth rate of 12.5% but with an increase of 8% in taxes collected, shortfalls loom. Under current law, however, no alternative source of funding is permissible so expenditures are strictly pay-as-you-go. To offset spiraling costs, deductibles were increased by 230% from 1981 to 1986: meaning an additional $1.1 billion was paid by claimants. On top of these changes, co-payments for 61-90 days of hospitalization more than doubled at the same time. In 1990, co-payments amounted to $157 daily and after 90 days were $314.

Part B, The Supplemental Medical Insurance Trust Fund, is financed from premiums, deductibles, co-payments, and general revenues. Premiums must cover 25% of all disbursements and in 1991 monthly premiums were $29.90; slated to rise to $41.80 in 1993. Under Part B, coverage was provided to 33 million people and paid roughly 80% of approved physician charges and certain home health and outpatient services such as laboratory, x-rays, and physical therapy. In those instances where physicians decline to accept assignment of Medicare as payment in full patients are liable for the remainder.

It is Part B that is growing most rapidly and where the containment debate is being waged. Sweeping revisions to Part B have occurred and more will take place. Under the five year fiscal plan of FY 1991, total Medicare outlays were legislated to be reduced by $44.1 billion. A total of $14.2 billion to be pared from Part B alone. New compliance surveillance efforts were also implemented to insure that Medicare is the secondary payer after private or employer-sponsored insurance. One dramatic facet of the compliance order is an extensive pooling of Social Security and IRS information augmented by Health Care Financing Administration data.

As part of the realignment of costs, fees to hospital-based physicians, primarily radiologists and pathologists, were reallocated from Part A to Part B—effectively shifting responsibility to recipients. Of course the major revision was the advent of the prospective payment system of DRGs as a means of curtailing automatic payments. The original contention was that suppliers and consumers used health care inefficiently, knowing they would be fully reimbursed. The latest five year expenditure reduction plan calls for providers and to a lesser extent beneficiaries, to bear the burden of reduced allowances. Physicians who participate in the system will be required to abide by new fee schedules and patients will be asked to pay a greater share.

Medicaid Coverage. While being old is not tantamount to living in a nursing home, 43% of those who reach age 65 in 1991 will eventually do so. That figure encompasses the one in seven men and the one in three women likely to spend at least a year in a nursing home before they die. In the face of long-term and protracted health care needs Medicaid is the only public program available. It is a means-tested program ostensibly providing pro-tection for the medically indigent, regardless of age. Successive revisions have left Medicaid so convoluted that it provides protection for fewer than half of all people falling below the poverty line. The remainder, as they say, fell between the cracks. It is a misperception to think of Medicaid as a safety net. Among the elderly, only 36% receive Medicaid and that includes those for whom the funds are used to purchase Medicare coverage when not otherwise covered by Social Security. Even at that, in 1987, 23.1 million persons received Medicaid coverage from the $45 billion contributed by Federal and state governments. Of the total, nearly $20 billion went to nursing home residents. Paradoxically, almost seven million fewer persons received Medicaid in 1987 than did four years earlier. The plight of the uninsured is one of those pernicious problems that is neither easily solved nor held at bay. We know, for example, that death rates among elderly poor on Medicaid are 50 percent higher than among those on Medicare. The basic question is: Does the right of citizenship include reasonable assurances of a sound and healthy life? Much of our ideology responds affirmatively. Besides, the State needs a healthy citizenry to fuel the economy. Yet the reality is something else.

At present Medicaid pays roughly 90% of all public expenditures for nursing homes and 48% of all residents receive Medicaid. Only four % of all public payments to nursing homes derive from Medicare. An alarming number of facilities are screening Medicaid patients, some going so far as to specify exactly which beds are Medicaid eligible. Many services are excluded from coverage and patients have to rely on their "personal needs allowance" of $30-$50 monthly for glasses, toothpaste, laundry, phone calls and sundry uncovered medical expenses. Cost-of-living-adjustments are not automatic and prior to the 1988 adjustment the previous allowance had been in place for 16 years. Even though spouses are permitted to retain incomes up to 150 percent of the poverty level, as of July, 1992, plus certain other assets not to exceed $1500 monthly, the provisions are anything but generous.

There are many who would willingly redefine the role of the State in providing even these assurances. Since the lifetime savings of the average person cannot buy four months in a nursing home, who is going to help? If the federal government does not do it and the patient cannot do it, where does responsibility rest? With the states? With families? With the health care industry? Neither easy questions nor easy answers here. The House of Representatives Aging Committee's Subcommittee on Health and Long-term Care attributes a sizeable portion of the elder abuse problem to pressures brought by the inability of care providers, adult children primarily, to find alternatives to family care (U.S. Senate, 1990). Clearly the family would be hard-pressed to do more. Interestingly, in Canada, where health and long-term care coverage is universal, intergenerational tension over the provision of such services is virtually non-existent. This is not to say no elderly Canadians are abused, only to note that a problem growing increasingly common in the United States is relatively less serious in Canada.

The government contends that approximately one-seventh of the U.S. population is medically indigent, without means of obtaining medical care. Does this mean there is no place for the poor or the old in the marketplace approach to health? Is their health not part of the compact? Are we now saying financial wherewithal is necessary to obtain the privileges of health among the citizenship? Under the Omnibus Budget Reconciliation Act of 1980, states were given greater flexibility in Medicaid reimbursement rates for nursing care and further discretion in determining eligibility. While tougher regulations and selective admission policies have reduced expenditures, it may be at the expense of those who have been denied care due to the government's restricted reimbursement policies (Harrington and Swan, 1984; Gibson et al, 1984).

The details of various subsections of Medicaid legislation are confusing to read and perplexing to anyone but an expert. Without attempting to bring even a modest degree of clarity to the discussion, it may still suffice to say that long-term care for chronic conditions is a distant goal at best. The reality is that something akin to universal health insurance may be necessary if older people are not to be hobbled with crippling expenses yet receive even an approximation of the quality of care we all desire when we are no longer capable of caring for ourselves.

The Quest For Equity. National health insurance has been debated since the first decade of the century. As we move through the last decade it continues as a controversial topic. The repeal of the short-lived Medicare Catastrophic Coverage Act of 1989 slowed whatever momentum had been building. Yet, with medical costs running well ahead of the Consumer Price Index, the issue will not go away. A real financing crisis looms and will keep attention focused. Because costs are so high, the elderly, and particularly the oldest-old requiring frequent medical attention, account for a disproportionate share of the health care dollar. Reconciling society-wide need, personal hardship, and public support is painful. During recessionary periods it becomes even more difficult to set priorities and appropriate realms of intervention. With all governmental spending under scrutiny, deep rescissions are undermining the types and extent of support the 34 million citizens, including 31 million elderly, receiving Medicare in 1991 may expect from governmental programs.

Federally sponsored health programs have been in for surgery. For example, certificates-of-need, to justify public beds in nursing homes, have become the order of the day as one way to dampen public expense. Yet there has been a hue and cry from the administration in Washington, D.C.,and from most quarters of the medical establishment, that any governmental intervention to control costs is too much. It is simply contrary to the "service for a profit" ideology upon which the country was founded. This same controversy has characterized health care from the first Federal policies and continues to circumscribe the debate (Walker, 1986). Such a premise clearly runs at cross purposes to a second ideological theme of equity and justice for all.

The longer people live the greater the risk of financial ruin, especially among those in declining health. There will apparently be little help from the public coffers. Something on the order of 36% of the $18.7 billion trimmed from the Federal budget during fiscal 1988 was carved from health programs. Through 1992 a projected "savings" of another $55.7 billion is envisioned by means of cuts and alterations in the cost-sharing formula (Iglehart, 1987).

Ironically, as new reimbursement regulations were formulated in 1991, the technology so highly touted only a few years earlier as the vehicle to improving the quality of health care, was being asked to demonstrate its cost-effectiveness else it be excluded from Medicare coverage. Should hi-tech medical care be ruled ineligible for governmental reimbursement, the result will be a *de facto* rationing of health care on the basis of ability to pay (Pear, 1991).

Of course shifting responsibility away from the government does not mean expenses will be curtailed, only that the source of payment will be elsewhere or medical care will be forgone. For the least advantaged segments of the population these changes are portentous. To reconcile rising costs with available funding will mean exploring options—increased taxation, incorporation of alternate revenues, changing the cost-sharing formula, altering eligibility, controlling reimbursement to physicians and hospitals (Aiken and Bays, 1984). Depending on which options are pursued and how change is undertaken, the health environment may be dramatically altered for those dependent on public programs. Imagine the consequences of limiting the availability of PET (positron emission tomography) diagnostic procedures to those wealthy enough to pay out-of-pocket. Clearly a new complex of values will have been implemented, one that implies fundamental changes.

While cause and effect are problematic, there is no denying the price tag on medical care has risen significantly since Medicare/Medicaid. We have also seen health care subverted to the political process. It is as if what it means to be ill can be reconstituted whenever third-party payers feel the pinch. A real quandary has been created since proportionate out-of-pocket costs for services covered by Medicare now exceed pre-Medicare levels. Where does culpability lie? Plausible answers are plentiful. What might be most salient, however, is that we have witnessed a movement of the definition of health and illness into the political arena. Two principal currents seem to rule the day: What generates the most support and what the vocal constituency feels is in their best interests—never mind what those who are ill or providing support to those who are ill feel is in their best interests. By the time current players are themselves ill or providing care, another group will have replaced them in the forum. There is no way around the fact that most cuts and compensatory measures have been settled on those groups who rely exclusively on Medicare/Medicaid. Does it have anything to do with their political voice?

The advent of DRGs was intended to bring about cost-containment. Hospital admission now carries with it DRG classification. The latter activates a predetermined range of permissible charges based on type of treatment and length of stay. Payments are capitation based on standardized reimbursements for 477 distinct disease groupings. As Walker (1986) and others point out, the year DRGs were implemented saw a decline of 7.5% in lengths of stay—puzzling to say the least. Had the medical establishment discovered a miracle cure? Had the system been out of kilter previously? Had patients been remiss in any of a variety of ways? No doubt advocates of one or another position see alternative answers. Still, it was generally agreed that waste was rampant and cost-containment appropriate. Estimates were that nearly $20 billion could be saved by elimination of unneeded laboratory tests, routine x-rays, or hospital-based terminal care (Beck, 1985). Yet, hi-tech medicine was sweeping the health-care field. Having the newest and most advanced apparatus may not automatically improve health care; it does, however, demand a steady supply of users in a market driven environment.

Who doubts it is laudable to have hospitals, providers and patients fully cognizant of the bottom line? With payment caps in place, the feeling was that providers would be more competitive by virtue of a marketing-of-services approach. Of course the same market mentality could also have negative consequences for patients, staff, or institutions. In fact, some critics contend it is exactly the free market approach that has fueled rapid inflation. Administrative expenses account for one-fifth to one-quarter of every dollar spent on health care in the U. S.— some estimates suggest this is twice as high as in other countries. The cost-cutting restraints of recent years have rendered many changes but they have not significantly altered the bureaucracy. Yet, in accounting, cross-subsidization is now out of the question. On the wards, complications must be serious enough to carry reclassification before a new course of treatment will be regimented. In the labs, the fewer tests the better. It sounds harsh but it makes sense too (Ginsberg, 1990). Having suggested that Medicare/Medicaid are market failures, the obvious question is where has the burden been shifted (Walker, 1986)? Unless the need for medical care has been vastly overdrawn or is largely artificial—and there is little evidence to suggest it is—shifting payments from one realm to another does not solve the problem. Recipients already pay 56% of physician fees over and above the 44% of approved charges covered by Medicare. How much more cost sharing can be expected? The growth in the "Medigap" insurance available to those who can afford supplemental coverage provides ample testimony of the extent to which federal programs leave glaring inadequacies. The figures are hard to come by but estimates are that the private insurance industry was selling policies to the tune of $8 billion annually as early as 1984 (Aiken and Bays, 1984). By 1991 there were 1.5 million policies in force from 130 different companies.

These trends are even more telling than first meets the eye. Reading closely it is clear that health care is increasingly a commodity to be bought and sold according to rules of the marketplace. If this is the case, the question of equity is compounded by the problem of governmental and industry pensions. If income is circumscribed by statute, as it is for those who rely primarily on Social Security, penalties will be levied if additional work is undertaken to purchase health care. In other words, working to secure medical attention will undermine pension benefits and leave the older person in need of medical attention in double jeopardy. Also—and this point is not readily apparent—by its very actions the government reinforces the notion of vendor profits. Without addressing the question of what is a legitimate charge, or focusing on demand, overuse, or governmental complicity, the vendor system remains intact at the expense of older users. While not in itself an illegitimate goal, caution must be exercised else it be reinforced under the guise of tightfistedness (Walker, 1986).

It seems the very least the government could do is to safeguard against potential abuses. The growth in medigap insurance has been dramatic, so too has been the number of forfeitures on which policy holders never collect a dime either in benefits or equity. Other restrictive or gatekeeper clauses imposed by the vendor limit benefits still further. When most people purchase long-term care insurance, between the ages of 55 and 60, they have not yet adapted to retirement income levels; nor do they think to buy policies that will adjust benefits for the inflation that will occur by the time they may attempt to claim benefits some twenty years hence. Then too, failure rates among insurance writers are high and guaranty or governmental fall-back protection varies from one state to the next.

As costs of long-term care escalate, the financial burden is crushing for patient and family alike. No one is spared but since two-thirds of all nursing home residents are women, they are especially hit. According to a 1988 report issued by the Brookings Institution, co-authored by a former director of the Congressional Budget Office, "...long-term care is a normal, insurable risk for the elderly, which should be covered under a general social insurance program..." (Rivlin and Wiener, 1988). The wording is noteworthy as it stresses the normalcy of long-term care as an expectable expense that should not entail welfare connotations. The report, which considers financing through higher payroll taxes on total earned incomes and not just Social Security ceilings, higher estate taxes, income tax surcharges, or higher Medicare premiums, recommends revisions to Medicare policy to provide long-term care coverage. As it is now, fewer than 1% of the elderly can afford the approximately $30,000-$40,000 required for one year in a nursing home in 1991.

Under Medicaid, the federal government's outlay for long-term care was approximately $20.6 billion in 1991. The Brookings Foundation report contends an additional $12 to $18 billion would provide total coverage for all elderly for the next three decades. It also suggests there is no real logic as to why the Federal government does not provide long-term insurance and underscores that impoverishment is hardly defensible. By using a Trust Fund approach, financial reserves could accumulate in the short run to offset any possible surge once protection became available. The latter, however, is unlikely as the prospect of institutionalization is not something insurance will make more attractive. Ironically, Medicare payments for home health and nursing benefits were reduced under a mandate by the Reagan administration by some $2.4 billion below what Congress authorized for the four-year period ending in 1988. It is as if all needs assessment studies of the previous several years had fallen on deaf ears—at least on ears more attuned to the federal deficit than the expense of personal and familial hardship.

As part of a series of recommendations commemorating the 20th anniversary of Medicare, a Harvard Medical School report looked toward the next millennium and attempted to address not only cost control, but service enhancement (Blumenthal, Schlesinger and Drumheller, 1986). Beginning from the premise that the Federal government ought to stay involved in ensuring adequate access to health, the report evaluated means of controlling costs, promoting fairness and simplicity in Medicare. The issue is whether a market-approach is best suited. What happens to the prospect of fairness when cost-containment is paramount? What happens to the 37 million Americans, including 300,000 elderly, who have no health insurance? Suggesting a variety of possible solutions, the report advocated flexibility based on ability to afford co-payments and premiums rather than blanket stipulations for all beneficiaries. One question we all need to ask if we are going to occupy the moral high ground is how can we not provide for long-term care whether it be given in institutions or at home? The report challenged the market model while being mindful of the need for fairness to providers as well as recipients (Blumenthal, Schlesinger and Drumheller, 1986).

In commenting on the changing health care climate, Iglehart (1987) identified three characteristics shaping service delivery. First, there are escalating expenditures, both public and private. To illustrate: in 1985, per capita medical costs were 51,721 for a total of $425 billion. These figures represent an 8.9% increase in that year alone, a year in which the inflation rate was 3.2% and the Gross National Product increased by 5.7%. The following year, 1986, health spending rose another 7.7% compared to a 1.1% increase in the Consumer Price Index. By 1988, national health expenditures had climbed to $539.9 million, or 11.1% of the GNP. In 1991 the national per capita cost for direct health expenditures had reached $2700. Second, since the Reagan administration demonstrated a willingness to circumvent Congressional intent, greater specificity has been incorporated into legislation and regulations to circumscribe possible discretionary actions by administration appointees. Third, lobbying efforts by those with vested interests in health care delivery are being stepped up. Whether, as Iglehart asserts, as a means of countering the "draconian" approach of the Reagan administration or merely to protect their own stewardship, they have become increasingly vocal (Iglehart, 1987). It is not too surprising that reductions in those health programs directly applicable to older persons were targets of major cost-cutting proposals throughout the 1980s. It is one thing to suggest delay or abolition of cost-of-living-adjustments in Social Security, quite another to rescind Medicare. Without Medicare and Medicaid there is nothing else for the bulk of those who claim benefits. Yet, through one means or another each has expanded more slowly than standard inflation measures would predict if they were closely indexed to the economy. Medicare has become a target of opportunity for cuts in domestic spending (Iglehart, 1985). In 1990 and again in 1991, further revisions were designed and implemented under OBRA provisions. As the FY 1992 Federal budget was drafted, even deeper cuts were on the table.

The Issue of Equity: Alternative Perspectives

With profit as the engine driving our nation, why should we be surprised when all else is secondary. Old age is not the culprit for the growing impoverishment that may accompany it, neither is it weakness of character. Social policies and statutes create the realities under which we live. Depending on how society chooses to provide for its elderly the scenario can be bright or bleak—it is a matter of writing the script. Neither in Canada, nor in most industrialized countries, do institutionalization and personal or familial destitution go hand-in-hand (Sheppard, 1990). In the United States it often does and even when medical benefits are obtained the picture is far from rosy. Yet, pitiful as they may be, current levels of Federal support are being challenged. The results are going to be catastrophic indeed. Should governmentsl policies bring *de facto* health care rationing, the quest for intergenerational equity can be abandoned. Hidden in the tangle of mandated budget reductions is the fact that sequestration of funds from health care to reduce the deficit is regressive, demanding the most of those least able to replace lost services.

As Green (1990) recently asked, "Why now this change of heart?" Prior to the crisis in the Persian Gulf the United States appeared on the eve of what was potentially the largest "peace dividend" in history. The upswing in the business cycle had not yet ebbed and the economy was doing well. The war put most other considerations on hold temporarily but as the war ended there were daily press accounts of calls for a further dismantling of welfare policies. Implicit in much of the discussion were questions of what is appropriate on the basis of age and potential. We heard too that the poorest group in the United States was comprised of children under the age of six. Undoubtedly their needs are many and ought not be sacrificed for any other age group. But neither should the needs of the elderly who were themselves children or adolescents during the Great Depression. They too were told that a better tomorrow was just around the corner.

Could it be the whole debate is a bit of a red herring? Might it not create a false "them" versus "us" mentality and sidestep examination of an ethic that pits one disadvantaged group against another? The question might be instead of what percentage of the GNP is accounted for by health-spending or Social Security, what is wrong with the GNP? Why is ours growing more slowly than that of other industrial countries? Our rate of growth has been stable at little more than 1% for over two decades. Then too the whole thrust of resource allocation has been reshaped in ten years; to the point where public opinion polls are detecting some real long-term skepticism about whether resources ought to be channeled toward the elderly when the budget crunch is in full force. What we are seeing is a real individualistic mentality, especially if special perquisites are not headed in my direction. But perhaps we are all looking in the wrong direction, distracted thereby from asking some hard questions.

The public ferment is growing, partly as a result of Americans for Generational Equity and its allies which opposed increased benefits for the aged throughout the latter 1980s. As a nation we developed a seemingly myopic view conveniently overlooking the consequences of the 1981 Omnibus Budget Reconciliation Act severely curtailing provisions for all low income groups (Quadagno, 1989). Relying on group averages to justify the allocation of resources without being cognizant that there are affluent elderly or children as well as desperately poor persons on either end of the age spectrum masks many devastating effects.

If poverty levels *per se* were used to justify entitlement, older black women, other minority elderly, young Hispanic populations and dependents in female-headed households would be at the front of the line. Lacking evidence that they are, distributive justice or intergenerational parity is harder to identify as a national priority. We need to ask in as forthright a fashion as possible, where does the money go? Do the majority of the elderly tuck it away in mattresses or channel it back into the economy? If it is the latter, and the evidence says it is, are not benefits helping sustain the economy anyway? Those who lack a second source of income in their old age use emoluments not to build nest eggs, but to keep the wolf at bay. Without those benefits coming from governmental sources, the responsibilities fall to their families—to the extent they were able to shoulder them. There is little evidence to suggest that the pockets of large numbers of older persons are lined with anything but poverty.

As Katz (1989] and others have pointed out, economic and social dependency may actually be a consequence of successful operation of the economy. Looking at poverty and defining dependency as social pathology is not likely to solve the problem. A far more fruitful perspective might be to acknowledge poverty as a concomitant of doing business as usual. Recognizing the underlying dimensions of our moral economy and creating a consensus on them may also suggest resolutions. One way of redressing the problem that would be ideologically acceptable to a majority lies in creating a more productive economy. More radical alternatives, revising the basis on which old age benefits are allocated, restructuring the regressive nature of Social Security taxes, or rethinking the market ideology upon which the infrastructure of the welfare system is predicated are plentiful. Paradoxically, underlying conservative or radical alternatives are some assumptions about the exchange value of the elderly as it is defined in terms of their importance and market value (Hendricks and Leedham, 1990). Some go further, saying inequities in old age, within, and between age categories are merely replications of life-long applications of a market-based assessment of personal worth (Hess, 1990). Excluded in the process are innumerable types of contributions to societal well-being. The participation of women who do not work outside the home but contribute significantly to the country's well-being is a case in point.

To put the issue of equity of access into perspective, and to suggest alternative modes of interpretation, it is necessary to establish what equity means. Leedham (1986) reviews three approaches to access as defined by the Office of Technical Assessment (U. S. Congress, 1985). First, a needs-based approach maintains all citizens have a right to sufficient care to optimize their functioning. A high ideal no doubt, but in an imperfect world, one that is elusive. Second, a market-based approach asserts all citizens have the right to purchase fulfillment of their needs at a cost reflecting true costs to the supplier. An ideal recognized as congruent with a competitive marketplace. Third, an adequate or decent minimum level of existence should be assured to all citizens with interventions as necessary to insure access to that level without undue hardship. The first may be too utopian, unrealizable given existing constraints and priorities. The second protects the competitive market ideology underpinning many western cultures. The third may not only be the most realistic but also the most flexible approach to locally determined needs (Leedham, 1986). It may also be a viable and practical means to focus resources on those in need, avoiding categorical inclusion as a means of achieving equity.

The latter alternative views older persons neither as needy nor homogeneous members of a social category. Fundamental to the development of possible alternatives is a recognition that much of the debate has taken place within the confines of a biased, albeit benign, view of older persons. Despite our compassionate ageism, not all are dependent by any stretch (Binstock, 1985). Not all require or desire well-intentioned intervention. In fact, rather than a social category in need of paternalistic protection, the elderly possess among them valuable resources imperiled by stereotypes. If social policy reflects a negative valuation of worth, it serves to circumscribe actors' perceptions of unequal worth and yield unequal treatment. Good ideas come not just from the young. Blocked from living up to their potential, older persons are also blocked from full participation in the decision-making process and from being resources to wider society.

What we have seen to date is categorical legislation—the regulation of mandatory retirement to make room for entering workers, alternating with flexible retirement when curtailing benefits becomes more important. What of a retirement system that would allow the willing and able to remain involved while protecting the honest right to state supported retirement for those who prefer to exit the labor force? Furthermore, what if, as is done in Sweden, the state assumed responsibility for levelling some of the social disadvantages carried into retirement? In this way, in the years when further disadvantages accrue with an increasing likelihood of impoverishment, the State provides essential protection. As Rein (1976) points out, only with equalization of resources can people gain equal dignity, self-respect and treatment. Whether the elderly of tomorrow or the day after face a life marked by adequacy or by dependency is contingent on policies formulated today.

Bibliography

Aiken, L. H. and K. D. Bays, 1984, "The Medicare Debate-Round One," *The New England Journal of Medicine.* 311,18, 1196-1200.

Beck, J., 1985, "Health Triage: Ending Useless Spending Would Help," *Kansas City Times*, September 15, 1985.

Binstock, R., 1985, "The Oldest Old: A Fresh Perspective on Compassionate Ageism Revisited," *Milbank Memoriai Fund Quarterly*, 63, 2, 420-451.

Blumenthal, D., Schlesinger, M., and P. B. Drumheller, 1986, "The Future of Medicare," *The New Enaland Journal of Medicine* 314,11 722-728.

Braun, D., 1991, *The Rich Get Richer: The Rise of Income Inequality in The United States and the World.* Chicago: Nelson-Hale.

Calasanti, T. M., and Bonanno, A., 1986, "The Status of Rural Elderly in Southern Italy. A Political. Economic View," *Aging and Society* 6, 1, 13-27.

Caplovitz, D., 1979, *Making Ends Meet: How Families Cope With Inflation and Recession.* Beverly Hills: Sage.

Clark, P. G., 1985, "The Social Allocation of Health Care Resources: Ethical Dilemmas in Age-Group Competition," *The Gerontologist* 25, 2, 119-125.

Crystal, S., 1984, *American's Old Age Crises: Public Policy and the Two Worlds of Aging.* New York: Basic Books.

Dowd, J. J., 1980, *Stratification Among the Aged.* Monterey, CA: Brooks/Cole.

Estes, C., 1979, *The Aging Enterprise.* San Francisco: Jossey-Bass Publishers.

____, 1983, "Austerity and Aging in the United States: 1980 And Beyond," in A. M. Guillemard (Ed.) *Old Age and the Welfare State.* Beverly Hills, CA: Sage, 169-185.

____, 1986, "The Politics of Aging in America," *Aging and Society* 6. 2, 121-134

Friedman, E. A. and D. J. Adamchak, 1983, "Societal Aging and Generational Dependency Relationship: Problems of Measurement and Conceptualization," *Research on Aging* 5,3, 319-38.

Gibson, R. M. et al, 1984. "National Health Care Expenditures, 1983," *Health Care Financing Review,* 6,2, 1-31.

Ginsberg, E., 1990, *The Medical Triangle: Physicians, Politicians and the Public.* Cambridge, MA: Harvard University Press.

Green, V. L., 1990. "Human Capitalism and Intergenerational Justice," *The Gerontologist,* 29.6, 723-4.

Harrington, C., and J. H. Swan, 1984, "Medicaid Nursing Home Reimbursement Policies, Rates and Expenditures." *Health Care Financing Review* 6,1, 39-49.

Hendricks, J., and C. D. Hendricks, 1986, *Aging In Mass Society,* 3/e, Boston: Little, Brown.

Hendricks, J., and C. L. Leedham, 1990, "Dependency or Empowerment? Toward a Moral and Political Economy of Aging," in *Moral and Political Economy of Aging.* M. Minkler and E. Estes (eds.) Amityville, NY: Baywood, 51-64.

Hess, B. B., 1990, "Gender and Aging: The Demographic Parameters," *Generations,* Summer, 12-15.

Iglehart, J. K., 1985, "Health Policy Report: The Administration's Assault on Domestic Spending and the Threat to Health Care Programs," *The New England Journal of Medicine* 312,8, 525-528.

Iglehart, J. K., 1987, "Health Policy Report: The Political Contest Over Health Care Resumes," *The New England Journal of Medicine,* 316,10, 639-644.

Investment Company Institute, 1987, *Mutual Fund Fact Book* Washington, DC:ICI.

Katz, M. B., 1989, *The Undeserving Poor.* New York: Pantheon Books

Kohli, M., 1989, "West Germany as an Aging Society: Political and Moral Economy," paper presented to XIV International Congress of Gerontology, Mexico.

Kutza, E. A., 1981, *The Benetits of Old Age: Social Welfare Policy for the Elderly*. Chicago: University of Chicago Press.

Leedham, C. L., 1986, "Models of Health and Medicine: Implications for Equity of Access Across the Lifecourse and For Aging Differently," paper presented to Gerontological Society of America annual meetings.

Levy, F., 1987, *Dollars and Dreams: The Changing American Income Distribution*. New York: Russell Sage Foundation.

Myers, G. C., 1985, Aging and Worldwide Population Change, in R. H. Binstock and E. Shanas (eds.) *Aging and the Social Sciences* 2/E. New York: Van Nostrand Reinhold Company, 173-198.

Myles, J., 1984a, "Does Class Matter? Explaining America's Modern Welfare State," Paper presented to the Conference on Theoretical Approaches to American Social Policies sponsored by the Center for the Study of Industrial Societies, University of Chicago, November.

Myles, J., 1984b, *Old Age in the Welfare State: The Political Economy of Public Pensions*. Boston: Little Brown and Company

Myles, J., and M. Boyd, 1982, "Population Aging and the Elderly," in D. Forcese and S. Richer (eds.) *Social Issues: Sociological Views of Canada*. Scarborough: Prentice-Hall, Canada, 258-285.

Navarro, V., 1987, "Federal Health Policies in the United States." *Milbank Memorial Fund Quarterly*, 65, 1, 81-111.

Nelson, G. M., 1982, "Social Class and Public Policy for the Elderly," in B. Neugartern (ed.) *Age or Need? Public Policies for Older People*. Beverly Hills, CA:Sage, 101-29.

Olson, L. K., 1982, *The Political Economy of Aging: The State, Private Power and Social Welfare*. New York: Columbia University Press.

Palmer, J. L, Smeedley, T., and B. B. Torrey, (eds.), 1988, *The Vulnerable*. Washington, D. C.: Urban Institute Press,

Pear, R., 1988, "Broader Medicare Is Urged To Cover Long-Term Cases" *The New York Times* February 7, p. 11,

Pear, R. 1991, "Medicare to Weigh Cost Factor in Reimbursement" *The New York Times*. April 21, p1.

Quadagno, J., 1984, "Welfare Capitalism and the Social Security Act of 1935," *American Sociological Review* 49,5. 632-47.

Quadagno. J., 1989, "Generational Equity and the Politics of the Welfare State" *Politics and Society*. 17, 3, 353-376.

Quadagno, J., and M. H. Meyer, 1990, "Gender and Public Policy," *Generations* Summer, 64-66.

Quinn, J., 1990, "Poverty in the Extremes: The Young and The Old in America," *The Gerontologist* 29,6, 837-839.

Rein, M., 1976, *Social Science and Public Policy*, New York: Penguin Books.

Rivlin, A. M., and Wiener, J. M., 1988, *Caring for the Disabled Elderly: Who Will Pay?*. Washington, DC. Brookings Institution,

Sheppard, H. L., 1990, "We Have Met the Elderly and They Are Us," *The New York Times Book Review* January, 21:p. 36.

Storey J. M., 1986, "Policy Changes Affecting Older Americans During the First Reagan Administration," *The Gerontologist* 26, 1, 27-31.

Thompson, E. P., 1971, "The Moral Economy of the English Crowd in the Eighteenth Century," *Past and Present*, 50, 76-136.

Townsend, P., 1981, "The Structured Dependency of the Elderly," *Aging and Society*, 1,1, 5-28.

U.S. Bureau of the Census, 1988, *Measuring the Effects of Benefits and Taxes on Income and Poverty: 1986*. Current Population Reports, Series P-60, No. 164-RD-l, Washington, D.C. USGPO.

U.S. Congress, Office of Technical Assessment, 1985, "Medicare's Prospective Payment System. Strategies for Evaluating Cost, Quality, and Medical Technology," Washington, D. C. USGPO

U. S. Senate, Select Committee on Aging, 1991, "Development on Aging," Vol 1, Washington, DC: USGPO.

U.S. Senate, Special Committee on Aging, 1985, "The Crisis in Medicare: Exploring the Choices." Washington, D. C.: USGPO.

U. S. Senate, Special committee on Aging, 1986, "Developments in Aging: 1985." Washington, D.C.,: USGPO.

U.S. Senate, Special Committee on Aging, 1991, "Developments in Aging: 1990." Washington, D. C.: USGPO.

Walker, G. K., 1986, "Reforming Medicare: The Limited Framework of Political Discourse on Equity and Economy," *Social Science and Medicine* 23,12, 1237-1250.

Weber, M., 1922, *Economy and Society*. Totowa. N. J.: Bedminster Press.

Epilogue

Initially, we will review the various papers from European societies where the welfare state and social assistance has its strongest roots (Sweden, Germany, France, Iceland and Italy). Next we will move to discuss Poland and the former USSR to review how more authoritarian states have constructed their systems. Then follows Switzerland, which is distinct if not unique when compared with other European countries. Finally, our attention will move to younger states which represent the more explicitly free-enterprise zones, namely Japan, Canada and the United States.

Eldercare and the Welfare State in Sweden

Of the countries discussed in these readings Sweden represents the most highly institutionalized, the most developed welfare state. As Sundström and Thorslund point out..."virtually all the elderly are above the poverty line...the welfare state has abolished one of the classic poverty traps: old age is no longer synonymous with misery for many aged persons" (currently the poverty rate among the elderly in the U.S. is 14%). Nevertheless retirement pay among the very oldest and among women leaves some older Swedes with an income on the edge of poverty. Older men have had less opportunity to generate higher incomes through the supplementary pensions schemes which are earnings related. Women also receive lower benefits; some may not have worked and were therefore ineligible for a supplementary pension; others, a fifth of whom are dependent on the basic pension either worked part-time or at rates of pay lower than men.

While the virtual eradication of poverty among the elderly is an enormous achievement, the array of medical and social services provided for the elderly is equally impressive. Sundström and Thorslund detail the extent to which geriatric care is associated with residence in one's own home or assistance with housing expenses. Municipalities commonly adapt homes to minimize difficulties with stairs and thresholds at no cost or via considerable subsidies, thereby enabling 92% of the elderly to maintain an independent existence. A wide variety of home help, nursing services and home visits by physicians are provided which also enables the elderly to continue to reside in their own homes. These services are provided free or are subject to a means test which is strongly weighted in favor of the less well-off. The extent to which a collectivist orientation predominates in the philosophy of care of the elderly is obvious from the following:

> A recipient of the basic pension may be entitled to a municipal housing allowance. This is a means-tested benefit and the rules for eligibility are determined by the municipality. In 1988, 31% of old-age pensioners received this type of benefit.

> The housing allowance is only one of a wide range of main and supplementary benefits which can be combined with the basic and ATP pensions.

> Pension amounts are set by government each year and are calculated according to a base amount which is related to the consumer price index. In approximate terms, the combined basic and ATP pension for a person with an average industrial worker's salary will equal just over 70% of his earlier net income (Swedish Institute, 1989).

Other provisions for the elderly enumerated by Sundström and Thorslund include sheltered accommodation, old-age homes, group dwellings; it is only in the nursing home sector that a medical model of care predominates.

How has Sweden been able to introduce a welfare state system that has been more extensive than other countries that have chosen to develop income support and social service systems which indemnify the population from both the cause and consequences of poverty? In terms of the concepts developed in the introduction, equity, uniformity, public accountability, collectivism, an institutionalized welfare state, and high wage economy—Sweden exemplifies in practice, to a varying but predominantly heightened degree, practical application of these principles. Only in the area of uniformity of provision does there seem to be a problem, particularly for service provisions for the elderly in their own home.

Recent data show wide variation across geographic areas, e.g., anywhere from 17% to 80% of the citizens 80 years or older receive home making services, depending upon the political jurisdiction in which they live. Sundström and Thorslund argue that these variations are due to a mixture of factors including regional and economic differences, political composition of an area and lastly, what the authors describe as local norms about "reasonable provision." Nevertheless, an uneven provision does not lead to negative outcomes. Several studies document the fact that very few of the aged are unsatisfied or need help and support. Why is this so? Perhaps, the informal system of family members and friends is still important in providing support for the elderly. Such informal services may indeed fill gaps in particular regions choosing to devote fewer resources to home care services. In other areas with higher rates of provision, the formal systems of care, presumably, replaces informal care giving. One might hypothesize that the political composition of the districts which allocate a relatively lower proportion of resources for the provision of home health care services encompasses a more individualistic or conservative political position, whereas districts providing higher rates of services, are characterized by a collectivistic or socialist orientation. A breakdown between high and low service areas would be interesting.

Another factor that characterizes some aspects of the welfare state is the extent of decentralization at the operational level. While policies and priorities for allocation of resources are established at the national level, cities and county councils have a unique degree of autonomy concerning the day-to-day operations of the Swedish welfare state. The local authorities levy taxes and many services are provided locally. This autonomy allows local political norms to operate and may lead to the diversity of services found within the various political jurisdictions. Yet in the absence of clear evidence of dissatisfaction among the population at-risk, or protests by or on behalf of elderly persons, one must assume the variation in service provision is not significant.

In all other respects, the concepts developed in the introduction are embraced and operationalized in Swedish society. Above all a collective orientation has been dominant in Swedish social, economic and political life, since the early 1930s. Both the political and the economic arms of the working-class are exceedingly successful in protecting working-class interests. The first trade union was formed in 1846 when the Typographic Association was established in Stockholm. As Sweden began to industrialize in the 1870s and 1880s, the first national trade unions came into being. Initially, as was the case in most European societies, they were craft unions, representative of the aristocrats of labor. Rapidly thereafter the trade unions expanded to cover all occupations and in 1898 a number of unions joined forces to create a central organization known as the Swedish Trade Union Confederation (LO). In 1902, the employers formed the Swedish Employers Confederation (SAF), creating the opportunity for wage bargaining to emerge on a national basis. Today, about 85% of the labor force is organized and unions now cover white-collar workers and professionals, each of whom developed their national organizations in the 1930s and 1940s. These developments have culminated in a climate of opinion in which collective bargaining is the norm for settling wage and salary disputes. Nevertheless, at the local level variation in the conditions of employment and remuneration are adjusted to reflect specific characteristics within relatively narrowly defined geographic locations.

Politically, the Social Democratic Labor Party has dominated Swedish politics since 1932. Together with occasional support from the Communist Party, now the Left Party, Sweden until recently, 1991, when a right wing government was elected, has been governed by the Social Democrats. Only briefly, during 1982-1986 were non-socialist coalition governments formed, involving the central, moderate and liberal parties, in different combinations. Above all the close bonds between the Social Democratic Labor Party and the trade union movement have ensured that working class interests predominate in virtually all areas of policy of concern to the working class movement. Few societies have done more to incorporate working class interests in the management of industries. In 1977, an act on employee participation in decision-making was passed by the Swedish parliament which required local union representation on the boards of directors of privately owned companies who have at least 25 employees. Even further support of working class interests arose from a parliamentary decision in 1983 which introduced a mechanism through which workers may acquire a financial interest in the companies in which they are employed. However, this decision has created the greatest possible disagreement between employers and employees, and it will be interesting to see what future developments occur.

The strength of the labor representation movement, both politically and economically, has generated what might best be described as a high wage economy. The totality of welfare state provisions, not all of which can be presented here, has created a welfare state system in which poverty through low wages or extensive levels of unemployment has been virtually eliminated.

Perhaps nothing is quite so remarkable as the structure and the responsibilities of the national labor market administration, consisting of the Labor Market Board—including union and employer representatives—the county labor boards and the local employment services. In Sweden, labor market policy emphasizes the generation of full employment. During 1987-88 there were a total of 893,000 people registered as job seekers at the employment agencies. At that time the total number of registered job openings was 756,000. Among those for whom no job could be found on the open market, relief work was available for 15,200 people. In the same year labor market training was available for an average of 39,000 workers thrown out-of-work through structural unemployment. Indeed, retraining of workers to ensure their future ability to hold down a job in the labor market is one of the most important and innovative aspects of Sweden's political economy. As part of this training some 43,200 people found employment through the assistance of government subsidized wage supplements. In 1989, a further 28,300 were employed in sheltered workshops. As is apparent, the commitment to full employment has been realistically operationalized in the Swedish economy.

The comprehensive welfare system is supported by a public sector which is easily proportionately the largest in the world. Public expenditure in 1990 accounted for 66% of Sweden's GDP. To support government activities, tax rates in Sweden are among the highest in the western world. Individuals pay both local and national income taxes, ranging from a low of 5% to 45% in the highest brackets. Local income tax is, however, proportional and averages across the nation to about 30%. The proportional component is, of course, regressive, but much of the social service provision is designed on a redistributive basis to make public transport, education, housing and so on, affordable to all segments of society. Certain tax ceilings operate at the higher levels, making it *impossible* for local and national income taxation to exceed 72% of income in any tax bracket. Other taxes on capital gains, gifts, inheritance and personal property exist, but again a ceiling makes it possible for even the highest taxed to keep 25% of income. As is the case with other European countries, indirect taxes of a value-added variety are important in the overall public revenue scene. The emergence of a highly developed welfare state together with the enormous strength of the political and economic arms of the working class movement might suggest that Swedish society is moving towards the establishment of a truly socialist society. Collectivist principles dominate the social and economic sectors of Swedish life, but, is this sufficient to declare the ultimate institutionalization of a socialist state? To answer this question we must define the broad parameters of a fully developed socialist system.

Much paper and ink has been expended in the pursuit of definitions of socialism and communism and whether or not socialism is simply a transition stage between capitalism and communism. The latter might be ignored for the time being, since the question first is: How might socialism be characterized and achieved within the current capitalist world system? A subsequent transition from socialism to communism is first dependent on the establishment of the former. Nevertheless, following Selden (1982:1034) most would acknowledge that the four distinctive institutional features listed below would be minimally necessary for a socialist state to exist:

1. *Ownership*. Transition from private ownership and control of the means of production to the predominance of cooperative, collective, and state forms.
2. *Plan and market*. Transition from predominant reliance on capital, market forces, and the law of value to the expanded role of planning (at the state center, in the regions, and in localities) directed toward accumulation, development of the productive forces, improving the people's livelihood, and reducing inequalities in the distribution of well-being.
3. *International position*. Socialist development necessitates progressively breaking the grip of international capital and redefining the position of the state within the world-economy without assuming a hegemonic position in interstate relations.
4. *Mastery by the immediate producers of work place and society*. Following the displacement of the dominance of capital (or of precapitalist elites) and the formation of state structures appropriate to the needs of the working classes, the most important conflict among groupings formed by processes

of the transition and throughout the transition is between the state and the immediate producers, the working classes.

Few, if any, of these features currently exist in Swedish society. Further, as we shall show below, (3) the *International Position* is absent and its absence is partly responsible for tax reform currently being introduced. But above all, the predominant principle of socialism is negated when a social system (in this case Sweden's) does not recognize that capital accumulation and profit are social products and belong as much to the workers as to the owners of the means of production and the state. Indeed, as we have already noted, the legislation of 1983 which enabled, most tentatively, workers to acquire a limited degree of ownership of private companies has generated the most serious disagreements between employers and employees that have occurred in Sweden in recent years.

Sweden might best be described as perhaps the leading example of welfare state capitalism. While market conditions and competition between capitals dominate the economy, mitigation of the worst features of capitalist exploitation of the work force have been significantly ameliorated. No one is bankrupted by illness or old age, legislation to promote social and economic equality between men and women—yet to be completely successful in operation—nevertheless is more highly developed than in all other western societies. One could go on. Sweden's welfare state as well as being highly developed seems well entrenched. However, as is only too obvious from the USA and the UK, certain aspects of the welfare state and attempts to privatize the public sector have come under attack from the Reagan/Bush/Thatcher/Major administrations. These attacks against the welfare state have been associated with changes in the tax structures of American and British society which have enabled the rich to get richer and the poor to become poorer (Braun, 1991), reducing the "safety net" in both societies just at a time when its protective mechanisms are most needed to combat high unemployment associated with yet another depression. (*En passant,* it is worth noting that capitalism has yet to develop a method of economic management to eliminate the dips and swings of economic activity whose consequences in terms of suffering are always borne disproportionately by waged and salaried workers.) The question therefore arises: Can the Swedish welfare state survive the tax reforms currently being introduced, reforms which are partly dictated by the international effects of the reduction in tax rates and welfare expenditures introduced by the U.S. in the 1980s?

As Sodersten states (1990:3)…"one major factor behind the Swedish tax reform of 1990 is international trends. But there are also very strong domestic reasons for such a reform... Until now the Swedish tax system has included high marginal tax rates, which have rewarded leisure, do-it-yourself activities, systematic tax planning and working in the unofficial ("black") economy."

Marginal tax rates on incremental income before the reforms amounted to 71.6%, i.e., if an employee received an additional SEK 100 in gross pay SEK 71.60 of this amount went toward national and local taxes. Since June, 1991 the marginal tax rate has been reduced to 50% using the following formula.

Taxable income SEK*	National income tax	National and local income tax
0-170,000	0%	30%
170,000-	20%	50%

*SEK 1 (Swedish Krona) = $U.S. 0.16 (approx.)
(ibid.:4)

However, many deductions have been reduced or eliminated thus broadening the tax base on earned income and reducing the cost of the reform to the government.

Taxation of income from capital has also been extensively revised and simplified introducing a uniform rate of 30% (details of these changes can be found in Sodersten (1990) the complexities of which need not concern us here). These changes in the tax code for earned income and income from capital are designed to be fiscally neutral but at a cost of approximately SEK 60 billion a year. The broadening of the tax base on earned income should increase tax revenues by SEK 15 billion per year. A value-added tax (VAT) is being imposed on energy for the first time and other VAT rates are being made more uniform and will yield an additional SEK 20 billion per year. Finally, the new system for taxing capital income is expected to yield SEK 25 billion per year.

As one might expect, the impact of these reforms will reduce the disposable income of the lowest 10% of households by 2.2%. "This is mainly related to the fact that this category of income earners has a very low labor force participation level, 33%, due to studies, military service, parental leave and the like." (ibid.:5) If dynamic effects are factored in, i.e., the incentives to work longer hours by reducing the marginal tax rates on earned incomes, all income categories will benefit from the reform.

While this sounds neatly sanguine, the disincentive for parental leave may have a negative impact upon women. While parental leave is available to both sexes, it is usually women who take time off from work to deal with children's illness, child rearing and care of the elderly. Women who choose to take advantage of the lower marginal tax rates may reduce their commitments to child and adult care.

Nevertheless, these changes in the tax code seem to have been constructed in support of distributive justice issues concerning vertical income distribution, which contrasts sharply with the so-called tax reforms of the Reagan era in the U.S.

> In 1981, when Reagan cut taxes and increased tax shelters for the rich, the concentration of wealth accelerated. A tax study prepared by the Congressional Budget Office in 1990 revealed that in the decade between 1980 and 1990, the real income of the poorest one-fifth of the population dropped by 3%, but the net federal tax for this income group increased by 16%. Meanwhile, the richest one-fifth of the population, with an average pre-tax income of $105,209, experienced a 32% increase in real income, and a 5.5% cut in their tax rate. (Zaldivot, 1990, quoted in Ropers, 1991, 62).

Time alone will tell whether tax reforms in Sweden will be compatible with the maintenance of a well developed and institutionalized welfare state. The reforms, drawing upon changes introduced in the U.S. in the 1980s, appear to have been designed to reward the rich. The reduction in tax rates and adjustments to VAT were also influenced by the growing conviction that Sweden will apply for membership of the EEC (supported nervously by the Social Democratic Labor party, but rejected by the Left Party). Should membership be achieved, the Swedish economy and its ability to support an institutionalized welfare state may be compromised, unless the hoped-for dynamic effects of the tax reforms improve the competitive position of Swedish industry.

On the other hand Holland, already a member of the EEC, vies with Sweden for top ranking in terms of welfare state provision. Perhaps the example of Sweden and Holland will shame the other members of the EEC to raise their standards for welfare state provision to match those of the Swedes and the Dutch. Hopefully Sweden and Holland will maintain their highly developed and institutionalized welfare provisions as an example to which other members of the EEC should aspire rather than be dragged down to the lowest common denominator of the less committed European nations.

Long Term Care and the Welfare State in Germany

Jaeckel's discussion of the problems Germany is facing when it attempts to meet the challenge of the fourth stage of the demographic transition—the growth in aged and the old-old proportion of the population—focuses attention upon the second theme we have tried to explore in these readings: the retrenchment or development of the welfare state. Current discussion and identification of the problems of providing long term care (LTC) for the elderly mirror, in some respects, similar uncertainties in the U.S. The major parameters of the problem include: 1) discussion of the ways in which needed care for the elderly can be provided both in institutions and in their own homes; 2) provision for the economic protection of caregivers, both related and unrelated; and 3) the generation of the spend-down phenomenon and subsequent pauperization of those who need care and services on a 24-hour basis in an institutional setting. As is the case in the U.S., identification of the problems is relatively straightforward, it is the development of an appropriate financing mechanism for LTC services which poses the greatest difficulty. Dependence on the private sector for a solution by extending the current forms of social and health insurance through increased premiums covered by employer and employee contributions, plus subsidies by either or both federal and local government to cover the unemployed or indigent attract support and criticism. While the private insurance industry savors the possibility of a growth in business and potential profit based on increased premiums levied against employees, the trade unions clearly object. Cost-sharing involving contributions from employees as well as federal and local government is objected to by all except working class groups. Nevertheless, as Jaeckel makes clear,"...the existing institutional infrastructure for the delivery of LTC services is severely underdeveloped...," and something must be done. Currently, LTC services are split between community and voluntary organizations on one side and specialized sub-units of the health care system on the other. Fragmentation predominates, especially in the voluntary sector when rivalries between agencies with varying religious, working class or so-called non-aligned orientations persist. These, together with other community-based ambulatory services, provide hopelessly inadequate coverage leading to neglect of the needs of the elderly persons or forcing the responsibility for care upon relatives, predominantly women, usually daughters or daughters-in-law. (Feminist researchers in both the UK and the USA have identified similar situations which place the burden of uncompensated care of the elderly upon the shoulders of women.)

Employers and right-wing politicians prefer either the status quo (uncompensated care by women), voluntaryism or the corporatist model—whether private-not-for-profit or private-for-profit—of self-insurance of the at-risk population to provide LTC services. All three mechanisms relieve local and central government from responsibility for LTC, and employers, if they cannot resist the upward pressure for wages and salary increases consequent to increased insurance premiums for self-insurance, can pass such costs on to consumers but only until such time as higher wages and salaries reduce the international competitiveness of German goods and services. If the solutions above are adopted, retrenchment, or at best, further limitation on the development of the welfare state in the German context are the most likely outcome.

The alternative would be to move toward a more developed form of the welfare state, the elements of which were outlined in the introduction. The major attraction of such an approach would be to take advantage of economies of scale, improved administrative efficiency and greater opportunity to control the rising costs of medical treatment associated with a single or monopsonistic payment system whose efficacy over alternative payment mechanisms is demonstrated by the British and Canadian system of medical care delivery. However, as we have demonstrated in the case of Sweden, a shift in such a collectivist direction is probably dependent upon the presence of a strong working class movement with an effective organization operating in both the political and economic spheres. Is such a shift likely?

The situation is exacerbated by the recent unification of the two Germanys. Even more disruptive is the economic upheaval or collapse that seems to pervade the Eastern German economy. East Germans expect to enjoy the same standards of living as their Western compatriots, yet Eastern industries cannot compete with their counterparts in the West. In terms of welfare provision, the previous West German economy will have to provide most of the funding to lift East Germans' levels to those of the rest of the country. Such increased expenditures will clearly make less attractive arguments in favor of increased federal and local commitments to fund LTC services.

On the other hand, contrary to the rather naive projections of some, particularly USA commentators—that the former USSR and its previous satellites will unquestioningly adopt the competitive principles of the market place—a commitment to more gradual change, together with retention of a collectivist orientation in social and medical services, may be retained. It is already evident that Poland is slowing down its conversion to a capitalist economy because of the enormous disruption and lowered standards of living which seemingly inevitably accompany conversion to a market place economy. Other Eastern Europeans and Soviets will soon learn, if they do not already know, that with the exception of Sweden, relative deprivation or even poverty for significant proportions of the population are the inevitable concomitants of capitalist economies. If such views become widespread, then the new Germany may be associated with increased support for collectivist perspectives in the political and economic areas. Should this occur, development rather than retrenchment of welfare state capitalism may ensue.

As the EEC moves toward a political union, it will be interesting to observe the outcome in terms of cross-national welfare provisions. The outcome will center on what becomes the common denominator. The British under Thatcher were nervous of the probability that UK welfare services would have to be raised, in certain areas, to the more advanced levels existing in Holland, Germany, France and elsewhere. Pessimists might suppose a move towards the mean, while optimists might hope for a rise in standards of welfare provision to match the more institutionalized forms of the welfare state existing in Holland and Scandinavia.

The Welfare State of France

Wallimann's chapter on France is useful for casting light upon the debate concerning the development or retrenchment of the welfare state. Despite an incumbent Socialist President, it is clear that both social and economic policies have been designed to assist capital accumulation at the expense of social protection and distributive justice. Following the recession of 1981-83, unemployment peaked at 2.68 million in 1987 and part of this loss of jobs consisted of structural unemployment in mining, steel and automobile production after the introduction of government policies designed to "streamline" the work force. In addition, the rise in part-time employment reduced the earning capacity of the work force. By contrast, over roughly the same period corporate profits, after depreciation, grew by 160% in real terms, while salaries and wages increased by only 12%. The unemployed, small businesses and the lower echelons of the working class bore the brunt of economic restructuring which fueled the substantial increase in profits in the corporate sector. Moreover, these changes were accompanied by restructuring of parts of the social insurance system which, by switching insurance coverage from the *régimes spéciaux* to the less extensive provision of the *régime général,* reduces the costs of the reproduction of the labor force both to the state and to the private sector. In addition, both direct and indirect taxes are minimally progressive (the latter in virtually any system of taxation are by definition regressive) imposing a further burden on the unemployed and the poorly paid.

In attempts to alleviate the problems of unemployment and to improve the conditions of others living at or below poverty levels, an elaborate locally-based system of guaranteed minimum income for social integration (RMI) was introduced in the late 1980s. These systems as in Sweden focus upon re-training workers made redundant through structural changes in the economy and emphasize the acquisition of new work skills. Unfortunately the schemes are subjected to fierce means testing, and allowable income support during retraining and while gaining job experience is set low, presumably to encourage re-entry into the "normal" labor force. Wallimann also argues that the staffing of the RMI agencies is inadequate and that insufficient state and local monies are available to make the system a success. The observer might ask: given the enormous increase in profits which occurred in France during the 1980s, why some of this surplus might not have been diverted to further enhance the RMI legislation and programs and thus speed up the re-integration of the truly disadvantaged into the main stream of economic life.

In 1969 France adopted minimum wage legislation which by 1989 stood at F 5,074/month (roughly $U.S. 923/month whereas in the U.S. the minimum wage of $3.75/hour nets $600/month assuming an 8 hour, 5 day, 4 week month) thus placing the French economy close to or in the 'high' wage group of nations. Such a strategy can only be successful, however, if measures for reducing unemployment and re-training workers displaced by structural unemployment are vigorously and effectively pursued. From the above it is apparent that success in this component of welfare state capitalism is yet to be achieved. The mechanisms are in place, but either the political will to fully implement them is lacking or the strength of the working class political and economic representative movements are insufficient to impose such a policy on the French government.

The Development of Geriatric Services in Iceland

Of the readings commissioned for this book the case of Iceland by Wieland is unique. While its cultural affinities are with Denmark and other Scandinavian countries, it is distinguished from them and other European and North Atlantic communities by the rapidity of social and economic changes which have transformed Iceland in less than one hundred years. In the late 19th century, barter and exchange were the principal media for the exchange of goods and services with money transactions playing a minor part. Today, Iceland has developed a welfare state whose coverage is as complete as that of their far wealthier and larger Scandinavian cousins. Long-term care for the elderly is of high quality and retention of personal residence attracts no fixed penalty; this is not the case in Britain, Switzerland, Germany or the United States where personal wealth must be surrendered to cover nursing home costs. It should be emphasized, however, that the high rate of institutionalization among the elderly is a consequence of the dearth of home care services, a situation which is currently being addressed, but whose resolution is made more difficult by—with the exception of Reykjavík and Akuneyoi—low population densities and difficulties of transportation and communication across the vastness of the Icelandic wastes.

The modernization of Icelandic society commenced with the introduction of large powered fishing boats at the turn of the century; making commercial fishing a viable industry and encouraging the development of subsidiary industries of fish processing, packaging and export. Nevertheless Iceland had to await the advent of World War II before prosperity spread throughout the society. In Orwellian terms, Iceland became 'Air-strip 1' as the American and British military poured men, machinery and money into the country turning *cottors* (landless farmers/laborers) into middle-class wage earners.

While the emergence of prosperity made it possible to finance a welfare state, its genesis seems to be closely associated with the aspects of Icelandic culture. A collectivist approach associated with a strong identification with and support for left wing political parties was important but the absence of significant class distinctions, a commitment to the nobility of satisfying and productive work and pride in its performance seemed to be responsible for an additional component of social solidarity. Such values were important in a subsistence economy, especially where the harshness of the work environment on sea or land required tenacity, even courage, to till the land or harvest the sea.

One should also note that in a barter and exchange economy, the acquisition of surplus value is difficult, reducing the possibility for some to accumulate value at the expense of others. The harshness of the environment and the seasonal nature of farming and fishing also gave support to a collectivist orientation and value system since all 'hands' were needed to cooperate to the mutual benefit of all during the heights of agricultural activity and the peaks of tidal, climatic and ocean conditions. In this sense, a collective orientation stemming from an economically imposed need for mutual support and cooperation resonated with the collective ideology of socialistic politics. (Incidentally, recall the socialist movement in central Canada related to the nature of agricultural work in the region). It will be interesting to see if the relatively low-level of capital accumulation in the past which in turn reduced the possibility of the emergence of class antagonism will survive continuing modernization. Perversely, if recent events in the former USSR and Eastern Europe continue to lower the military tensions between East and West, the economy of Iceland may experience less favorable circumstances than in the recent past. Iceland's military value to North America may decline thereby leading to a reduction of USA's military presence on 'Air-strip 1.' In these circumstances the increase in Iceland's affluence may be halted, jeopardizing the ability of its economy to support a welfare state apparatus.

On a more positive note, it is interesting to acknowledge the extent to which the elderly tend to remain in the work force, despite the presence of a well-developed pension and social and medical security system. "In 1980, over 70% of Icelanders aged 65-69 were fully or partly employed, while over 40% of those 70-74 and 15% older than 75 retained jobs (Wieland, p. 90)." Some undoubtedly worked because they had to but others may have stayed in work because of the positive connotations and satisfactions associated with work from an earlier less affluent time which still persist. If the economy does face further austerity, such a spirit may help to preserve a commitment to the humanistic ideologies which ultimately underpin the existence of the welfare state.

Distributive Justice, Contradictions and Rationality
in Mature Capitalism: Services for the Aged in Italy

Bonanno and Calasanti provide an excellent socio-historical account of
the emergence of health and social services in Italy particularly as they relate to
elderly care. The analysis highlights the historical configuration of class
tensions to the Italian setting and the ways in which working class pressure
through the parties of the left and the trade union movement was initially
successful in agitating for the decommodification of health and social services
in the late 19th and early 20th centuries. In 1917 and 1920 old age and
sickness insurance was mandated for employed workers, but of course did
nothing to ameliorate the sufferings of the unemployed.

During the Fascist regime (1920-1945) both the Socialist Party and CGIL
(the national trade union) were outlawed and the legislation of 1917 and 1920
was rescinded. The brief interregnum in which health and social services were
beginning to be decommodified was reversed except for the continuation of
public assistance at a basic minimum for the absolutely deprived. Even more
regrettable was the introduction of a crude form of political patronage or
clientelism which accompanied the re-privatization of health care services and
social insurance. Such crude political maneuvering was clearly designed to
assuage criticism of the oppression and excesses of the Fascist regime. In
practical terms bureaucratic inefficiencies were manifest. Mechanisms for the
coordination of various health agencies broke down and duplication of provider
groups led to waste and unnecessary administrative overhead. Apart from the
advantages of clientelism for the Fascists, the privatization of health and social
services was part of the regime's strategy to advance the interests of capital.
Reduction in public expenditure on these areas enabled more government
monies to be redirected into the military-industrial complex, a procedure
notorious for improving the profitability of basic extracting and processing
industry and manufacturers of military hardware.

Unfortunately, as state support for health services for the elderly increased in the postwar era, the tradition of clientelism was preserved. This
tradition coupled with a multiplicity of decentralized providers maintained the
waste and inefficiencies of the pre-war era. The strength of the working class
movement, while able to push for improvement in state provision for health and
social services, tended to increase even further the advantages of elite working
groups in the monopoly sector. Once again the utility of Offe's categorization,
as outlined in our introduction for the analysis of the interrelationships among
the state, the working class and welfare provision is evident.

In the mid 1970s Italy, like many other Western capitalist welfare states,
was severely affected by the world-wide decline of trade which accompanied
the steep increase in energy costs. Consequently, the state's ability to enhance

or even maintain welfare expenditures was truncated. The relative improvements of the economy, in the 1980s, was accompanied by increased activity in what Bonanno and Calasanti describe as the peripheral labor sector (akin to our elaboration of Offe's notion of the residual labor sector described in the introduction) characterized by low labor costs through low wages, intermittent or part-time employment and the absence or avoidance of fringe benefits. In addition, the Italian economy was affected by the problem of structural unemployment; a problem which we have already seen in the economies of France, Germany and Sweden and potentially in Iceland and will also be seen to affect most of the other countries yet to be discussed.

Economic policy in Italy took the path followed by many other capitalist welfare states; that of trying to increase the rate of accumulation to improve the overall performance of the economy. Reductions in public expenditures were favorite options adopted, as we have already seen in France and Sweden, and we will also see in some of the other countries to be discussed. Italy was no exception. Previous commitments to expand health and social service provision for the elderly were largely abandoned and these changes were accompanied by a growing 'medicalization' of the definition of the problem (Binney, et. al., 1990). Rather than focussing on the causes of the social disadvantages of elderly persons, their problems were defined and treated in terms of a medical model. Again one may suppose that the spin-offs from medical treatment, providing as they do for increased activity and profits in the medical and medical supply sectors of the economy, tend to support the further accumulation of private capital.

Bonanno and Calasanti go on to elaborate the essential conflict between capital accumulation, the need to develop or maintain the welfare state, and the consequences of this tension for the issue of distributive justice in the following terms:

> First, the State's role in mature capitalism contradicts the achievement of distributive justice. That is, within advanced capitalism there is conflict between the State's need to both foster accumulation and to maintain legitimation. On the side of accumulation, the bourgeoisie pressures the State for actions which will increase profits. The State also has a vested interest here as it relies on accumulation to finance its existence. At the same time, legitimation, popular support, is necessary either in material or ideological form. Welfare spending is one material legitimative strategy. These social expenditures are resisted by the bourgeoisie, however, as they are contradictory to accumulation. As the State must also be concerned with accumulation, legitimation through expenditures is carried out only if a strong push from below exists.

As Bonanno and Calasanti point out, this dilemma can only be resolved by the decommodification of both medical and social systems of care. In the care of the elderly the elimination of the profit motive from both systems is a dominant requirement because alleviation of the problems of elderly persons are dependent upon the coordination and integration of both medical and social services. Such integration of social and medical service provision can only be accomplished within the parameters of an institutionalized welfare state system. To date the development of the welfare state in Italy has stopped short of full institutionalization. Further pressures from the working class movement will be necessary if Italy is to move in the direction of Sweden which provides the necessary range of services, pensions and medical care to protect the elderly from social isolation and relative deprivation.

The Elderly and Social Policy in Poland

After reading Hrynkiewiz, Stanega-Piasek and Supinska's chapter, one's emotions are tightly strung. During World War II five million Poles died in the fighting and many more were left permanently "injured," thus totally disrupting their social and working lives. The authors argue that the low educational levels characteristic of current generations of elderly persons stem from the horrendous disruption or even destruction of the school system consequent to war-time conditions.

The establishment of state capitalism after World War II under the auspices of the Communist Party, led to further disruption of the social system. In turn, this forced intellectuals and the well-educated to accept the constraints of a totalitarian form of government or to work in positions or occupations in which they were over-qualified. The Polish economy, attached to the Soviet monolith, adopted a mode of industrialization based on a low-wage structure accompanied by the extraction by the state of the maximum amount of surplus value which could be squeezed from the industrial and agricultural sectors alike.

Such conditions should not surprise anyone familiar with the social history of both the agricultural and industrial revolutions in Western European countries and North America. In Britain, Belgium, France, Germany and the United States the early stages of both revolutions were financed in much the same fashion—maximization of the rate of extraction of surplus value from the workforce. In Britain, in the late 18th and early 19th centuries, farm laborers were driven from the land or forced to work for starvation wages as agriculture moved from subsistence to for-profit farm production. Cottage industries were gradually destroyed and the displaced workers forced to survive in the atrocious working and living conditions which prevailed in early industrial towns. In America, a century later, the 'muckrakers' of the late 19th and early

20th century exposed similar conditions in America's rural areas, extraction industries, food processing plants and industrializing towns.

In Britain and Western Europe, as the productive energy of industrial development was realized, standards of living improved. Life for the working class, particularly skilled workers, gradually improved due in part, to the rise of economic (the trades unions) and political (socialist, social democratic parties) working class protest movements. Pressure from the working class protest movement was also partially responsible for the emergence of welfare state capitalism, but as was noted in the introduction, the persistence of a low wage sector within the economy and an underdeveloped welfare state remains even in the USA today.

What is so poignant in the Polish case, and that of other Eastern European Communist systems is that the rhetoric of Communism includes protection of the working class from gross exploitation during the processes of modernization and industrial development. As Hrynkiewicz, et. al. make clear, the Polish government was unable to modernize the Polish economy without recourse to the exploitation of the working class, a process tried, tested and confirmed by the mode of development of earlier industrializing societies. Had Poland, the USSR and the other Iron curtain countries been able to achieve industrialization, together with rising standards of living distributed in some relatively equitable fashion, then recent events in Eastern Europe and the USSR might have been different. A slow rate of increase in standards of living together with a basic lack of political and individual freedom in the Communist countries were a formula for disaster.

The propensity of certain Western socio-political analysts to credit the Cold War and the arms race as a successful strategy in the "defeat" of Communism is probably correct. In addition to the need for capital accumulation in the early phases of modernization and industrialization in the East, it was also necessary to divert further components of surplus value into the armaments industry. Western rhetoricians forget or conveniently ignore the fact that France, Britain and the United States, however half-heartedly, committed troops to defeat the Russian revolution of 1917.

Once the foundations for the Cold War after World War II were laid by Churchill in his infamous Iron Curtain speech in Fulton, Missouri, the arms race was inevitable. The West, given the higher development of productive capacity stemming from its historically fortunate earlier process of industrialization, was more easily able to absorb this form of wasteful expenditure without depressing, too obviously and too overtly, the standards of living of both the working and middle classes. Indeed, the impetus provided by the arms race to traditional heavy industry, to the growth and expansion of improved weapons technology and, to the whole paraphernalia of peripheral industries linked to arms production led to marked improvements in the standards of living of working and middle class groups following World War II.

In the East, the hostility of the Western nations towards the Russian Revolution of 1917 were to be long remembered. After World War II when the West again turned against the revolutionary governments established in Eastern Europe after the cessation of hostilities, Russia and its satellites had little option but to join the arms race to protect their national and geographical entities. But for Eastern Europe and Russia, in the early or middle stages of modernization and industrialization, the diversion of economic resources into armament production and prestige products—such as space exploration whose major purpose was to demonstrate the ability of the East to compete with the West in this particular form of conspicuous consumption—was a much more expensive proposition. Capital accumulation to support modernization and industrialization was already an enormous burden to be born by the producers of wealth. The additional burden of financing expenditures on armaments probably contributed significantly to the already extant forces which depressed the ability of the economy to produce consumer as well as capital goods. In this way the ultimate failure of state capitalism was assured.

Paradoxically, the military "adventures" of Western powers against the 1917 revolution, the subsequent isolation of the USSR and the instigation of the Cold War and the arms race after World War II, may have enabled the totalitarian regimes of the Soviet Union and many of its satellites to survive longer than would otherwise have been the case. The acquiescence of the Soviet and East European peoples to the harsh repression of state capitalist bureaucracies under the domination of Communism may be in part due to the "artificial" internal unity generated by fear of Western aggression. Soviet and other East European leaders could demand sacrifices in the economic sphere and loyalty to the state, however oppressive its impact on the daily lives of its citizens, by pointing to the need to defend itself against Western aggression. In this way the Cold War was antithetical to the interests of both the East and the West, since its instigation and continuation was against the interests of the common people in both nation groups.

Under these circumstances it is surprising that Poland managed to incorporate the basic components of a welfare state ideology, including fiscal support and medical and social services for the elderly, when the demands on the public purse were so overwhelming that support of the processes of modernization and industrialization and even the survival of the very state had to take precedence. Notions of fairness and equity, essential components of the socialist creed which underpins Communist ideology, obviously played an important part as Hrynkiewicz, et. al. demonstrate. Sentiments of atonement to those who sacrificed so much and fought so hard against Fascism are also apparent in the supports available to aged veterans. But even a Communist government operating under the principles of state capitalism must pay attention to the problem of hegemony. Pensions, social and medical care services, day centers, old people's homes, day care and so on are part of the system of eldercare in Poland, however, incomplete the coverage may be. Hrynkiewicz, et. al., also make clear that on occasion policies are "modified" in accordance with the establishment's interpretation of the broader socio-economic needs which affect the extent and depth of support for the elderly. Ages and rates of reimbursement for the retired population have been adjusted either to encourage the elderly to leave the work force or to continue to work in accordance with the then perceived needs of the economic situation.

Moreover, many services which enable the elderly to continue a social existence in the larger community and to maintain an independent life style in their own homes are the responsibility of a confused mix of quasi-public and private charitable organizations. The state also seems to rely upon family loyalty to provide for the care of the elderly when formal provisions are wanting or inadequate. Such circumstances, however, are not unique to Poland or other Eastern European societies, but are also to be found in Western countries where the lack of formal provision thrusts the care of the elderly back upon the shoulders of the younger generation, particularly the daughters or daughters-in-law of the grand-parental generation. Indeed in the U.S. the staff of emergency rooms are beginning to report incidents of "elderly dumping." Relatives are apparently taking their sick and debilitated elders whose constant needs for care and attention have exhausted the care-giver's ability to cope, to hospital emergency rooms whereupon the relatives leave, leaving the subsequent responsibility for the care of the elderly in the hands of the hospital.

The authors of "The Elderly and Social Policy in Poland" demonstrate throughout their chapter a complete and sophisticated understanding of the major dimensions of the needs which must be addressed if the elderly are to be able to live out the seventh stage of man and woman in a tolerable and civilized fashion. At present significant aspects of these needs are not met. In Poland, as is the case in other nations, East and West, development rather than retrenchment of the welfare state is what is required.

Primary Health Care and the Elderly in the former USSR

Muzafarov and Kurleutov, using the Alma-Ata declaration of 1978, provide a clear statement of the requirements to integrate medical and social systems of care if the needs of the elderly are to be adequately met. Arguing that the cornerstones of justice and equity should be the foundation of geriatric care, they outline the five major principles that should guide the development of service provision for the elderly.

1.   Equitable distribution of health services and their accessibility;
2.   Extensive community involvement in the development of health systems;

3. Health promotion and disease prevention;
4. Technologies which are scientifically grounded and are socially and economically acceptable;
5. Taking into account mutual and direct influence of all spheres of human activity on health and health systems.

The authors then go on to describe the changing demographic structure of the population of the former USSR which differs in only a few respects from those of other complex industrial societies. In the USSR the aging of the population shows somewhat wider variation than that of most other Western societies. In the Asian republics, especially in the rural areas, the age distribution has yet to shift towards the elderly since falling family size, although evident, started at a later date than in the rest of the country.

Nevertheless, the themes which would be related to a discussion of the circumstances of the elderly in the West are mirrored in the authors' accounts of conditions in the USSR in the 1980s. Many pensioners would return to work if suitable occupational circumstances existed. While maximum pension rates provide 70-75% of previous salaries and wages, it should be noted that the rate, high in relation to previous income, is based on low wage rates compared with other countries at a similar stage of development. State capitalism has extracted surplus value from the work force at a rate higher than the average of Western economies, to fuel the country's armament industries and to support geographic and political ambitions in Europe, Asia and elsewhere.

Many pensioners face difficulties with activities of daily living and the USSR, like any other industrialized country, must provide a variety of support systems, sheltered housing, sheltered workshops, day care centers, home health care and other support services, long term care and so on—if the needs of the elderly are to be addressed. Like the U.S., the USSR of the 1980s had a shortage of physicians appropriately trained in geriatric medicine to provide the specialist knowledge of procedures and treatment regimes dictated by the specific bio-medical condition of the elderly.

Shortcomings in the care of the elderly are not simply restricted to the medical care sector. Muzafarov and Kurleutov describe the complex mix of formal and informal services for the elderly. These include: 1) Charity Society programs, 2) Red Cross programs, and 3) the integrated, intersectorial target program "Care." All three are described as community health projects and the extent of community involvement and "volunteerism" is laudable. One is, however, left with the impression of a lack of integration and coordination among these programs. The funding of these programs is unclear and the essay conveys the impression of a lack of fiscal support from the government sector whether national or local. The medico-social "Care" program, for example, is very recent, dating from 1987 and financial support is derived from the budget of the local Soviets of people's deputies and monies allocated to their account from local enterprises. The authors provide no indication of the level of such funding. Apparently, much remains to be done if the necessary infrastructure for the care of the elderly is to be developed—purpose built housing units, daycare centers, adaptation of houses and the like.

What does seem to be innovative in the former USSR setting is the encouragement given to industrial and production enterprises to become involved in the care of their own elderly workers. In some industrial settings the factory or production unit is already engaged in providing housing for its work force. In the early stages of the Soviet revolution one of the objectives was to provide crèches at all work sites. Such objectives were, however, soon "lost" during the horrendous circumstances of the civil, political and economic disruptions of the 1920s and 1930s. After World War II such "social" reforms were neglected as the Soviet Union tried to rebuild its economic infrastructure either destroyed or diverted by the struggle for survival. Additional strains on the economy imposed by the arms and space races not only reduced the availability of consumer goods but also prevented the allocation of scarce resources to the development of welfare services.

Advocates for domestic programs and further development of the welfare state in the West are hoping that part of the "Peace Dividend" can be utilized to improve medical and social service provision to the deprived and disadvantaged. The targets are legion; unemployment in the UK and the USA, refurbishing and reconstruction of hospitals and the expansion of geriatric care in the British NHS, providing adequate medical care for the uninsured in America, and so on, and so on. In the former USSR, in the short term, any "Peace Dividend" will first have to address the restructuring of the country's economy. Subsequently, more resources might be allocated to welfare provision. Integration of the work place, housing and support for the elderly holds much promise since the aging of the population has been accompanied by improvements in the health status and capacity of the "young-old." It might be that continued employment opportunities, for the elderly, perhaps at a reduced pace, would enable them to maintain their previous identification with and satisfaction from employment and might be a corrective to the economic consequences of an aging population.

The one thing we can be sure of is the continuation of the dynamism and changes in the structure of social systems. The welfare state must be responsive to changing social and economic conditions. We must continuously review and rethink the basic structure of the Welfare State to adapt it to the new needs of an ever-changing world. Aging is not new but the roles of the elderly have changed out of all recognition since the agricultural and industrial revolutions. Now is the time to explore the roles of the elderly using new insights and encouraging initiatives to enable senior citizens to expand their horizons. Let the search continue.

Social Policy in Switzerland

Of the countries discussed in this volume Switzerland represents the society whose welfare state is one of the least developed. This is reflected in Fragnière's presentation where the bulk of the argument centers upon an explanation of the reasons for this parlous state of affairs. Before commenting on Fragnière's arguments the editors have chosen to include a brief account of geriatric care and associated support services in Switzerland.

The twenty-six Cantons of Switzerland with their 6.3 million people have relatively independent health care policies. Some 50% of medical expenses are covered in Switzerland through a combination of communal, cantonal and federal funding sources. Over 95% of the population, as of 1979, is covered by either private (577 companies) or public insurance programs. In 1980, article 34 of the federal constitution required citizens to participate in a medical insurance plan.

Major hospitals and the majority of nursing homes are owned and operated by government or by private non-profit foundations. Salaried physicians, as in Britain, work in and control the hospitals. Private fee-for-service general internists and specialists deliver ambulatory medical care to the aged and non-aged. This latter group of physicians do *not* have hospital privileges; some may practice in smaller specialized private hospitals.

Insurance schemes, whether public or private, reimburse more for the technical and diagnostic procedures than for socio-clinical consultations and assessments. The bulk of medical expenditure went in 1975 to hospitals 45% and to private medicine, 32%. Home health care and social work services are both under-developed by British and other European standards. Throughout the 1970s the public component of medical care insurance has declined relative to the private sector and Swiss citizens are paying ever increasing private insurance premiums. Swiss industry does not and has never paid a significant proportion of health insurance premiums; currently only 1% of the total premium. Recently public meetings were held to discuss and debate who or what is to blame for this cost explosion in medical care.

Overall data on the Swiss medical care system are hard to locate because of the decentralized nature of government. A less satisfactory but adequate alternative is to focus upon one Canton's health care system for the aged. The Canton of Geneva is a good choice for several reasons. Informally, the Canton was requested by the confederation to undertake a Research and Development function in developing an improved geriatric care system. While Geneva is richer than other Swiss Cantons, its health care system is not atypical and is similar to those of Zurich, Bern, Lausanne and Basel.

By 1983, for a population of 340,000 with 13% aged 65 or older, there existed the following components partially integrated in a geriatric care system:

1) two new geriatric hospitals (80 and 276 beds), 2) two day hospitals and five day care centers for the disabled and frail elderly, 3) some 1,800 sheltered housing units with nurses on call, 4) a strong geriatric community nursing and home-health aide service (with 80 teams), 5) a geriatric ambulatory center (with five teams consisting of physicians, a physical therapist, a social worker and a psychologist to visit nursing homes and the residency of homebound persons), 6) a geriatric-liaison service at the 2,000 bed university cantonal hospital (created to improve discharge planning, inpatient care, as well as to prevent unnecessary hospital admissions) and since 1965, 7) a geriatric psychiatric service for persons 65 and older, (300 out of 600 beds at the university psychiatry hospital).

Of the 58 nursing homes and boarding homes that exist in the Canton, the majority of beds (55%) and the larger facilities are government or foundation operated (non-profit). Many Cantons in Switzerland have no for-profit nursing homes, in sharp contrast to the robust private sector in the U.S. where at least 75% are for-profit.

Switzerland's social, political and economic infrastructure is a strange mix of democratic and anti-democratic tendencies. Switzerland was the last western society to grant women the vote in 1971. The Federal Assembly consists of two chambers: the National Council whose members are elected by proportional representation and the Council of States with two members from each Canton who may be appointed or elected. Once elected or appointed the members tend to remain in power and rarely suffer defeat or recall. Council members have incomes averaging three times the average citizen (108,000 SRF = U.S. $53,000) and a complex patronage system ensures that deputies of the bourgeois parties are linked to the industrial and banking interests of Switzerland. In the 1980s over 80% of all deputies belonged to one or more management boards. These appointments are typically granted after a deputy is elected and these appointments carry with them substantial incomes. Recently, for example, 39 Radical Party deputies represented 284 banks, multi-nationals and companies and Christian Democrats represented 344 banks, industrial trusts and armament plants. Upon leaving the Federal Assembly these relationship are further cemented with right-wing deputies moving into leadership positions with major firms, e.g., to the Board of Nestlé and Vice-Presidency of Sandoz.

Swiss banks are notorious for the strict provisions of privacy which protect bank accounts. Consequently Swiss banks have been suspected and on occasions it has been proven that they have provided havens for funds acquired illegally by individuals and corporations. Banks also affect the internal market by playing off one Canton against another to secure lower taxes or fewer regulations to place or maintain their business premises in a particular location.

The tax system with its heavy emphasis upon sales is one of the least progressive in the industrial world. While taxes on wealth, inheritance, capital gains, corporate income and military exemption contribute to federal income, they do so at a low level with the major source of federal and local revenues derived from salary and wages through both direct and indirect taxation. It is not surprising that 10% of the Swiss population owns 90% of private wealth or that less than 2% control two-thirds of the country's wealth. In addition, Switzerland spends less *per capita* on health and welfare services than does the U.S.

On the other hand, the possibility of direct as opposed to representative democracy is made possible through the provisions for the federal popular initiative and the referendum. In the case of the former any 100,000 citizens can demand a modification of the federal constitution. The legislative referendum enables 50,000 citizens to demand that a federal law (or a federal ruling of general application) must also be subjected to a vote by the electorate before it can be enacted.

Such gross inequities in the distribution of wealth might be supposed to encourage the development of a rigorous working class protest movement but this is not the case. A partial explanation may be associated with the high proportion of immigrant labor in the Swiss economy. In 1972 some 23% of the population and 27% in the peak month of August were immigrants, the vast majority of whom have no rights of permanent residence. Moreover their employment opportunities, like foreign workers all over Europe tend to be restricted to the less well-paid and arduous jobs at the bottom of the employment structure. When tight monetary policy ensues and trade is depressed such workers can be exported back "home" and in this way insulating the Swiss work force from the vicissitudes of the trade cycle so characteristic of capitalism. These circumstances may also help to explain why the various worker-oriented political parties have so little influence in Swiss politics.

Fragnière discusses these and associated issues in a sophisticated, abstract and generic fashion. He confirms our view concerning the under-development of the welfare state in Switzerland and documents the extent to which conservative forces advocate even further reductions in federal responsibility for welfare provision in favor of privatization.

It is surprising that a modern complex society can continue to survive in Europe where other nations provide much more comprehensive welfare systems designed to alleviate the circumstances of the less well-off without following suit. Switzerland's traditional isolationism has undoubtedly contributed to this important role within international banking, through the provision of 'invisible' earnings which underpin much of the country's economic activity, links it to the world of multinational corporations. In addition, it is able to attract immigrant labor at relatively low levels of social and economic costs from surrounding countries at a lower level of industrialization and economic development. This comparative economic advantage is likely to decline as the European Economic Community improves the economies of the less developed countries on the Continent. Switzerland may then be forced to address the inequities characteristic of its current, social, economic and political structure and move towards a welfare state capitalist system more similar to those of its neighbors.

Health and Medical Care for the Aged in Japan

Kinoshita's account of the provision of geriatric care in Japan is a fascinating narrative of rapid changes in a societal context of even broader social change. "Before 1945 Japan had an institutionalized patriarchical family system in which the status of aged parents was secured and filial responsibility was rigidly prescribed." Today the family has become more 'nucleated' with the proportion of single and aged couple households increasing rapidly, a trend likely to continue over the next three decades.

During the period 1973-1982 an almost unique experiment in free medical care for the elderly emerged at the instigation of a bottom-up grass-roots movement which eventually became national policy. As Kinoshita makes clear, a convincing explanation of this phenomenon awaits development but the changing demographic characteristics of Japanese society (a rapidly increasing number of elderly persons) and the breakdown of the traditional family structure referred to above probably played their parts. As the elderly became more isolated and their sons and daughters were highly integrated into the economic sector, the traditional pattern of filial responsibility for the care of the elderly was severely strained or completely disrupted. When the elderly became sick with either acute or chronic illness episodes, their kin were no longer in a position to provide the necessary care and attention. While the then current system of Health Care Insurance was highly complex and fractionated, a minimal payment infrastructure nevertheless existed which could be modified to provide free medical care for the elderly. The program varied by locale both by age and in terms of completeness; eligible ages varied between 60 and 80 years and in some jurisdictions income restrictions limited eligibility.

While the changing demographic pattern and the disruption of the traditional family structure were partially responsible for the introduction of free medical care, the major impetus for the reforms stemmed from the shift in the political climate in Japan in the late 1960s and early 1970s. In this period socialists and socialist-coalition candidates were successfully elected to governorships and mayoralties favoring the adoption of left-wing policies and welfare reforms in local and regional jurisdictions. Such strong sentiments in favor of reform at the local level forced the national government dominated by the conservative Liberal Democratic Party to support the provision of free medical care nationally. The movement also made possible other improvements in pension, social security and welfare services in general, starting Japanese society on the path towards a welfare state.

Unhappily such progress was soon halted and free medical care eliminated with the re-introduction of charges. Free care eliminated barriers to both hospital and ambulatory care leading to increases in utilization when those previously barred from access presented for treatment. Since 1983 the elderly are required to make co-payments, albeit at low levels, when they need medical care. Other measures designed to contain costs, or at least cost increases, of providing medical care for the elderly have also been imposed by the introduction of a new reimbursement mechanism similar to that of the Diagnostic Related Groups under Medicare in the U.S. Not surprisingly, the patient care outcomes in Japan were similar to those which occurred in the U.S.—many hospitals attempted to discharge long-stay hospitalized aged patients. Further parallelism of the two countries' decision-making procedures is to be found in the reaction to the problem of long-term stay. Local jurisdictions are being encouraged and sometimes required to provide long-term care facilities for the aged as well as improve home-care services, thus relieving the National Government of these responsibilities. In this way local politicians must "take the heat" for either inadequate service provision or raising taxes to finance appropriate levels of care. In the UK this shift of responsibility from state to local government is taken one step further by imposing limitations upon the taxation power of local authorities. The consequence of these policy shifts and changes in the care of the elderly is to thrust back upon the family the responsibility for geriatric care. The outcome in welfare state capitalist societies and mixed economies alike is most unfortunate for middle and low-income families. Changes in the world economy have reduced the previously favorable balance of trade of the advanced societies leading to declining standards of living for large segments of the middle and working class. Many families in these segments, faced with falling incomes, particularly for male wage earners, have struggled to maintain family income by more and more women seeking paid employment outside the home full or part-time. Care of the elderly in the domestic sector is often predominantly the responsibility of daughters or daughters-in-law rather than sons or sons-in-law, just when more women are unavailable for such tasks and the high incidence of divorce complicates the situation even further.

The defeat of the grassroot and socialist inspired free medical care for the elderly in Japan was clearly the consequence of a variety of factors, the oil price rises of the early and late seventies, the failure of socialist administrations at the regional and local levels and an electoral system weighted heavily in favor of the more conservative rural areas. In part the failure may also be associated with the lack of success of socialist parties at the level of national politics in Japan. Without a strong presence of working class interest groups in both the political and economic sectors of modern societies, welfare policies which help ameliorate the adverse conditions of labor in capitalist or mixed economies are always at risk. The history of the defeat of the free medical care experiment in Japan is a clear example of this risk.

Health Care in Canada

As was suggested in the introduction and as has become clear in comments emerging in the epilogue, some aspects of the issue of distributive justice have been effectively dealt with in the Canadian medical care system. Equity is assured since no Canadian is barred from access to medical care, primary, secondary or tertiary, through inability to pay. Services are available at zero cost at point of delivery. Uniformity is less complete since hospital services, particularly in the tertiary care sector, are not available in sparsely populated districts or regions. While physicians are remunerated on a fee-for-service basis, they are not allowed to bill payments in excess of the payment schedules negotiated between the provinces and doctors' organizations.

Administrative overhead is low, consequent upon a monopsonistic payment system which eliminates the duplication of bureaucracies in the insurance system and removes the cost of profit from medical insurance. Controls over hospital expansion and limitation of overall budgets are weaker but generate some attention to cost control measures. Nevertheless the system is predominantly physician-oriented or physician-dominated, as Chappell makes clear in her analysis of the system and its ability to meet the needs of elderly citizens.

The national insurance scheme has established a medical (physician) and an institutional (hospital and long-term care) focus within the Canadian health care system. Community services have developed, almost as an afterthought and without coordination and integration from the national government. This has resulted in what Chappell calls a lack of appropriateness in the provision of services for the elderly.

Appropriate care of the elderly, particularly if they are to maintain an independent existence in their homes, requires a combination of services which blend medical and social support in the community. Chappell classifies such appropriate care under three broad categories: "*basic* (necessary for the maintenance of the person and include assistance, for example, with preparing food or bathing), *supportive* (helping the individual to cope with the indirect effect of illness such as providing personal attention, company or reassurance), and *remedial or therapeutic* (requiring professional intervention and treatment such as medical, nursing or family counselling)."

Community based services for the elderly vary considerably among the provinces. The variation includes the need for physician certification, age restrictions and user fees. In Manitoba, however, the system could be defined as a template which other provinces, or for that matter other societies, might do well to match. A range of services are available, after an initial assessment by a nurse and a social worker which provide partial or complete coverage under the classification referred to above. Such services are provided at no cost to the recipient.

While the lack of uniformity across provinces in the provision of community care is to be regretted the federal government has expressed awareness and a commitment to resolution of the problem, a commitment to expansion rather than retrenchment of the welfare state. It will be interesting to see if the political will to address this issue is maintained in the near future and whether or not both the federal government and provinces will commit more resources to expand community care.

A note of guarded optimism might be recorded here. As Chappell notes: "...Canada's founding fathers emphasized Peace, Order and Good Government..." as founding principles of the state culminating in much greater support for social democratic redistributive and welfare policies in contrast to the dominant laissez-faire tradition in the United States which generates opposition to such measures. Indeed, welfare state capitalism is apparent in Canadian society, albeit less extensively than in some Western European countries. The federal government administers a number of income-maintenance measures, including the Canada Pension Plan, Canada Assistance Plan, old-age security pensions, family allowances, youth allowances and unemployment insurance. These programs reduce poverty throughout all stages of the life cycle including a minimal level of income support to the elderly, thus reducing poverty rates at all ages compared to the United States, for example. The fact that all Canadians are protected against medical care costs since medical services are provided at zero cost at point of delivery, must add to the financial stability of both individuals and families. In contrast, the leading cause of family bankruptcies in the United States is medical care costs.

Chappell's comments on the lack of accountability of the Canadian medical care system to the body politic are particularly insightful. The ownership of the means of production of medical services, hospitals and doctors' offices remain largely in private hands but with decision-making power shared between hospital management, governments and private physicians. Both fiscal accountability and utilization review are difficult to achieve in a system where decision-making is shared between three groups, two of which, hospital management and physicians, represent the interests of producers. In such a situation representation of patient interests becomes the responsibility of government and currently the representation of patient interests can only be achieved indirectly.

Moreover, government can only represent the interests of patients if a body of data, routinely collected, is available to evaluate the success or failure of treatment regimens and the comparative costs of the enormous variety of medical procedures. Chappell argues that insufficient research dollars are available to instigate and maintain these forms of accountability. But Canada is not alone. Britain has pioneered the development of QALYS, quality of life indicators which attempt to assess both the costs of and the contribution to improved socio-biological conditions of patients associated with various medical procedures, with an emphasis upon high-tech and high cost intervention strategies. Interestingly the data base generated by DRGs and the prospective payment system for Medicare patients in the U.S. could provide the necessary information for evaluating the efficacy and cost-effectiveness of major medical procedures on the subsequent well-being of patients.

Ultimately, the expansion or retrenchment of service provision for the aged will depend in Canada, as elsewhere, on the balance of political forces. In Canada the major political parties are the Progressive Conservative Party and the Liberal Party. The PC favors individualism, free enterprise and free trade whereas the Liberals place greater emphasis upon government intervention to promote the general welfare. Recently the New Democratic party, a social democratic grouping associated with the labour movement has increased its representation in the House of Commons. Currently almost 30% of non-agricultural workers are unionized, thereby creating another force likely to support welfare state development. Improvements in community care for the elderly may be dependent on the fortunes of Liberal and New Democratic politicians and the continued existence of the trade unions. Certainly the presence of such political groupings has been in part responsible for the development of the welfare state in Canada today.

Governmental Responsibility:
Adequacy or Dependency for the Aged in the U.S.

Hendricks' chapter provides a masterful overview of the development of pension policy, geriatric services and the impact of general fiscal policy and tax structures on the condition of the elderly in the United States today. The Social Security system, introduced in the depth of the Great Depression, was designed as much to correct the problems of capital accumulation in the American economy as it was meant to alleviate the problems of unemployment and loss of income in later life. Moreover the pension component was couched in terms of social insurance rather than welfare provision since benefit levels were tied to previous earnings. It also excluded workers in marginal occupations (what the editors refer to as the residual labour power sector, following Offe but with modifications) and even today part-time, seasonal and low-paid workers must depend upon the provisions of Title I of the Social Security Act (Old Age Assistance as amended in 1973) which Hendricks rightly argues maintains the distinction between the "needy" and "deserving" elderly.

It should also be noted that the earned benefit portion of Title II is only marginally redistributive and the marginality of the system further emphasizes the regressive nature of the Social Security "tax." The situation in terms of retirement pensions is even worse, through the relatively poor performance of the private sector. Only 46% of American workers participate in private pension schemes and the financial security of some of these schemes has been compromised by the poor management of many private insurance companies, the deregulation of the Savings and Loan Industry during the Reagan administration, the distortion of money markets and investments by S & Ls in ridiculous real estate speculation to which deregulation gave rise and the development of the "junk bond" market. Together with extortions in defense industries, financial mismanagement in virtually all branches of the investment and money markets and downright thievery ["white collar" crimes so characteristic of American and Japanese business and financial operations, plus the international thefts of BCCI (Bank of Crooks and Criminals International)] the stability of even the largest financial institutions are suspect. While Western powers have rejoiced at the failures of state capitalism in the USSR and Eastern Europe, a more prudent reaction might be to look to the problems that capital accumulation and the struggle for profits has generated in the competitive and mixed economies of welfare state capitalist societies.

The above circumstances do not augur well for future generations of American retirees and the proportion who find themselves living in poverty after retirement may well exceed the current 14% who find themselves in this condition; poverty rates amongst the U.S. elderly population that rank among the highest in the industrialized world. "In addition to the elderly who fall below the poverty line, another one-fifth of the elderly hover just above it, existing at 125% of the poverty threshold (Ropers, 1991:47)." This situation will assuredly worsen if some private insurance schemes become insolvent or if rates of Social Security and Supplemental Security Income do not keep up with inflation and the growing numbers of elderly Americans.

The etiology of poverty among the elderly is not sudden. The vast majority of the elderly poor have probably been poor throughout their lives. Those living a little above, at, or below the poverty level have probably "enjoyed" such circumstances throughout the six preceding stages of man (with apologies to Shakespeare). The Industrial Revolution in America, as was the case with most other industrial nations, was financed in part by the payment of near-starvation wages—just above the minimal cost of the social reproduction of the labor force—to segments of the working class. In the American case wage levels could be pushed to the lowest possible extremes since massive immigration from Europe and the influx of illegal or quasi-legal Mexicans provided new recruits to the labor force throughout the industrial revolution and in the case of Hispanics, well beyond.

Today the low wage sector persists in the U.S. economy and continues to grow. Well-paid semi- and skilled jobs are declining in the manufacturing sector as companies as disparate as General Motors and Schwinn bicycles "export" their manufacturing operations to Mexico and South Korea respectively. Growth in the U.S. economy is highest in service industries, including health care where wages are particularly low; where part-time work and consequent absence of benefits condemns significant segments of the American working class to continuous poverty. All they can expect in old age is indeed dependency. This bleak picture of the current and future prospects of those in the residual labor power sector contrasts sharply with the favorable tax "reforms" introduced during the Reagan era for the already wealthy.

Hendricks goes on to describe and analyze the current crisis in the medical care industry and the reductions in Medicare and Medicaid coverage consequent upon various changes in the operation of both medical plans. Elderly Americans, on average, now pay more in terms of out-of-pocket medical expenses than they did in 1964, before Medicare and Medicaid were introduced, and this in constant dollars. There is little point in reproducing Hendricks' arguments here or to refer to earlier documentation of the parameters of the medical care funding crisis which were outlined in the introduction to these essays.

What is worth emphasizing is Hendricks' endorsement of Walker's (1986:1210) argument which exposed the limited extent of political debate over health care provision in the U.S. She argued

> ...that realistic debate concerning principles which might influence the form, structure, financing and organization of American medical care is restricted to only two alternatives, liberalism and conservatism. Both positions ignore significant questions such as: What are the reasons which support the application of subsidies to *both* the private and public medical care sector? Who really owns and controls the production process in the medical care industry? Why is it assumed that price competition and the other allocation mechanisms of the market place will distribute medical "goods and services" appropriately when much medical care is defined as a right rather than a privilege? Is the concept of profit even applicable to the treatment of illness, disease and suffering?

Walker goes on to show how the current legislative proposals and changes in the funding of Medicare are creating a dualistic form of medical care in the U.S.—one for the poor and one for the rich. Is this the direction in which the American public really wishes to travel?

Five years later, in the period leading up to the Presidential election of 1992, the parameters of the debate concerning the provision of medical care in the U.S. seem hardly to have changed at all. The Republican Party recently (February 1992) has proposed an unrealistic set of suggestions to address the problems facing the medical care industry and the Democrats' proposal ignores the basic principles which might resolve the crisis, such as the introduction of a monopsonistic payment system, elimination of the wasteful duplication of for-profit and not-for-profit health insurance, lack of funding for long-term care, inadequate funding of domiciliary-based services and lack of control over the dissemination of increasingly expensive medical technologies. Even the relatively successful Canadian model which limited the cost explosion of medical care while still preserving competent services and resolving the problem of funding long-term care, is largely ignored. Why is this?

No single answer is possible. Competing capitals, for example, take very different positions. The private insurance industry argues vehemently in favor of the status quo. Profits can and are being made from the medical care industry and it continues to be one of the most profitable sectors of the U.S. economy. U.S. automakers, on the other hand, favor the introduction of some form of national health insurance which would relieve them of the requirement to fund this "fringe" benefit for their work force. The CEO of the Chrysler Corporation has stated that the cost of each unit it produces includes $500-$600 to provide medical care benefits for its employees. Both industries generously fund PACs to lobby Congress in their behalf. Of these two interest groups, which one will prevail?

Futurologists of whatever basic disciplinary persuasion—economists, political scientists, sociologists—are usually wrong but we will hazard a guess. The insurance industry is an enormously important part of the capital accumulation process which also reaches into every other sector of the economy through the investment process. Even more, insurance funds are an integral component of the financial infrastructure of capitalism whose profits must be protected if commercial banking, stock markets and commodity exchanges, national and international are to survive.

The ultimate solution to the medical care funding crisis is, of course, decommodification of medical care, the elimination of the market place from the production and supply of medical services. Canada has moved toward this position. Physicians may not charge more to patients than the rates set by negotiations between physicians' organizations and the provinces. A monopsonistic payment system was introduced eliminating the administrative waste and profits associated with a mix of insurance companies, some for-profit others not-for-profit. We guess that the American insurance industry will do all it can to prevent the introduction of a medical care system which will provide cost-savings for automobile manufacturers; the automakers will lose! Neither the present administration nor the Democrats will demonstrate sufficient political will to threaten the profits of the health insurance and medical industries.

But above all, the interests of ordinary people are unlikely to receive much of a hearing in this debate. One of the reasons for the limited nature of political discourse in the United States is the absence of a vigorous working class representative movement. There are no equivalents of social democratic (Canada) or labor parties (Britain, Scandinavia) on the U.S. political scene. The American trade union movement is weak and has gown weaker in recent years. Welfare state capitalism has advanced furthest in those countries with a vigorous organized working class protest movement where their combined political and economic strength has forced concessions from governments who must ultimately adjudicate between the interests of capital and labor if hegemony is to be maintained. The welfare state is unlikely to advance in the U.S. until labor representation is powerful enough to persuade government to limit the power of capital to the ultimate benefit of all.

Conclusions and Afterword

Of the countries described in this volume none escapes without some criticism of the services provided for the elderly within its particular form of a welfare state. Even in Sweden, one of the most advanced welfare states, some pensioners, particularly women, subsist on incomes close to the poverty margin in that country and variations in the extent and accessibility of home care services to the elderly are considerable in different locales. Nevertheless, in most other respects the welfare state in Sweden indemnifies its citizens against the major effects of a capitalist economy based on the profit motive and the extraction of surplus value from the producers of wealth.

But when realistic legislation designed to redistribute profit from businesses to their work forces was introduced, and this to a modest extent, the social consensus in favor of continued advances in welfare state capitalism was halted. In September of 1991 the alliance of the Social Democratic and Left Parties was defeated at the polls. Political analysts in Sweden attribute part of the reasons for this electoral defeat to the decision in 1983 which introduced a mechanism through which workers could acquire a financial interest in and access to the profits through share ownership of the companies in which they were employed. This, together with earlier legislation in 1977 which required union representation on the boards of directors of privately owned companies, would have shifted Sweden from welfare state capitalism towards the development of a truly socialist state where the workers were enabled to share in the profits they had generated. Both the logic of, and the values and morality embedded in the principles of the welfare state culminate in the establishment of socialism. This the Swedish electorate rejected in the early Fall of 1991.

While the above scenario may have contributed to the defeat of the left in Sweden, other external forces played their part as we argued in our comments on 'Geriatric Care and the Welfare State in Sweden.' Indeed Swedish analysts pointed to the tax 'reforms' in the USA as examples of 'enlightened' taxation policy that Sweden ought to follow and which were introduced in 1990-91. Arguments in favor of considerable reductions in the marginal rate of taxation were also presented to adjust Sweden's economy to face entry into the EEC, or if not, to provide it with a more competitive economy able to withstand competition from EEC countries.

Such interaction effects emphasize the difficulties facing states that have advanced welfare provisions. If leading economies, the U.S. and Japan, Swiss banking, the IMF and the World Bank all support traditional investment policy where investors expect to make profits from loans to countries less fortunate than themselves, then the economies of advanced industrial social systems which favor welfare provisions designed to nullify or ameliorate the conditions of the elderly, single parent families, the unemployed—in short the poor—are placed in jeopardy. In this way countries that continue to foster a 'low' wage economy or a significant 'low' wage sector within the overall economic structure (the U.S. and the U.K.) are residual compared with an institutionalized welfare state (the U.S., Switzerland, and in the case of South Africa, total absence of provision for the majority of the population), encourage capital accumulation at the expense of welfare provision (France and Italy), who stop short of or make little or no attempt to decommodify medical care (just about all), make it difficult for societies committed to welfare state capitalism to survive.

In the developing countries, none of which are clearly represented in this collection, the primitive stages of capital accumulation take precedence over other considerations, including the introduction of a welfare state. In Latin America hereditary or recently entrenched elites exercise political power, own the means of production and natural resources and control the peasantry in a manner more characteristic of Feudal society than the, albeit hesitant, steps towards real democracy that can be discerned in some developed societies. In Africa de-colonialization has often been accompanied by political de-stabilization whose economic consequences, documented by sources as disparate as WHO, UN, AID, IMF and the World Bank, have resulted in precipitous declines in productivity, particularly in agriculture. In the Middle East, the Far East and Asia the rate of primitive capital accumulation has varied considerably between different nation states. Japan was able to build upon a nascent industrial structure, initially through the comparative advantage of a low wage structure, to create an economy which can now compete with the U.S. and Europe. South Korea is following a similar path and is now able to produce automobiles at a lower cost per unit than Japan. Many of the 'parts' are produced in Japan and the finished product assembled in South Korea. It is at the assembly stage that lower labor costs produce the most competitive advantage. In Hong Kong, Singapore and to a lesser extent Taiwan, entrepot trading positions have created, together with low wages, the opportunity for rapid capital accumulation.

In other Asian and Far Eastern countries the transition from under-developed to a developing society status has been less dramatic, less evident. Some countries are the victims of political instability—Laos, Cambodia, Vietnam, Indonesia and Sri Lanka—akin to the situation in Africa. Others like Pakistan, India and China have been frustrated by population growth where the pressure of numbers has placed brakes upon the rate of advancement. In the Philippines its situation as 'Airstrip 2' and 'Naval Haven' to the United States has improved the economy which may now be jeopardized as the U.S. armed forces are withdrawn. The Philippines, like Iceland may experience a sharp reduction in income if the thaw in the cold war continues as the military potential of the USSR and its satellites decreases.

Multinational corporations are of course aware of the forces and cir-cumstances outlined above and are ever-ready to exploit these conditions in the pursuit of profit. Where political stability exists, associated with a low wage economy, corporations which were previously dependent upon Western economies where a high wage structure persists in the monopoly and to a lesser extent in the competitive employment sector, the advantage for switching production facilities to societies which can provide an abundance of cheap labor is obvious. Consequently workers who previously enjoyed reasonable salaries as skilled or semi-skilled workers in mass production factories in Western societies find themselves out of work or forced to accept employment in the growing low-wage service sector in the U.S., the U.K., etc., etc. Workers in developing societies are subject to gross exploitation, like workers in the West during the industrial revolution, while workers in advanced societies are deprived of a standard of living which they previously enjoyed and were led to believe would continue is a consequence of the continuing success of the capitalist system of production.

To repeat, profits are generated by paying people less than they have added to the value of a product in the production process whether the product is a durable or consumer good or a service. The lower the cost of labor the higher the rate of profit. In a free market economy capital movements are unrestrained which enable multinational corporations to exploit low wage conditions wherever they may exist. Poland and the former USSR may soon become new havens for international capital if, as appears likely, the low wage aspect of their economies established under communism persists under the new govern-ment structures which are emerging in the USSR and Eastern Europe. Such 'investment opportunities' (i.e. the possibility of increasing the rate of profit) will increase the flow of capital from the developed to the developing world. These capital movements in turn deplete the capital of the donor countries to the detriment of wage, salary and employment structures in developed societies.

The unemployed workers of Flint, Michigan are conscious of the impact of the flight of capital. They look askance at advertisements to 'buy American' when the cars so advertised, previously produced at the GMC plant in Flint are now built in Mexico. To whom do they turn to seek redress for their grievances? The trade unions have been reduced to impotent fury. No political party which consistently represents the interests of the working class exists in America. Unemployment benefits cease after 26 weeks and irony of ironies, you are no longer counted among the unemployed after benefits cease.

The essence of the welfare state is ultimately dependent on the maintenance of employment at wages capable of guaranteeing independent existence. Depending at any stage of the life cycle is a measure of the overall failure of government to respond responsibly to the needs of its citizens. Governments respond to power within the social system. The power of capital and its ability to influence governments to act in its interests is so obvious it does not need explanation. The interests of the working class are only acknowledged when governments need the loyalty and sacrifice of the work force. Sadly, improvements in the standard of living of working class groups often occur during war-time. Under normal conditions the working class can only expect to exercise power and influence government by collective action, both politically and economically. Recent American and British administrations have recognized this fact and have introduced measures designed to limit the power of the trade union movement. Political rhetoric is also built around the glorification of the profit motive; self-interest, greed and the pursuit of profit are portrayed as the highest virtues. On Interstate 70 in the Midwest a billboard reads "Guns, God and Guts made America Great: Keep all Three!"

As these essays make clear, development and refinement of existing welfare state provisions, rather than retrenchment, are required if the condition of the elderly is to be improved. In general the welfare state and in particular services for the elderly are best developed in societies with a strong and entrenched working class movement. If the welfare state is to survive and improve it will be because working class groups have managed to survive and to increase their power situation relative to capital in the constant struggle over the allocation of scarce resources.

References

Binney, E. A., C. L. Estes and S. R. Ingman "Medicalization, Public Policy and the Elderly: Social Services in Jeopardy? *Social Science and Medicine* 7,30, (1990), 761-71.

Braum, D. 1991 *The Rich Get Richer.* Chicago: Nelson-Hale.

Ropers, R. H. *Persistent Poverty: The American Dream Turned Nightmare.* New York, Plenum Press, 1991.

Selden, M. "Socialism or 'Post-Revolutionary Society'? " in Christopher K. Chase-Dunn (ed) *Socialist States in the World System* Beverly Hills, Sage Publication, 1982. pp 101-109.

Sodersten, B. "The Swedish Tax Reform: How will it affect the Economy?" *Current Sweden*, Published by the Swedish Institute, no 375, October, 1990. Stockholm, Sweden. pp 1-10.

The Swedish Institute. "The Care of the Elderly in Sweden" Fact Sheets on Sweden, Stockholm, December 1989, 1-4

Walker, G. " Reforming Medicare: The Limited Framework of Political Discourse on Equity and Economy" *Social Science and Medicine,* 23,12, (1986), 1237-1250.

Contributors

Allessandro Bonanno is Associate Professor of Rural Sociology at the University of Missouri-Columbia. He has investigated topics such as aging, the structure of agriculture, regional and international development, and the State. He is the author of numerous journal articles and books, among them *Small Farms* (1987), *Sociology of Agriculture* (1989), *Agrarian Policies and Agricultural Systems* (1990), *The Agricultural and Food Sector in the New Global Era* (1992), *Retirement and the Welfare State* (1993, forthcoming, co-authored with Toni M. Calasanti). He received his Ph.D. in Sociology from the University of Kentucky.

Toni M. Calasanti is assistant professor of sociology at Virginia Polytechnic Institute and State University. Her current research is concerned with applying political economic and socialist-feminist approaches to aging, especially as these illuminate the intersections of domestic and paid labor, and retirement. Other interests include the greater incorporation of issues of diversity into socialist-feminist theory in general and to the study of retirement in particular. Recent publications have appeared in *The Sociological Quarterly* and *Social Problems*.

Neena L. Chappell has a Ph.D. in Sociology and is founding Director of the research Center on Aging at the University of Manitoba. She is author or co-author of three books and over 60 articles in refereed journals and chapters in books. Her research focuses on informal support, formal support, and social policy related to aging. She is an editorial board member of several gerontology journals and currently serves as President of the Committee on Aging of the International Sociological Association. Recently, she became the Director of Centre on Aging at University of Victoria.

Jean-Pierre Fragnière was born in Switzerland. He holds a doctorate in social sciences and education. A professor at the University of Geneva, he also serves as an advisor to the Swiss National Fund for Scientific Research. He is the co-founder of *Réalités Sociales*, a publishing company, and the author of numerous works on social policy and welfare.

Derek G. Gill is the Chair of the Department of Sociology and Anthropology, University of Maryland Baltimore County campus. Previously, he was with the Medical Sociology Research Unit, University of Aberdeen, and the Chief, Section of Behavioral Sciences, University of Missouri, Columbia.

He is the author of two books, *The British National Health Service: A Sociologist's Perspective* and *Illegitimacy, Sexuality and the Status of Women*. In addition he has published 40 articles in the areas of the sociology of health, human sexuality, the social correlates of pregnancy and comparative health care system analysis.

Jon Hendricks, Professor and Chair, Department of Sociology, Oregon State University has been a long-time contributor to social gerontology. He is a recent past-chair of Behavioral and Social Sciences Section of the Gerontological Society of America and is currently serving as the Associate Editor of the *International Journal of Aging and Human Development*. Hendricks is author or co-author of several books in gerontology and has authored many other scholarly contributions.

Jozefina Hrynkiewicz is a Research Fellow at the Institute of Applied Social Sciences, Warsaw University, where she teaches courses in social policy. Her research focuses on education and employment policy as well as living standards of various social groups. She collaborates with Parliament and government in preparing social policy programs in Poland, and since 1992, serves as an advisor to the prime-minister. She, along with Dr. Starega-Piasek and Dr. Supinska, is a participant in an international project "Shifts in the Welfare Mix-Social Innovation in Welfare Policies: The Case of Care for the Elderly" organized by the European Center for Social Welfare Policy and Research in Vienna, 1989-92.

Stanley R. Ingman is currently the Director of the Texas Institute for Research and Education on Aging, a joint program of the University of North Texas and of the Texas College of Osteopathic Medicine. He has co-edited a number of volumes, eg., (D. Gill), 1986. *Special Issue of Social Service Medicine*, entitled "Distributive Justice and Geriatric Care: Cross-National Perspective," (S. Spicker) *Vitalizing Long-Term Care*, (1985) and (A. Thomas) *Utopias and Topias in Health: Policy Studies*, (1975).

Martin Jaeckel is a Research Associate with Keystone University Research Corporation in Erie, Pennsylvania, where he conducts research on health promotion and disease prevention topics. He has taught sociology at Sangamon State University and at Saint Xavier College, and is currently also adjunct faculty at Gannon University. His general field of interest is health regulation and social welfare policy. His publications include: *The Image of the Mentally Ill* (1970), and a number of articles on research methodology. Other recent publications include: "Training Needs in the Chicago Eldercare Network" (1991), and "Public versus Private Long Term Care Insurance in the U.S.: Issues and Prospects" (1992).

Yasuhito Kinoshita is Director of Gerontology Center, Japan Senior Citizens Welfare Organization, a leading non-profit organization in Tokyo, Japan, for continuing care retirement centers. Dr. Kinoshita received his Ph.D.

in Human Development and Aging from the University of California, San Francisco in 1984. Based on his doctoral dissertation, he wrote with Christie W. Kiefer a book, *Refuge of the Honored: Social Organization at a Japanese Retirement Community* (1992). He also has numerous publications in Japanese in areas of social gerontology and medical sociology.

Ernest M. Kurleutov is joint author of *Primary Health Care in Kazakhstan*, which was published in Alma Ata, Kazakhstan. He is the Deputy Head of the WHO International Collaborating Center on Primary Health Care housed within the Institute of Regional Pathology in Alma-Ata, Kazakhstan.

Rustam R. Muzafarov is Chief of Health Management, Computer Technology Unit at the WHO International Collaborating Center on Primary Health Care in Alma-Ata, Kazakhstan. He has training in medicine, computer sciences, social medicine and gerontology.

Joanna Starega-Piasek is a Research Fellow at the Institute of Social Prophylaxis and Resocialization, Warsaw University. In the 1980s, she was the leader of a team preparing the social welfare reform in Poland, and the organizer of post-graduate courses for social workers. During 1990-91, she was the vice-minister of Labor and Social Welfare. She does research in social gerontology and social welfare problems.

Jolanta Supinska is a Research Fellow and Vice-director at the Institute of Social Policy, Warsaw University. She teaches courses and does research on social policy theory and practice, and social-demographic problems. She is the author of a theoretical book "Dilemmas of Social Policy," 1987.

Gerdt Sundström is senior researcher at the Institute of Gerontology in Jönköping and holds a doctorate in social work from the University of Stockholm, where he previously worked as a university lecturer. He has published and lectured in Sweden and abroad on old age care, family sociology and related fields.

Mats Thorslund is senior researcher and associate professor (sociology) with the Swedish Medical Research Council at the Department of Social Medicine, University Hospital in Uppsala. He is responsible for several local as well as nationwide studies regarding care of the elderly.

Isidor Wallimann, senior lecturer in sociology and social policy at the School of Social Work in Basel, Switzerland, is co-editor, with Michael Dobkowski, of *Towards the Holocaust: The Social and Economic Collapse of the Weimar Republic, Genocide and the Modern Age: Etiology and Case Studies of Mass Death, Research in Inequality and Social Conflict* and *Genocide* (forthcoming). He is the author of *Estrangement: Marx's Conception of Human Nature and the Division of Labor* and the editor of *Selbstverwaltung: Erfahrungen und Perspektiven in der Schweiz* (forthcoming). He has also published on Max Weber and in the areas of ethnic relations, youth protest, deviance, the welfare states, industrial relations, and the sociology of work.

G. Darryl Wieland conducted ethnographic fieldwork in the Westfjörd area of Iceland between 1976 and 1978, focusing on aging and social change in a small community. Since then, he has published several works in gerontological and medical anthropology, concerning not only the Icelanders but ethnic minorities in the United States. Since 1982, as Senior researcher at the Sepulveda VA Geriatric Research, Education, and Clinical Center, and Assistant Research Professor at the UCLA Multicampus Division of Geriatric Medicine and Gerontology, his efforts have been chiefly directed at research and development in the fields of comprehensive geriatric assessment, functional status and quality-of-life assessment, and long-term care. He is currently an investigator in several large-scale projects to determine the clinical and cost-effectiveness of various health services innovations in geriatric care, including programs specifically targeted to ethnic minorities.

Index